YUZU THE PET VET

3

By **MINGO ITO**

In collaboration with
NIPPON COLUMBIA CO., LTD.

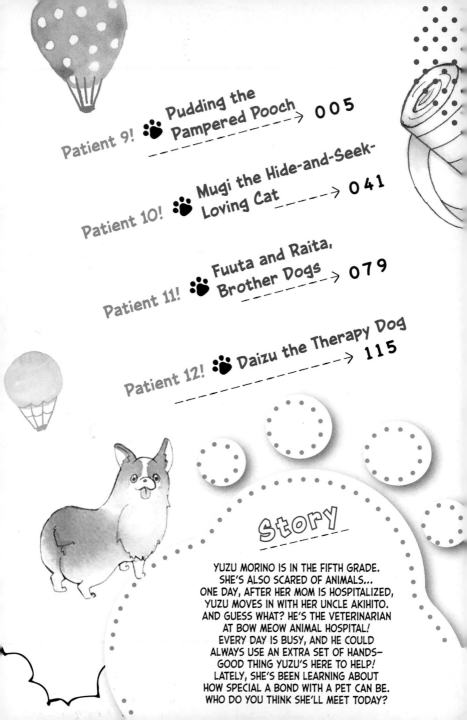

Story

YUZU MORINO IS IN THE FIFTH GRADE. SHE'S ALSO SCARED OF ANIMALS... ONE DAY, AFTER HER MOM IS HOSPITALIZED, YUZU MOVES IN WITH HER UNCLE AKIHITO. AND GUESS WHAT? HE'S THE VETERINARIAN AT BOW MEOW ANIMAL HOSPITAL! EVERY DAY IS BUSY, AND HE COULD ALWAYS USE AN EXTRA SET OF HANDS— GOOD THING YUZU'S HERE TO HELP! LATELY, SHE'S BEEN LEARNING ABOUT HOW SPECIAL A BOND WITH A PET CAN BE. WHO DO YOU THINK SHE'LL MEET TODAY?

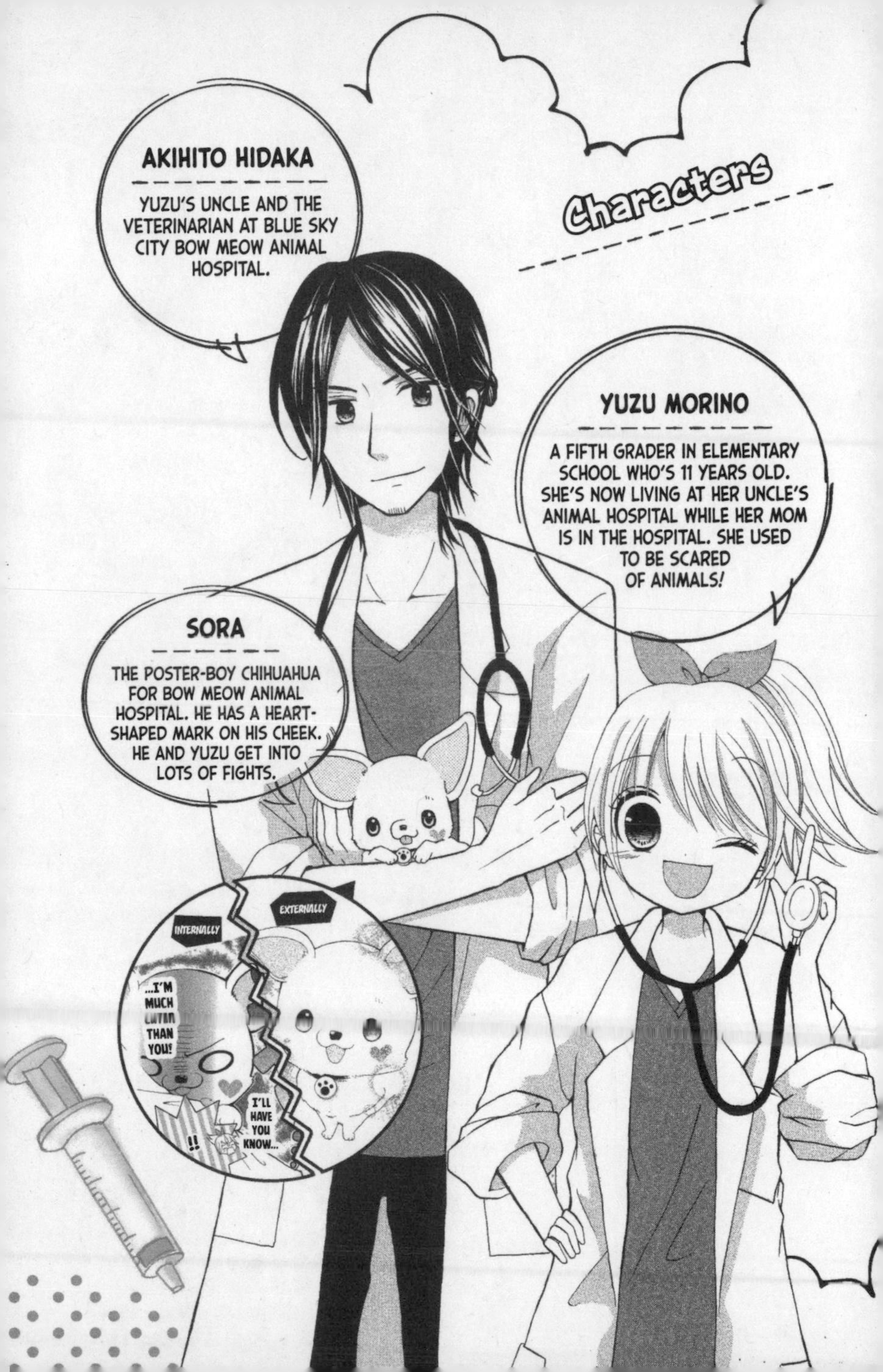
Characters
AKIHITO HIDAKA
YUZU'S UNCLE AND THE VETERINARIAN AT BLUE SKY CITY BOW MEOW ANIMAL HOSPITAL.
YUZU MORINO
A FIFTH GRADER IN ELEMENTARY SCHOOL WHO'S 11 YEARS OLD. SHE'S NOW LIVING AT HER UNCLE'S ANIMAL HOSPITAL WHILE HER MOM IS IN THE HOSPITAL. SHE USED TO BE SCARED OF ANIMALS!
SORA
THE POSTER-BOY CHIHUAHUA FOR BOW MEOW ANIMAL HOSPITAL. HE HAS A HEART-SHAPED MARK ON HIS CHEEK. HE AND YUZU GET INTO LOTS OF FIGHTS.
EXTERNALLY
I'LL HAVE YOU KNOW...
INTERNALLY
...I'M MUCH CUTER THAN YOU!
!!

YUZU THE PET VET

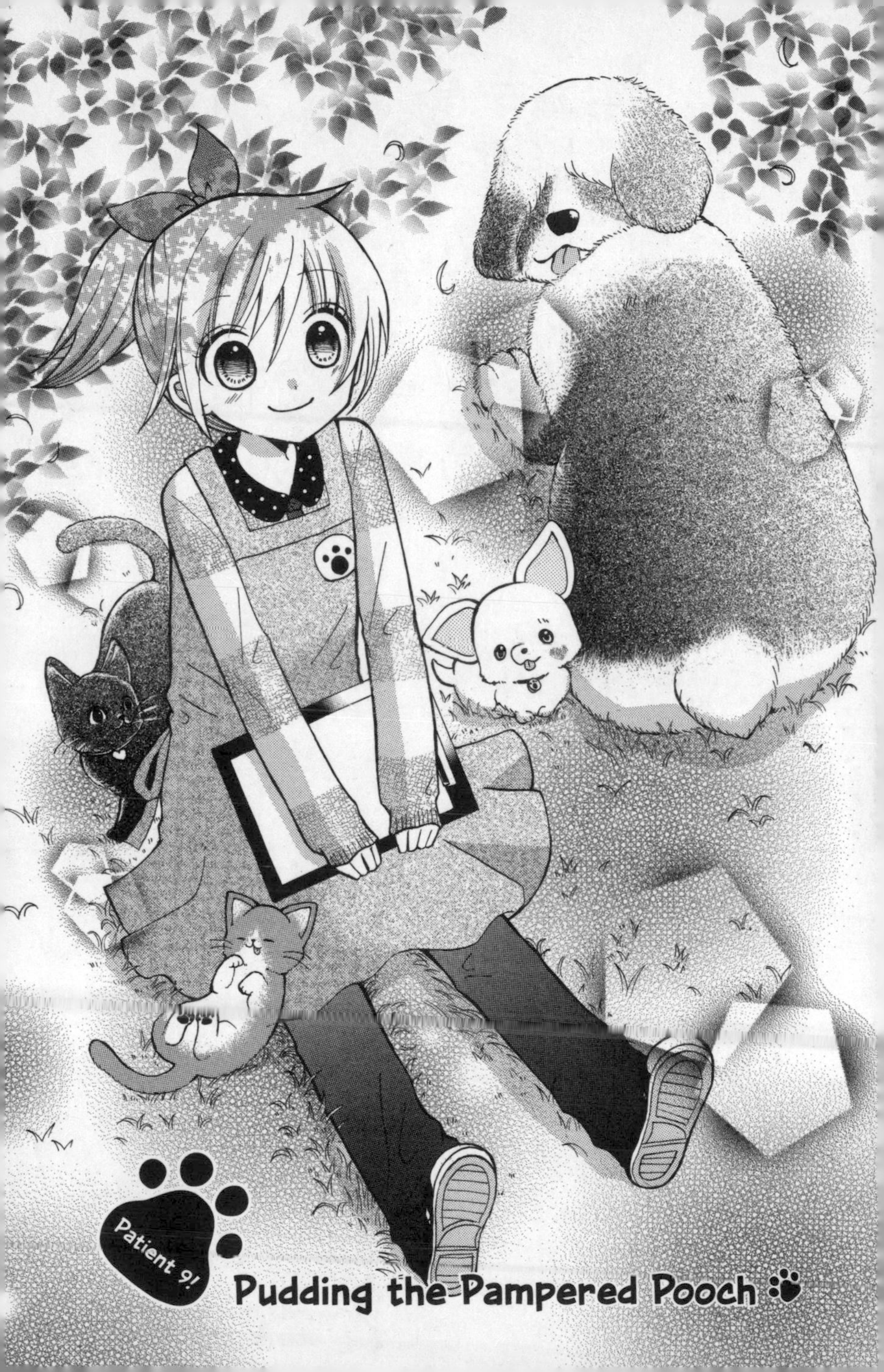
Patient 9!
Pudding the Pampered Pooch

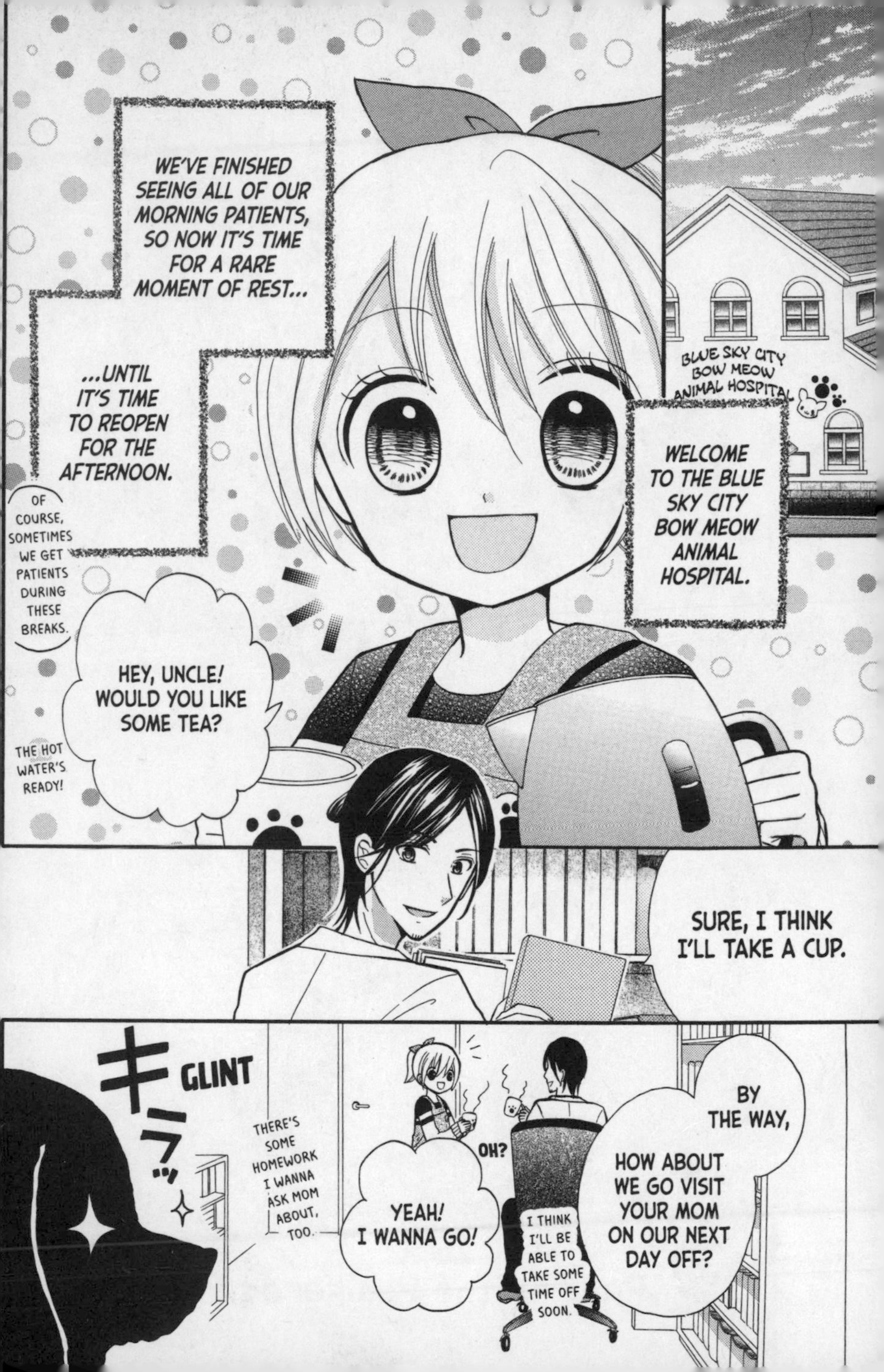
BLUE SKY CITY BOW MEOW ANIMAL HOSPITAL
WELCOME TO THE BLUE SKY CITY BOW MEOW ANIMAL HOSPITAL.
WE'VE FINISHED SEEING ALL OF OUR MORNING PATIENTS, SO NOW IT'S TIME FOR A RARE MOMENT OF REST...
...UNTIL IT'S TIME TO REOPEN FOR THE AFTERNOON.
OF COURSE, SOMETIMES WE GET PATIENTS DURING THESE BREAKS.
HEY, UNCLE! WOULD YOU LIKE SOME TEA?
THE HOT WATER'S READY!
SURE, I THINK I'LL TAKE A CUP.
BY THE WAY,
HOW ABOUT WE GO VISIT YOUR MOM ON OUR NEXT DAY OFF?
I THINK I'LL BE ABLE TO TAKE SOME TIME OFF SOON.
OH?
YEAH! I WANNA GO!
THERE'S SOME HOMEWORK I WANNA ASK MOM ABOUT, TOO.
キラッ
GLINT

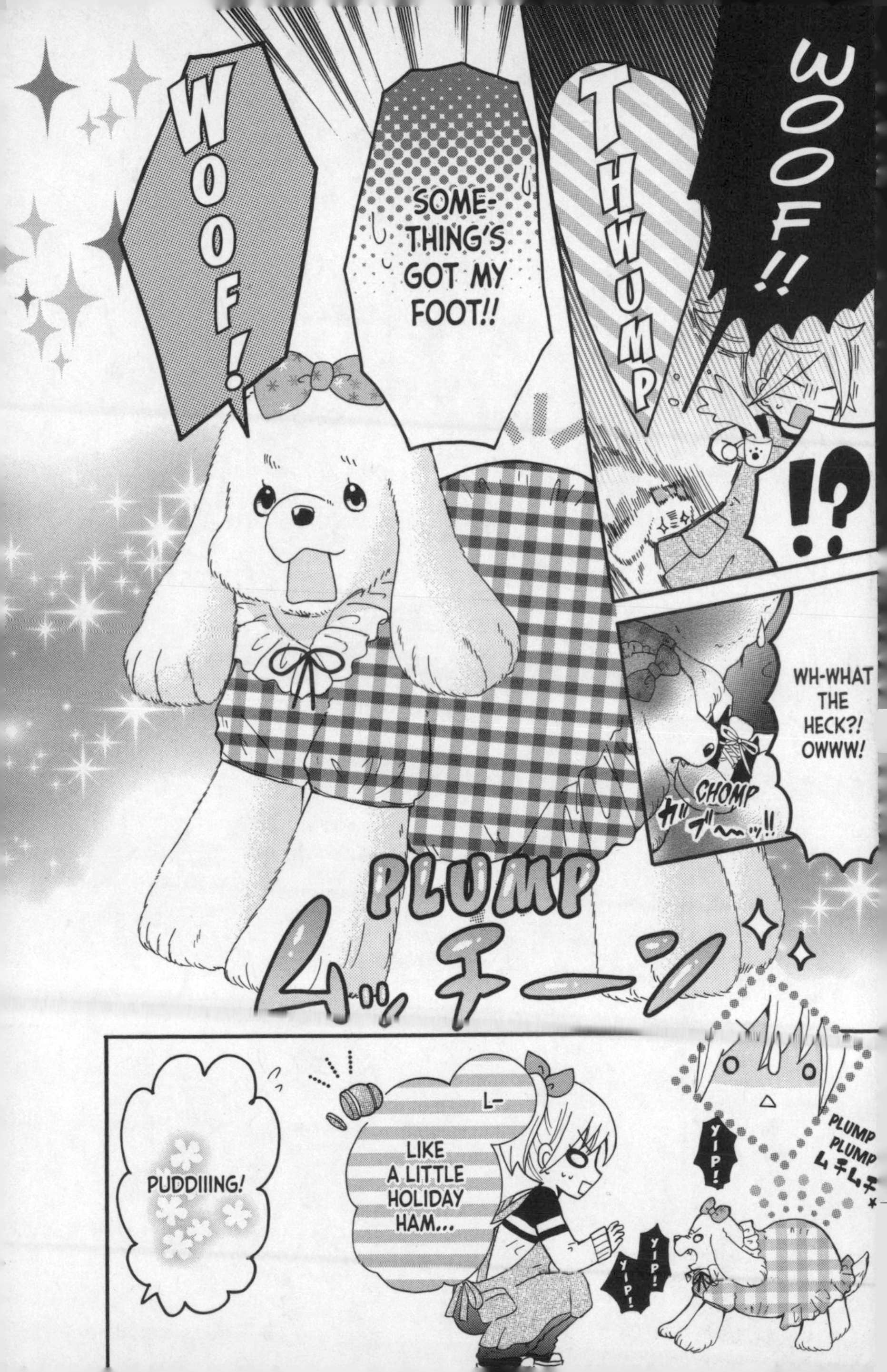
WOOF!!
THWUMP
!?
WH-WHAT THE HECK?! OWWW!
CHOMP
SOME-THING'S GOT MY FOOT!!
WOOF!
PLUMP
YIP!
PLUMP PLUMP
YIP!
YIP!
YIP!
L-
LIKE A LITTLE HOLIDAY HAM...
PUDDIIING!

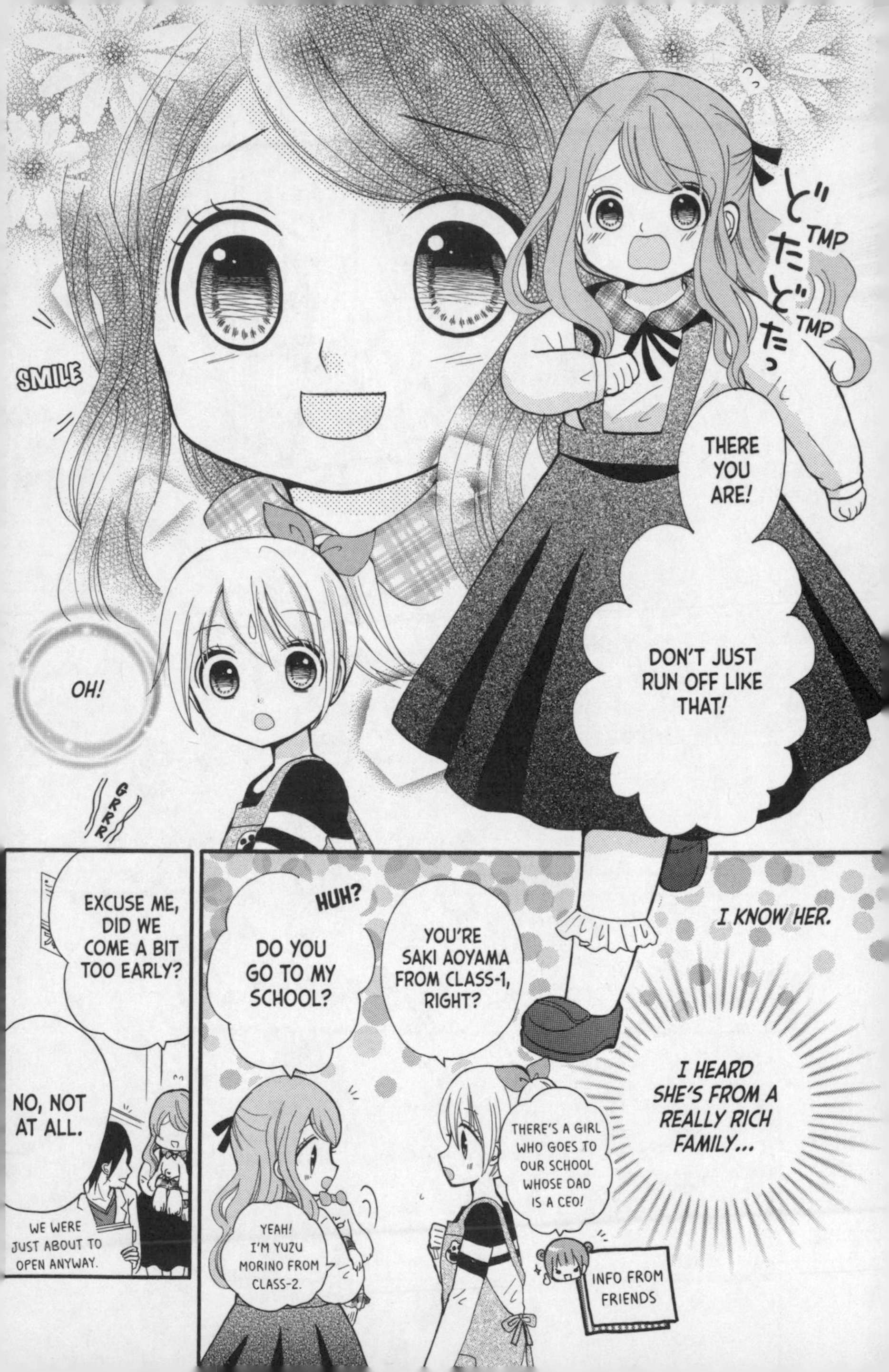
どた
TMP
どたっ
TMP
THERE YOU ARE!
DON'T JUST RUN OFF LIKE THAT!
SMILE
OH!
GRRR
I KNOW HER.
I HEARD SHE'S FROM A REALLY RICH FAMILY...
THERE'S A GIRL WHO GOES TO OUR SCHOOL WHOSE DAD IS A CEO!
INFO FROM FRIENDS
YOU'RE SAKI AOYAMA FROM CLASS-1, RIGHT?
HUH?
DO YOU GO TO MY SCHOOL?
YEAH! I'M YUZU MORINO FROM CLASS-2.
EXCUSE ME, DID WE COME A BIT TOO EARLY?
NO, NOT AT ALL.
WE WERE JUST ABOUT TO OPEN ANYWAY.

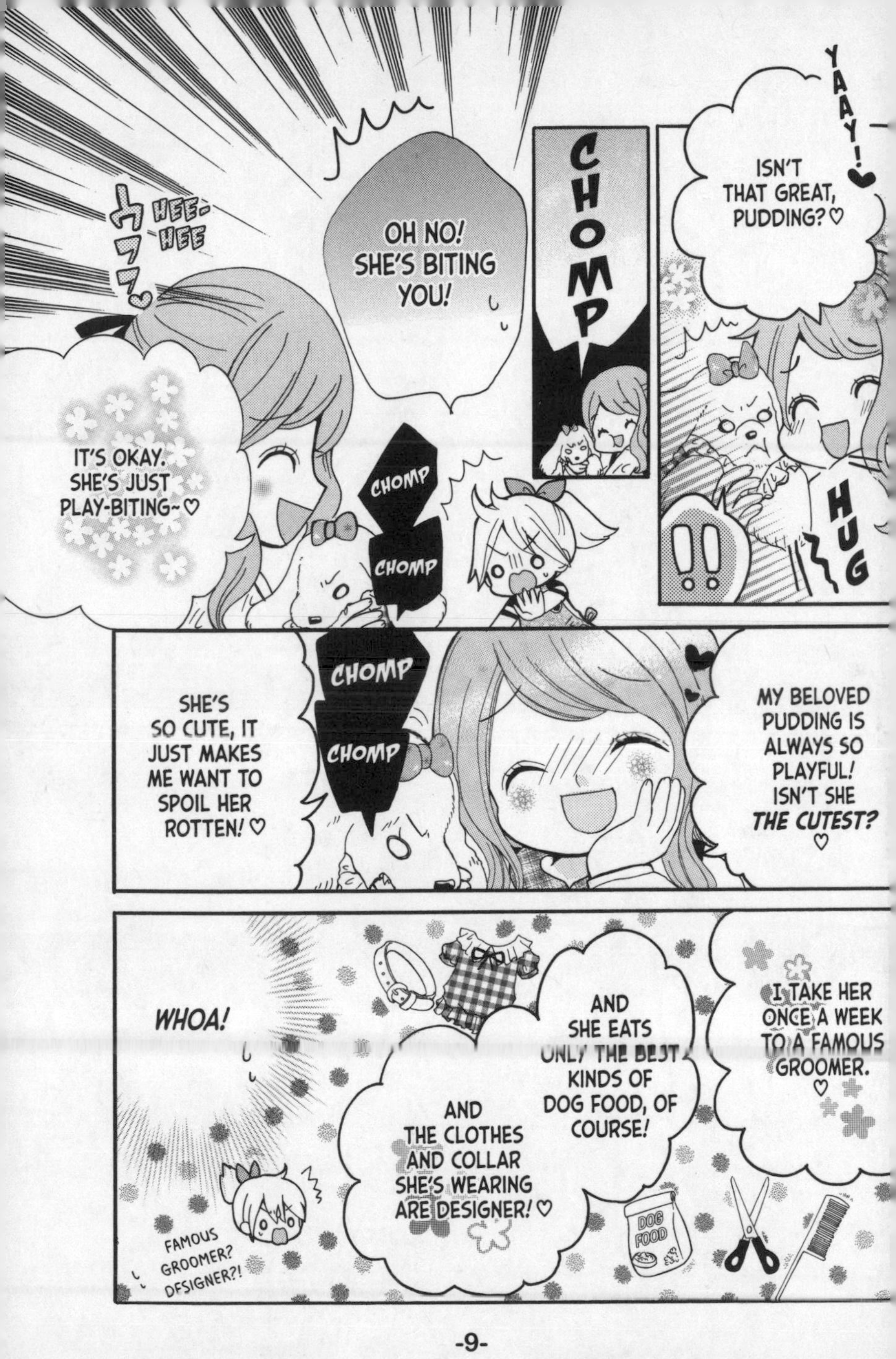
YAAY!
ISN'T THAT GREAT, PUDDING? ♡
!!
HUG
CHOMP
OH NO! SHE'S BITING YOU!
HEE-HEE
CHOMP
CHOMP
IT'S OKAY. SHE'S JUST PLAY-BITING~ ♡
MY BELOVED PUDDING IS ALWAYS SO PLAYFUL! ISN'T SHE *THE CUTEST?* ♡
CHOMP
CHOMP
SHE'S SO CUTE, IT JUST MAKES ME WANT TO SPOIL HER ROTTEN! ♡
I TAKE HER ONCE A WEEK TO A FAMOUS GROOMER. ♡
AND SHE EATS ONLY THE BEST KINDS OF DOG FOOD, OF COURSE!
AND THE CLOTHES AND COLLAR SHE'S WEARING ARE DESIGNER! ♡
DOG FOOD
WHOA!
FAMOUS GROOMER? DESIGNER?!

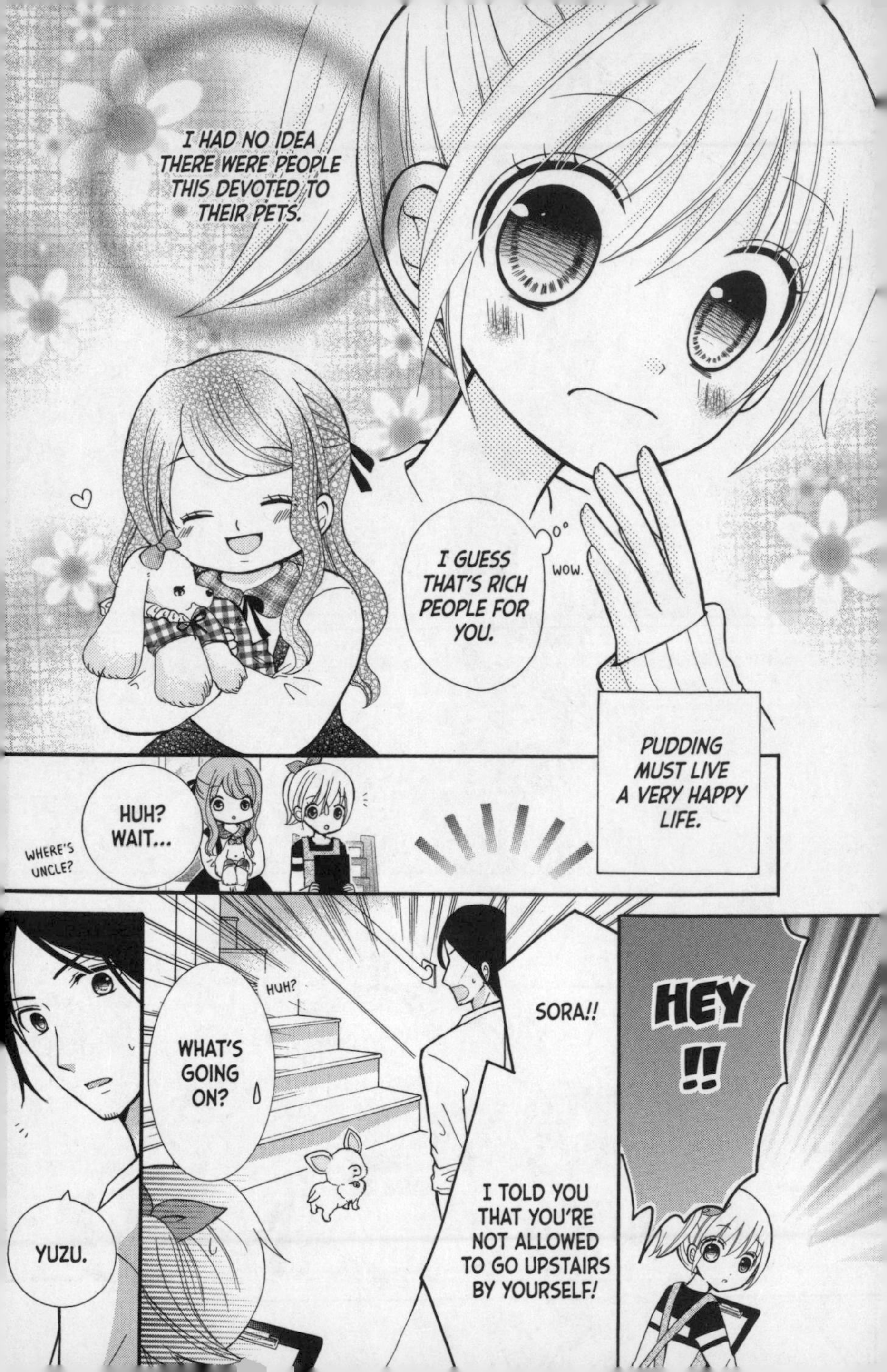
I HAD NO IDEA THERE WERE PEOPLE THIS DEVOTED TO THEIR PETS.
WOW.
I GUESS THAT'S RICH PEOPLE FOR YOU.
PUDDING MUST LIVE A VERY HAPPY LIFE.
HUH? WAIT...
WHERE'S UNCLE?
HEY !!
SORA!!
I TOLD YOU THAT YOU'RE NOT ALLOWED TO GO UPSTAIRS BY YOURSELF!
HUH?
WHAT'S GOING ON?
YUZU.

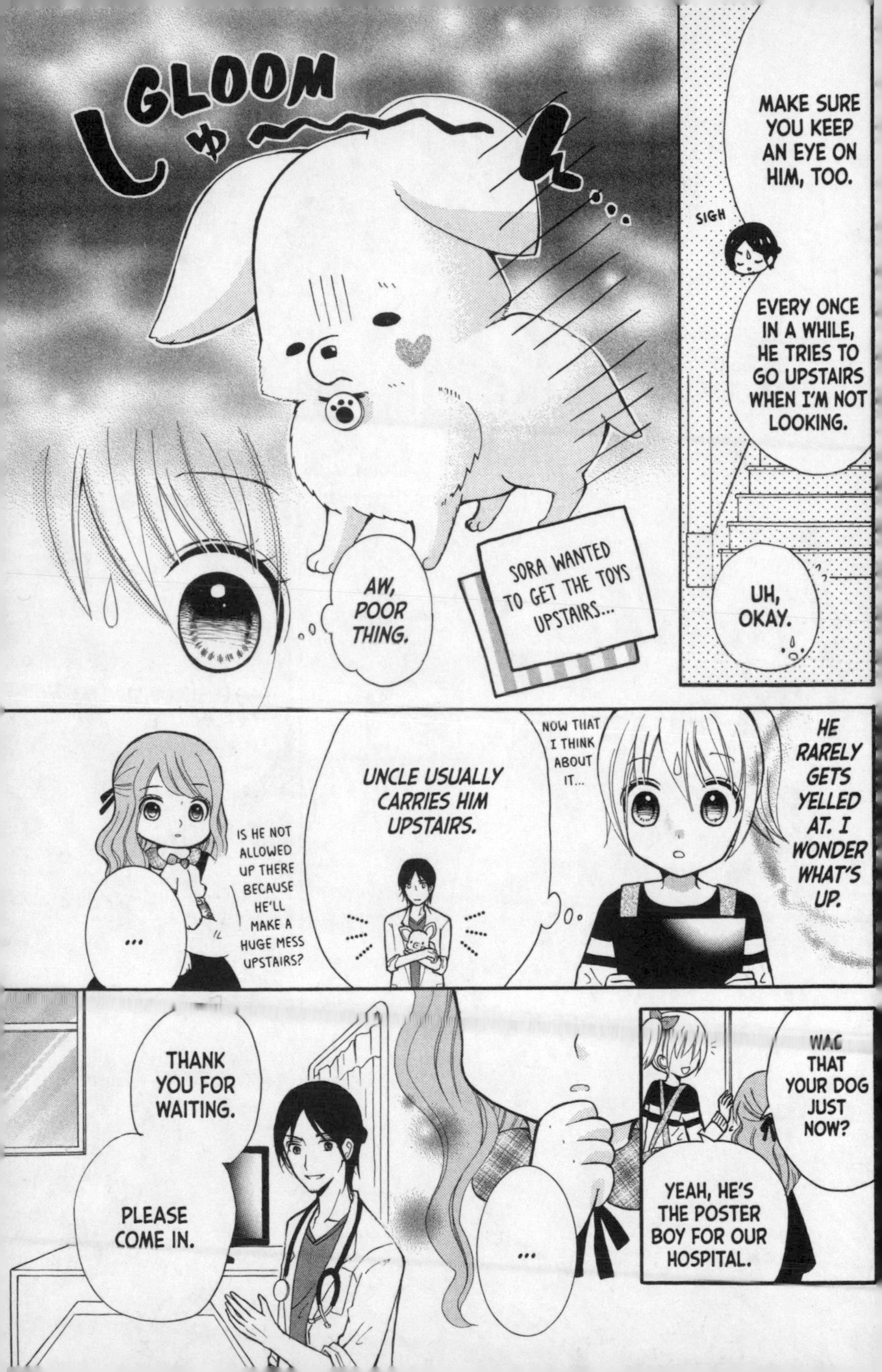
MAKE SURE YOU KEEP AN EYE ON HIM, TOO.
SIGH
EVERY ONCE IN A WHILE, HE TRIES TO GO UPSTAIRS WHEN I'M NOT LOOKING.
UH, OKAY.
GLOOM
しゅ～ん
SORA WANTED TO GET THE TOYS UPSTAIRS...
AW, POOR THING.
HE RARELY GETS YELLED AT. I WONDER WHAT'S UP.
NOW THAT I THINK ABOUT IT...
UNCLE USUALLY CARRIES HIM UPSTAIRS.
IS HE NOT ALLOWED UP THERE BECAUSE HE'LL MAKE A HUGE MESS UPSTAIRS?
...
WAS THAT YOUR DOG JUST NOW?
YEAH, HE'S THE POSTER BOY FOR OUR HOSPITAL.
...
THANK YOU FOR WAITING.
PLEASE COME IN.

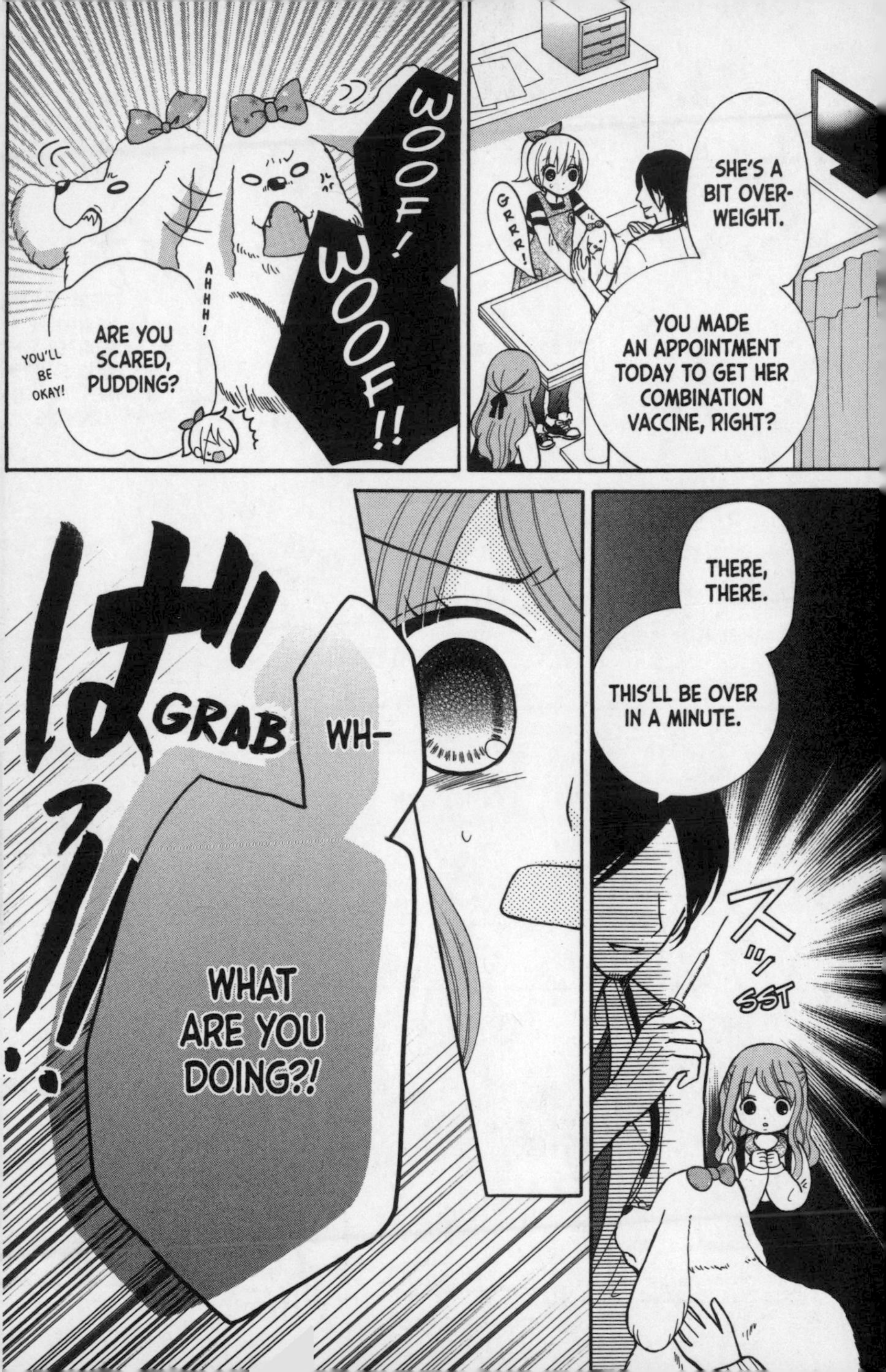
SHE'S A BIT OVER-WEIGHT.
YOU MADE AN APPOINTMENT TODAY TO GET HER COMBINATION VACCINE, RIGHT?
GRRR!
WOOF! WOOF!!
AHHHH!
ARE YOU SCARED, PUDDING?
YOU'LL BE OKAY!
THERE, THERE.
THIS'LL BE OVER IN A MINUTE.
SST
WH-
GRAB
WHAT ARE YOU DOING?!

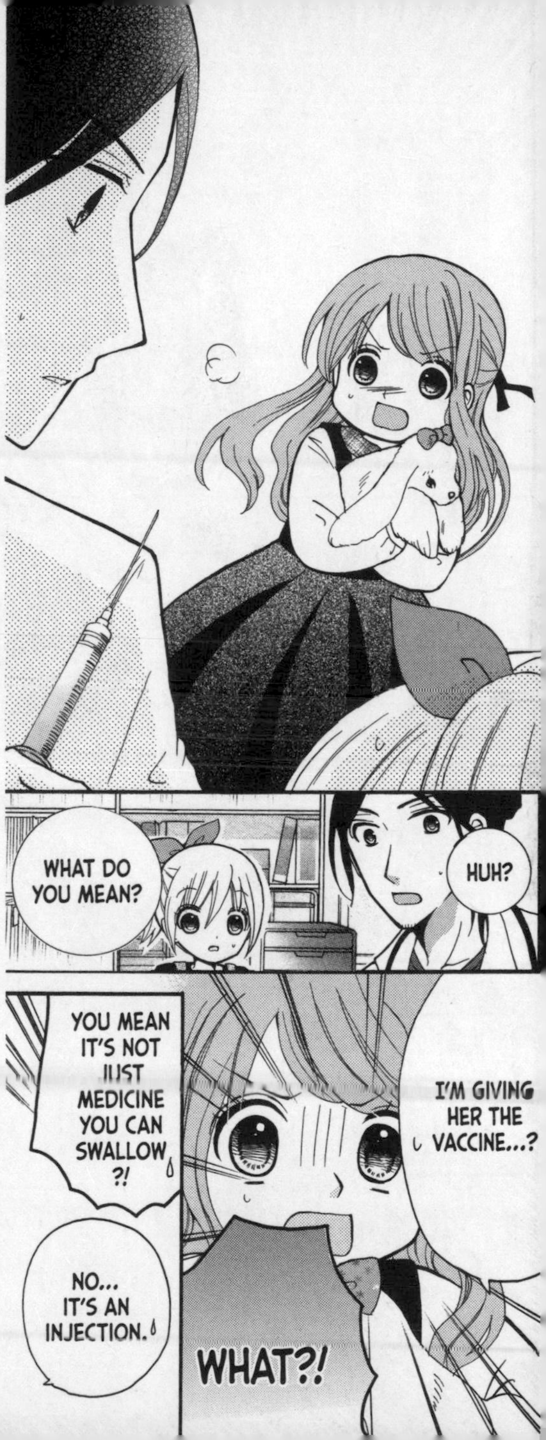
HUH?
WHAT DO YOU MEAN?
I'M GIVING HER THE VACCINE...?
YOU MEAN IT'S NOT JUST MEDICINE YOU CAN SWALLOW?!
NO... IT'S AN INJECTION.
WHAT?!

GREETINGS.

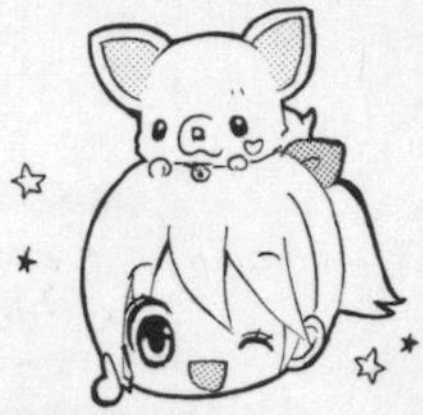

THANK YOU SO VERY MUCH FOR PURCHASING *YUZU THE PET VET* VOLUME 3!

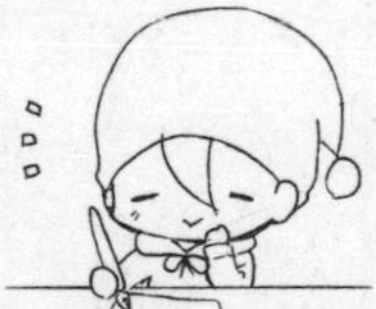

EVER SINCE I STARTED WORKING ON THIS SERIES, I FIND MYSELF WATCHING CATS AND DOGS WHENEVER I COME ACROSS THEM. I'M SORRY FOR ACTING SO SKETCHY! (LOL)

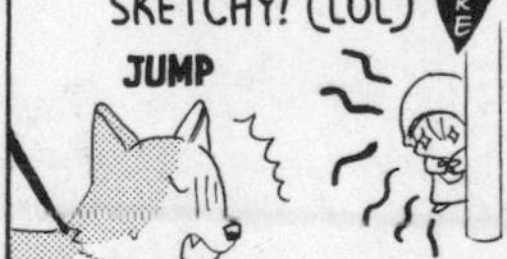
STARE
JUMP

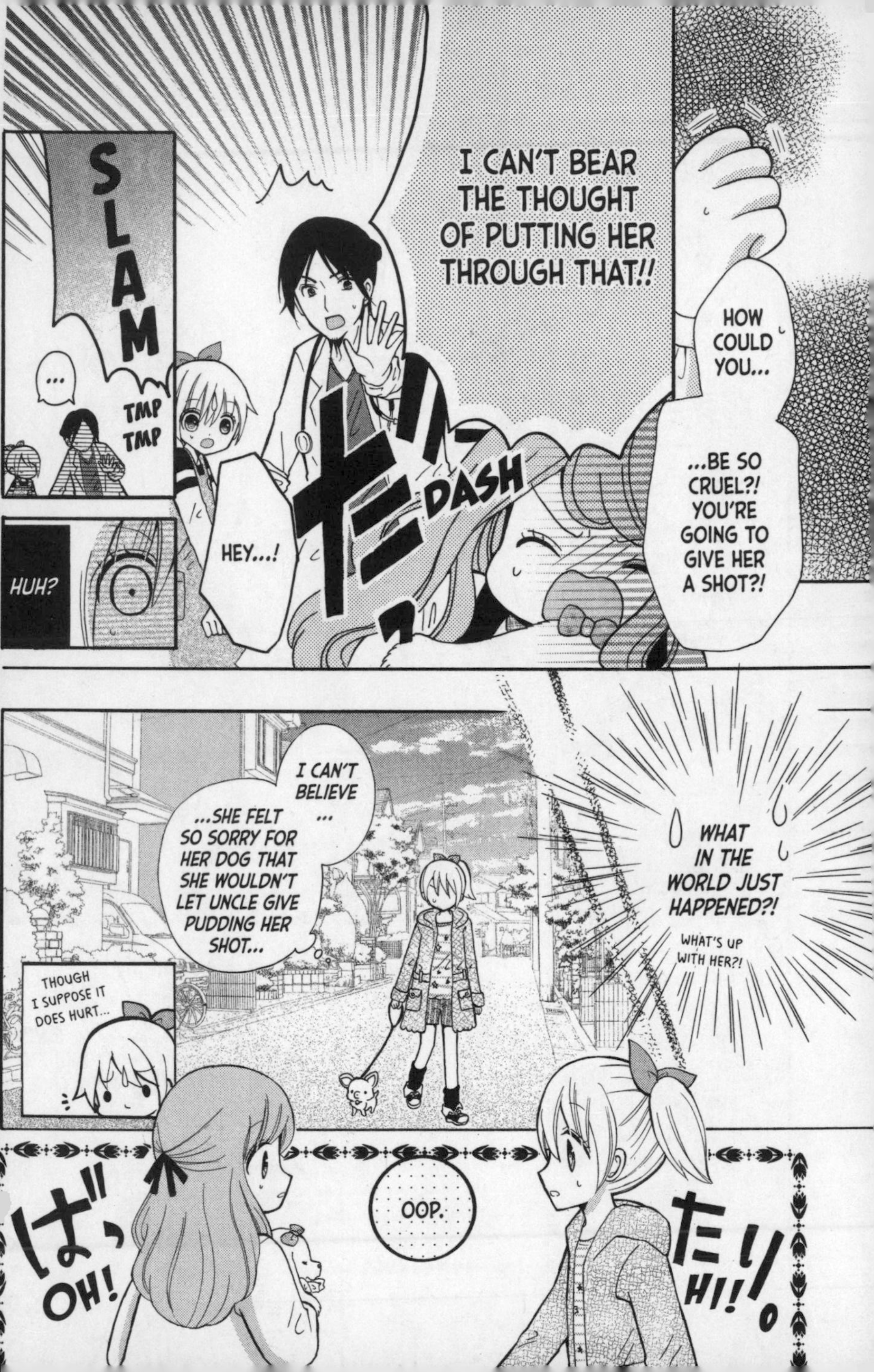
HOW COULD YOU...
...BE SO CRUEL?! YOU'RE GOING TO GIVE HER A SHOT?!
DASH
I CAN'T BEAR THE THOUGHT OF PUTTING HER THROUGH THAT!!
HEY...!
SLAM
TMP TMP
...
HUH?
WHAT IN THE WORLD JUST HAPPENED?!
WHAT'S UP WITH HER?!
I CAN'T BELIEVE...
...SHE FELT SO SORRY FOR HER DOG THAT SHE WOULDN'T LET UNCLE GIVE PUDDING HER SHOT...
THOUGH I SUPPOSE IT DOES HURT...
たりっ
HI!
OOP.
ばっ
OH!

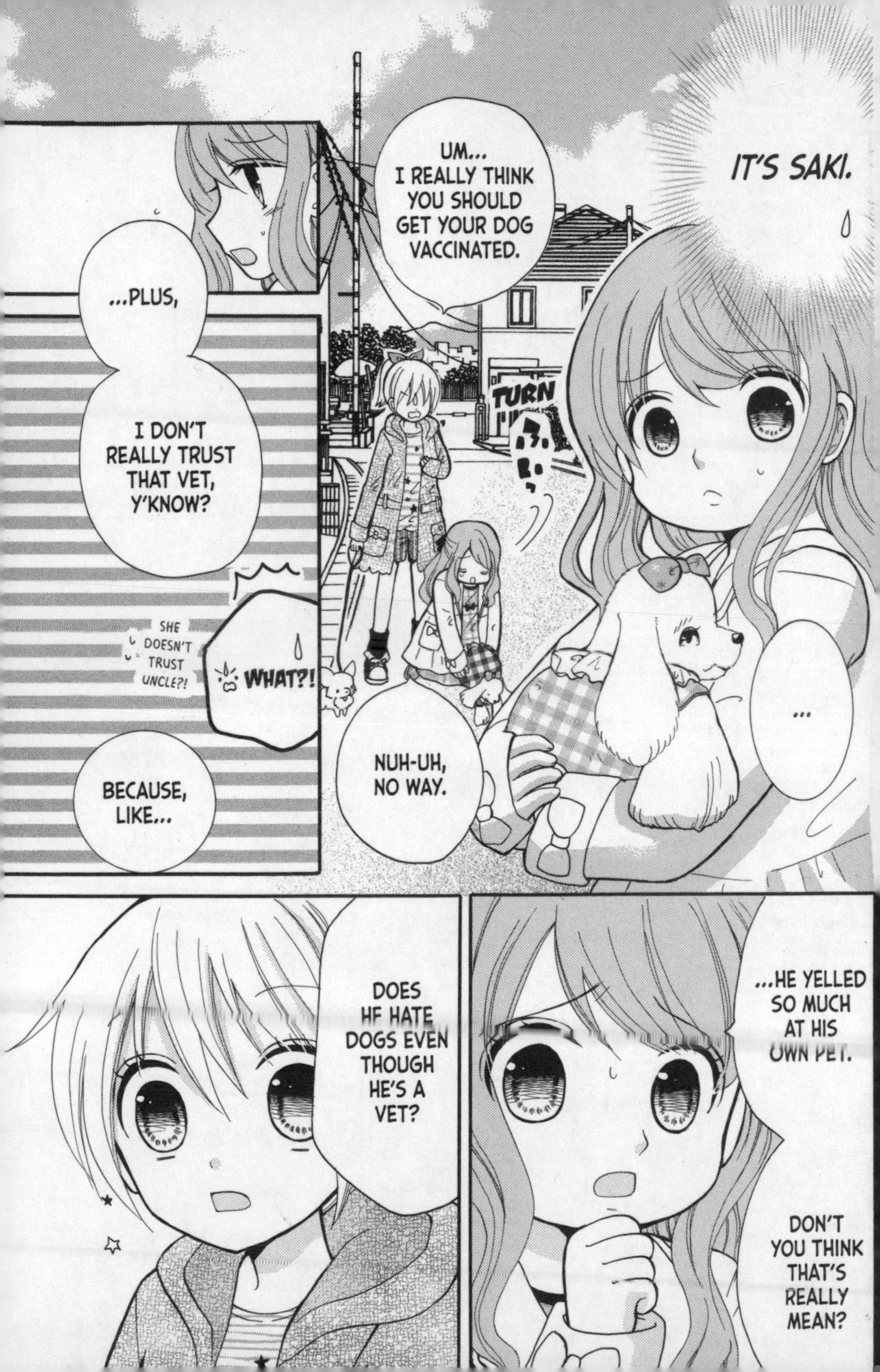
IT'S SAKI.
...
UM... I REALLY THINK YOU SHOULD GET YOUR DOG VACCINATED.
TURN
NUH-UH, NO WAY.
...PLUS, I DON'T REALLY TRUST THAT VET, Y'KNOW?
WHAT?!
SHE DOESN'T TRUST UNCLE?!
BECAUSE, LIKE...
...HE YELLED SO MUCH AT HIS OWN PET.
DON'T YOU THINK THAT'S REALLY MEAN?
DOES HE HATE DOGS EVEN THOUGH HE'S A VET?

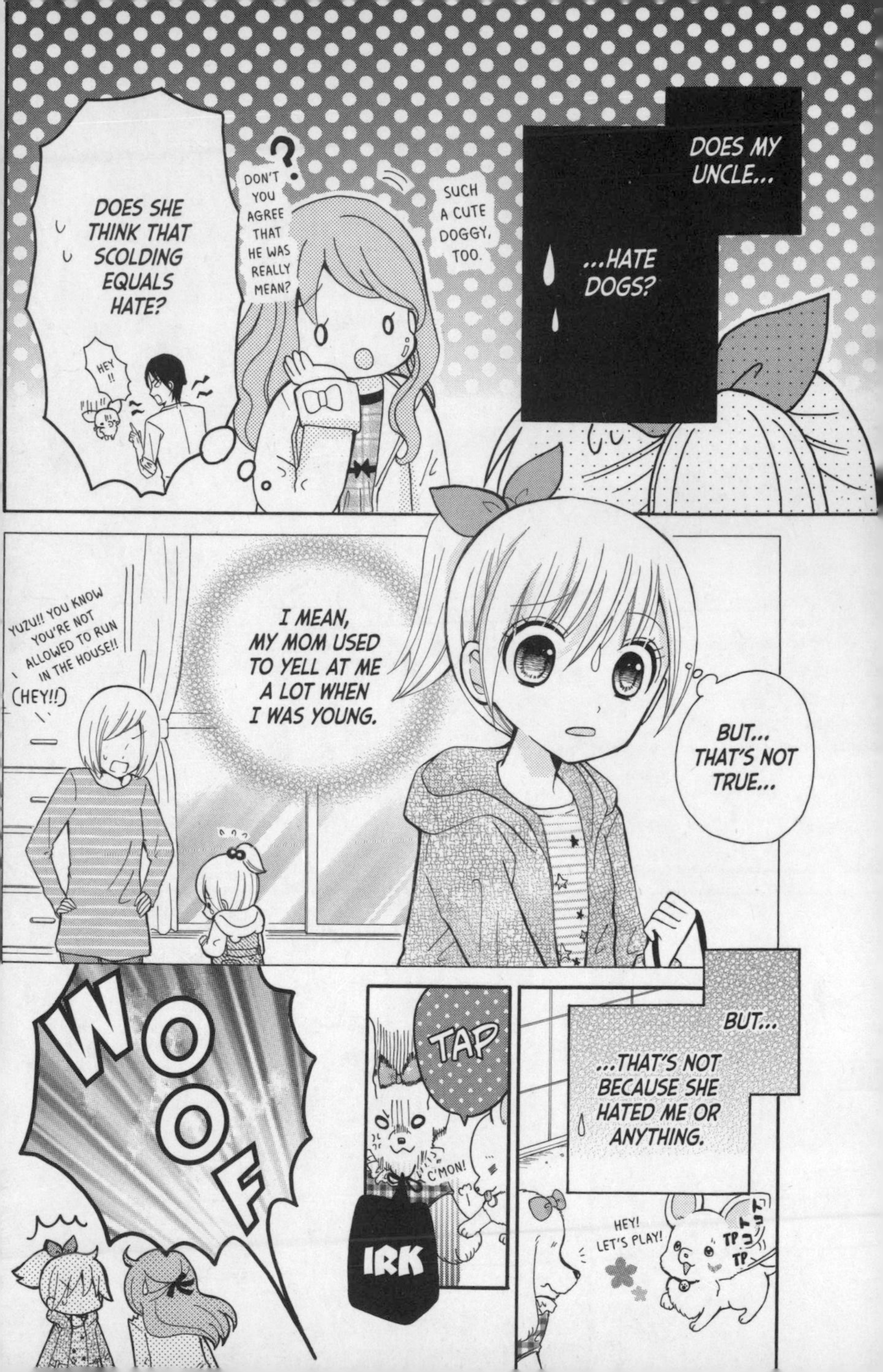
DOES MY UNCLE...
...HATE DOGS?
SUCH A CUTE DOGGY, TOO.
DON'T YOU AGREE THAT HE WAS REALLY MEAN?
DOES SHE THINK THAT SCOLDING EQUALS HATE?
HEY!!
BUT... THAT'S NOT TRUE...
I MEAN, MY MOM USED TO YELL AT ME A LOT WHEN I WAS YOUNG.
YUZU!! YOU KNOW YOU'RE NOT ALLOWED TO RUN IN THE HOUSE!!
(HEY!!)
BUT...
...THAT'S NOT BECAUSE SHE HATED ME OR ANYTHING.
HEY! LET'S PLAY!
TP TP
TAP
C'MON!
IRK
WOOF

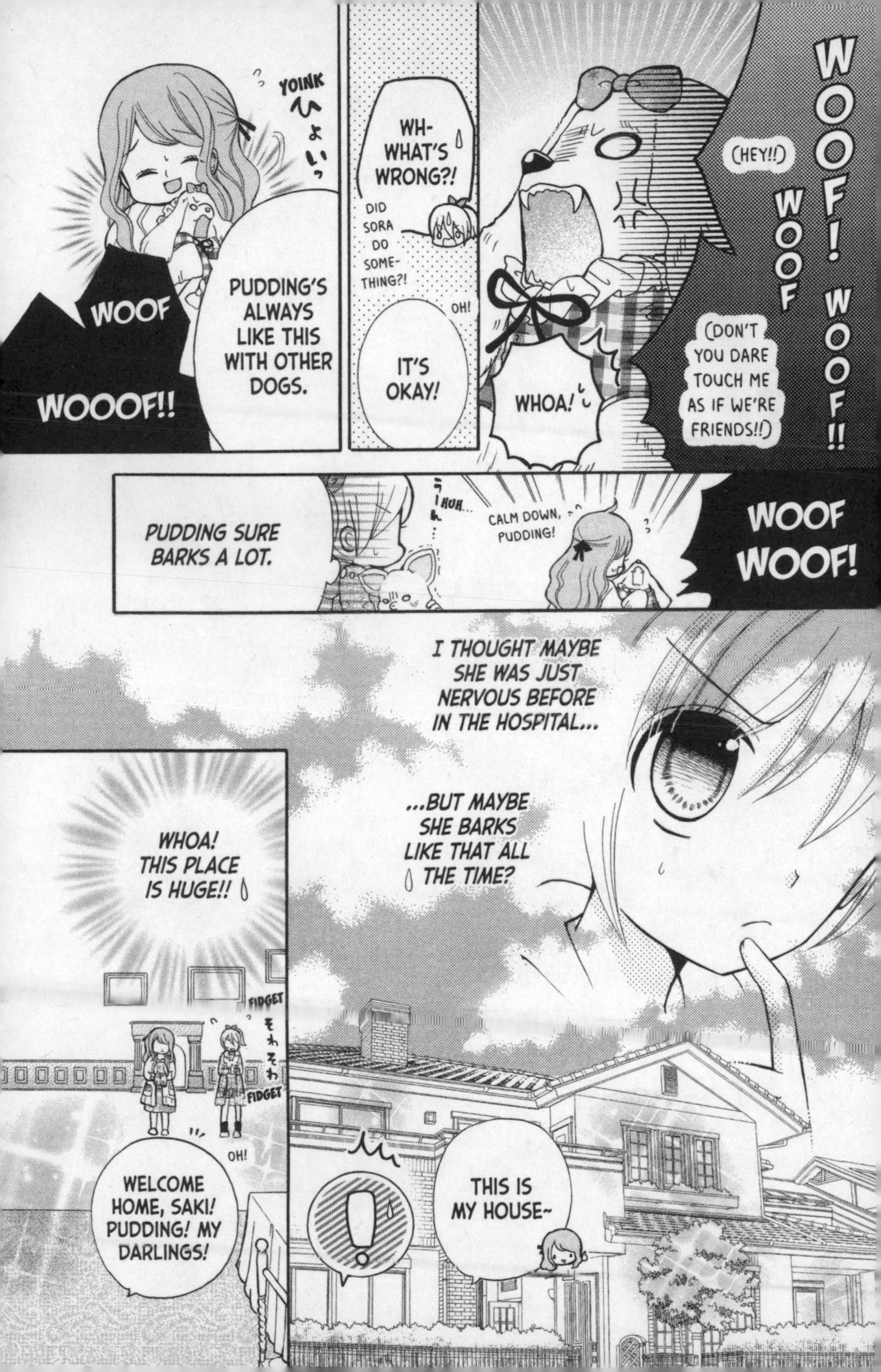
WOOF! WOOF!!
WOOF WOOF
(HEY!!)
(DON'T YOU DARE TOUCH ME AS IF WE'RE FRIENDS!!)
WHOA!
WH-WHAT'S WRONG?!
DID SORA DO SOME-THING?!
OH!
IT'S OKAY!
YOINK
ひょいっ
PUDDING'S ALWAYS LIKE THIS WITH OTHER DOGS.
WOOF
WOOOF!!
WOOF WOOF!
CALM DOWN, PUDDING!
HUH...
うーん…
PUDDING SURE BARKS A LOT.
I THOUGHT MAYBE SHE WAS JUST NERVOUS BEFORE IN THE HOSPITAL...
...BUT MAYBE SHE BARKS LIKE THAT ALL THE TIME?
THIS IS MY HOUSE~
!
WHOA! THIS PLACE IS HUGE!!
FIDGET
そわそわ
FIDGET
OH!
WELCOME HOME, SAKI! PUDDING! MY DARLINGS!

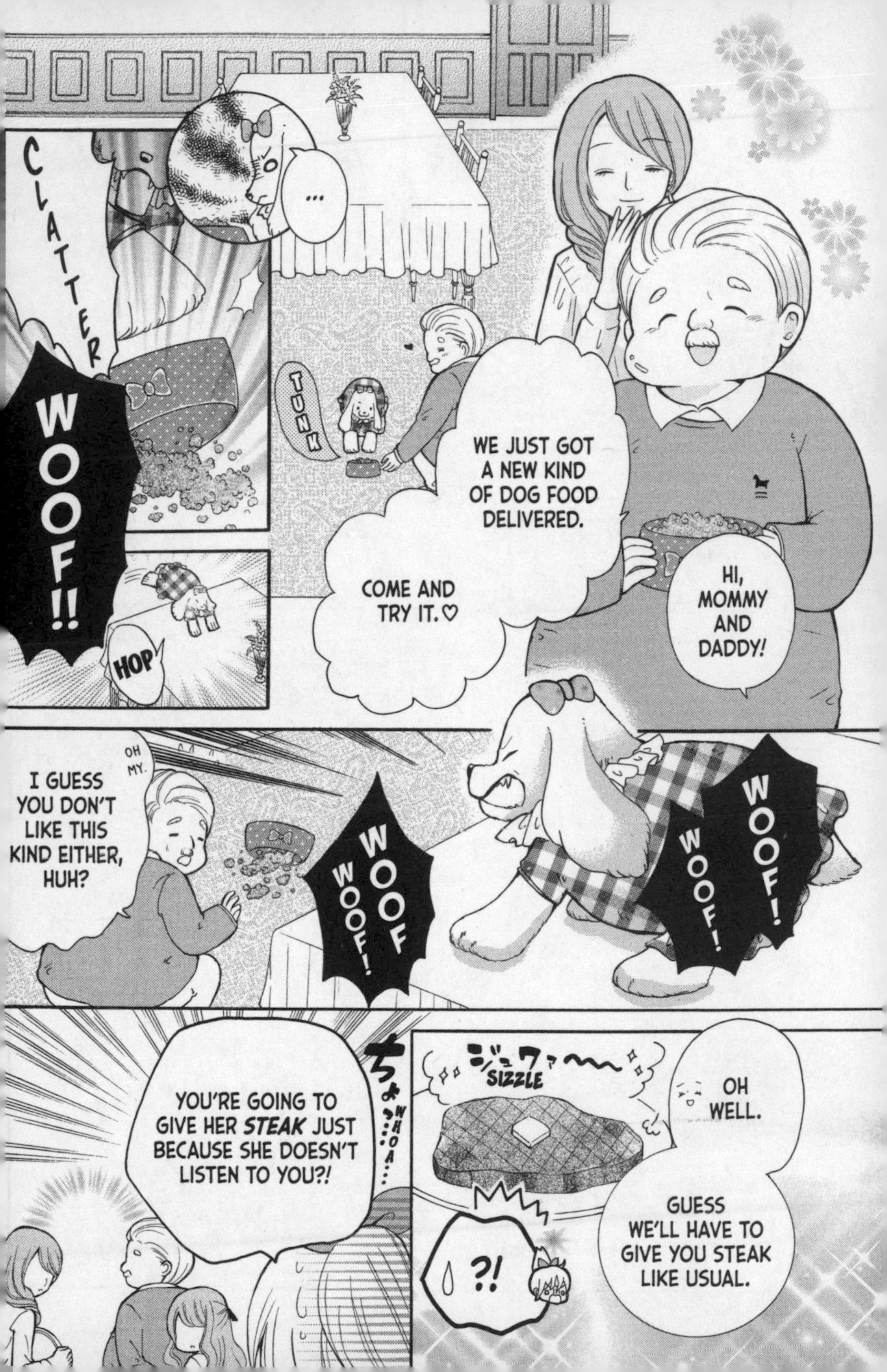
WE JUST GOT A NEW KIND OF DOG FOOD DELIVERED.
COME AND TRY IT. ♡
HI, MOMMY AND DADDY!
TUNK
...
CLATTER
WOOF!!
HOP
WOOF! WOOF!
WOOF WOOF!
OH MY.
I GUESS YOU DON'T LIKE THIS KIND EITHER, HUH?
OH WELL.
ジュワァ〜〜
SIZZLE
GUESS WE'LL HAVE TO GIVE YOU STEAK LIKE USUAL.
?!
ちょ?!
WHOA...
YOU'RE GOING TO GIVE HER *STEAK* JUST BECAUSE SHE DOESN'T LISTEN TO YOU?!

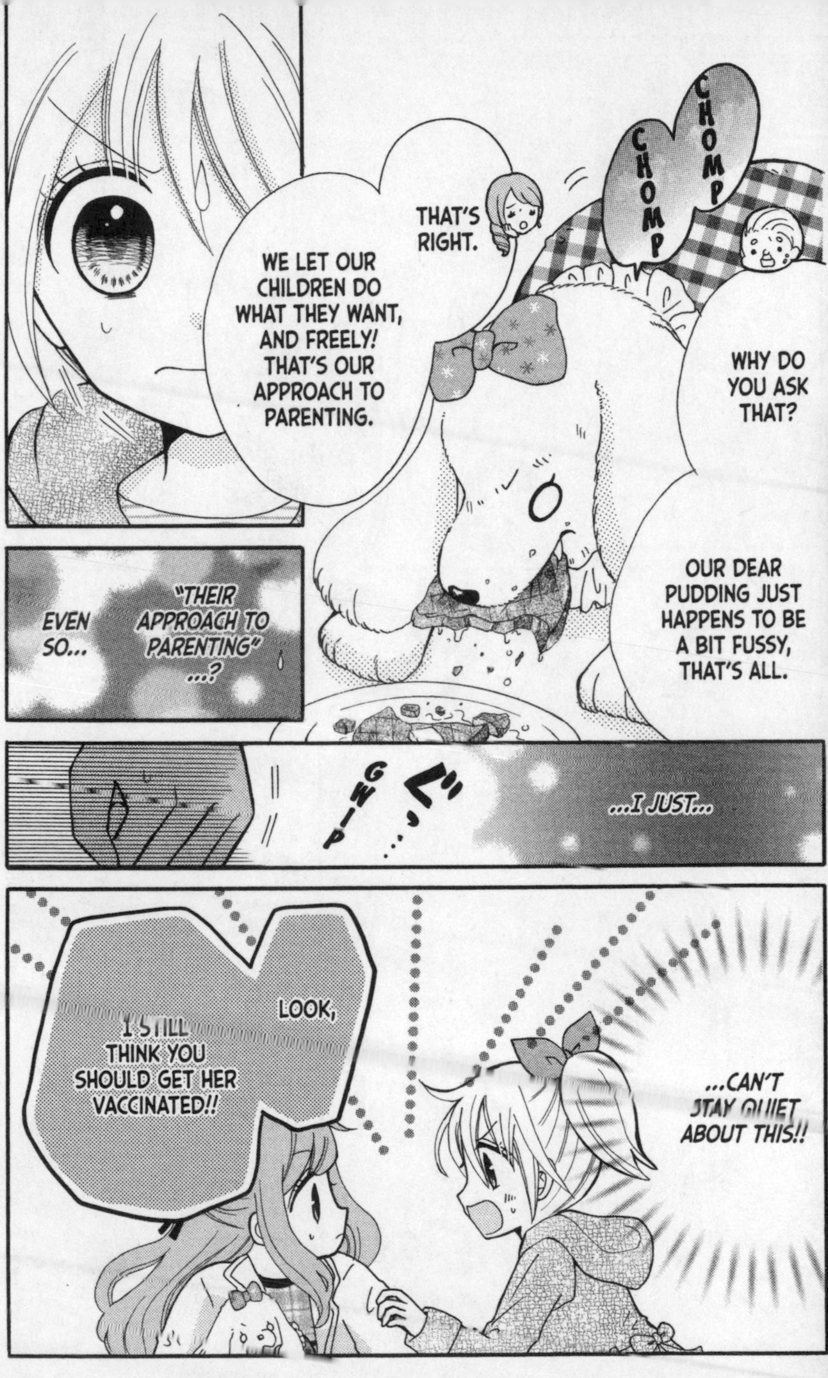
CHOMP CHOMP
WHY DO YOU ASK THAT?
OUR DEAR PUDDING JUST HAPPENS TO BE A BIT FUSSY, THAT'S ALL.
THAT'S RIGHT.
WE LET OUR CHILDREN DO WHAT THEY WANT, AND FREELY! THAT'S OUR APPROACH TO PARENTING.
"THEIR APPROACH TO PARENTING" ...?
EVEN SO...
...I JUST...
GWIP
...CAN'T STAY QUIET ABOUT THIS!!
LOOK,
I STILL THINK YOU SHOULD GET HER VACCINATED!!

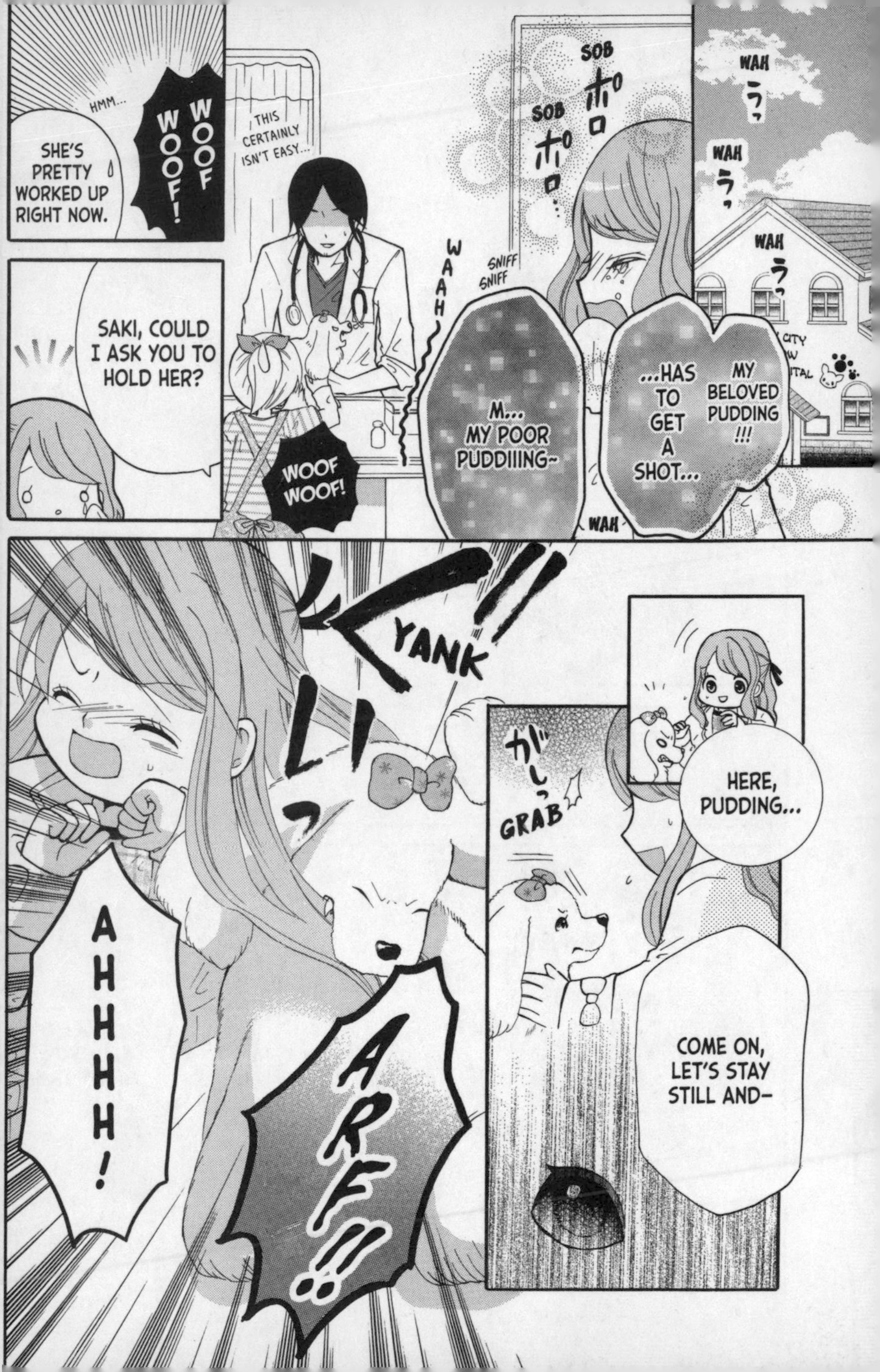
WAH
ラっ
WAH
ラっ
WAH
ラっ
SOB
ホロ
SOB
ホロ…
SNIFF SNIFF
WAAH~
MY BELOVED PUDDING!!!
...HAS TO GET A SHOT...
M... MY POOR PUDDIIING~
WAH
THIS CERTAINLY ISN'T EASY...
WOOF WOOF!
HMM...
WOOF WOOF!
SHE'S PRETTY WORKED UP RIGHT NOW.
SAKI, COULD I ASK YOU TO HOLD HER?
HERE, PUDDING...
がしっ
GRAB
COME ON, LET'S STAY STILL AND–
ぐいっ
YANK
ARF!!
AHHHH!

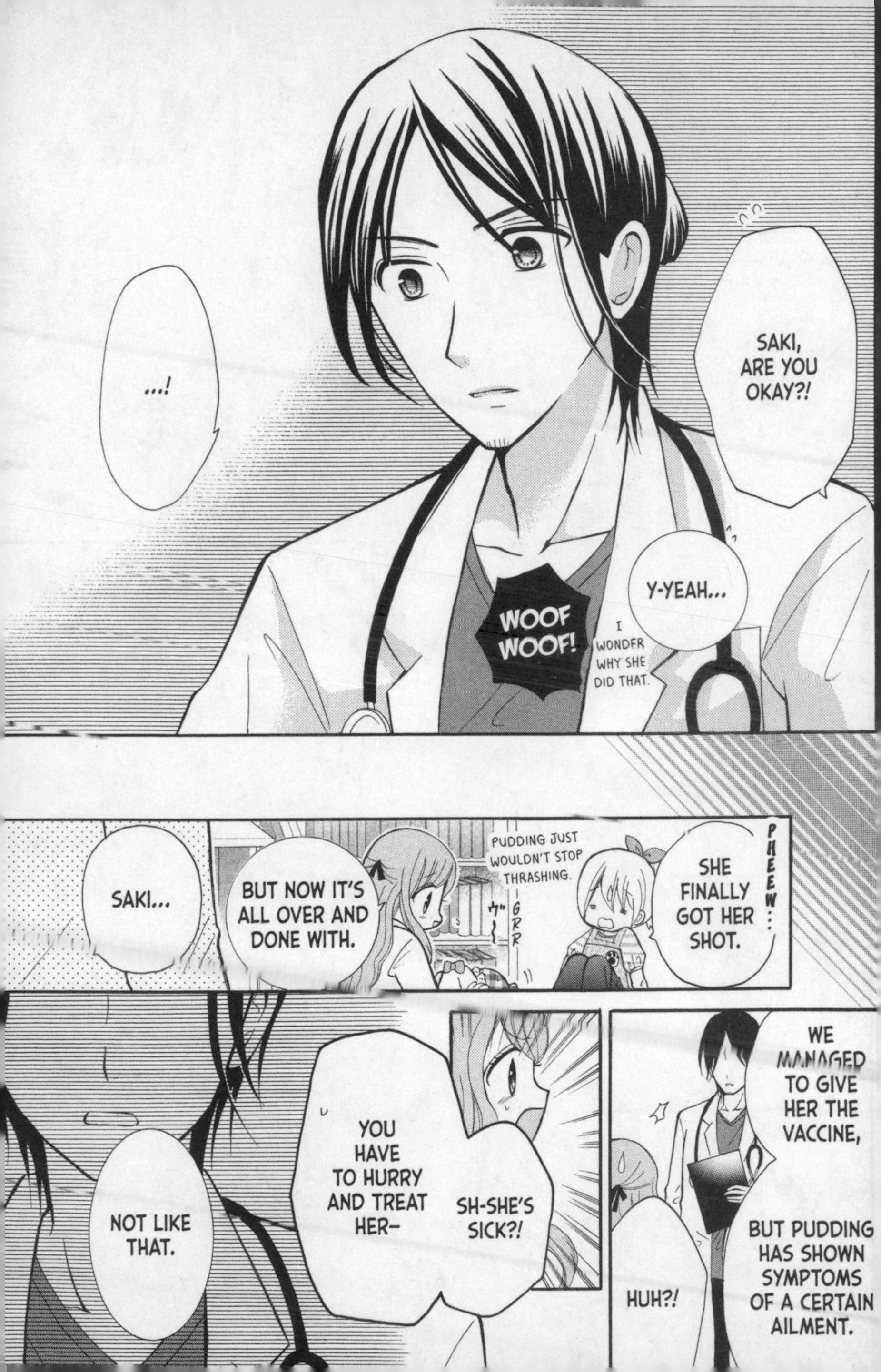
SAKI, ARE YOU OKAY?!
...!
Y-YEAH...
I WONDER WHY SHE DID THAT.
WOOF WOOF!
PHEEW...
SHE FINALLY GOT HER SHOT.
PUDDING JUST WOULDN'T STOP THRASHING.
GRR
BUT NOW IT'S ALL OVER AND DONE WITH.
SAKI...
WE MANAGED TO GIVE HER THE VACCINE,
BUT PUDDING HAS SHOWN SYMPTOMS OF A CERTAIN AILMENT.
HUH?!
SH-SHE'S SICK?!
YOU HAVE TO HURRY AND TREAT HER–
NOT LIKE THAT.

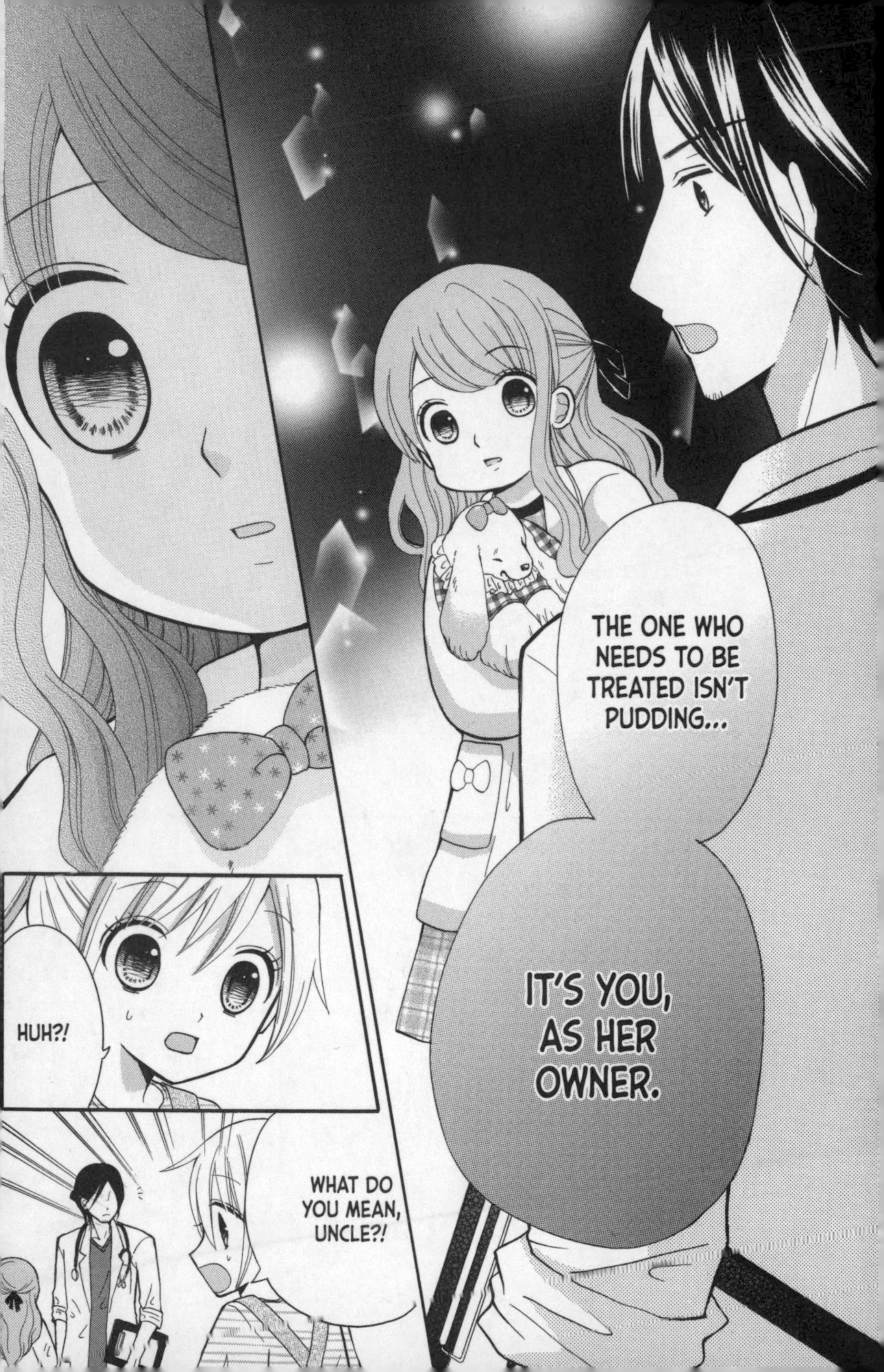
THE ONE WHO NEEDS TO BE TREATED ISN'T PUDDING...
IT'S YOU, AS HER OWNER.
HUH?!
WHAT DO YOU MEAN, UNCLE?!

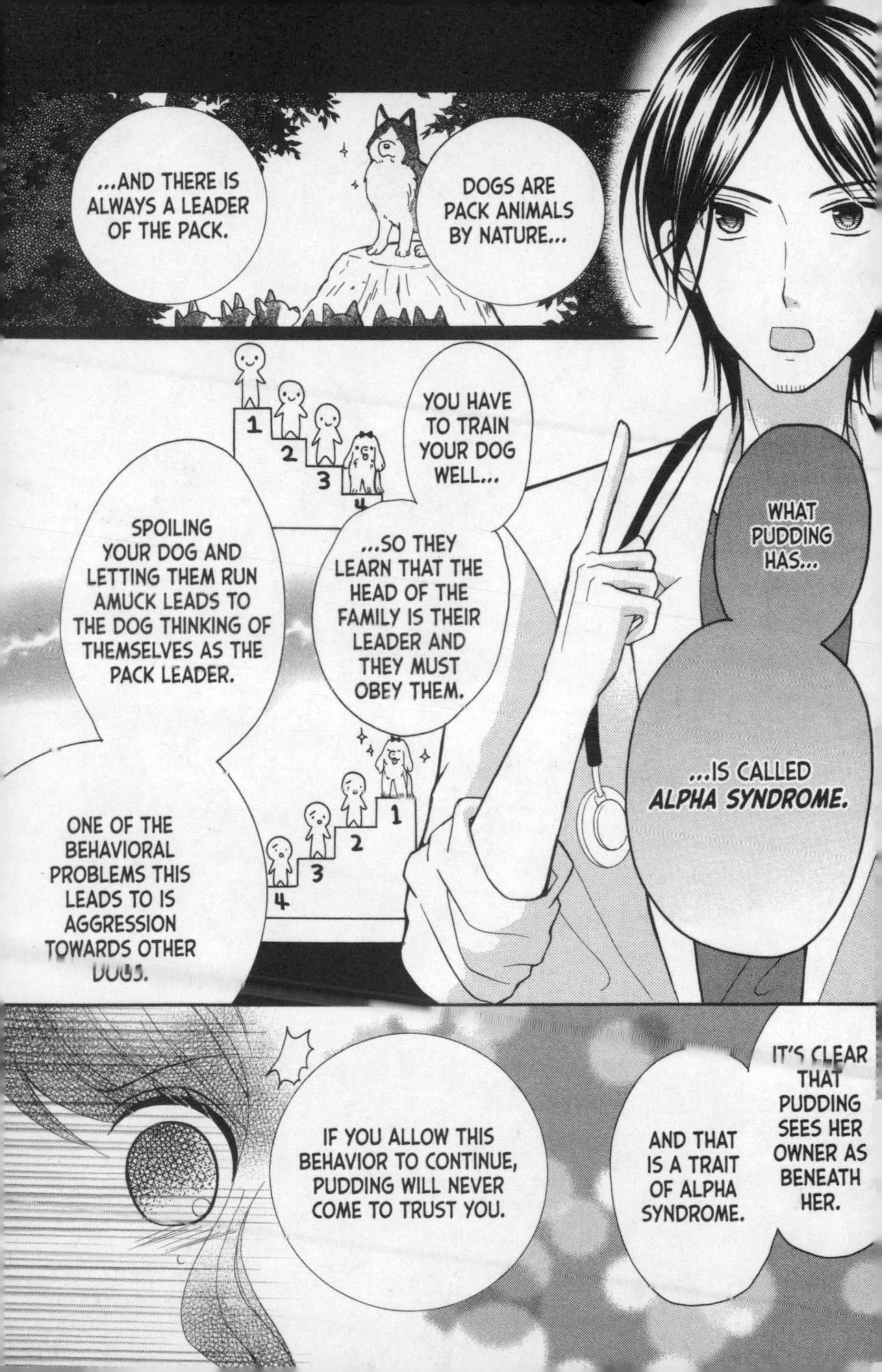
DOGS ARE PACK ANIMALS BY NATURE...
...AND THERE IS ALWAYS A LEADER OF THE PACK.
YOU HAVE TO TRAIN YOUR DOG WELL...
...SO THEY LEARN THAT THE HEAD OF THE FAMILY IS THEIR LEADER AND THEY MUST OBEY THEM.
1
2
3
4
SPOILING YOUR DOG AND LETTING THEM RUN AMUCK LEADS TO THE DOG THINKING OF THEMSELVES AS THE PACK LEADER.
1
2
3
4
ONE OF THE BEHAVIORAL PROBLEMS THIS LEADS TO IS AGGRESSION TOWARDS OTHER DOGS.
WHAT PUDDING HAS...
...IS CALLED ALPHA SYNDROME.
IT'S CLEAR THAT PUDDING SEES HER OWNER AS BENEATH HER.
AND THAT IS A TRAIT OF ALPHA SYNDROME.
IF YOU ALLOW THIS BEHAVIOR TO CONTINUE, PUDDING WILL NEVER COME TO TRUST YOU.

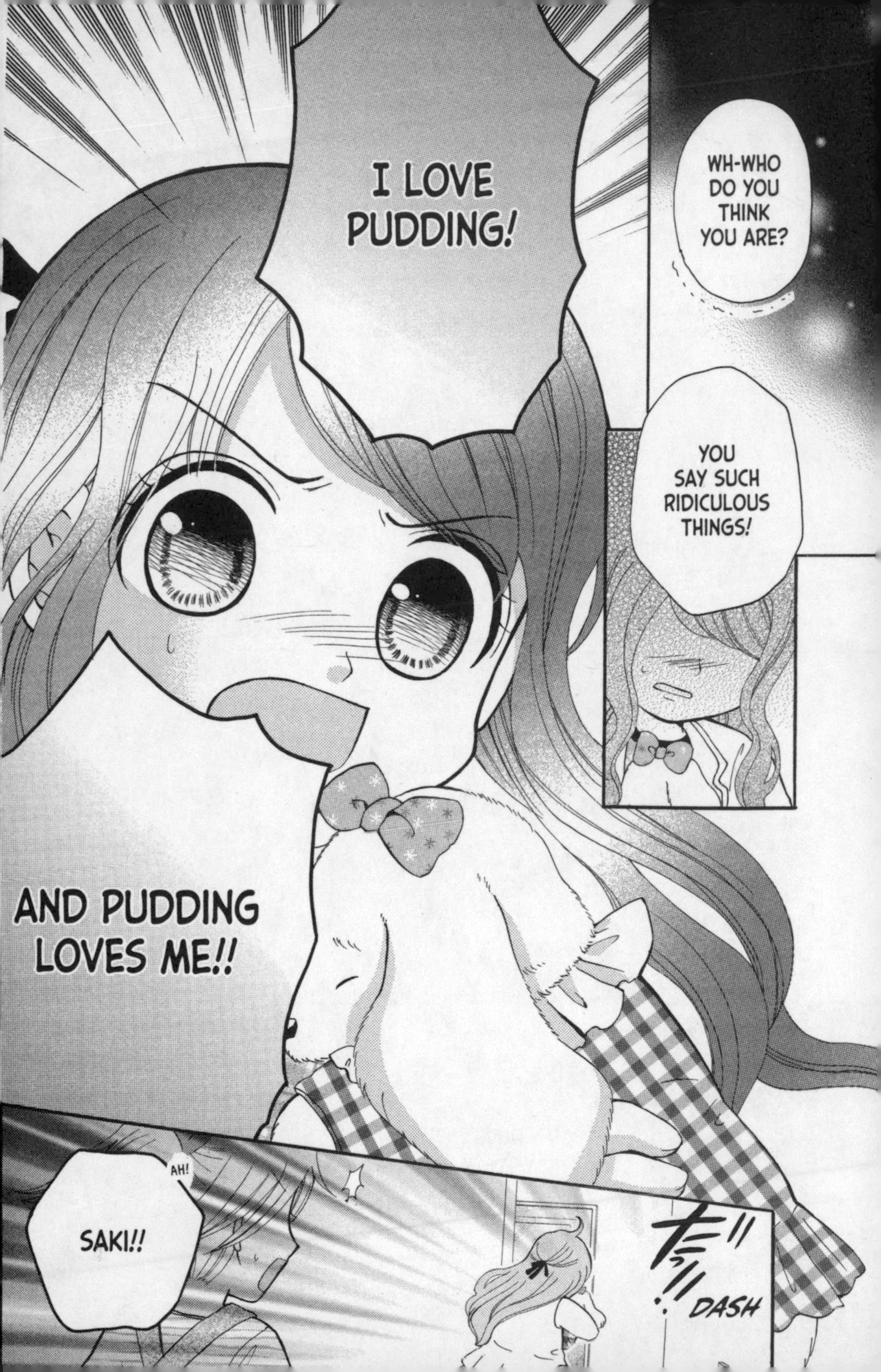
WH-WHO DO YOU THINK YOU ARE?
YOU SAY SUCH RIDICULOUS THINGS!
I LOVE PUDDING!
AND PUDDING LOVES ME!!
DASH
AH!
SAKI!!

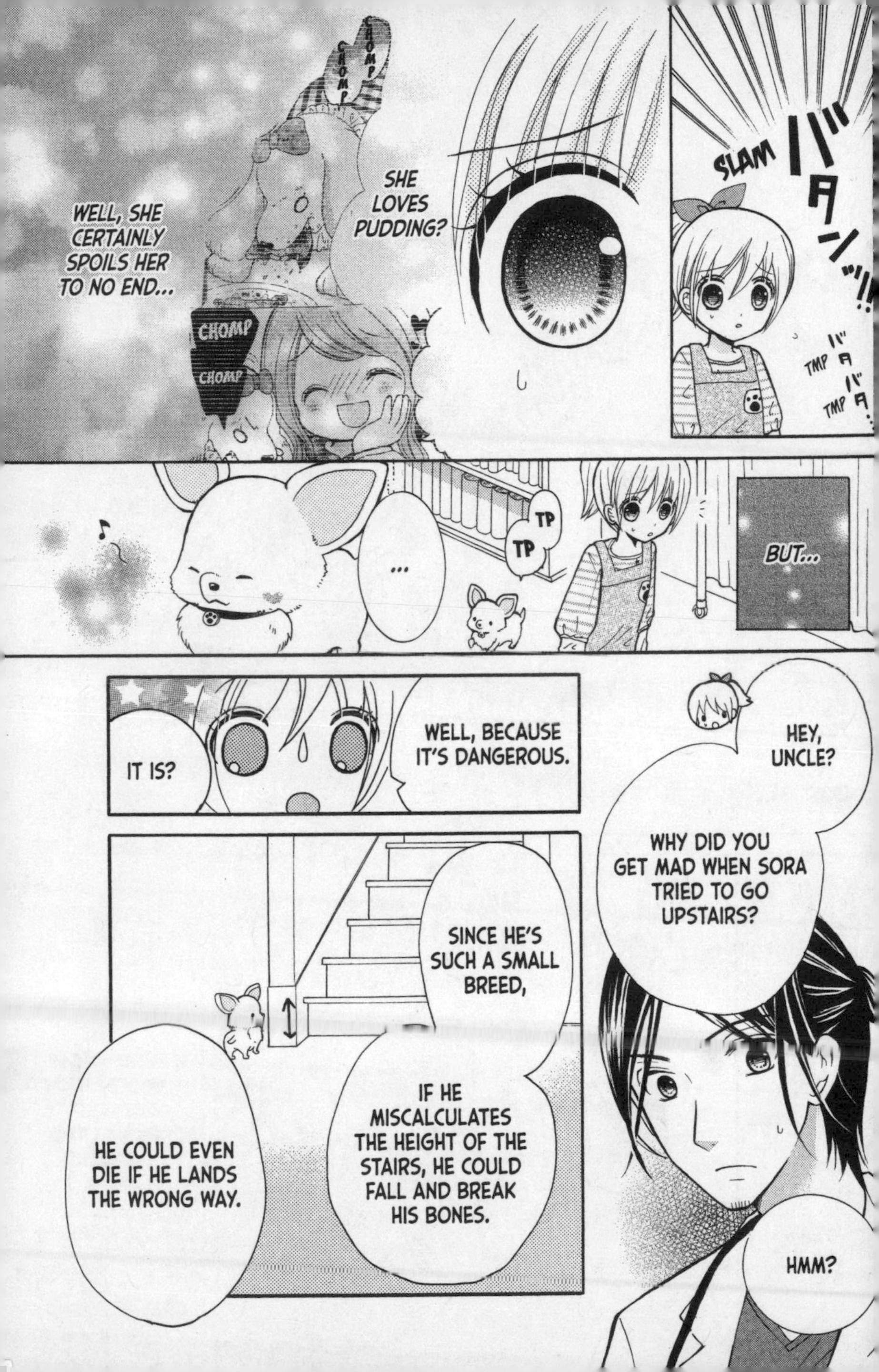
SLAM
バタンッ!!
TMP
バタ
TMP
バタ
CHOMP
CHOMP
SHE LOVES PUDDING?
WELL, SHE CERTAINLY SPOILS HER TO NO END...
CHOMP
CHOMP
BUT...
TP
TP
...
HEY, UNCLE?
WHY DID YOU GET MAD WHEN SORA TRIED TO GO UPSTAIRS?
HMM?
WELL, BECAUSE IT'S DANGEROUS.
IT IS?
SINCE HE'S SUCH A SMALL BREED,
IF HE MISCALCULATES THE HEIGHT OF THE STAIRS, HE COULD FALL AND BREAK HIS BONES.
HE COULD EVEN DIE IF HE LANDS THE WRONG WAY.

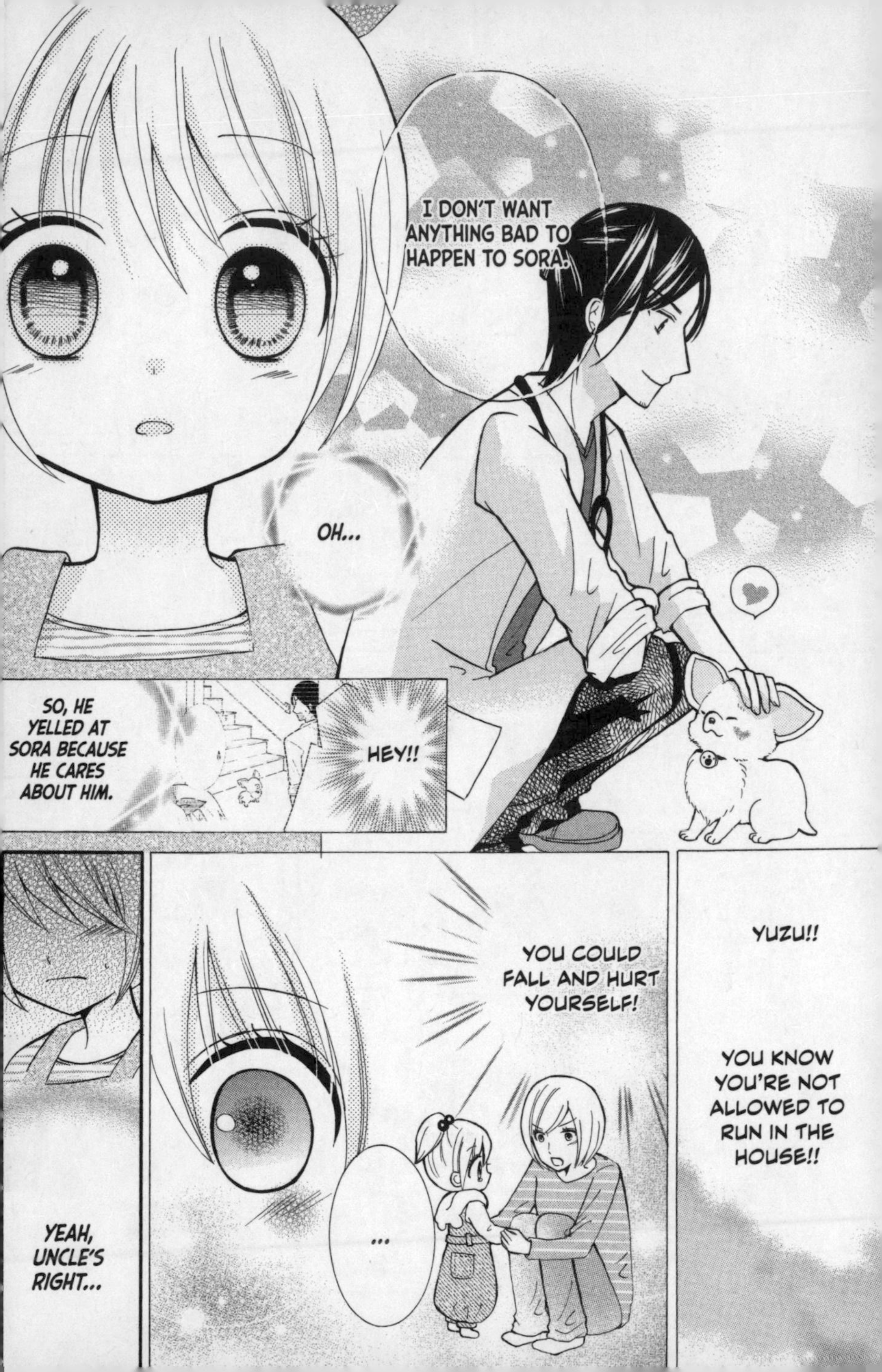
I DON'T WANT ANYTHING BAD TO HAPPEN TO SORA.
OH...
HEY!!
SO, HE YELLED AT SORA BECAUSE HE CARES ABOUT HIM.
YUZU!!
YOU KNOW YOU'RE NOT ALLOWED TO RUN IN THE HOUSE!!
YOU COULD FALL AND HURT YOURSELF!
...
YEAH, UNCLE'S RIGHT...

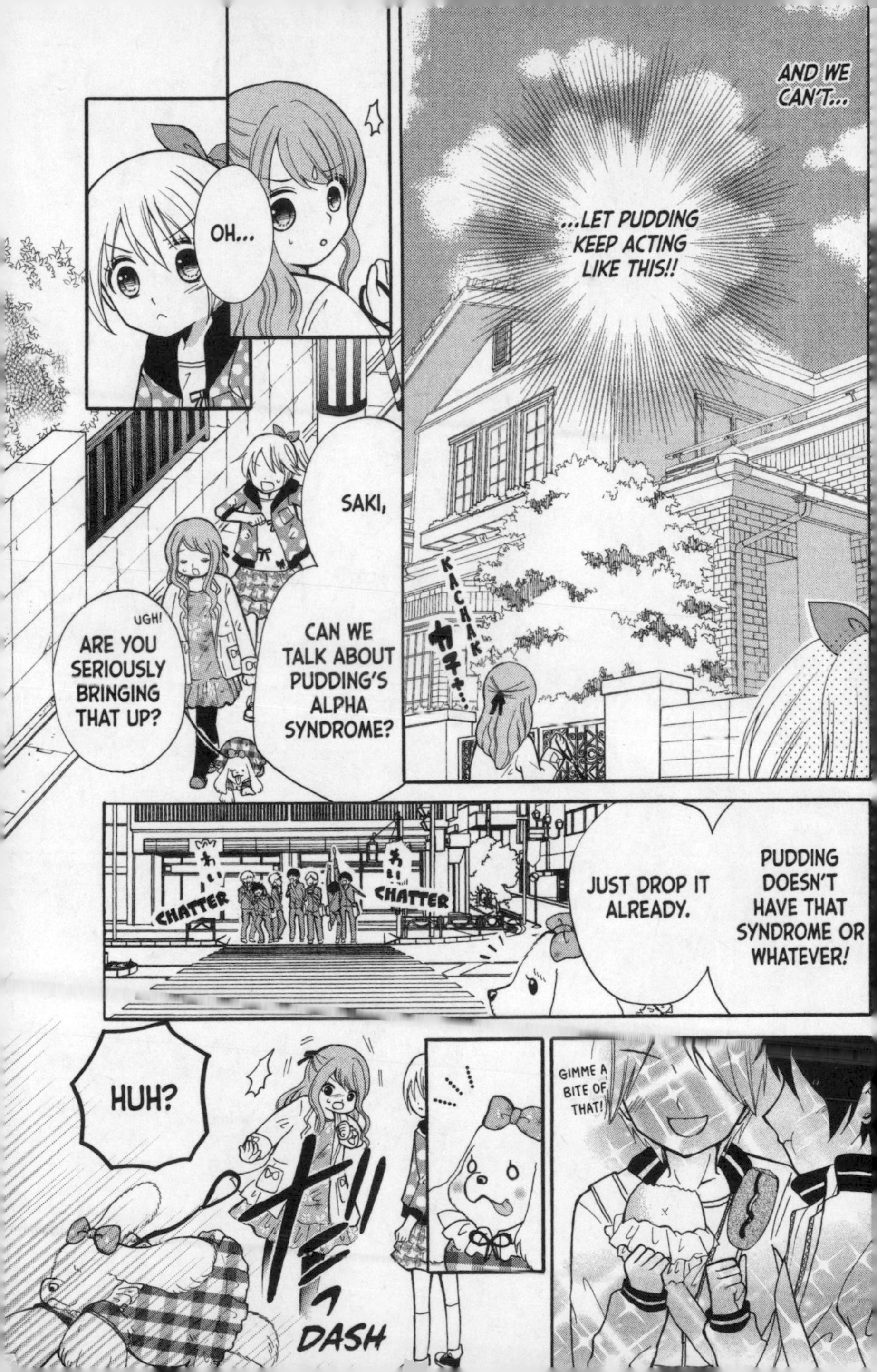
AND WE CAN'T...
...LET PUDDING KEEP ACTING LIKE THIS!!
KACHAK
OH...
SAKI,
CAN WE TALK ABOUT PUDDING'S ALPHA SYNDROME?
UGH!
ARE YOU SERIOUSLY BRINGING THAT UP?
PUDDING DOESN'T HAVE THAT SYNDROME OR WHATEVER!
JUST DROP IT ALREADY.
CHATTER
CHATTER
GIMME A BITE OF THAT!
...!!
HUH?
DASH

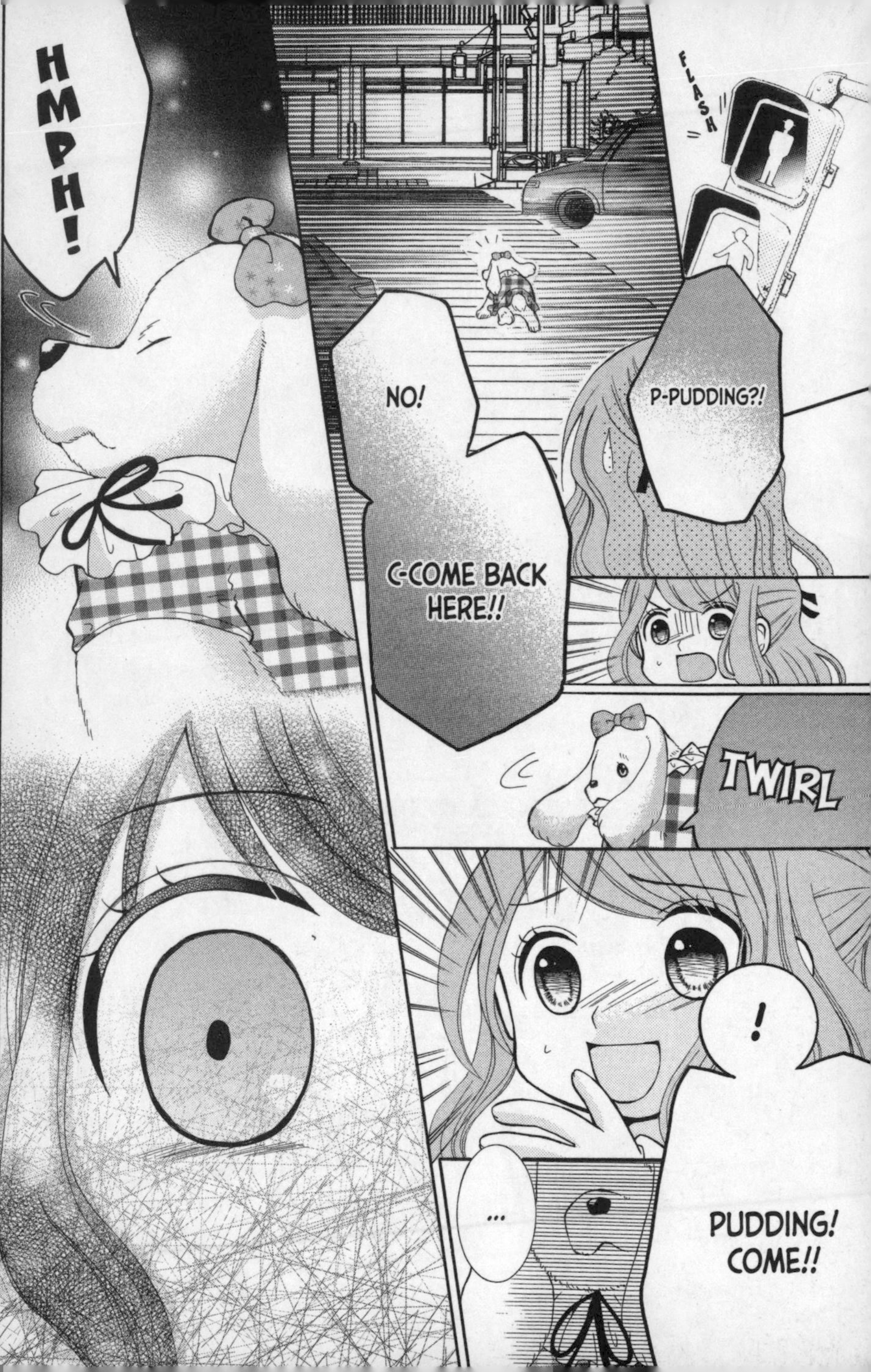
FLASH
P-PUDDING?!
NO!
C-COME BACK HERE!!
TWIRL
!
PUDDING! COME!!
...
HMPH!

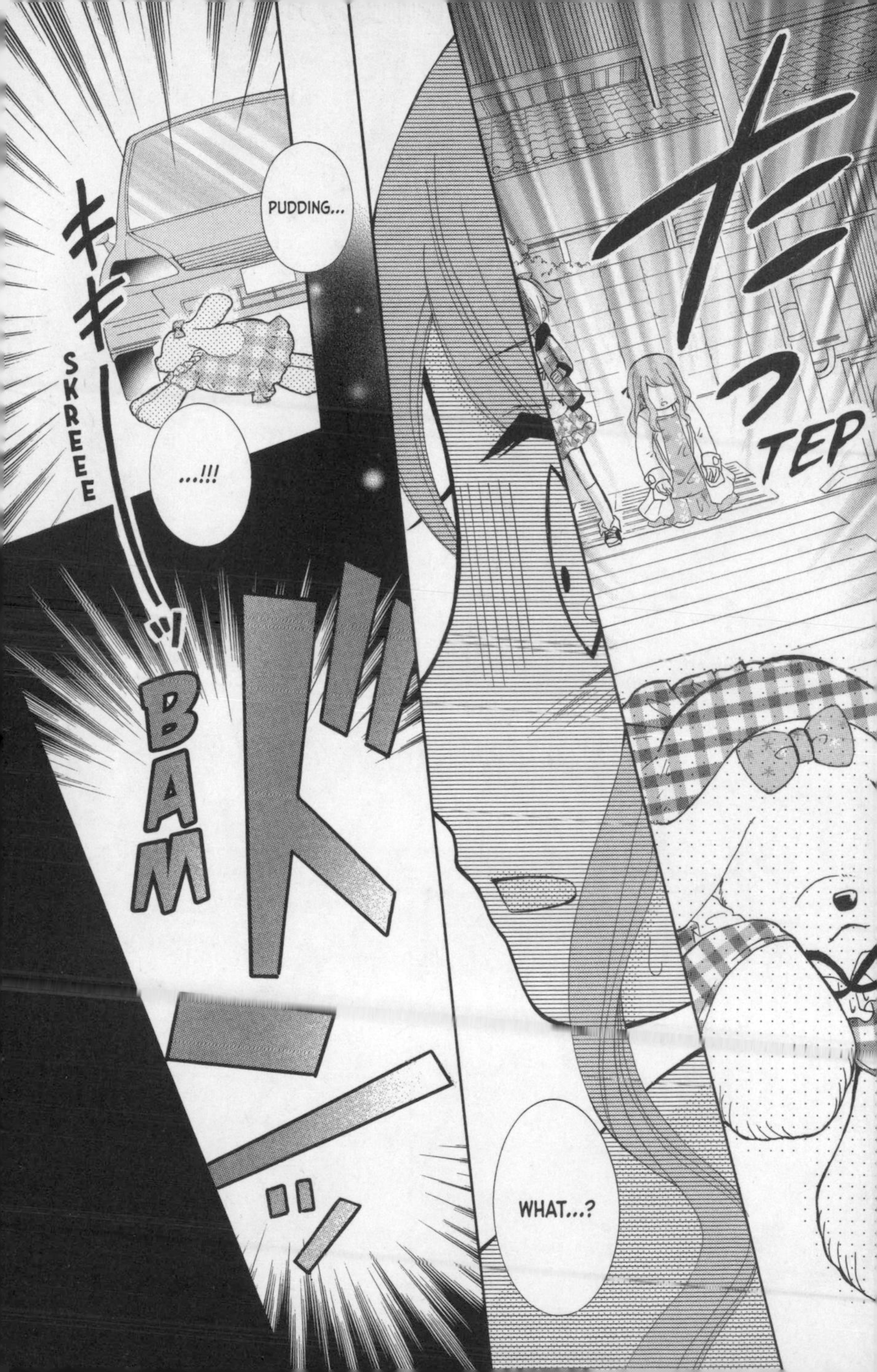
TEP
PUDDING...
...!!!
SKREEE
BAM
WHAT...?

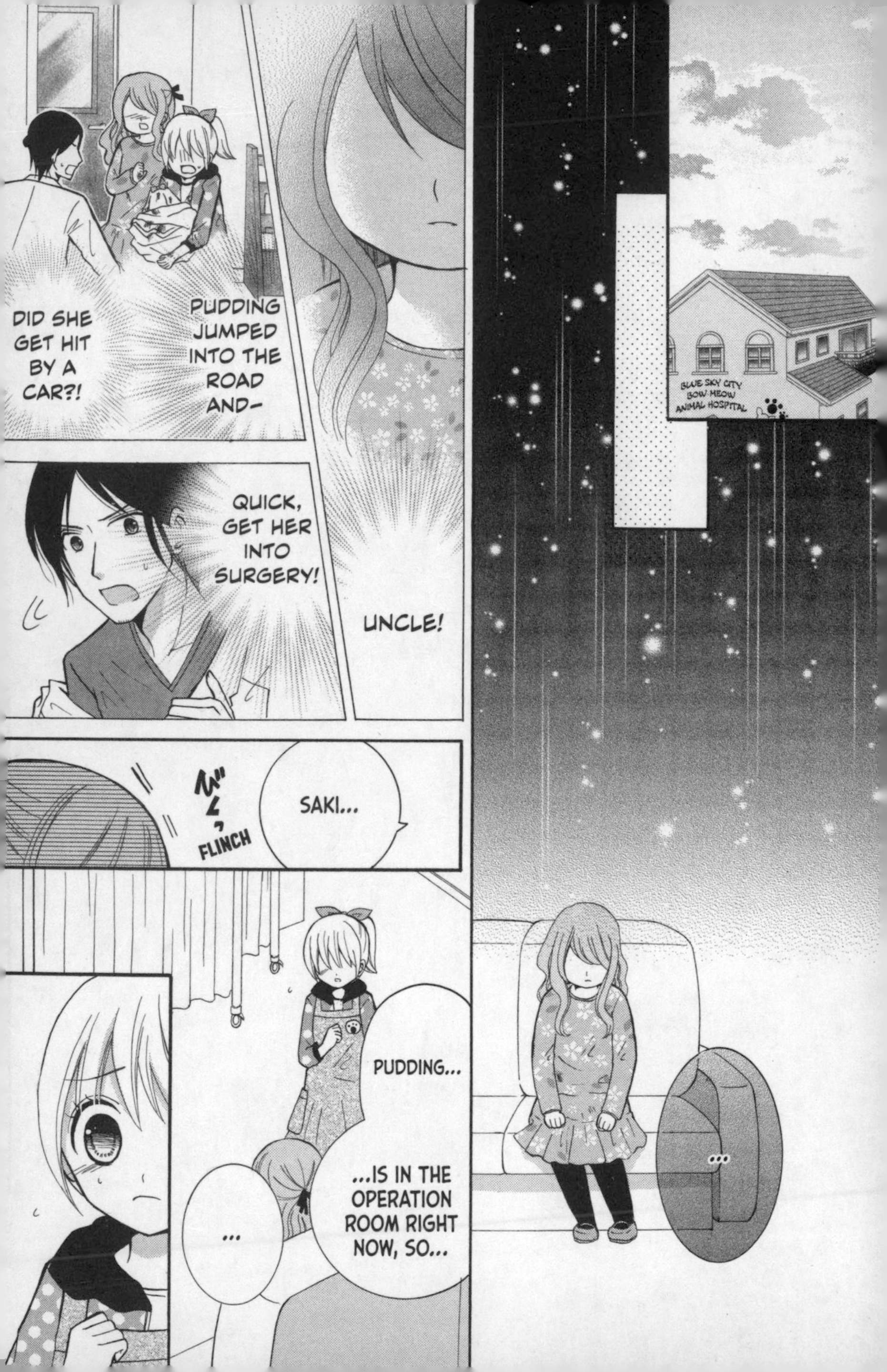
BLUE SKY CITY
BOW MEOW
ANIMAL HOSPITAL
...
UNCLE!
PUDDING JUMPED INTO THE ROAD AND—
DID SHE GET HIT BY A CAR?!
QUICK, GET HER INTO SURGERY!
SAKI...
FLINCH
PUDDING...
...IS IN THE OPERATION ROOM RIGHT NOW, SO...
...

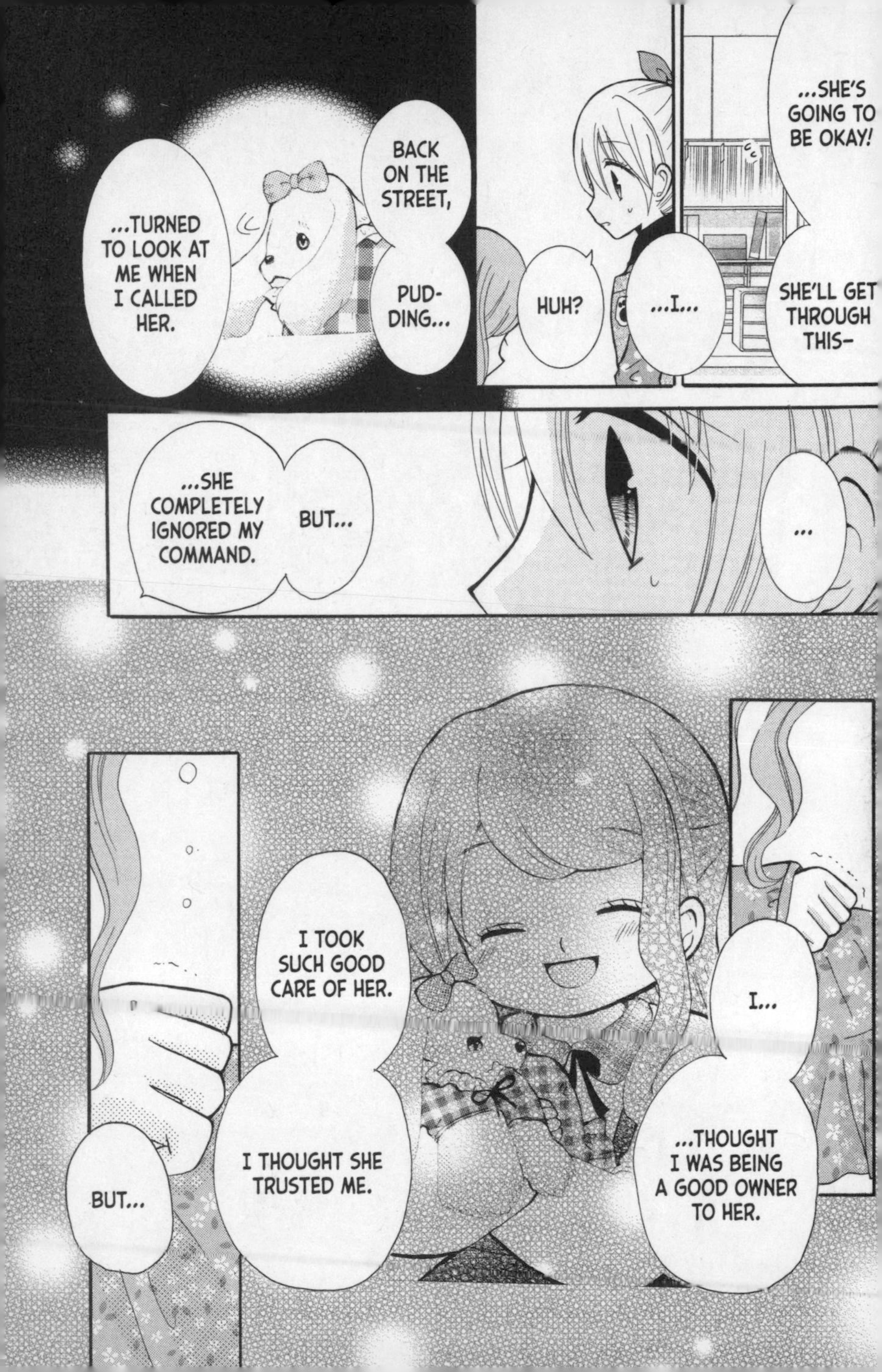
...SHE'S GOING TO BE OKAY!
SHE'LL GET THROUGH THIS–
...I...
HUH?
BACK ON THE STREET,
PUD-DING...
...TURNED TO LOOK AT ME WHEN I CALLED HER.
...
BUT...
...SHE COMPLETELY IGNORED MY COMMAND.
I...
...THOUGHT I WAS BEING A GOOD OWNER TO HER.
I TOOK SUCH GOOD CARE OF HER.
I THOUGHT SHE TRUSTED ME.
BUT...

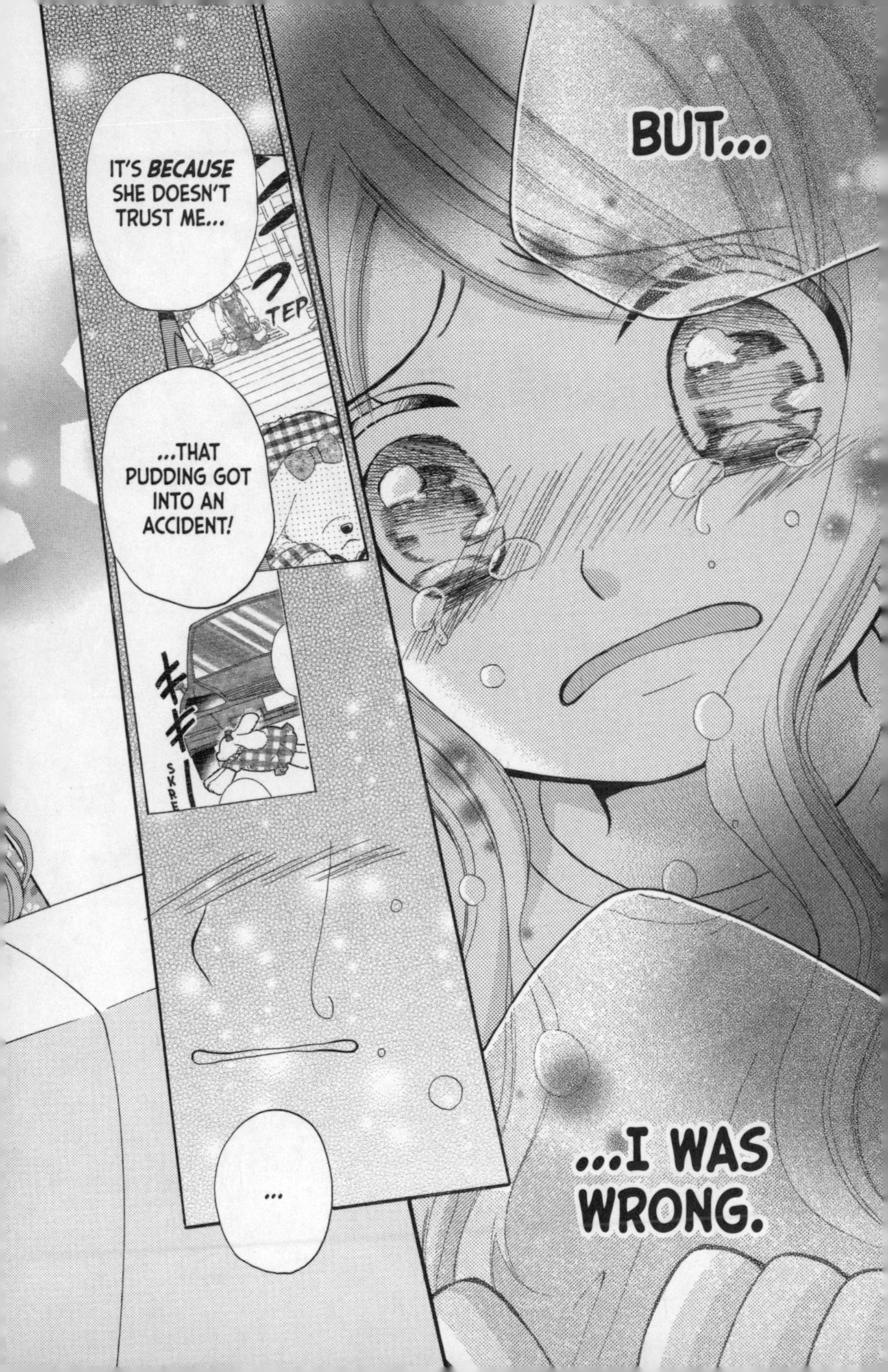
BUT...
IT'S *BECAUSE* SHE DOESN'T TRUST ME...
TEP
...THAT PUDDING GOT INTO AN ACCIDENT!
SKRE
...
...I WAS WRONG.

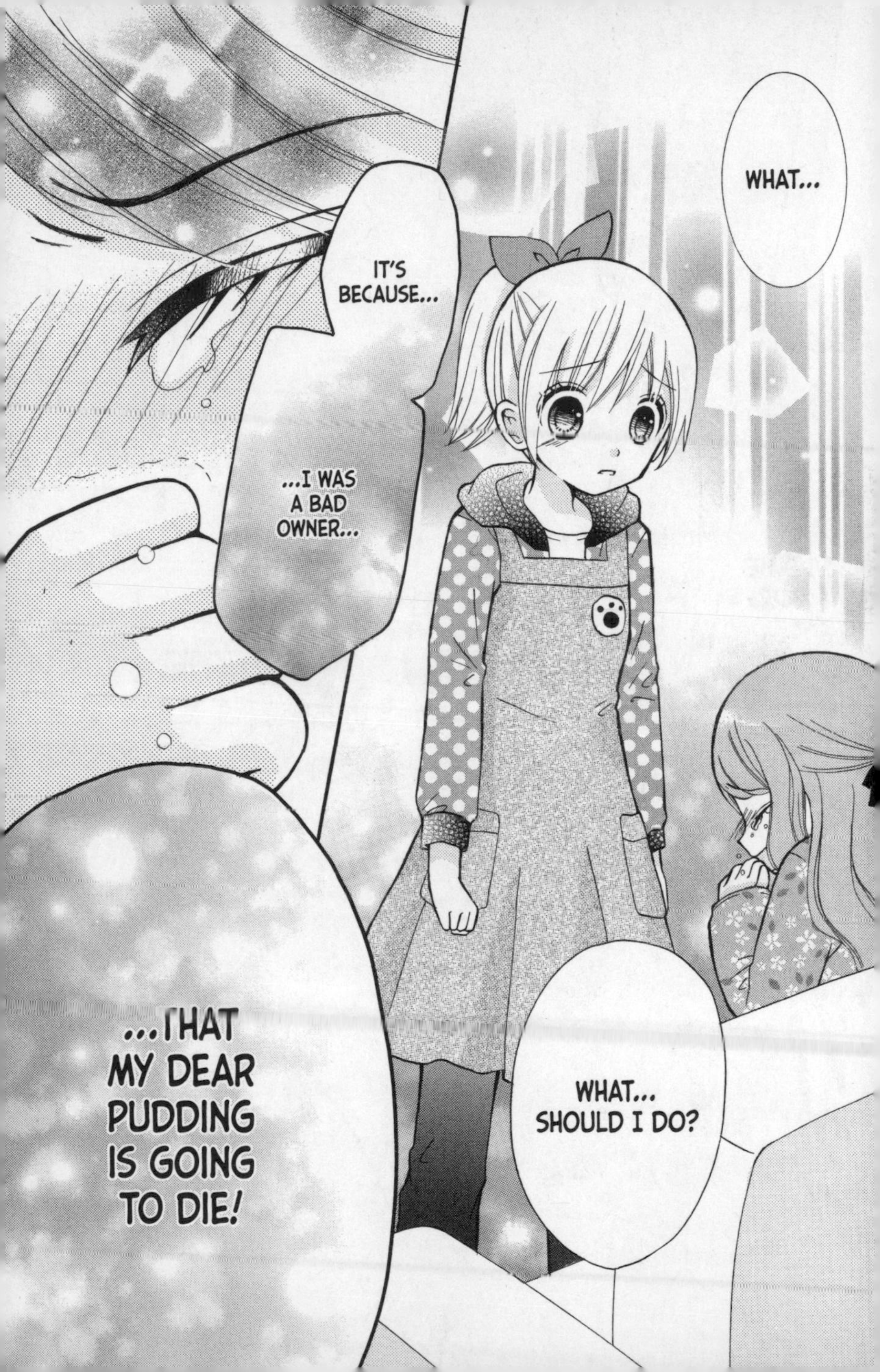
WHAT...
IT'S BECAUSE...
...I WAS A BAD OWNER...
...THAT MY DEAR PUDDING IS GOING TO DIE!
WHAT... SHOULD I DO?

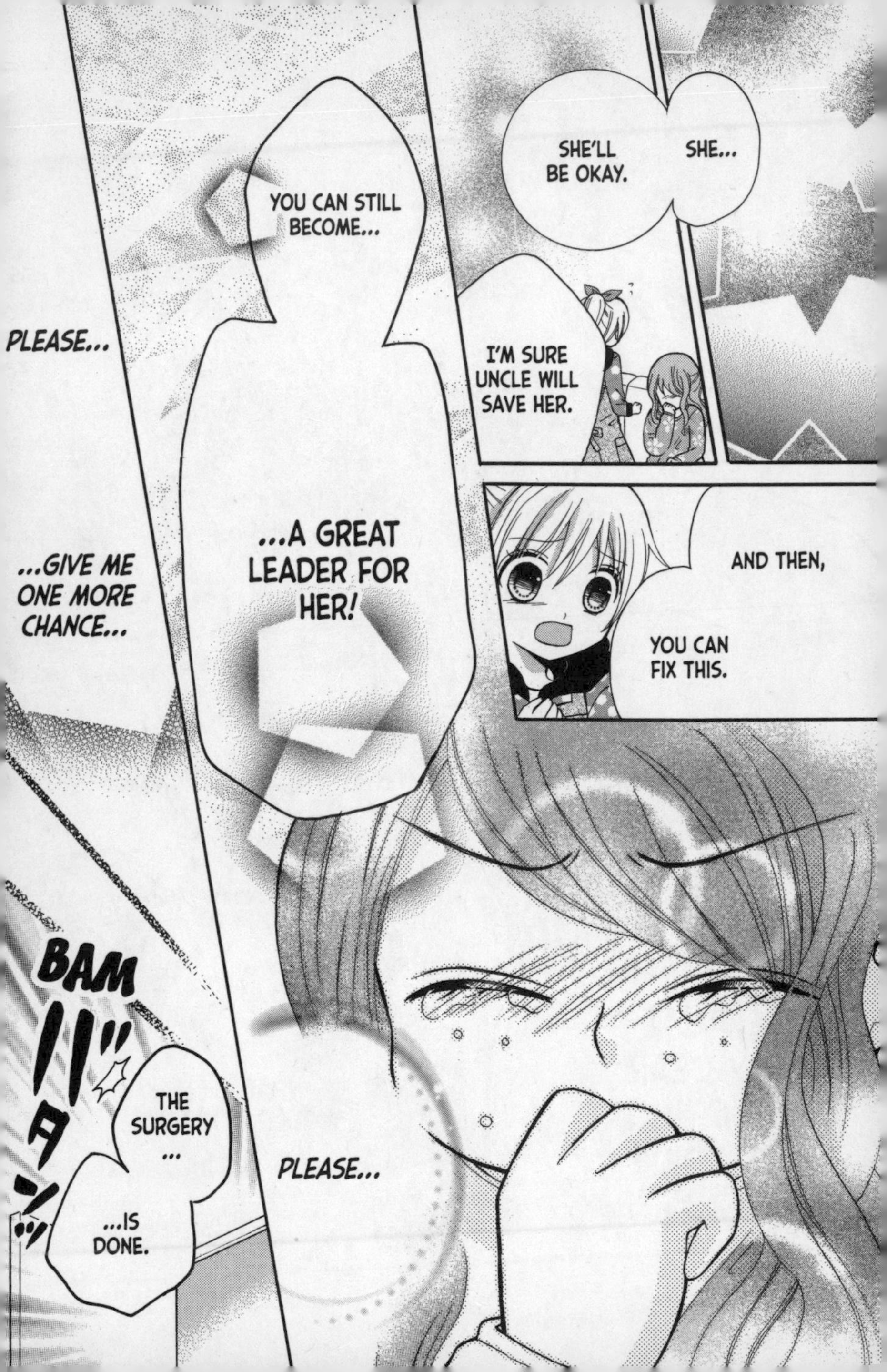
SHE...
SHE'LL BE OKAY.
I'M SURE UNCLE WILL SAVE HER.
AND THEN,
YOU CAN FIX THIS.
YOU CAN STILL BECOME...
...A GREAT LEADER FOR HER!
PLEASE...
...GIVE ME ONE MORE CHANCE...
PLEASE...
BAM
THE SURGERY ...
...IS DONE.

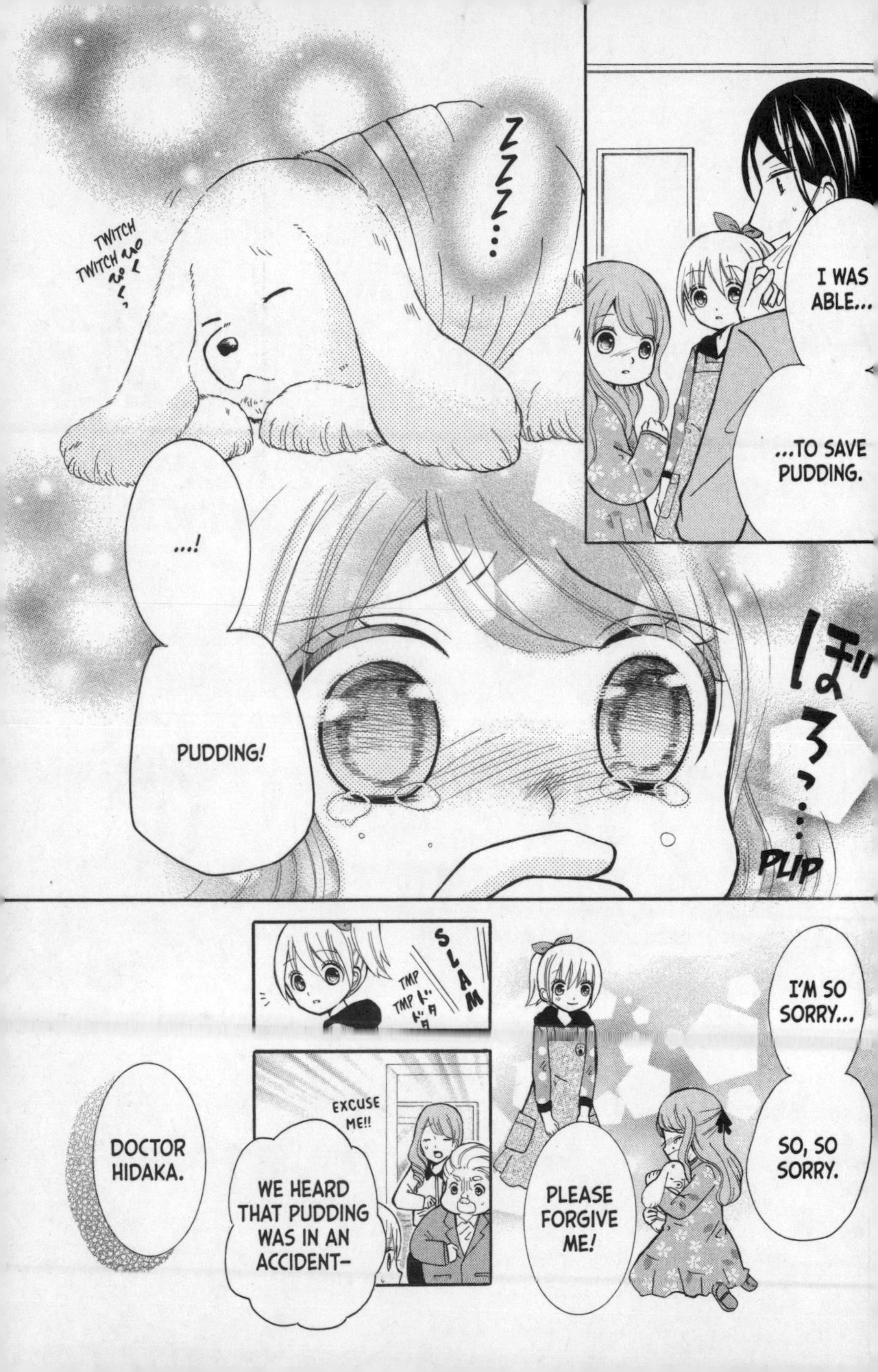
I WAS ABLE...
...TO SAVE PUDDING.
ZZZ...
TWITCH TWITCH
...!
PUDDING!
ぼろっ...
PLIP
I'M SO SORRY...
SO, SO SORRY.
PLEASE FORGIVE ME!
SLAM
TMP TMP
EXCUSE ME!!
WE HEARD THAT PUDDING WAS IN AN ACCIDENT–
DOCTOR HIDAKA.

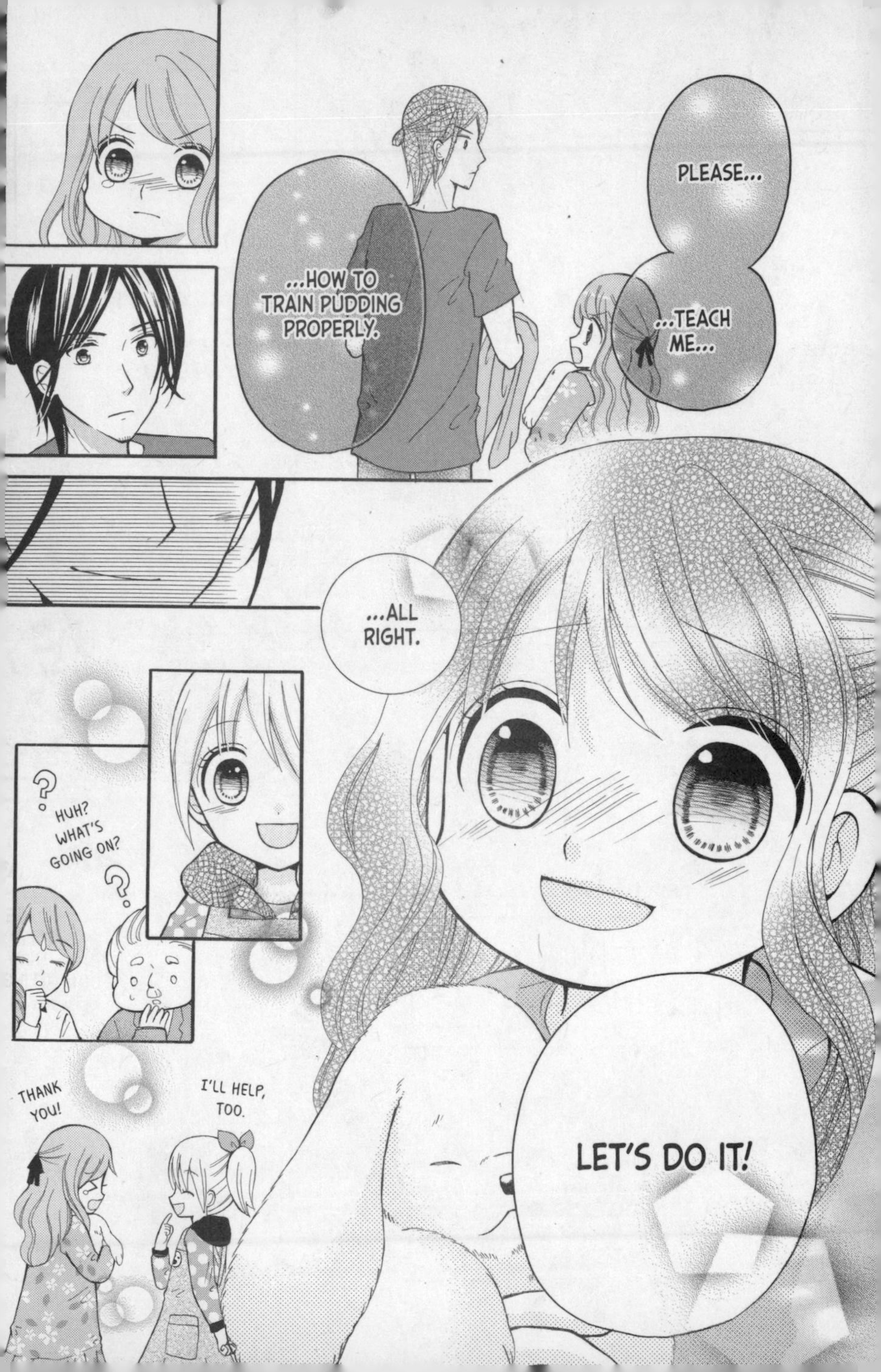
PLEASE...
...TEACH ME...
...HOW TO TRAIN PUDDING PROPERLY.
...ALL RIGHT.
LET'S DO IT!
HUH? WHAT'S GOING ON?
I'LL HELP, TOO.
THANK YOU!

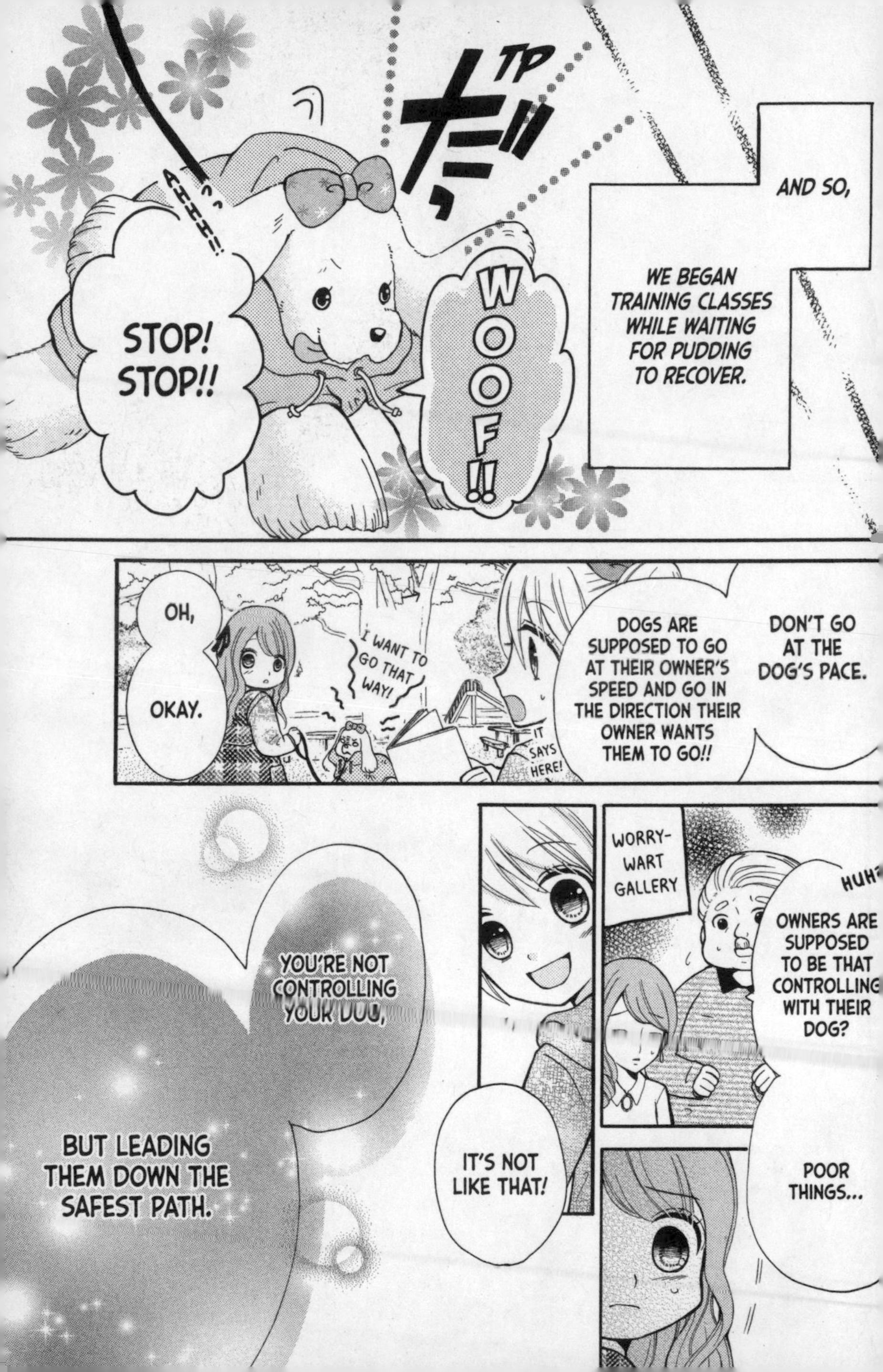
AND SO,
WE BEGAN TRAINING CLASSES WHILE WAITING FOR PUDDING TO RECOVER.
TP
WOOF!!
AHHHH!!
STOP! STOP!!
DON'T GO AT THE DOG'S PACE.
DOGS ARE SUPPOSED TO GO AT THEIR OWNER'S SPEED AND GO IN THE DIRECTION THEIR OWNER WANTS THEM TO GO!!
IT SAYS HERE!
I WANT TO GO THAT WAY!
OH,
OKAY.
HUH?
OWNERS ARE SUPPOSED TO BE THAT CONTROLLING WITH THEIR DOG?
WORRY-WART GALLERY
POOR THINGS...
IT'S NOT LIKE THAT!
YOU'RE NOT CONTROLLING YOUR DOG,
BUT LEADING THEM DOWN THE SAFEST PATH.

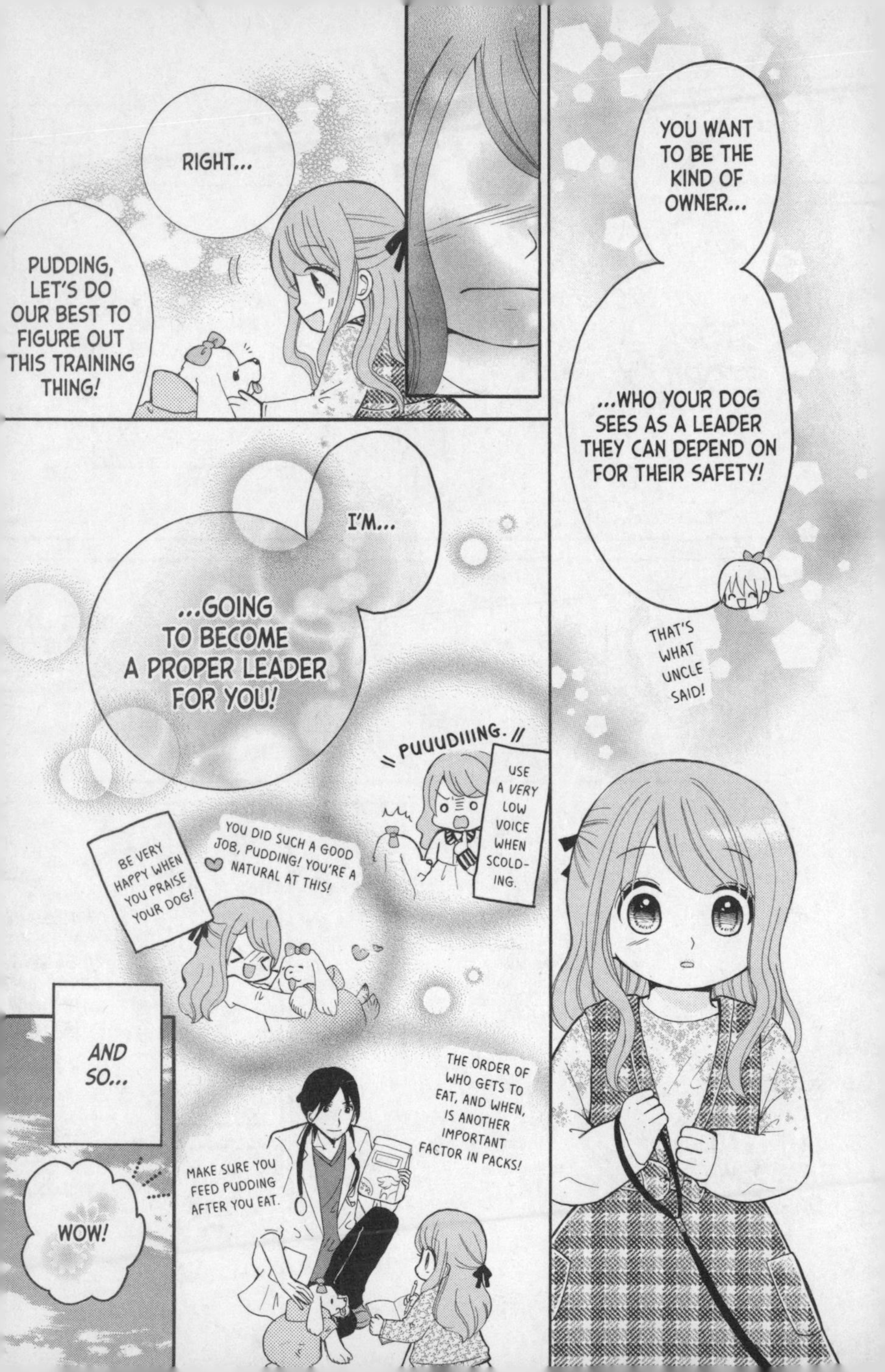
YOU WANT TO BE THE KIND OF OWNER...
...WHO YOUR DOG SEES AS A LEADER THEY CAN DEPEND ON FOR THEIR SAFETY!
THAT'S WHAT UNCLE SAID!
RIGHT...
PUDDING, LET'S DO OUR BEST TO FIGURE OUT THIS TRAINING THING!
I'M...
...GOING TO BECOME A PROPER LEADER FOR YOU!
PUUUDIIING.
USE A VERY LOW VOICE WHEN SCOLD-ING.
YOU DID SUCH A GOOD JOB, PUDDING! YOU'RE A NATURAL AT THIS!
BE VERY HAPPY WHEN YOU PRAISE YOUR DOG!
THE ORDER OF WHO GETS TO EAT, AND WHEN, IS ANOTHER IMPORTANT FACTOR IN PACKS!
MAKE SURE YOU FEED PUDDING AFTER YOU EAT.
AND SO...
WOW!

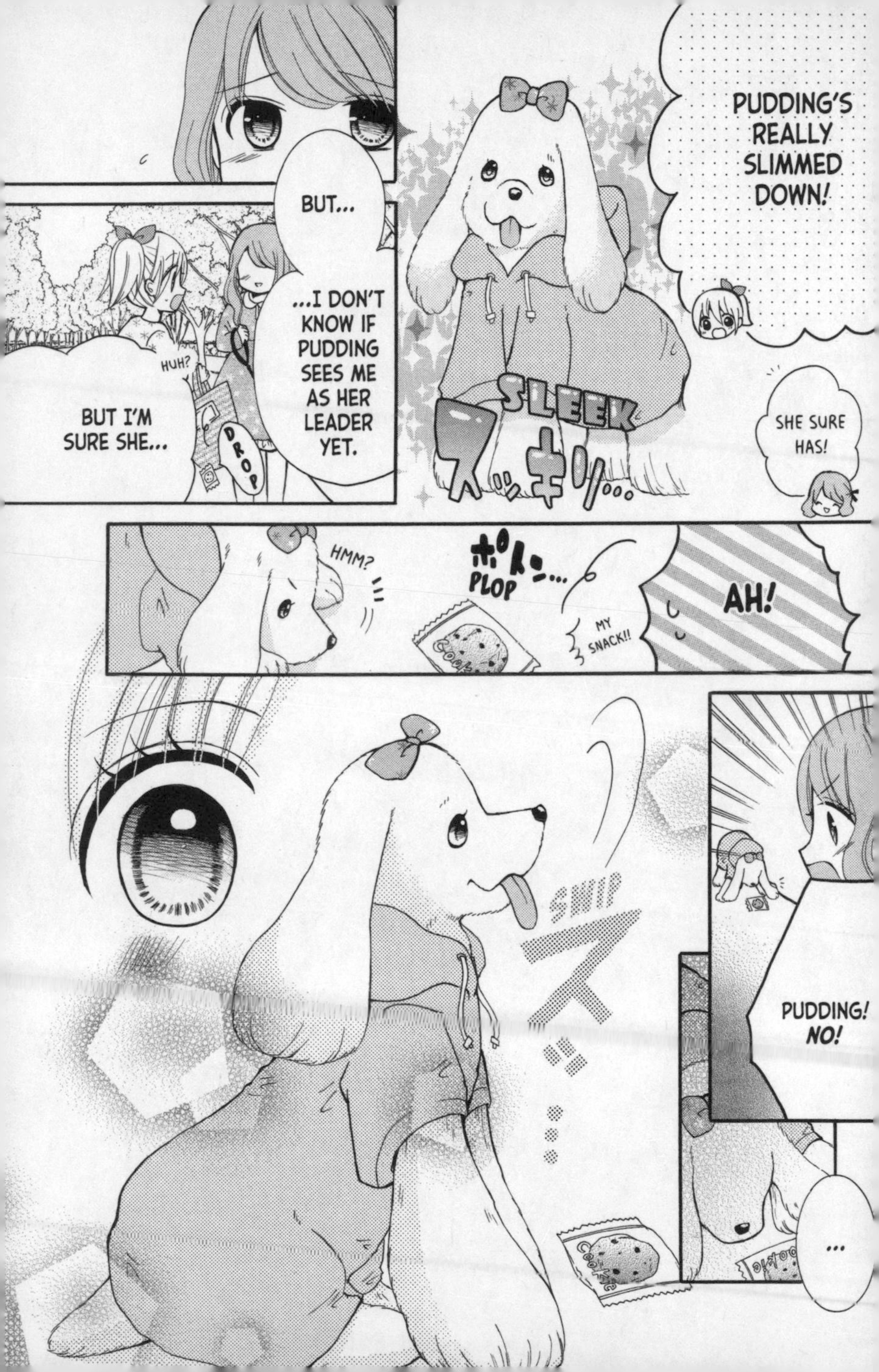
PUDDING'S REALLY SLIMMED DOWN!
SLEEK
SHE SURE HAS!
BUT...
...I DON'T KNOW IF PUDDING SEES ME AS HER LEADER YET.
HUH?
BUT I'M SURE SHE...
DROP
AH!
MY SNACK!!
PLOP
HMM?
PUDDING! NO!
...
SWIP

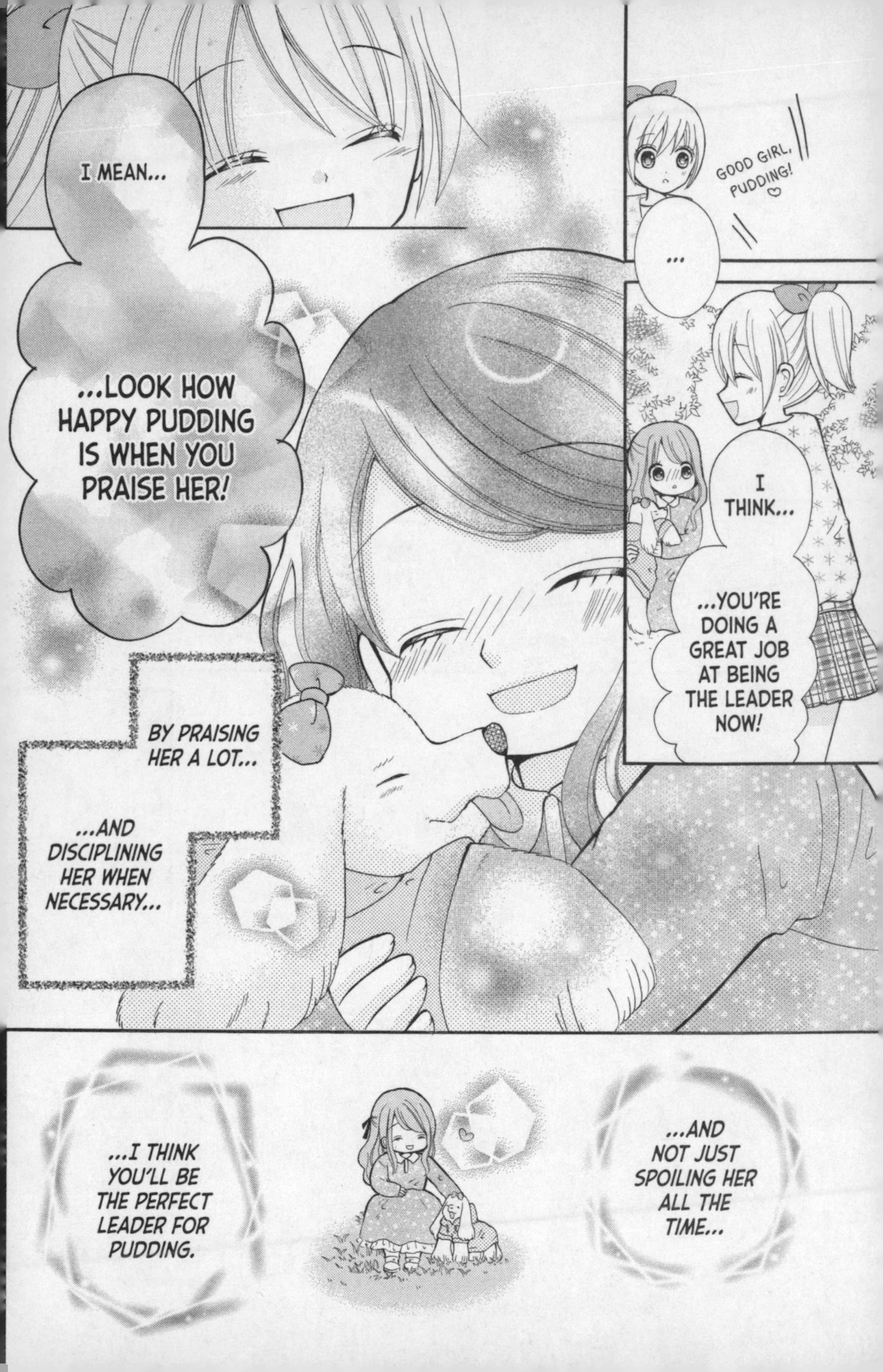
GOOD GIRL, PUDDING! ♡
...
I THINK...
...YOU'RE DOING A GREAT JOB AT BEING THE LEADER NOW!
I MEAN...
...LOOK HOW HAPPY PUDDING IS WHEN YOU PRAISE HER!
BY PRAISING HER A LOT...
...AND DISCIPLINING HER WHEN NECESSARY...
...AND NOT JUST SPOILING HER ALL THE TIME...
...I THINK YOU'LL BE THE PERFECT LEADER FOR PUDDING.

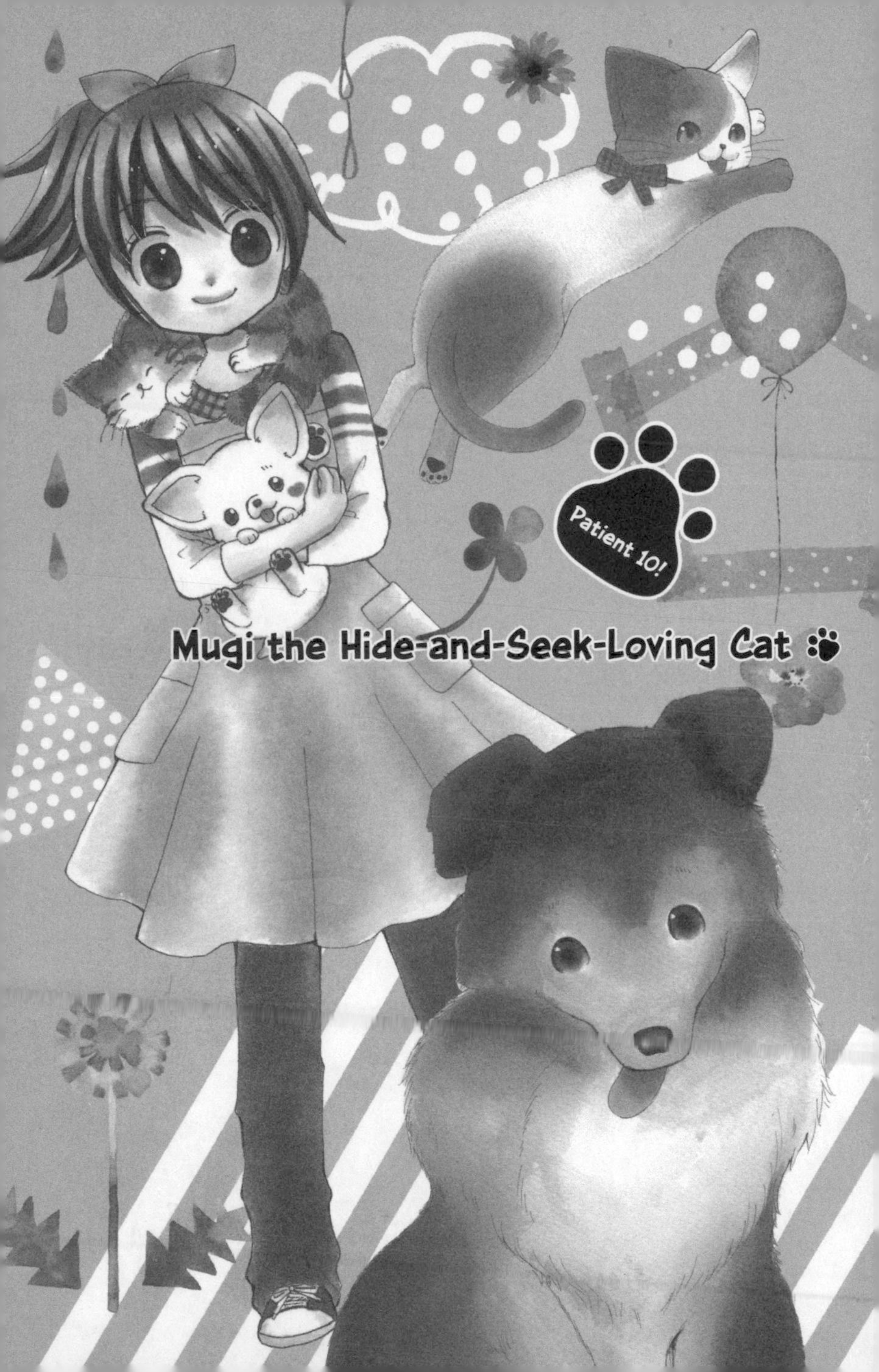
Patient 10!
Mugi the Hide-and-Seek-Loving Cat

YUZU THE PET VET

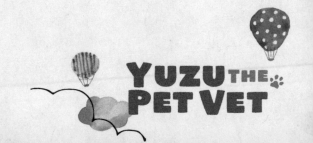

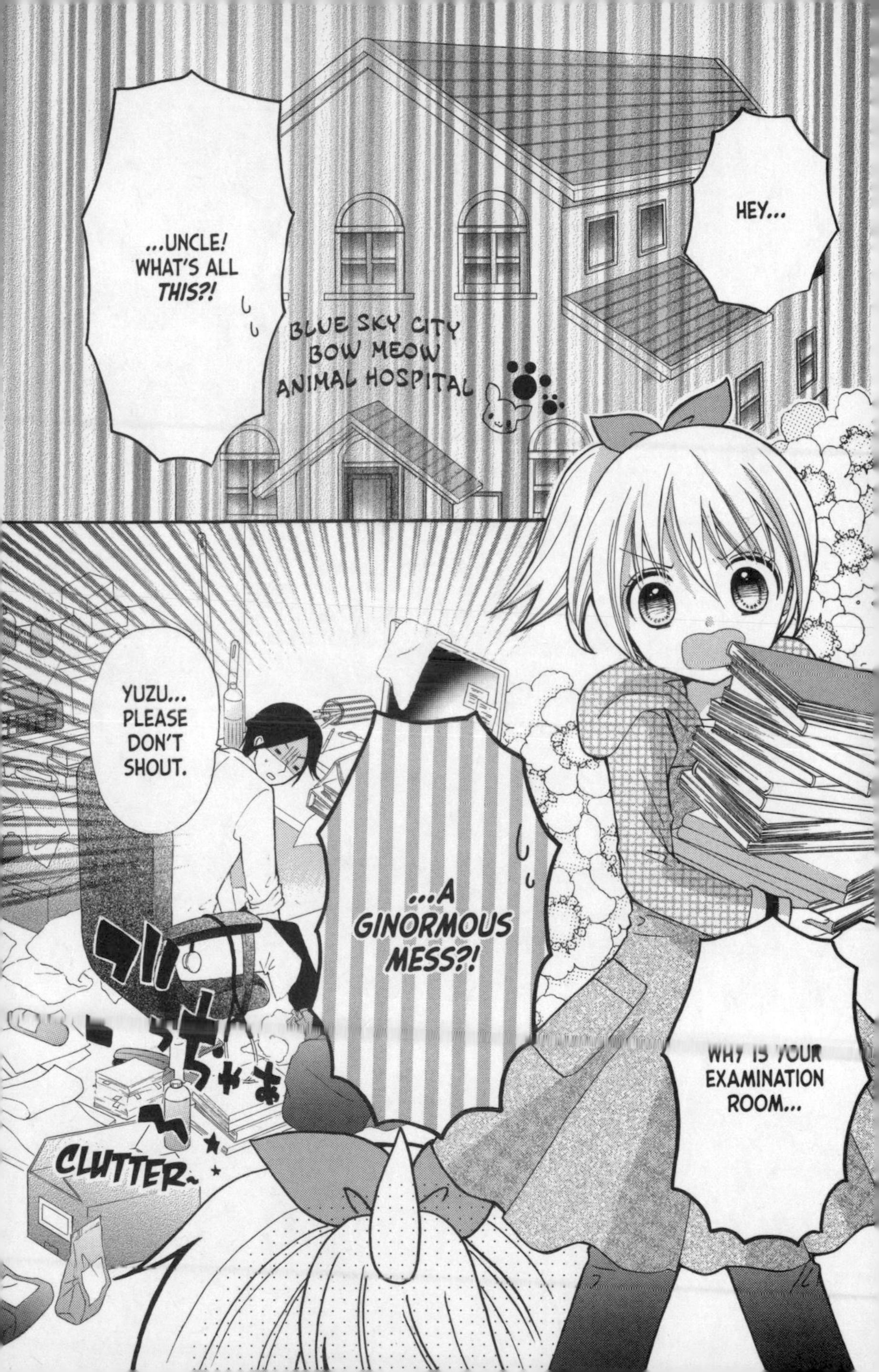
HEY...
BLUE SKY CITY BOW MEOW ANIMAL HOSPITAL
...UNCLE! WHAT'S ALL *THIS?!*
WHY IS YOUR EXAMINATION ROOM...
...A GINORMOUS MESS?!
YUZU... PLEASE DON'T SHOUT.
CLUTTER~

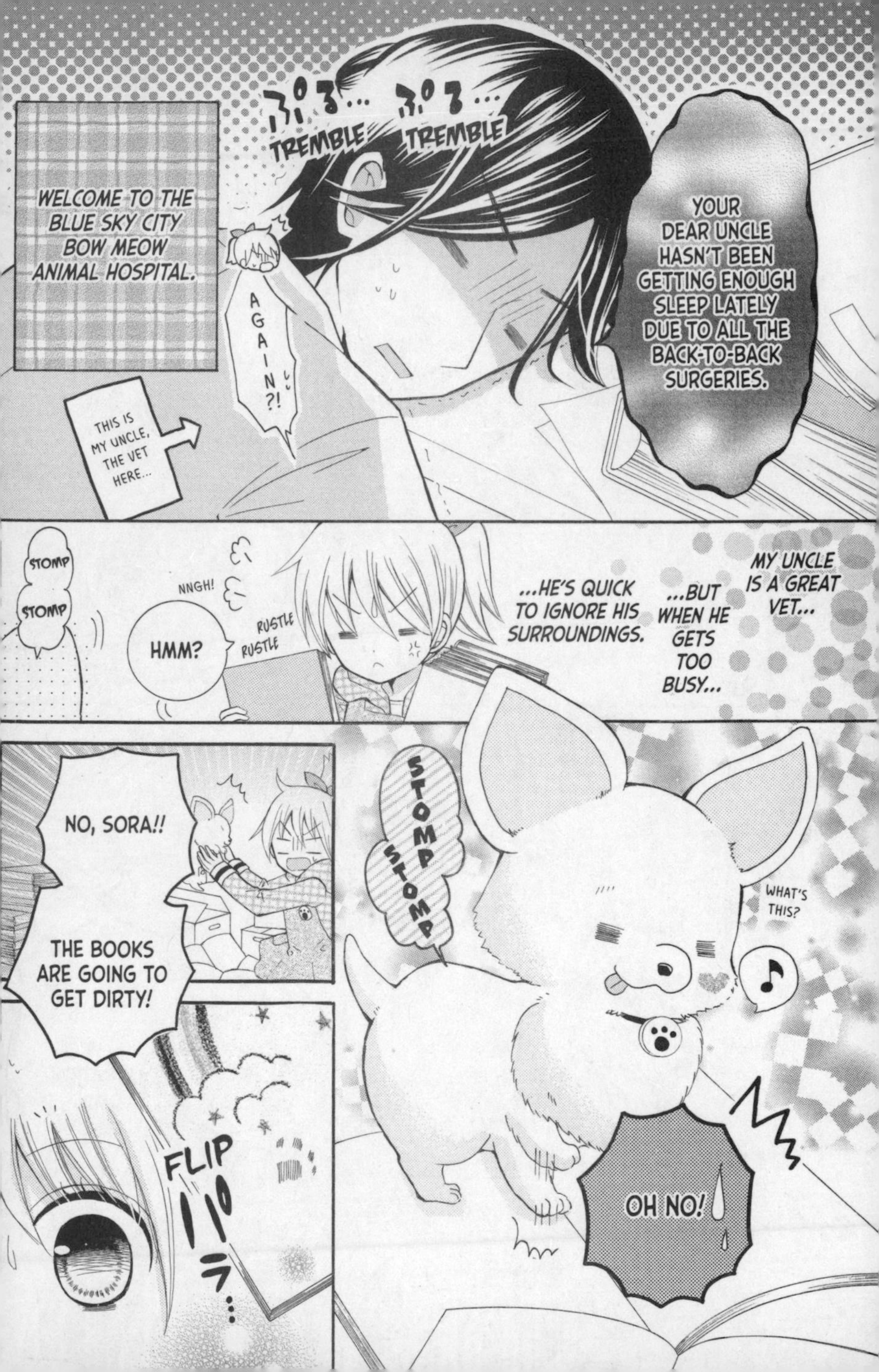
TREMBLE TREMBLE
YOUR DEAR UNCLE HASN'T BEEN GETTING ENOUGH SLEEP LATELY DUE TO ALL THE BACK-TO-BACK SURGERIES.
WELCOME TO THE BLUE SKY CITY BOW MEOW ANIMAL HOSPITAL.
AGAIN?!
THIS IS MY UNCLE, THE VET HERE...
MY UNCLE IS A GREAT VET...
...BUT WHEN HE GETS TOO BUSY...
...HE'S QUICK TO IGNORE HIS SURROUNDINGS.
RUSTLE RUSTLE
NNGH!
HMM?
STOMP
STOMP
STOMP STOMP
WHAT'S THIS?
♪
OH NO!
NO, SORA!!
THE BOOKS ARE GOING TO GET DIRTY!
FLIP

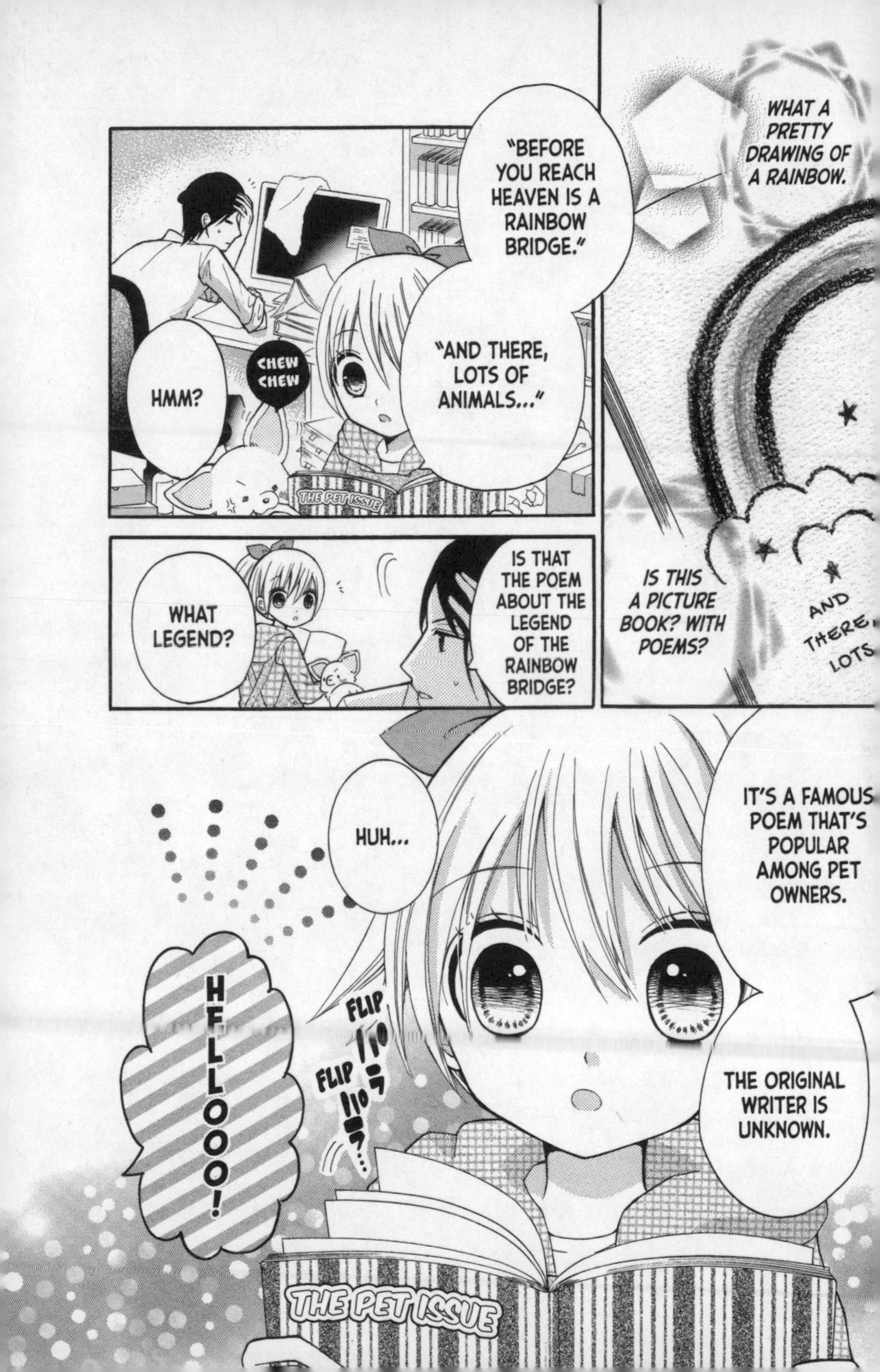
WHAT A PRETTY DRAWING OF A RAINBOW.
AND THERE, LOTS
IS THIS A PICTURE BOOK? WITH POEMS?
"BEFORE YOU REACH HEAVEN IS A RAINBOW BRIDGE."
"AND THERE, LOTS OF ANIMALS..."
CHEW CHEW
HMM?
THE PET ISSUE
IS THAT THE POEM ABOUT THE LEGEND OF THE RAINBOW BRIDGE?
WHAT LEGEND?
IT'S A FAMOUS POEM THAT'S POPULAR AMONG PET OWNERS.
THE ORIGINAL WRITER IS UNKNOWN.
HUH...
FLIP FLIP
HELLOOO!
THE PET ISSUE

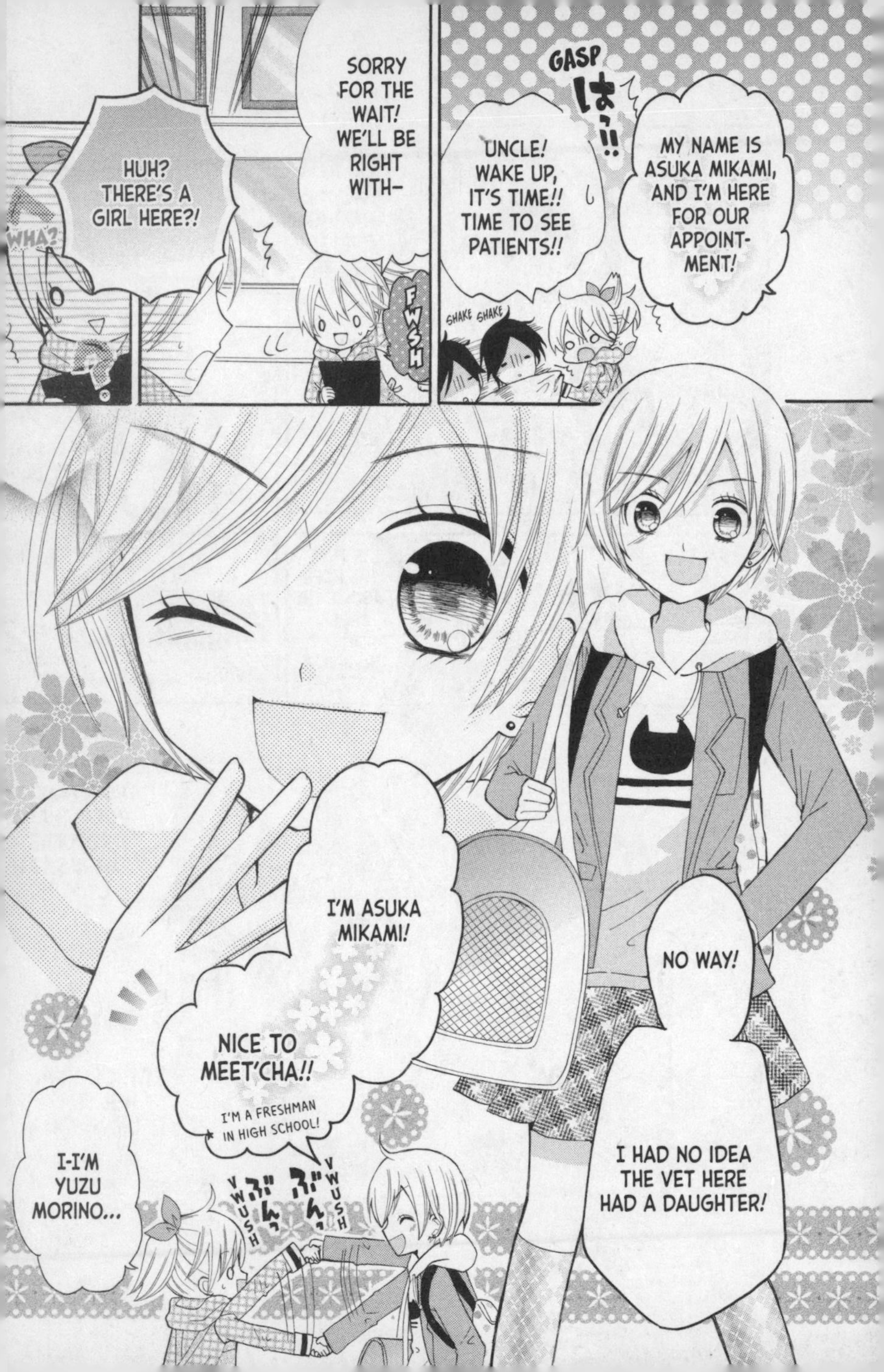
GASP
はっ!!
MY NAME IS ASUKA MIKAMI, AND I'M HERE FOR OUR APPOINT-MENT!
UNCLE! WAKE UP, IT'S TIME!! TIME TO SEE PATIENTS!!
SHAKE SHAKE
SORRY FOR THE WAIT! WE'LL BE RIGHT WITH–
FWSH
HUH? THERE'S A GIRL HERE?!
WHA?
NO WAY!
I HAD NO IDEA THE VET HERE HAD A DAUGHTER!
I'M ASUKA MIKAMI!
NICE TO MEET'CHA!!
I'M A FRESHMAN IN HIGH SCHOOL!
VWUSH
ぶんっ
VWUSH
ぶんっ
I-I'M YUZU MORINO...

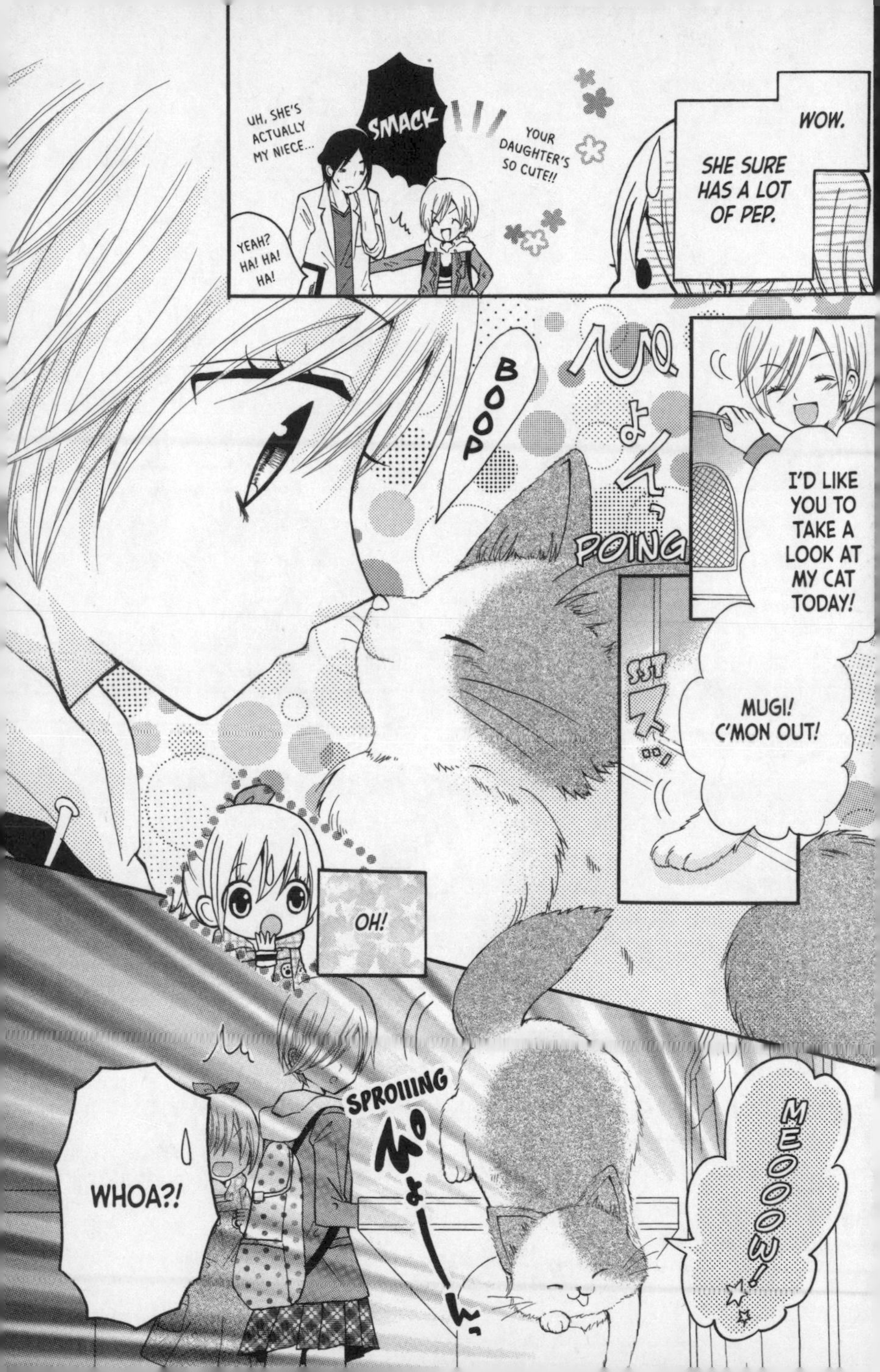
WOW.
SHE SURE HAS A LOT OF PEP.
YOUR DAUGHTER'S SO CUTE!!
SMACK
UH, SHE'S ACTUALLY MY NIECE...
YEAH? HA! HA! HA!
I'D LIKE YOU TO TAKE A LOOK AT MY CAT TODAY!
MUGI! C'MON OUT!
SST
POING
BOOP
OH!
MEOOOW!
SPROIIING
WHOA?!

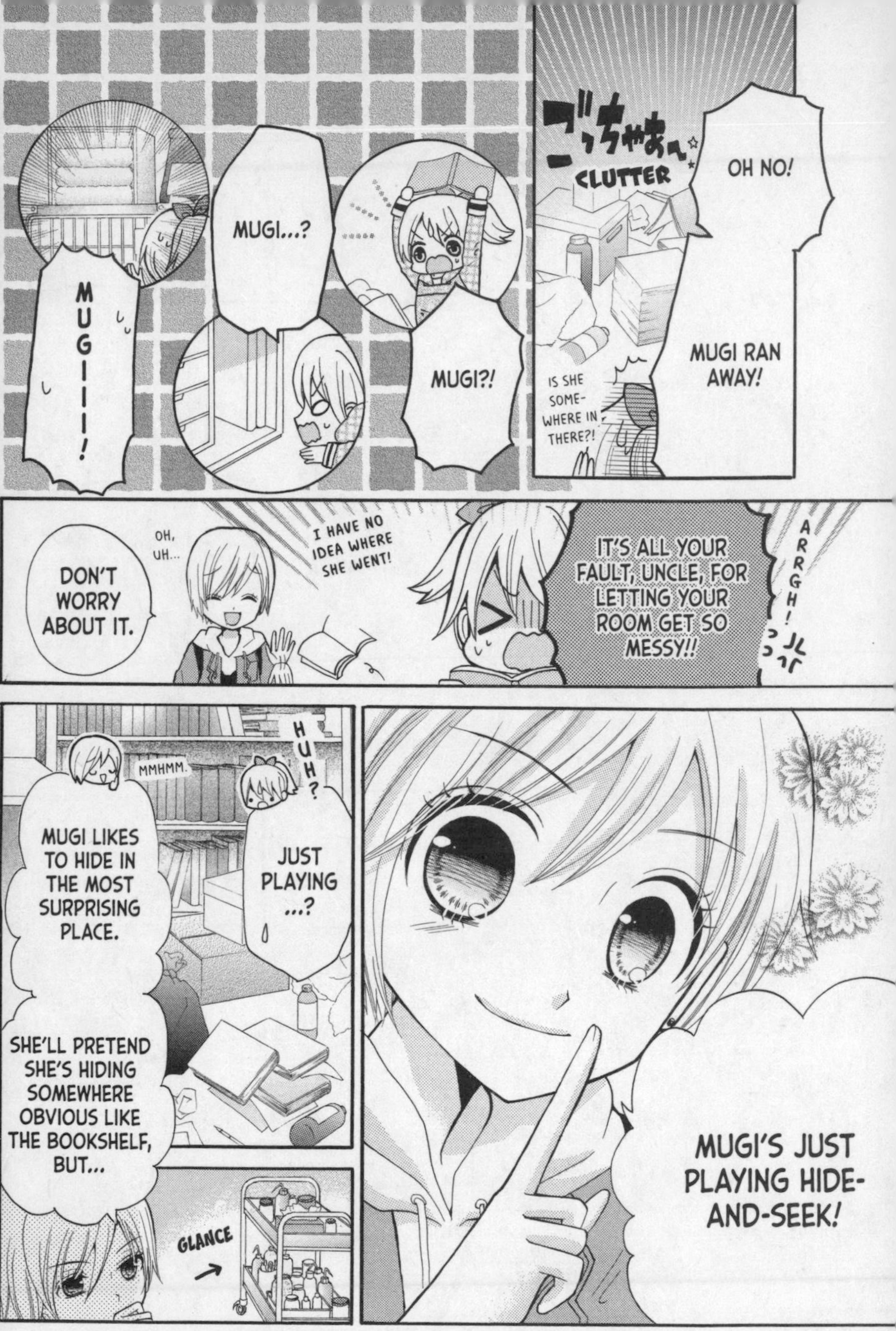
CLUTTER
OH NO!
MUGI RAN AWAY!
IS SHE SOMEWHERE IN THERE?!
MUGI?!
MUGI...?
MUGIIII!
ARRGH!!
IT'S ALL YOUR FAULT, UNCLE, FOR LETTING YOUR ROOM GET SO MESSY!!
I HAVE NO IDEA WHERE SHE WENT!
OH, UH...
DON'T WORRY ABOUT IT.
MUGI'S JUST PLAYING HIDE-AND-SEEK!
HUH?
JUST PLAYING...?
MMHMM.
MUGI LIKES TO HIDE IN THE MOST SURPRISING PLACE.
SHE'LL PRETEND SHE'S HIDING SOMEWHERE OBVIOUS LIKE THE BOOKSHELF, BUT...
GLANCE

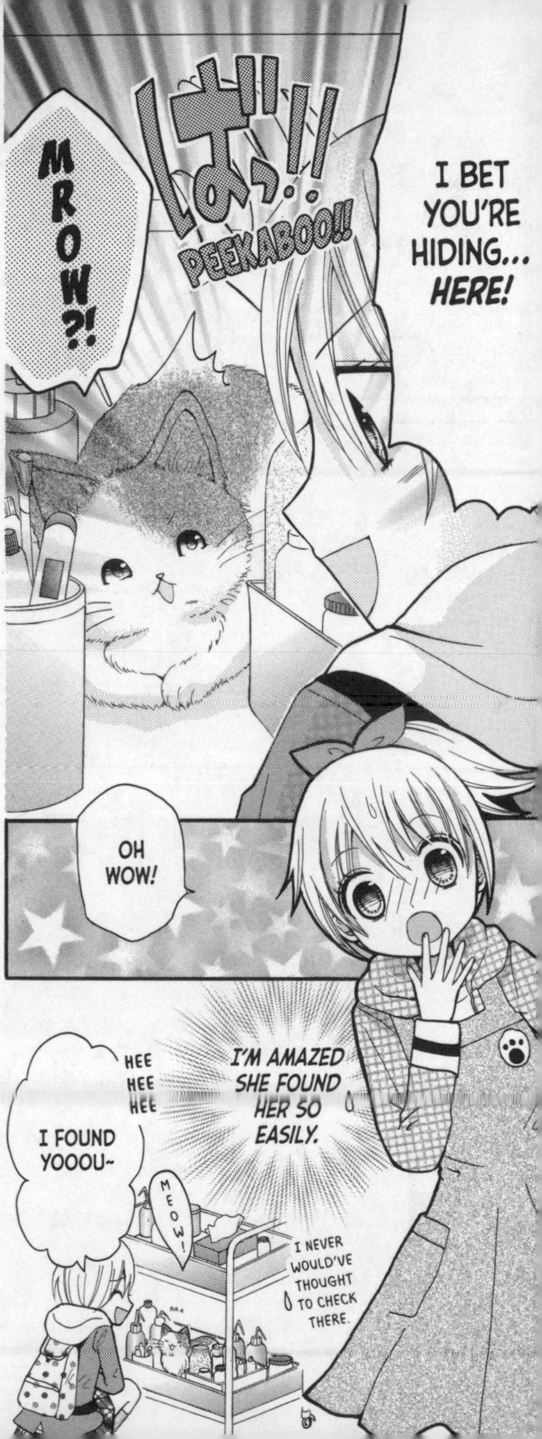
I BET YOU'RE HIDING... *HERE!*
ぱっ!!
PEEKABOO!!
MROW?!
OH WOW!
I'M AMAZED SHE FOUND HER SO EASILY.
I NEVER WOULD'VE THOUGHT TO CHECK THERE.
HEE HEE HEE
I FOUND YOOOU~
MEOW!

LETTERS!

I BELIEVE THAT MANGA ARTISTS GET THE MOST MOTIVATION FROM THE ✧LETTERS✧ THEY GET FROM THEIR READERS.

READING ABOUT YOUR THOUGHTS AND SEEING YOUR FANART OF YUZU AND SORA MAKES ME SO HAPPY! I CAN'T HELP BUT READ YOUR LETTERS OVER AND OVER AGAIN! AND LOTS OF MY READERS OWN PETS, JUST LIKE I THOUGHT!✧

I'M ALWAYS SO HAPPY TO READ ABOUT YOUR PETS!

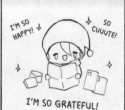

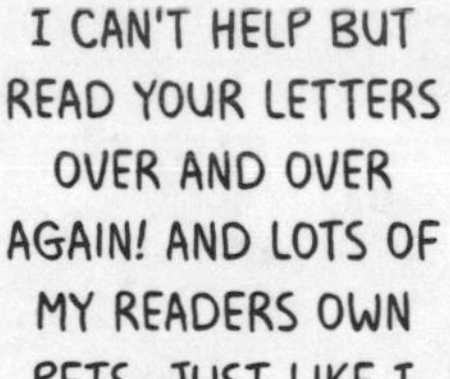
I'M SO HAPPY!
SO CUUUTE!

I'M SO GRATEFUL!

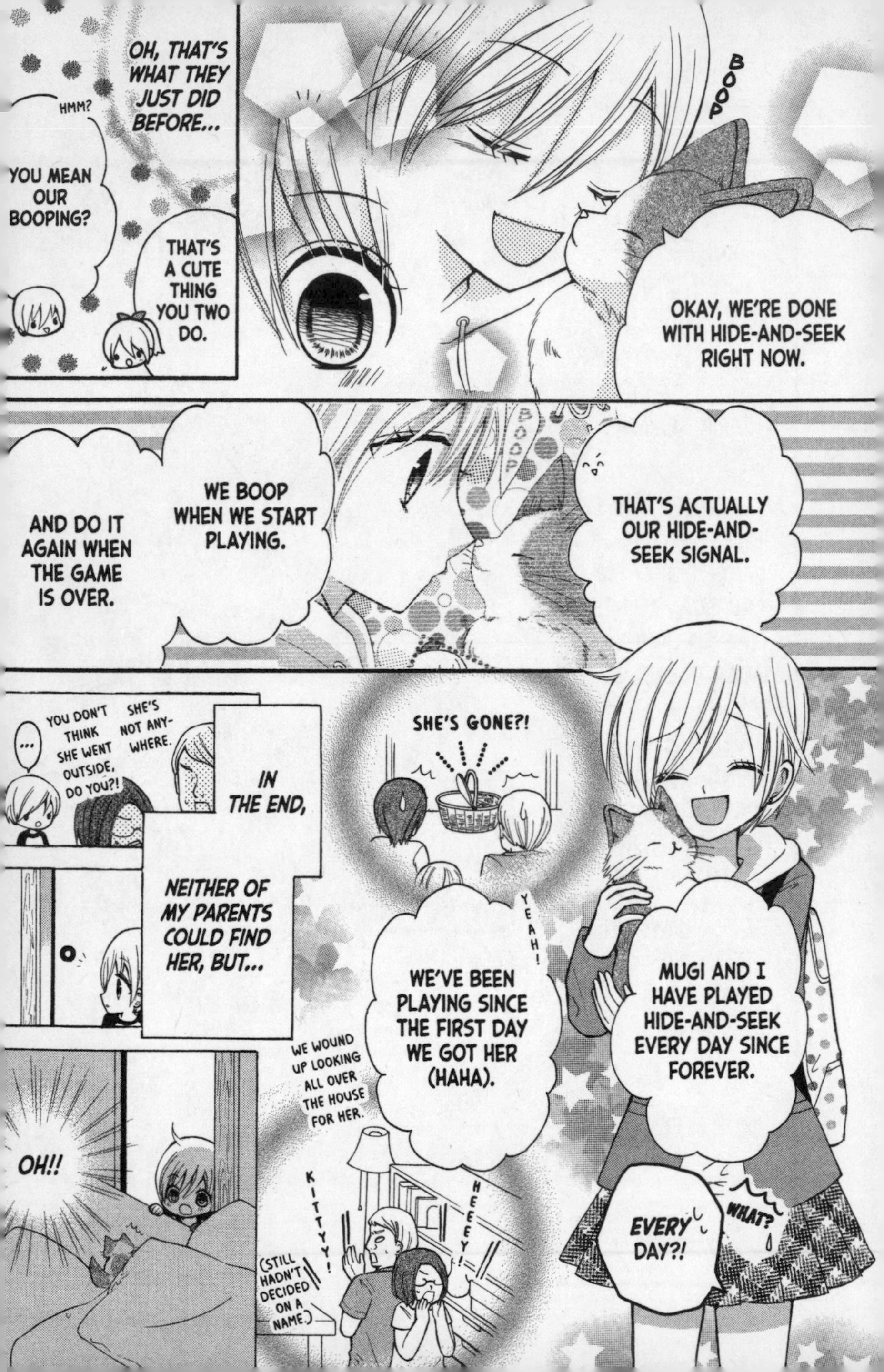
BOOP
OKAY, WE'RE DONE WITH HIDE-AND-SEEK RIGHT NOW.
OH, THAT'S WHAT THEY JUST DID BEFORE...
THAT'S A CUTE THING YOU TWO DO.
HMM?
YOU MEAN OUR BOOPING?
BOOP
THAT'S ACTUALLY OUR HIDE-AND-SEEK SIGNAL.
WE BOOP WHEN WE START PLAYING.
AND DO IT AGAIN WHEN THE GAME IS OVER.
MUGI AND I HAVE PLAYED HIDE-AND-SEEK EVERY DAY SINCE FOREVER.
WHAT?
EVERY DAY?!
YEAH!
WE'VE BEEN PLAYING SINCE THE FIRST DAY WE GOT HER (HAHA).
SHE'S GONE?!
WE WOUND UP LOOKING ALL OVER THE HOUSE FOR HER.
HEEEY!
KITTYY!
(STILL HADN'T DECIDED ON A NAME.)
SHE'S NOT ANYWHERE.
YOU DON'T THINK SHE WENT OUTSIDE, DO YOU?!
...
IN THE END,
NEITHER OF MY PARENTS COULD FIND HER, BUT...
OH!!

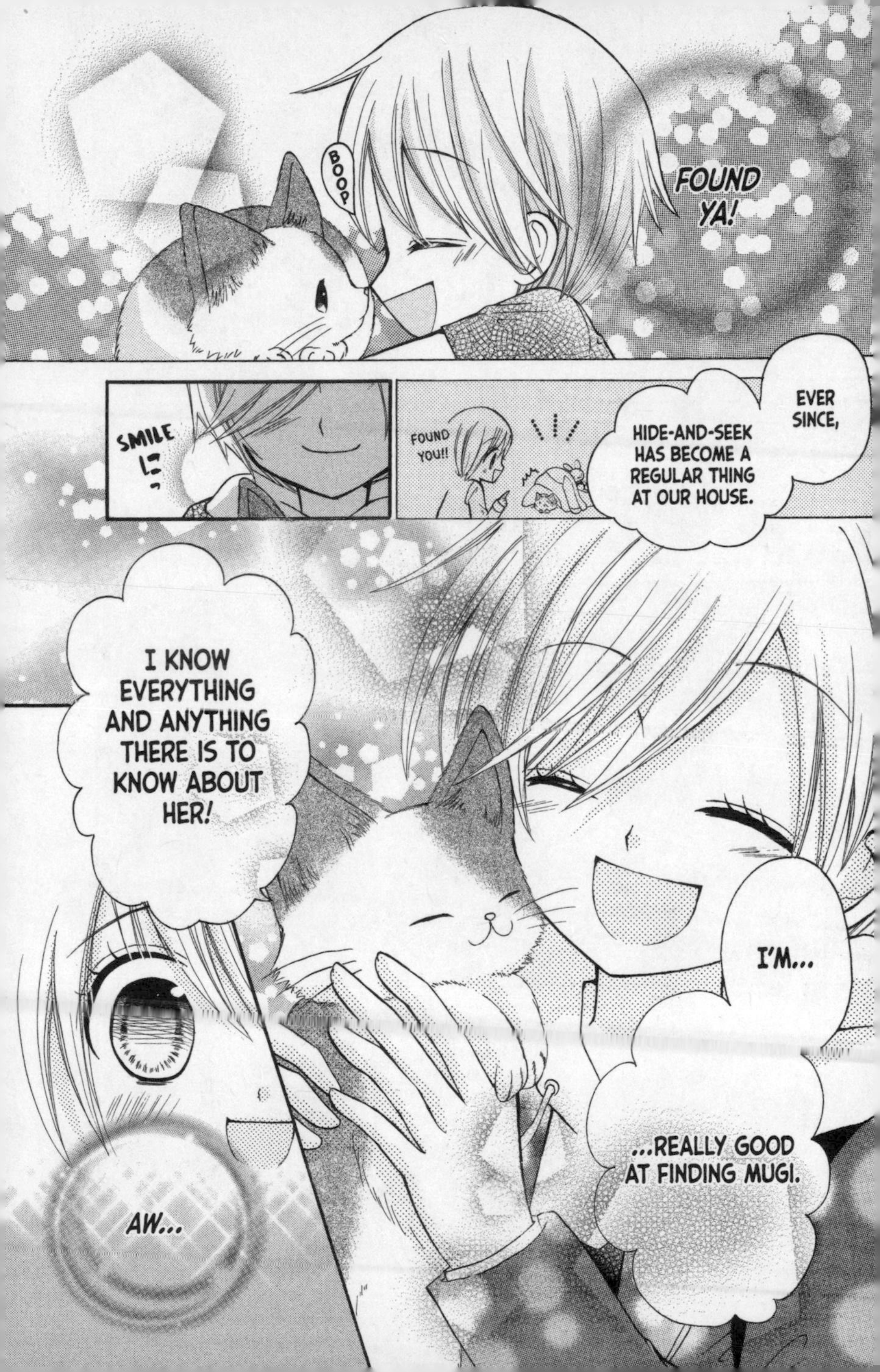
FOUND YA!
BOOP
EVER SINCE,
HIDE-AND-SEEK HAS BECOME A REGULAR THING AT OUR HOUSE.
FOUND YOU!!
SMILE
I'M...
...REALLY GOOD AT FINDING MUGI.
I KNOW EVERYTHING AND ANYTHING THERE IS TO KNOW ABOUT HER!
AW...

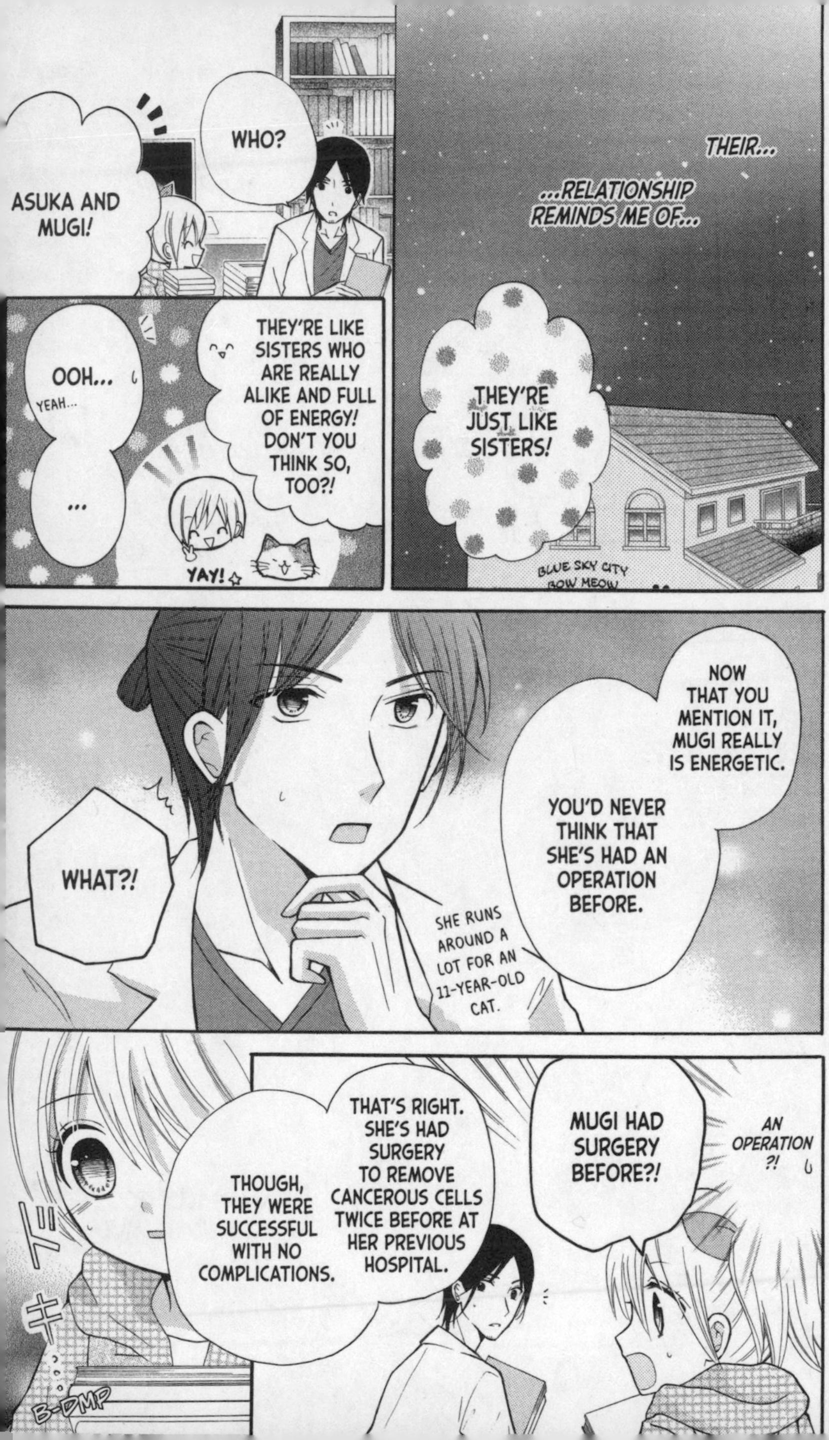
THEIR...
...RELATIONSHIP REMINDS ME OF...
THEY'RE JUST LIKE SISTERS!
BLUE SKY CITY BOW MEOW
WHO?
ASUKA AND MUGI!
THEY'RE LIKE SISTERS WHO ARE REALLY ALIKE AND FULL OF ENERGY! DON'T YOU THINK SO, TOO?!
YAY!
OOH... YEAH...
...
NOW THAT YOU MENTION IT, MUGI REALLY IS ENERGETIC.
YOU'D NEVER THINK THAT SHE'S HAD AN OPERATION BEFORE.
SHE RUNS AROUND A LOT FOR AN 11-YEAR-OLD CAT.
WHAT?!
AN OPERATION?!
MUGI HAD SURGERY BEFORE?!
THAT'S RIGHT. SHE'S HAD SURGERY TO REMOVE CANCEROUS CELLS TWICE BEFORE AT HER PREVIOUS HOSPITAL.
THOUGH, THEY WERE SUCCESSFUL WITH NO COMPLICATIONS.
B-DMP

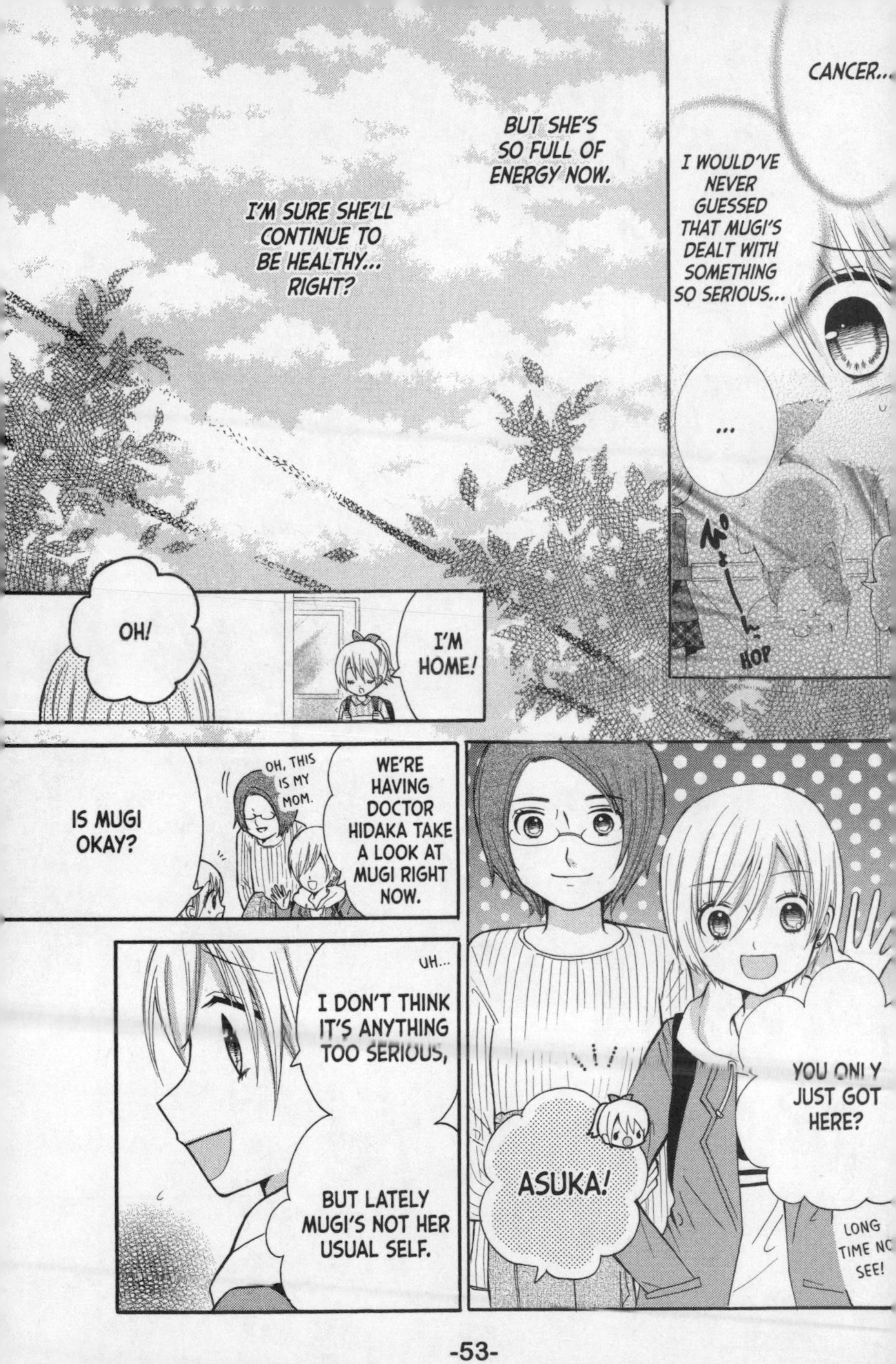
CANCER...
I WOULD'VE NEVER GUESSED THAT MUGI'S DEALT WITH SOMETHING SO SERIOUS...
...
HOP
BUT SHE'S SO FULL OF ENERGY NOW.
I'M SURE SHE'LL CONTINUE TO BE HEALTHY... RIGHT?
I'M HOME!
OH!
YOU ONLY JUST GOT HERE?
LONG TIME NO SEE!
ASUKA!
WE'RE HAVING DOCTOR HIDAKA TAKE A LOOK AT MUGI RIGHT NOW.
OH, THIS IS MY MOM.
IS MUGI OKAY?
UH...
I DON'T THINK IT'S ANYTHING TOO SERIOUS,
BUT LATELY MUGI'S NOT HER USUAL SELF.

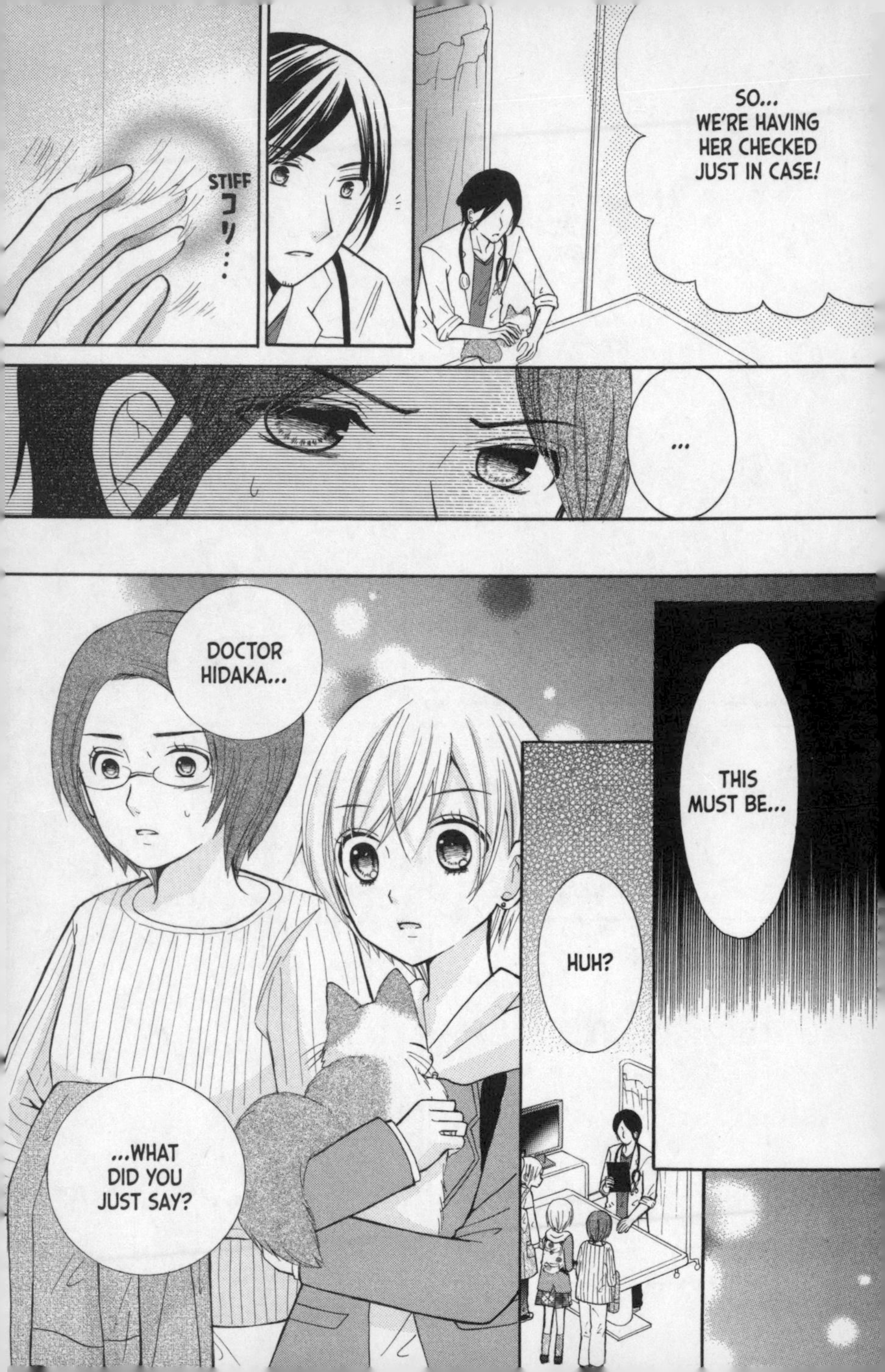
SO... WE'RE HAVING HER CHECKED JUST IN CASE!
STIFF
コリ・・・
...
THIS MUST BE...
HUH?
DOCTOR HIDAKA...
...WHAT DID YOU JUST SAY?

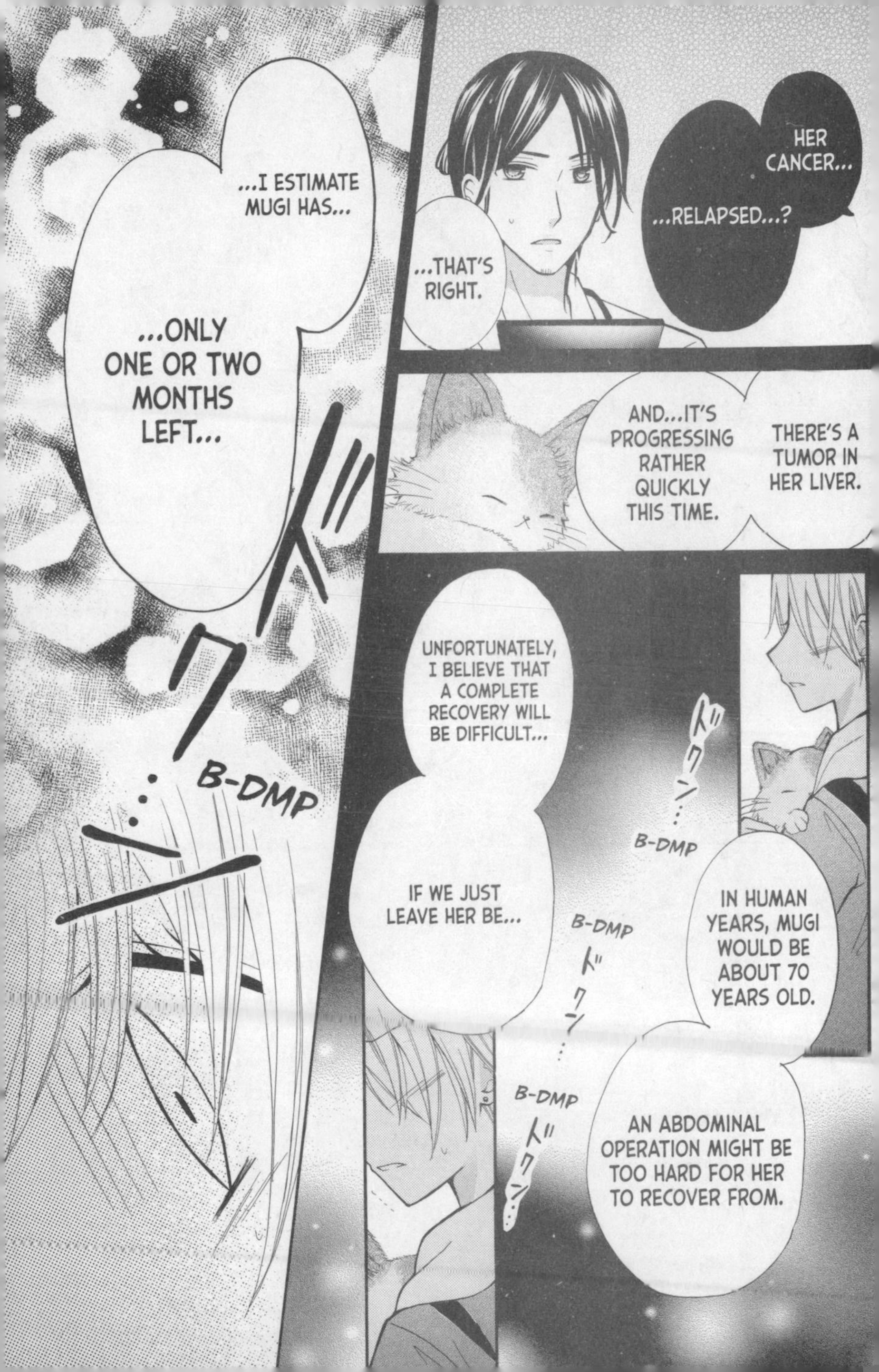
HER CANCER...
...RELAPSED...?
...THAT'S RIGHT.
THERE'S A TUMOR IN HER LIVER.
AND...IT'S PROGRESSING RATHER QUICKLY THIS TIME.
IN HUMAN YEARS, MUGI WOULD BE ABOUT 70 YEARS OLD.
AN ABDOMINAL OPERATION MIGHT BE TOO HARD FOR HER TO RECOVER FROM.
UNFORTUNATELY, I BELIEVE THAT A COMPLETE RECOVERY WILL BE DIFFICULT...
IF WE JUST LEAVE HER BE...
B-DMP
B-DMP
B-DMP
...I ESTIMATE MUGI HAS...
...ONLY ONE OR TWO MONTHS LEFT...
B-DMP

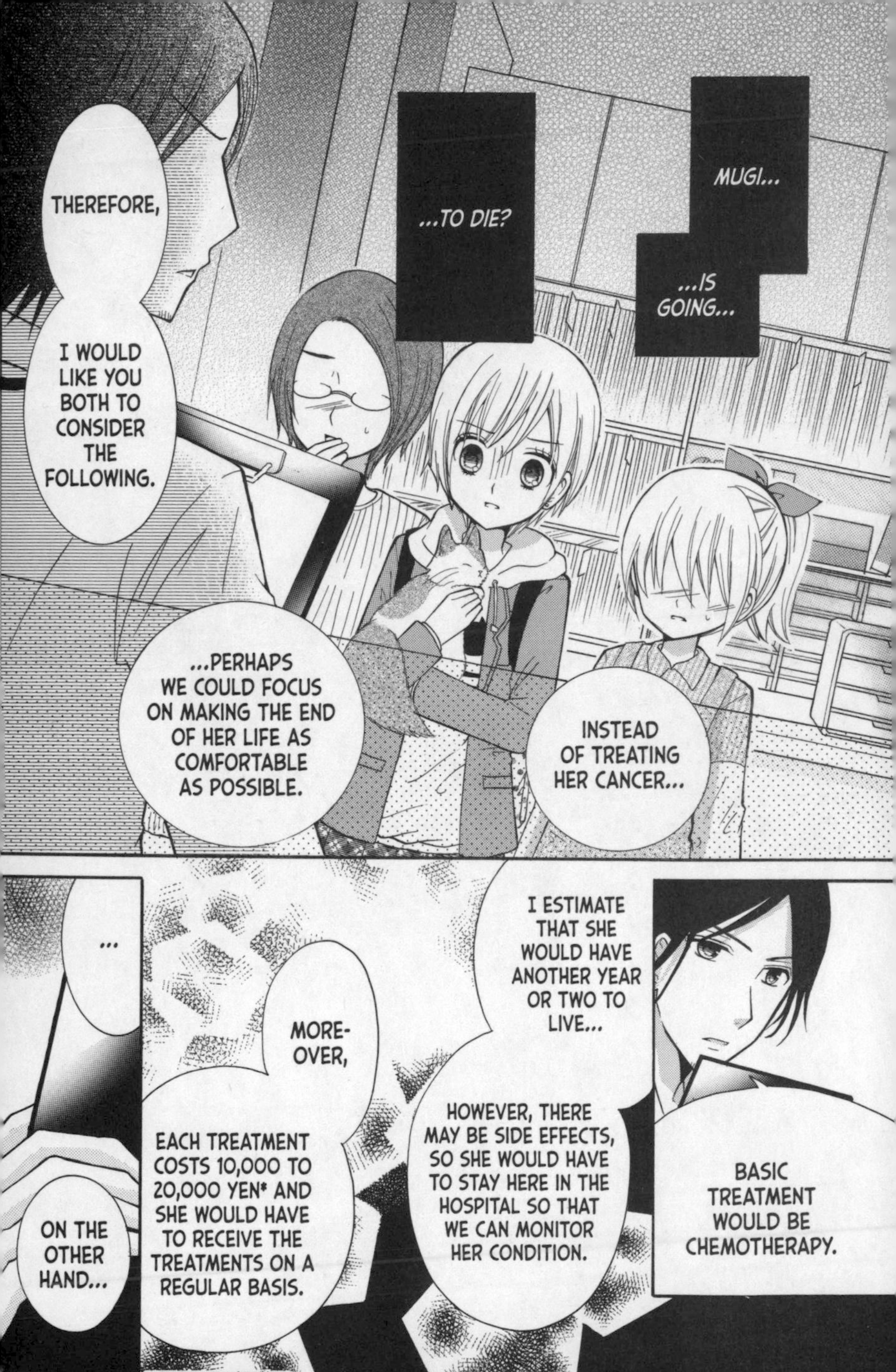
MUGI...
...IS GOING...
...TO DIE?
THEREFORE,
I WOULD LIKE YOU BOTH TO CONSIDER THE FOLLOWING.
INSTEAD OF TREATING HER CANCER...
...PERHAPS WE COULD FOCUS ON MAKING THE END OF HER LIFE AS COMFORTABLE AS POSSIBLE.
BASIC TREATMENT WOULD BE CHEMOTHERAPY.
I ESTIMATE THAT SHE WOULD HAVE ANOTHER YEAR OR TWO TO LIVE...
HOWEVER, THERE MAY BE SIDE EFFECTS, SO SHE WOULD HAVE TO STAY HERE IN THE HOSPITAL SO THAT WE CAN MONITOR HER CONDITION.
MORE-OVER,
EACH TREATMENT COSTS 10,000 TO 20,000 YEN* AND SHE WOULD HAVE TO RECEIVE THE TREATMENTS ON A REGULAR BASIS.
ON THE OTHER HAND...
...

*APPROXIMATELY $100-$200.

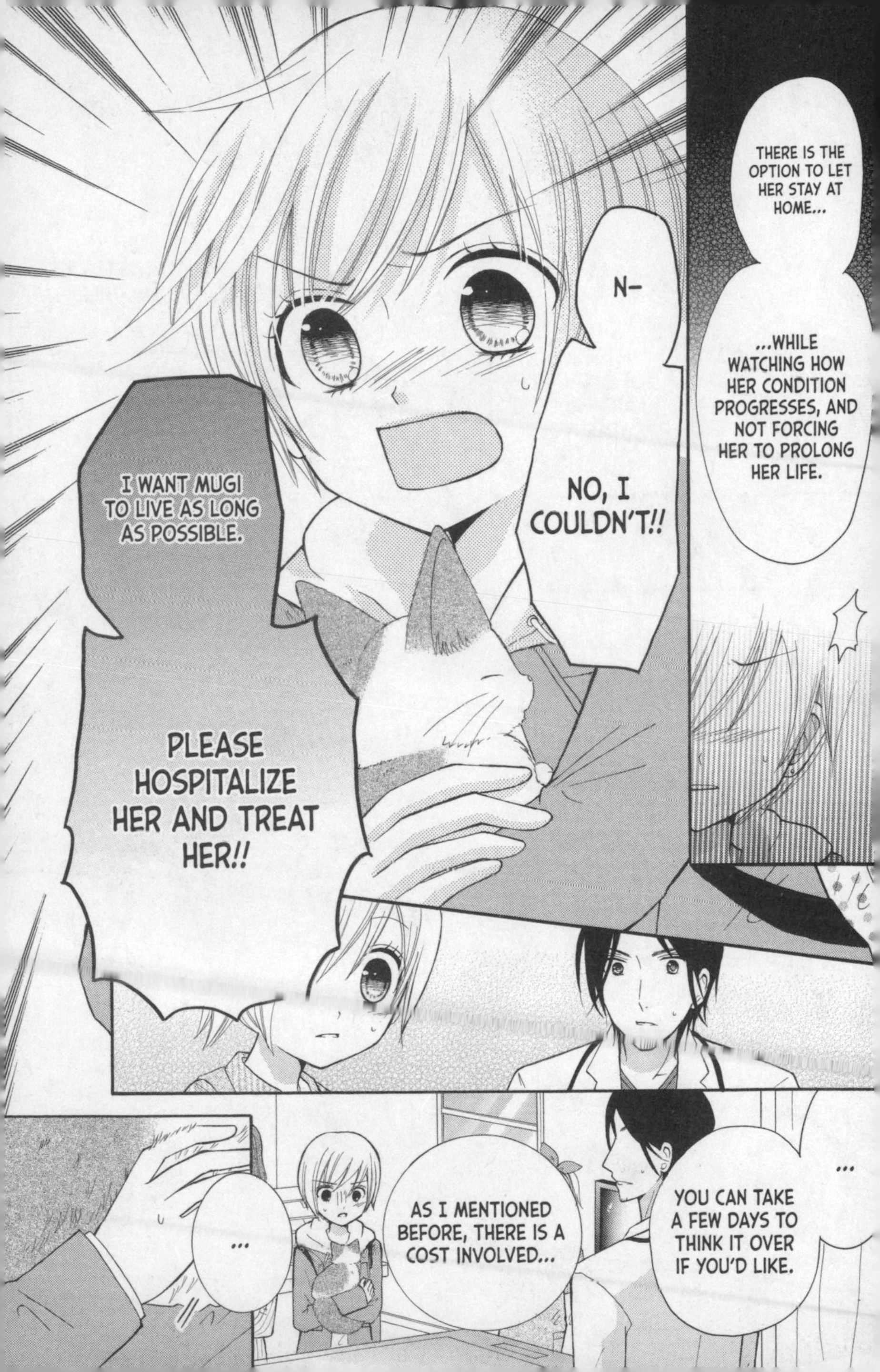
THERE IS THE OPTION TO LET HER STAY AT HOME...
...WHILE WATCHING HOW HER CONDITION PROGRESSES, AND NOT FORCING HER TO PROLONG HER LIFE.
N-
NO, I COULDN'T!!
I WANT MUGI TO LIVE AS LONG AS POSSIBLE.
PLEASE HOSPITALIZE HER AND TREAT HER!!
...
YOU CAN TAKE A FEW DAYS TO THINK IT OVER IF YOU'D LIKE.
AS I MENTIONED BEFORE, THERE IS A COST INVOLVED...
...

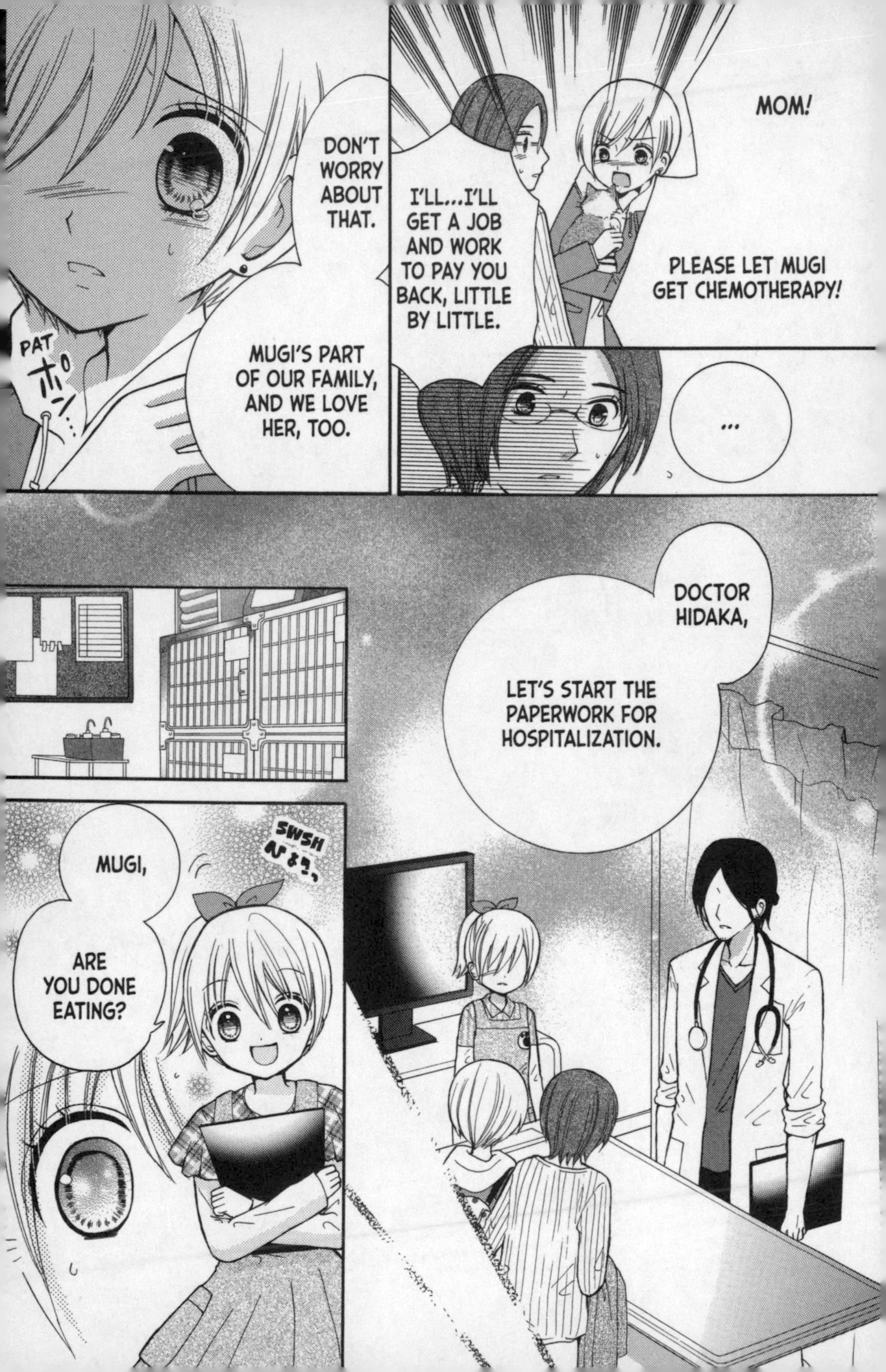
MOM!
PLEASE LET MUGI GET CHEMOTHERAPY!
I'LL...I'LL GET A JOB AND WORK TO PAY YOU BACK, LITTLE BY LITTLE.
...
DON'T WORRY ABOUT THAT.
PAT
MUGI'S PART OF OUR FAMILY, AND WE LOVE HER, TOO.
DOCTOR HIDAKA,
LET'S START THE PAPERWORK FOR HOSPITALIZATION.
SWSH
MUGI,
ARE YOU DONE EATING?

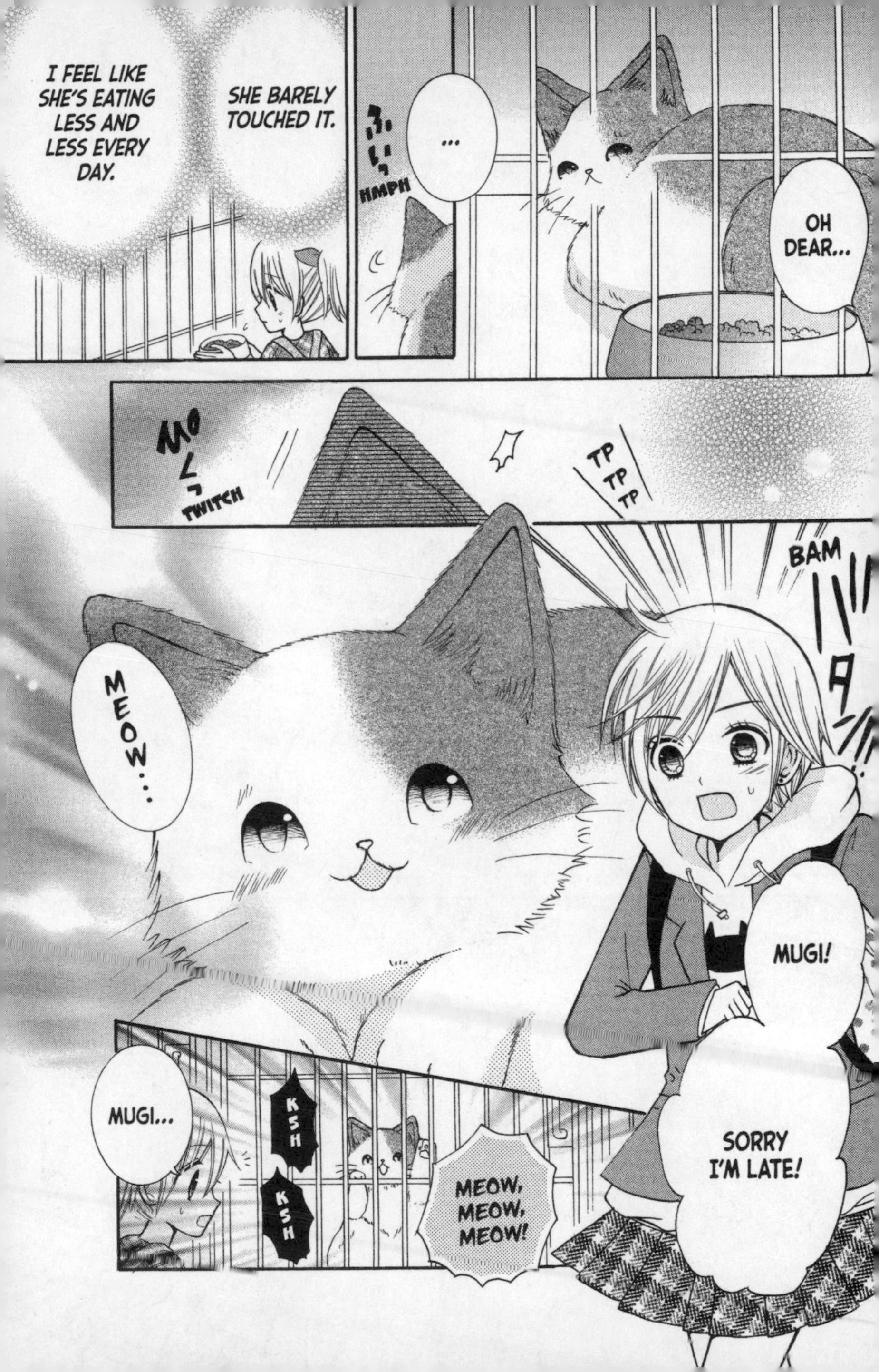
OH DEAR...
...
HMPH
SHE BARELY TOUCHED IT.
I FEEL LIKE SHE'S EATING LESS AND LESS EVERY DAY.
TP TP TP
TWITCH
BAM
MUGI!
SORRY I'M LATE!
MEOW...
MEOW, MEOW, MEOW!
KSH
KSH
MUGI...

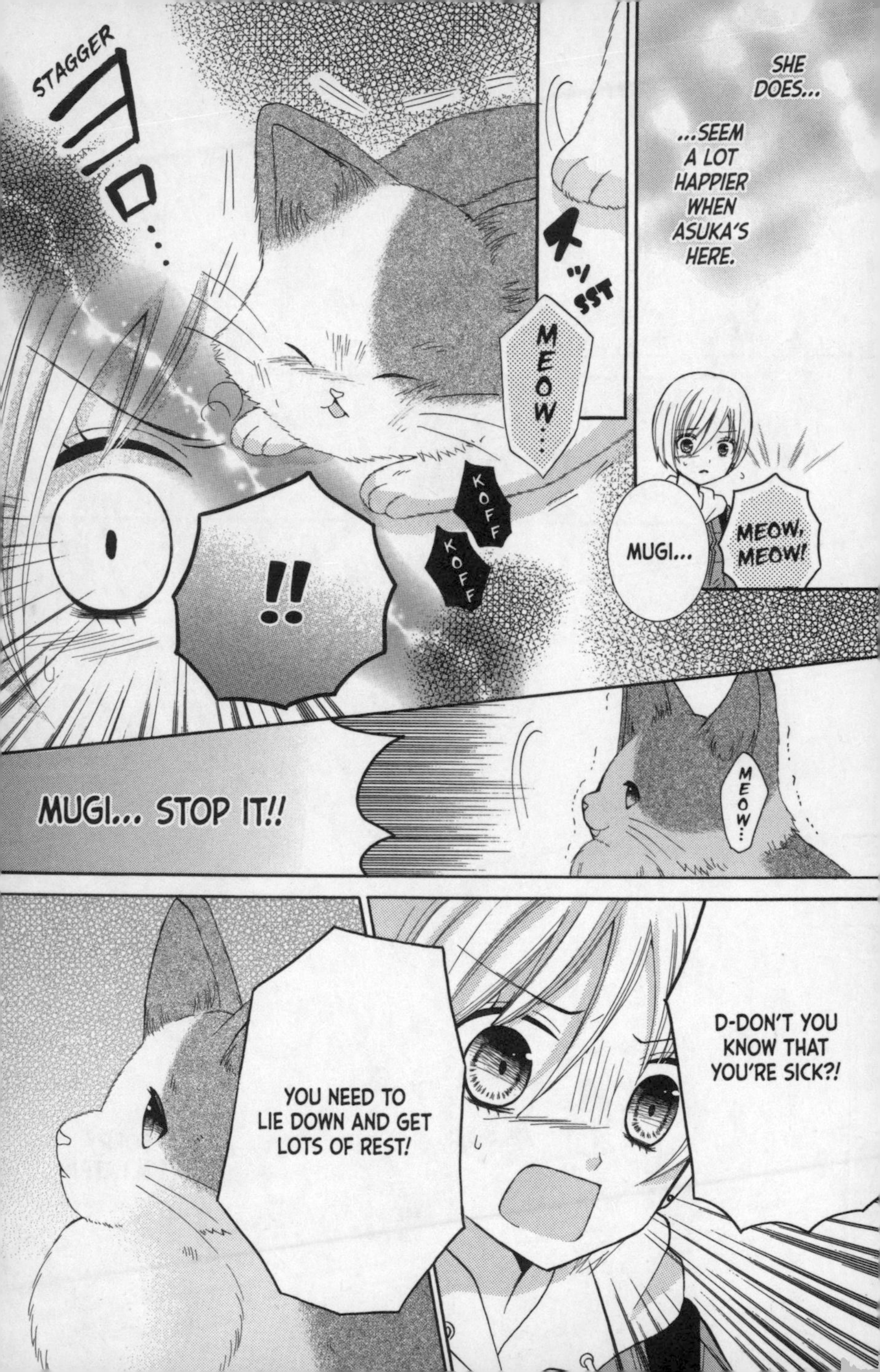
SHE DOES...
...SEEM A LOT HAPPIER WHEN ASUKA'S HERE.
MEOW, MEOW!
MUGI...
SST
MEOW...
KOFF KOFF
STAGGER
!!
MEOW...
MUGI... STOP IT!!
D-DON'T YOU KNOW THAT YOU'RE SICK?!
YOU NEED TO LIE DOWN AND GET LOTS OF REST!

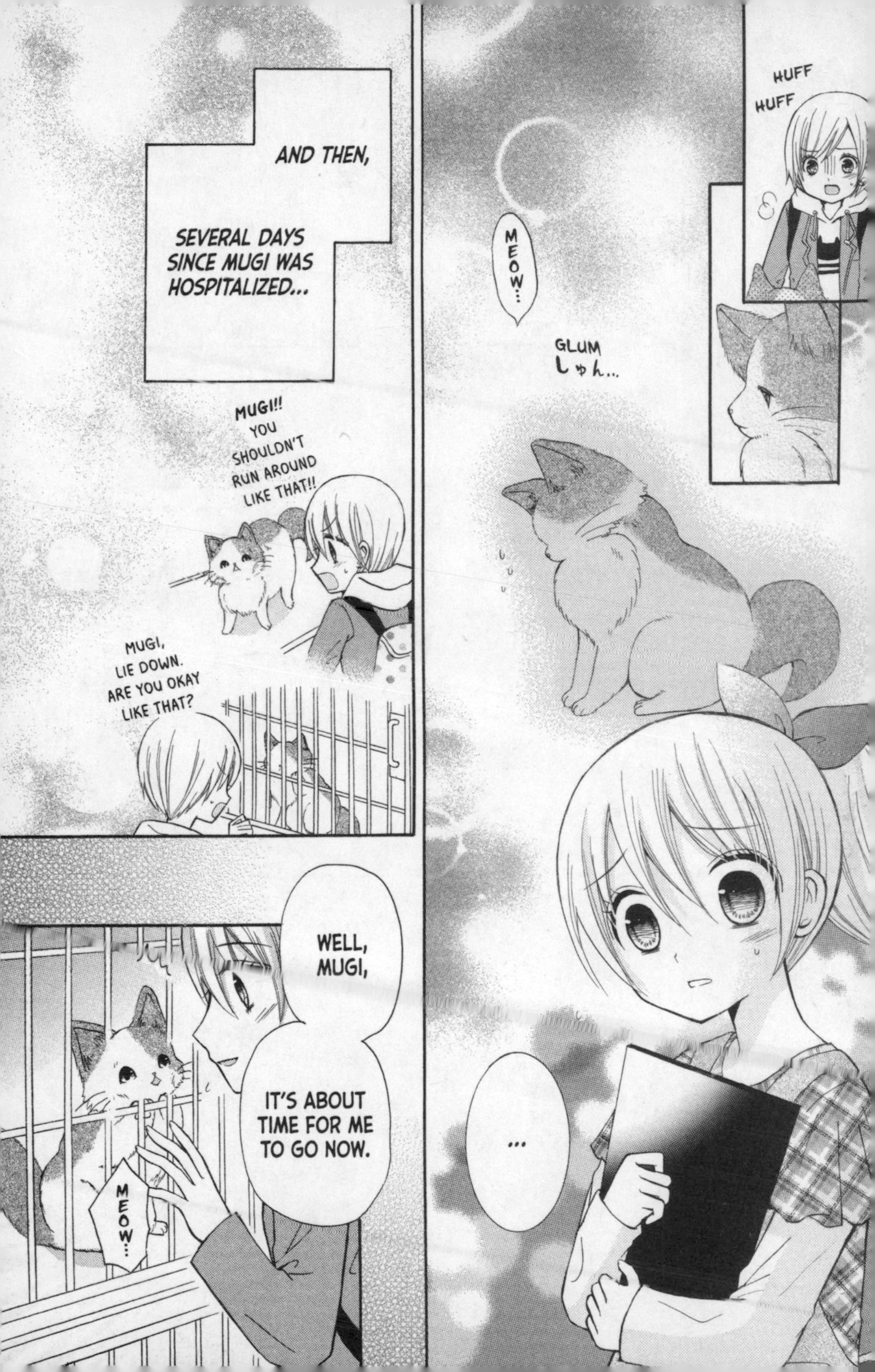
HUFF
HUFF
MEOW...
GLUM
しゅん...
...
AND THEN,
SEVERAL DAYS SINCE MUGI WAS HOSPITALIZED...
MUGI!! YOU SHOULDN'T RUN AROUND LIKE THAT!!
MUGI, LIE DOWN. ARE YOU OKAY LIKE THAT?
WELL, MUGI,
IT'S ABOUT TIME FOR ME TO GO NOW.
MEOW...

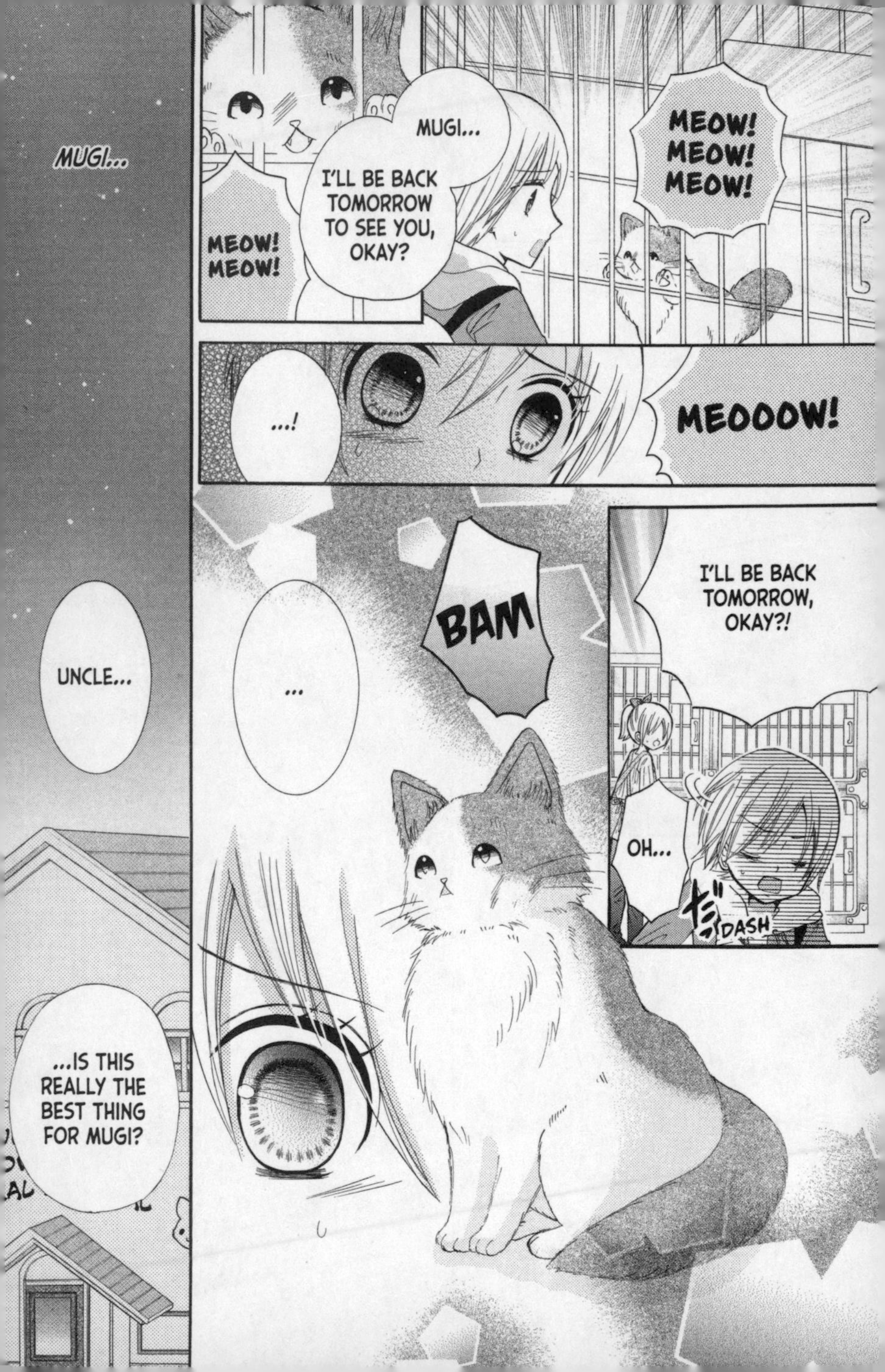
MEOW! MEOW! MEOW!
MUGI...
I'LL BE BACK TOMORROW TO SEE YOU, OKAY?
MEOW! MEOW!
MEOOOW!
...!
I'LL BE BACK TOMORROW, OKAY?!
OH...
DASH
BAM
...
MUGI...
UNCLE...
...IS THIS REALLY THE BEST THING FOR MUGI?

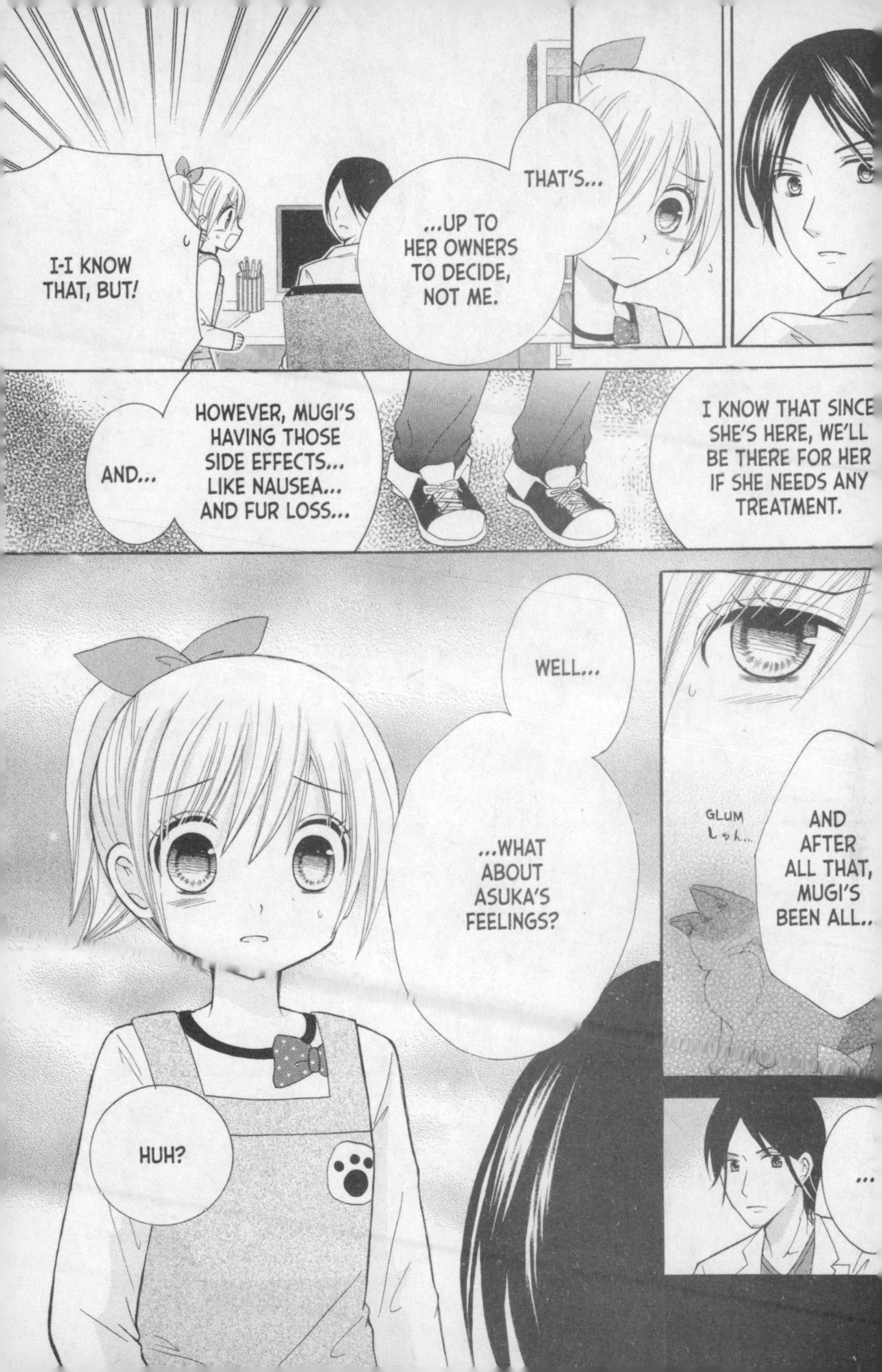
THAT'S...
...UP TO HER OWNERS TO DECIDE, NOT ME.
I-I KNOW THAT, BUT!
I KNOW THAT SINCE SHE'S HERE, WE'LL BE THERE FOR HER IF SHE NEEDS ANY TREATMENT.
HOWEVER, MUGI'S HAVING THOSE SIDE EFFECTS... LIKE NAUSEA... AND FUR LOSS...
AND...
AND AFTER ALL THAT, MUGI'S BEEN ALL...
GLUM
しゅん...
...
WELL...
...WHAT ABOUT ASUKA'S FEELINGS?
HUH?

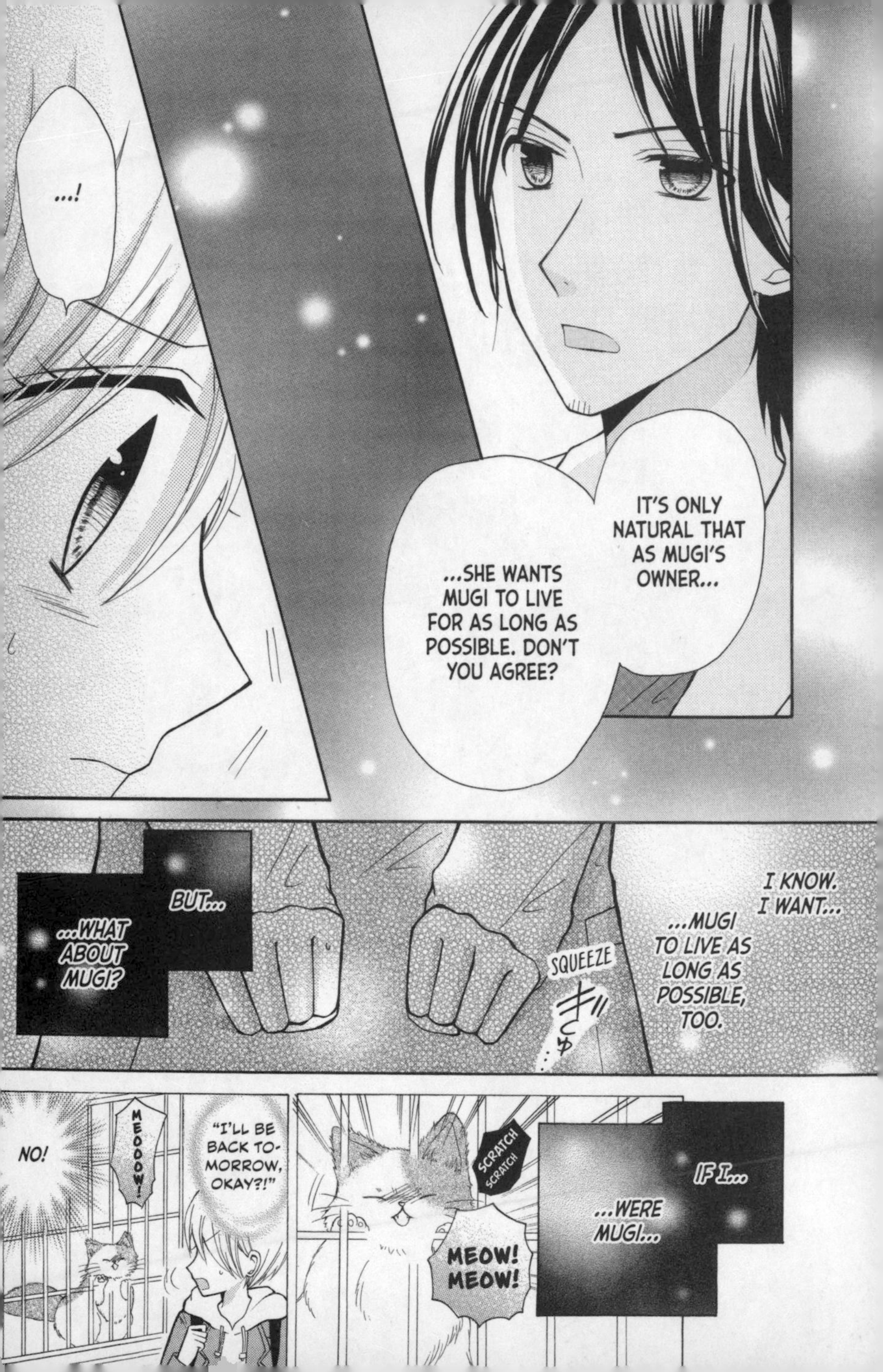
IT'S ONLY NATURAL THAT AS MUGI'S OWNER...
...SHE WANTS MUGI TO LIVE FOR AS LONG AS POSSIBLE. DON'T YOU AGREE?
...!
I KNOW. I WANT...
...MUGI TO LIVE AS LONG AS POSSIBLE, TOO.
SQUEEZE
BUT...
...WHAT ABOUT MUGI?
IF I...
...WERE MUGI...
SCRATCH SCRATCH
MEOW! MEOW!
MEOOOW!
"I'LL BE BACK TO-MORROW, OKAY?!"
NO!

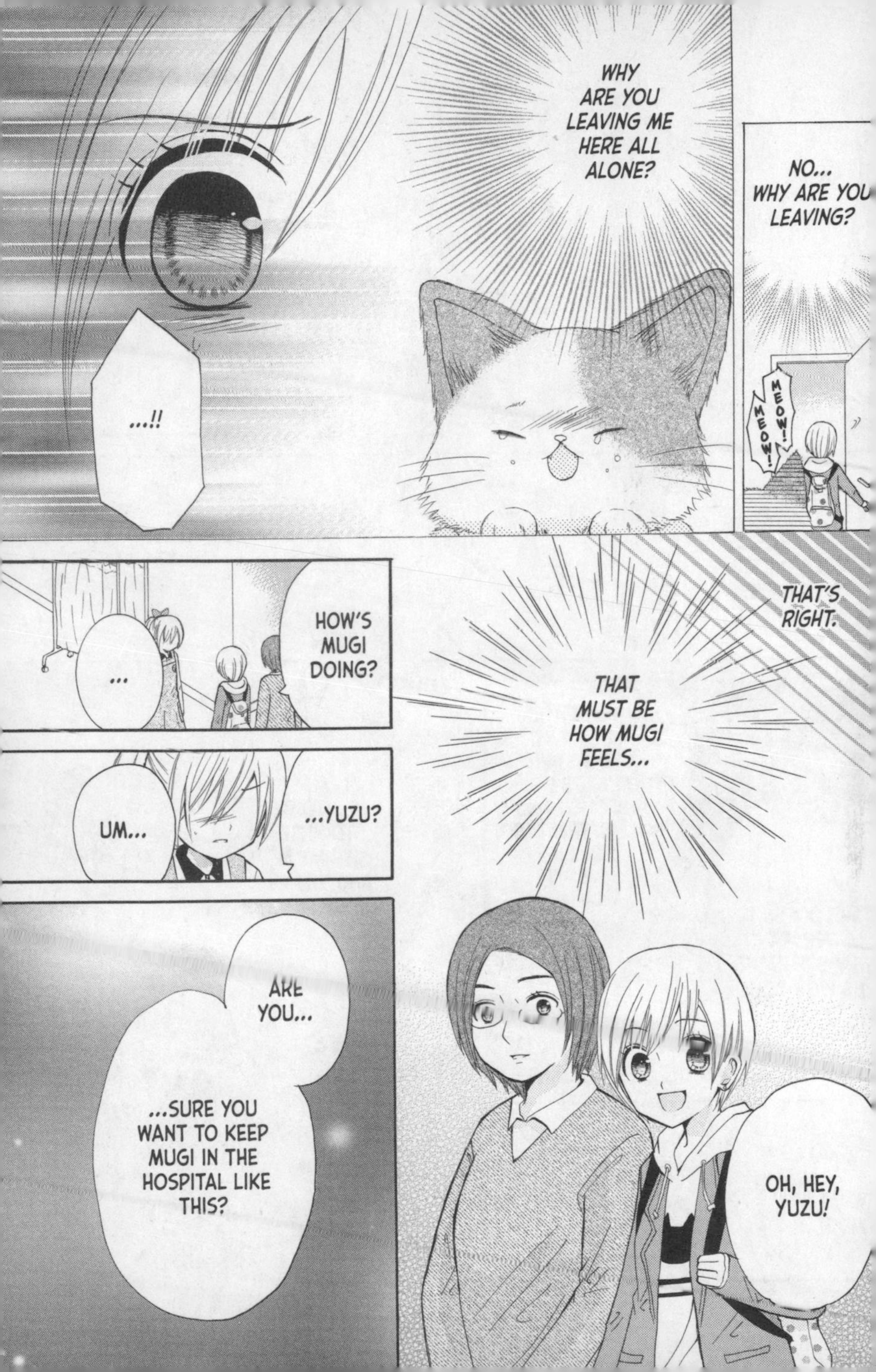
NO... WHY ARE YOU LEAVING?
MEOW! MEOW!
WHY ARE YOU LEAVING ME HERE ALL ALONE?
...!!
THAT'S RIGHT.
THAT MUST BE HOW MUGI FEELS...
OH, HEY, YUZU!
HOW'S MUGI DOING?
...
...YUZU?
UM...
ARE YOU...
...SURE YOU WANT TO KEEP MUGI IN THE HOSPITAL LIKE THIS?

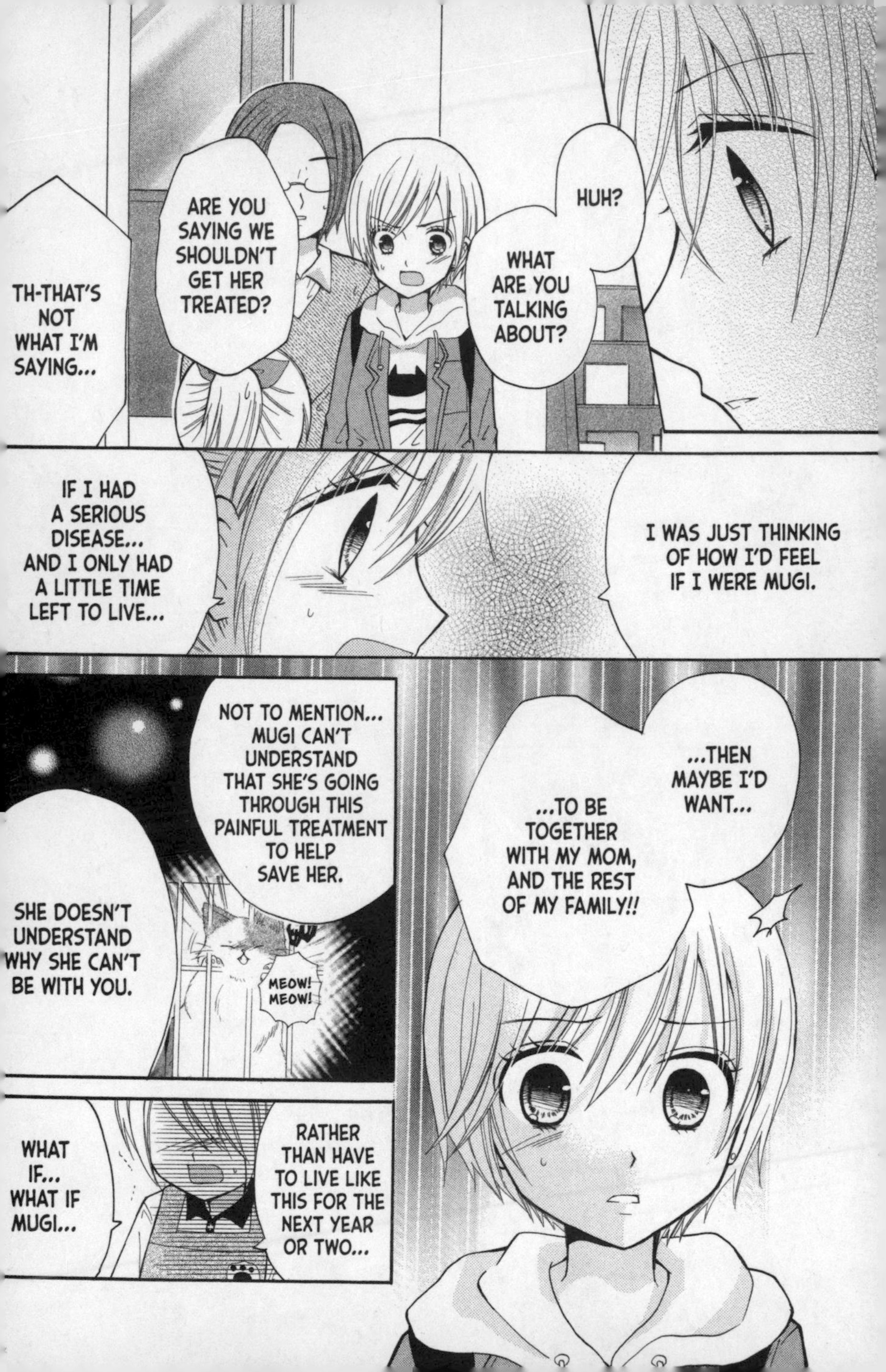
HUH?
WHAT ARE YOU TALKING ABOUT?
ARE YOU SAYING WE SHOULDN'T GET HER TREATED?
TH-THAT'S NOT WHAT I'M SAYING...
I WAS JUST THINKING OF HOW I'D FEEL IF I WERE MUGI.
IF I HAD A SERIOUS DISEASE... AND I ONLY HAD A LITTLE TIME LEFT TO LIVE...
...THEN MAYBE I'D WANT...
...TO BE TOGETHER WITH MY MOM, AND THE REST OF MY FAMILY!!
NOT TO MENTION... MUGI CAN'T UNDERSTAND THAT SHE'S GOING THROUGH THIS PAINFUL TREATMENT TO HELP SAVE HER.
SHE DOESN'T UNDERSTAND WHY SHE CAN'T BE WITH YOU.
MEOW! MEOW!
RATHER THAN HAVE TO LIVE LIKE THIS FOR THE NEXT YEAR OR TWO...
WHAT IF... WHAT IF MUGI...

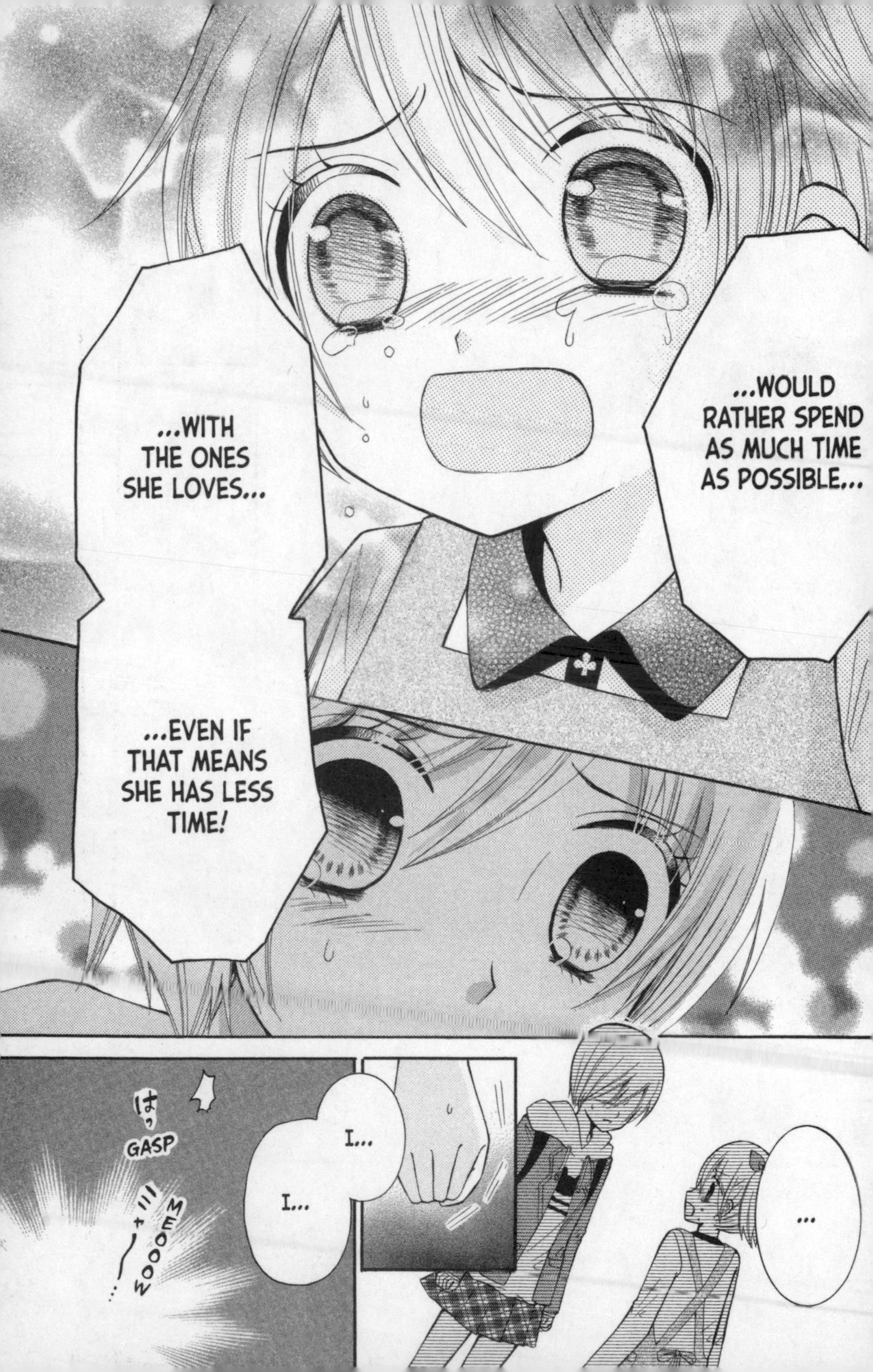
...WOULD RATHER SPEND AS MUCH TIME AS POSSIBLE...
...WITH THE ONES SHE LOVES...
...EVEN IF THAT MEANS SHE HAS LESS TIME!
...
I...
I...
はっ
GASP
ミャ〜…
MEOOOW

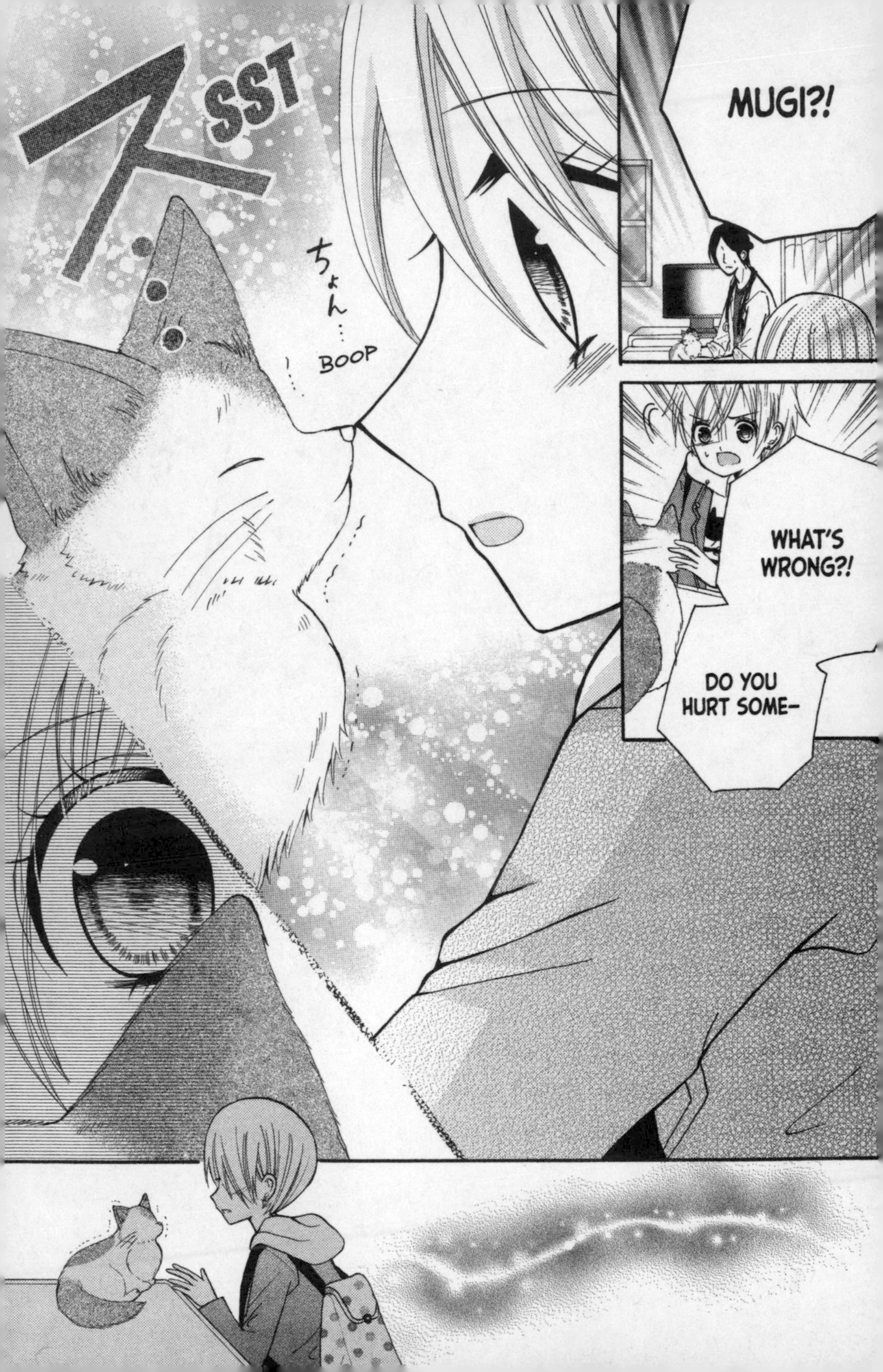
MUGI?!
WHAT'S WRONG?!
DO YOU HURT SOME-
SST
ちょん…
BOOP

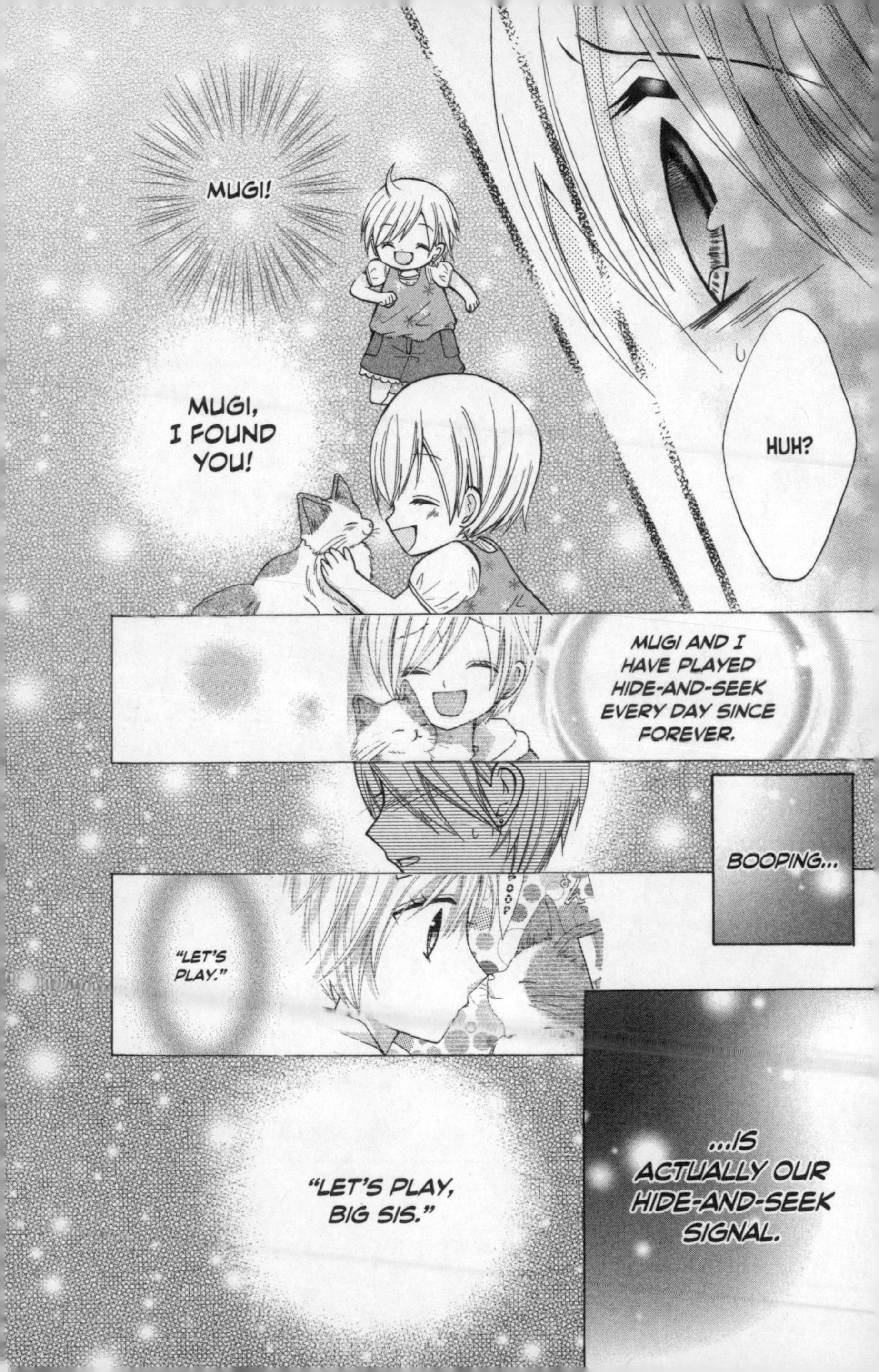
HUH?
MUGI!
MUGI, I FOUND YOU!
MUGI AND I HAVE PLAYED HIDE-AND-SEEK EVERY DAY SINCE FOREVER.
BOOPING...
"LET'S PLAY."
...IS ACTUALLY OUR HIDE-AND-SEEK SIGNAL.
"LET'S PLAY, BIG SIS."

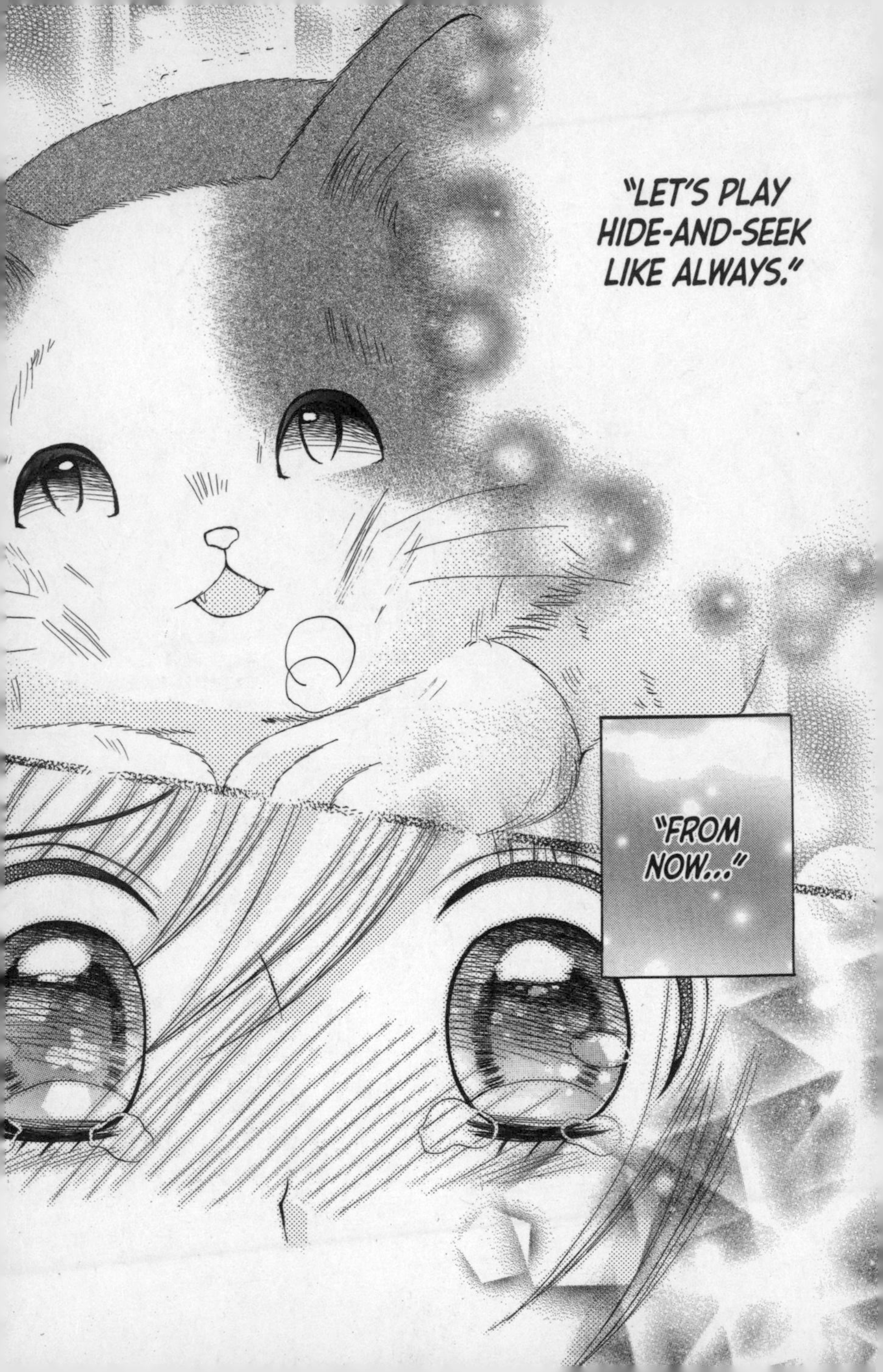
"LET'S PLAY HIDE-AND-SEEK LIKE ALWAYS."
"FROM NOW..."

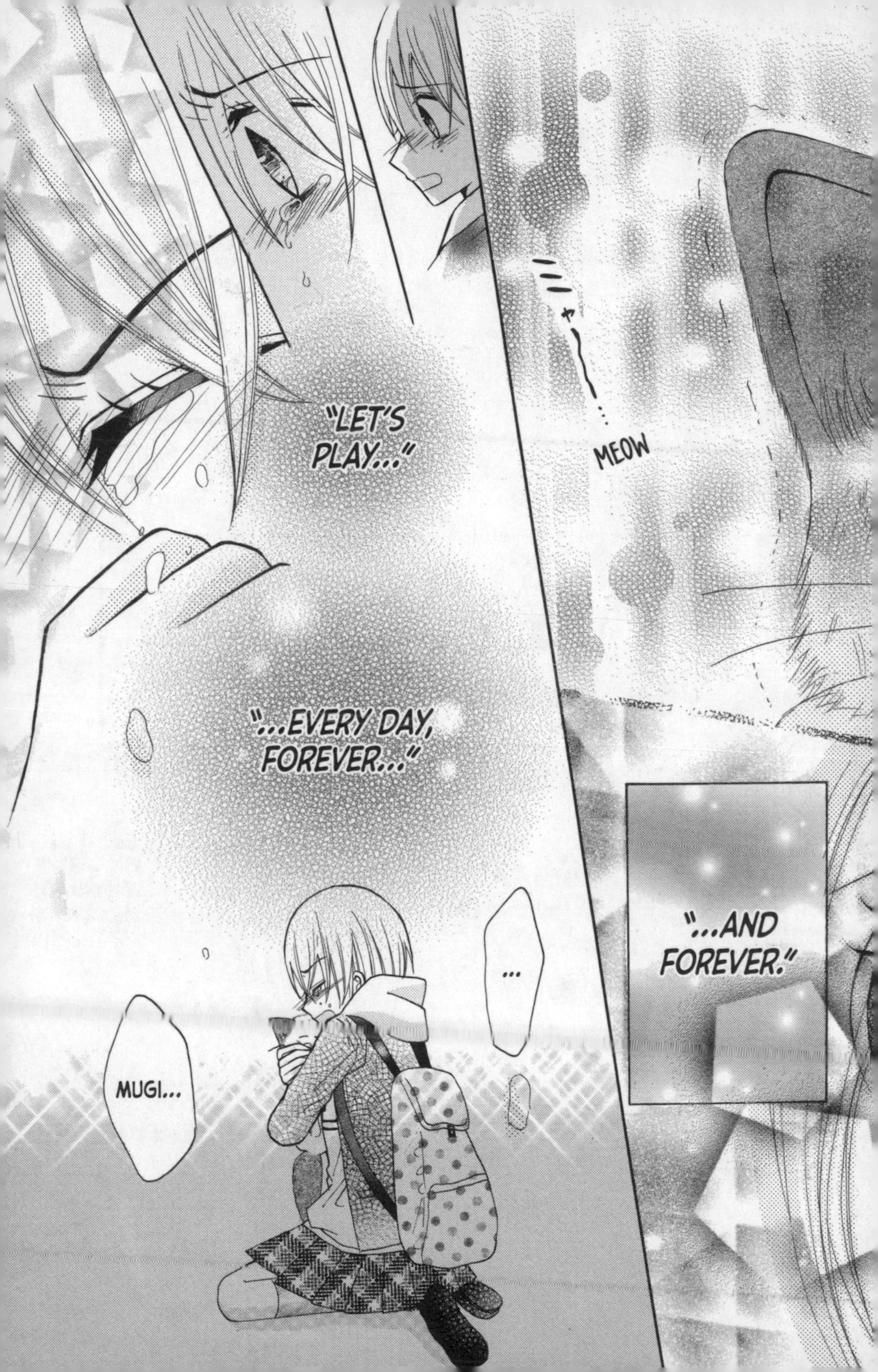
ニャ〜…
MEOW
"LET'S PLAY..."
"...EVERY DAY, FOREVER..."
"...AND FOREVER."
...
MUGI...

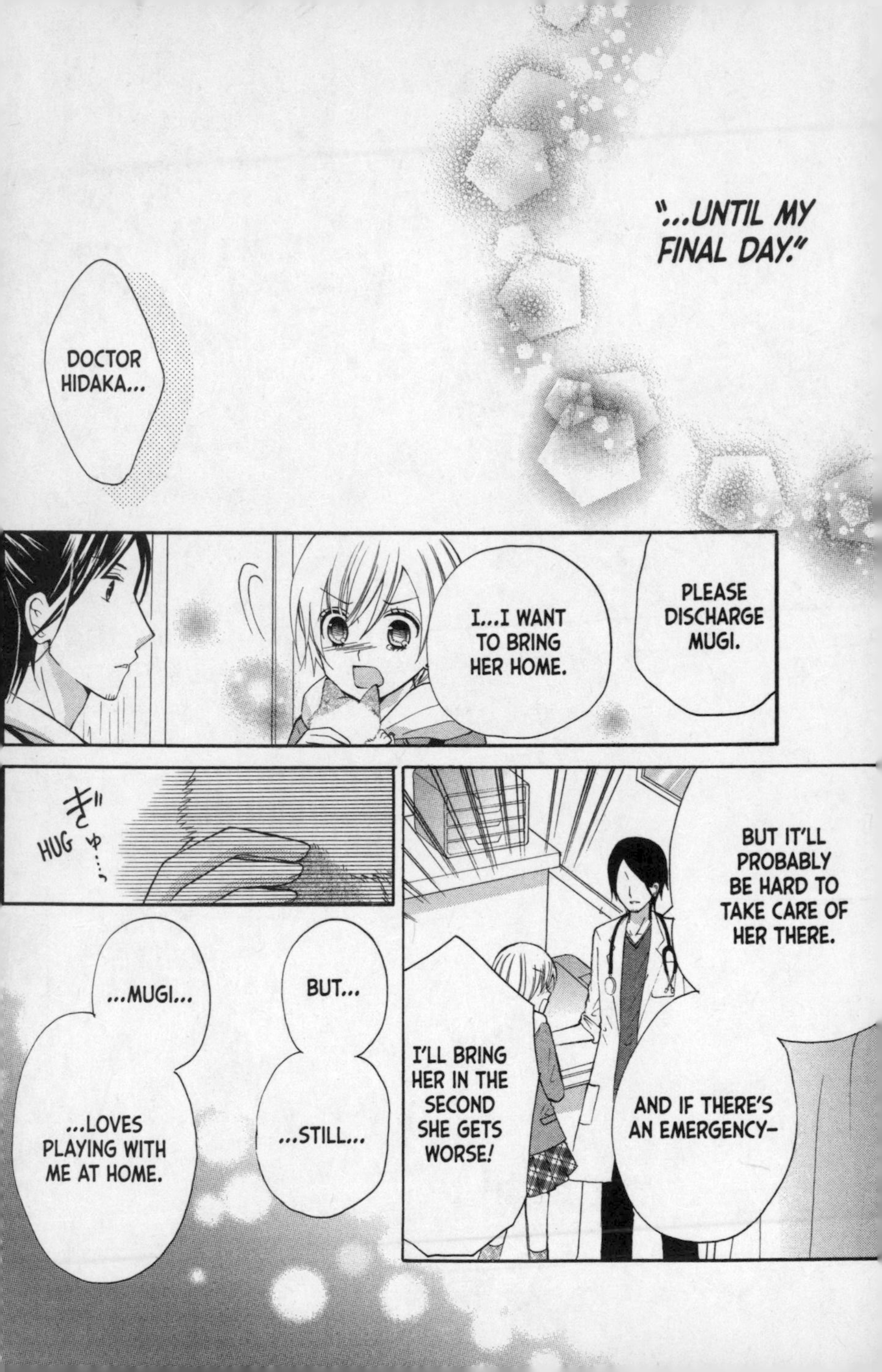
"...UNTIL MY FINAL DAY."
DOCTOR HIDAKA...
PLEASE DISCHARGE MUGI.
I...I WANT TO BRING HER HOME.
BUT IT'LL PROBABLY BE HARD TO TAKE CARE OF HER THERE.
AND IF THERE'S AN EMERGENCY–
I'LL BRING HER IN THE SECOND SHE GETS WORSE!
HUG
ぎゅ…
BUT...
...STILL...
...MUGI...
...LOVES PLAYING WITH ME AT HOME.

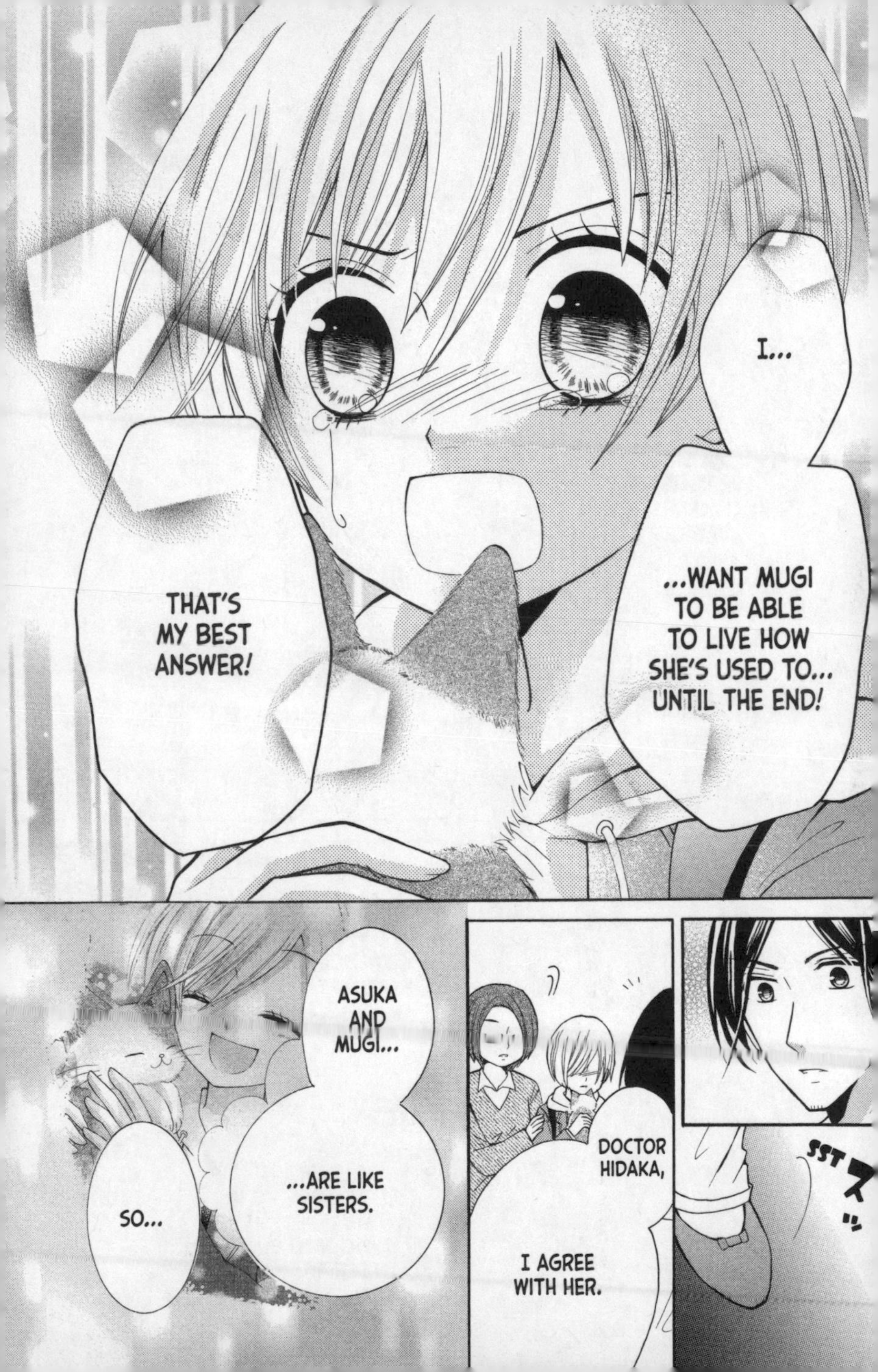
I...
...WANT MUGI TO BE ABLE TO LIVE HOW SHE'S USED TO... UNTIL THE END!
THAT'S MY BEST ANSWER!
SST ス"
DOCTOR HIDAKA,
I AGREE WITH HER.
ASUKA AND MUGI...
...ARE LIKE SISTERS.
SO...

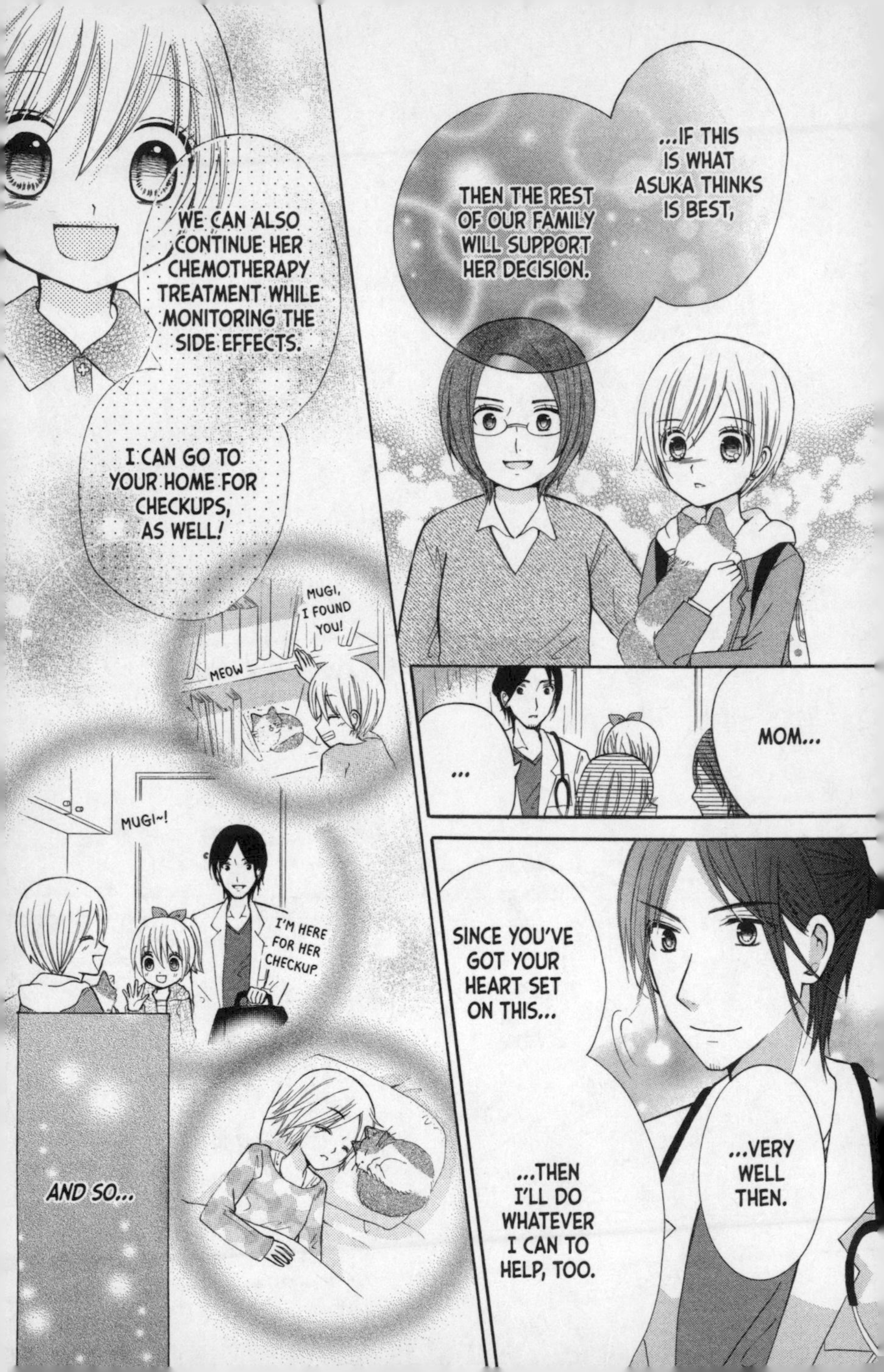
...IF THIS IS WHAT ASUKA THINKS IS BEST,
THEN THE REST OF OUR FAMILY WILL SUPPORT HER DECISION.
MOM...
...
SINCE YOU'VE GOT YOUR HEART SET ON THIS...
...VERY WELL THEN.
...THEN I'LL DO WHATEVER I CAN TO HELP, TOO.
WE CAN ALSO CONTINUE HER CHEMOTHERAPY TREATMENT WHILE MONITORING THE SIDE EFFECTS.
I CAN GO TO YOUR HOME FOR CHECKUPS, AS WELL!
MUGI, I FOUND YOU!
MEOW
MUGI~!
I'M HERE FOR HER CHECKUP.
AND SO...

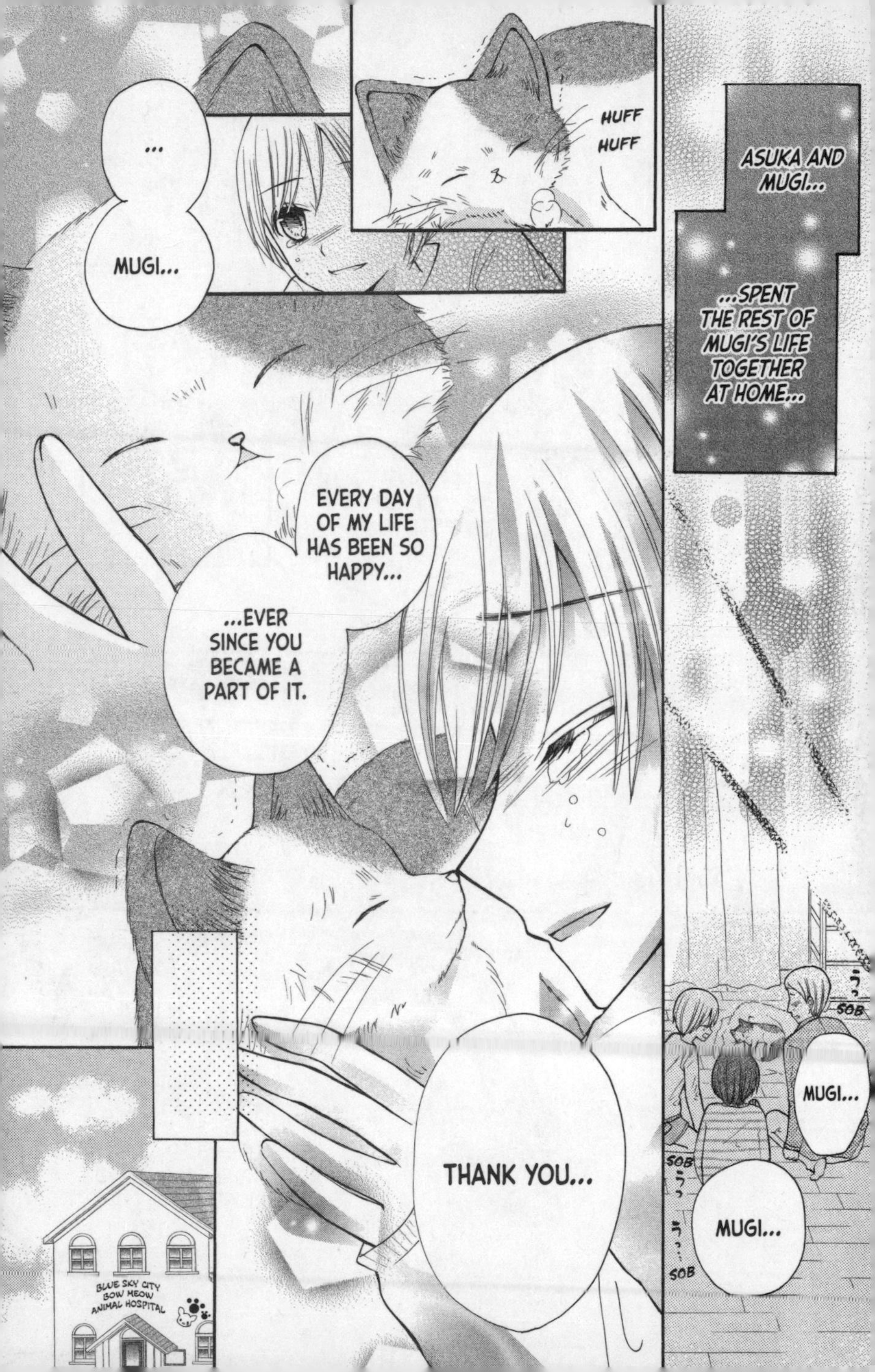
ASUKA AND MUGI...
...SPENT THE REST OF MUGI'S LIFE TOGETHER AT HOME...
SOB
MUGI...
SOB
MUGI...
SOB
HUFF HUFF
...
MUGI...
EVERY DAY OF MY LIFE HAS BEEN SO HAPPY...
...EVER SINCE YOU BECAME A PART OF IT.
THANK YOU...
BLUE SKY CITY BOW MEOW ANIMAL HOSPITAL

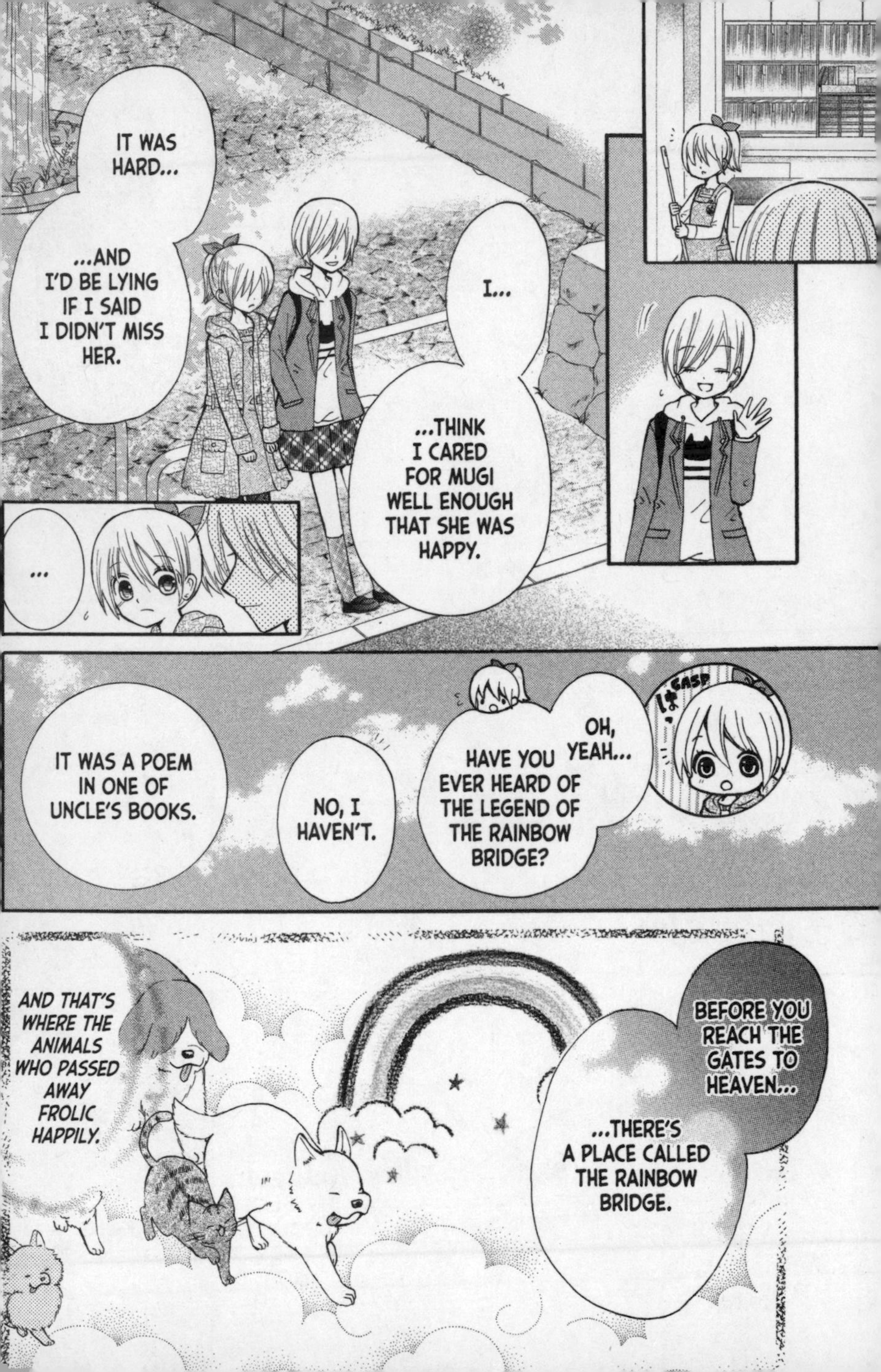
I...
...THINK I CARED FOR MUGI WELL ENOUGH THAT SHE WAS HAPPY.
IT WAS HARD...
...AND I'D BE LYING IF I SAID I DIDN'T MISS HER.
...
GASP
OH, YEAH...
HAVE YOU EVER HEARD OF THE LEGEND OF THE RAINBOW BRIDGE?
NO, I HAVEN'T.
IT WAS A POEM IN ONE OF UNCLE'S BOOKS.
BEFORE YOU REACH THE GATES TO HEAVEN...
...THERE'S A PLACE CALLED THE RAINBOW BRIDGE.
AND THAT'S WHERE THE ANIMALS WHO PASSED AWAY FROLIC HAPPILY.

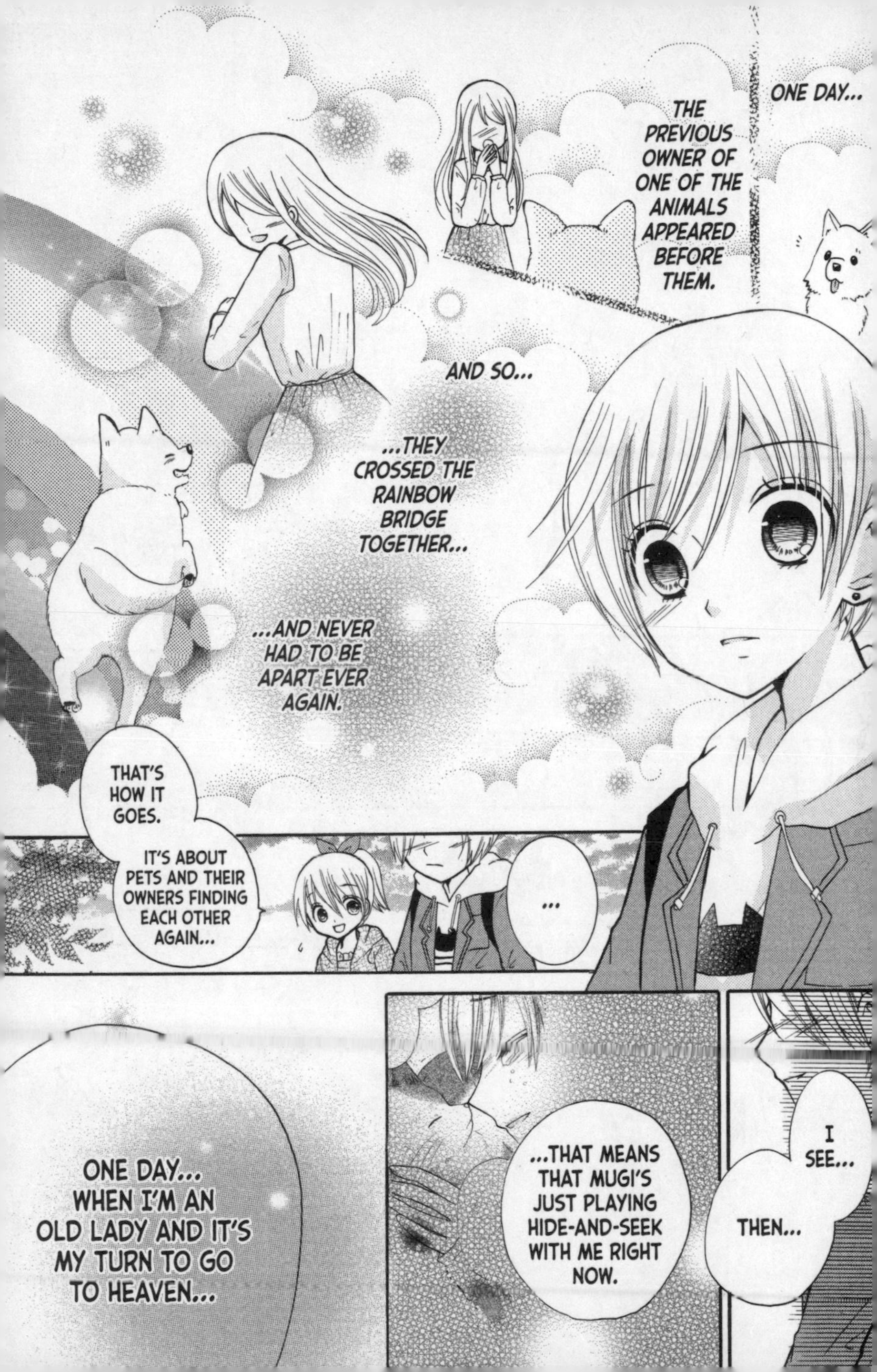
ONE DAY...
THE PREVIOUS OWNER OF ONE OF THE ANIMALS APPEARED BEFORE THEM.
AND SO...
...THEY CROSSED THE RAINBOW BRIDGE TOGETHER...
...AND NEVER HAD TO BE APART EVER AGAIN.
THAT'S HOW IT GOES.
...
IT'S ABOUT PETS AND THEIR OWNERS FINDING EACH OTHER AGAIN...
I SEE...
THEN...
...THAT MEANS THAT MUGI'S JUST PLAYING HIDE-AND-SEEK WITH ME RIGHT NOW.
ONE DAY... WHEN I'M AN OLD LADY AND IT'S MY TURN TO GO TO HEAVEN...

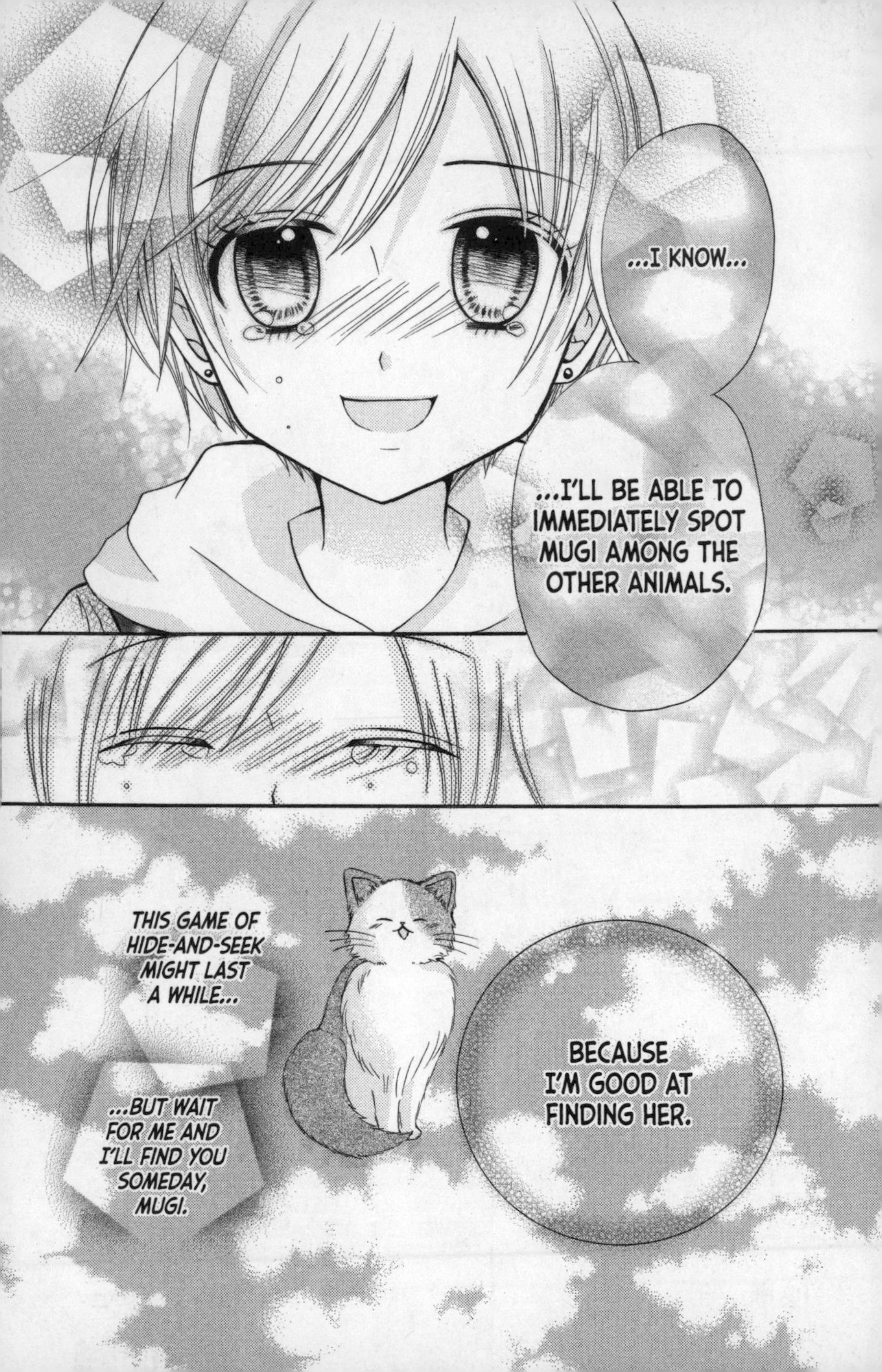
...I KNOW...
...I'LL BE ABLE TO IMMEDIATELY SPOT MUGI AMONG THE OTHER ANIMALS.
BECAUSE I'M GOOD AT FINDING HER.
THIS GAME OF HIDE-AND-SEEK MIGHT LAST A WHILE...
...BUT WAIT FOR ME AND I'LL FIND YOU SOMEDAY, MUGI.

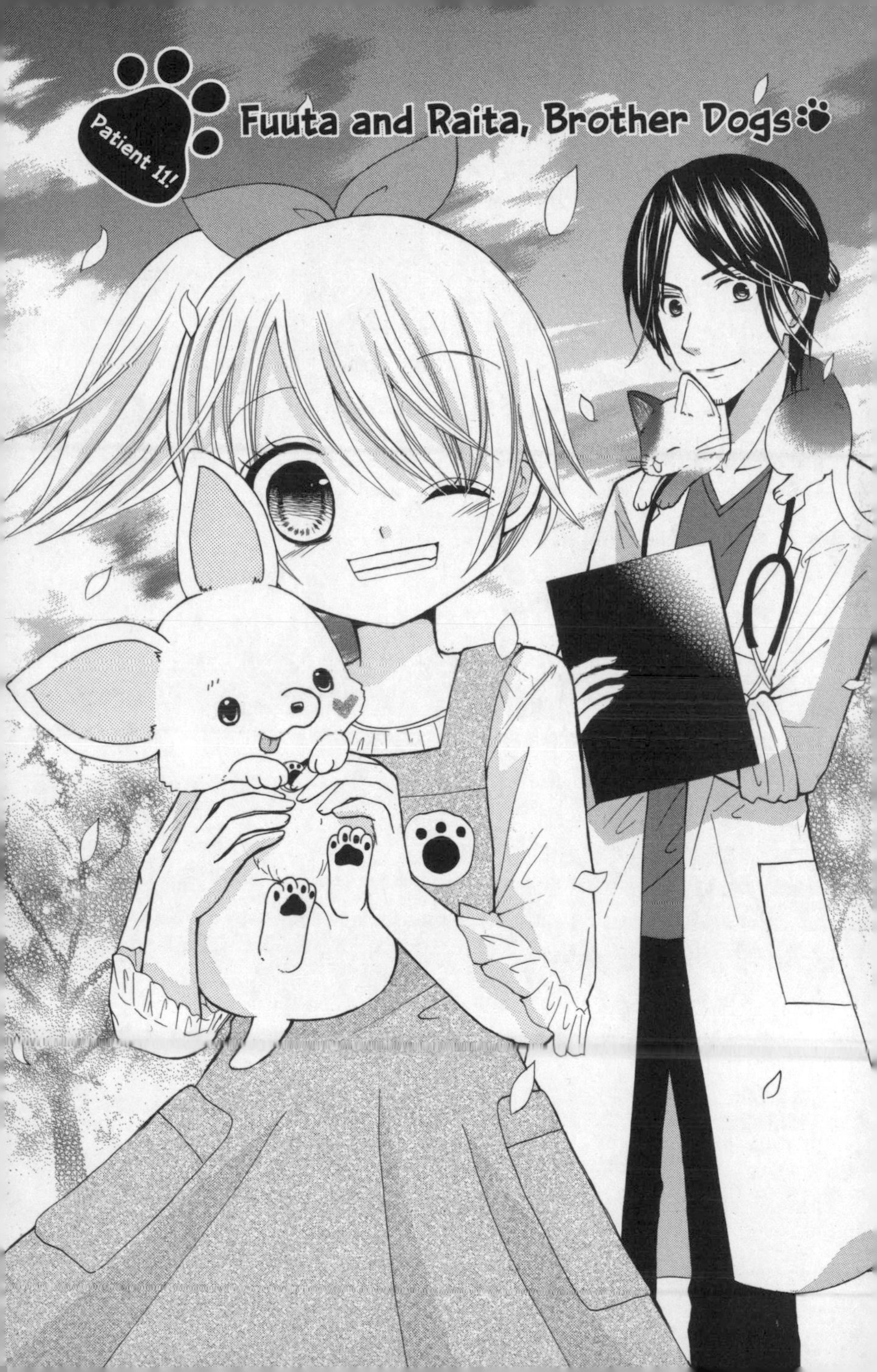
Patient 11!
Fuuta and Raita, Brother Dogs

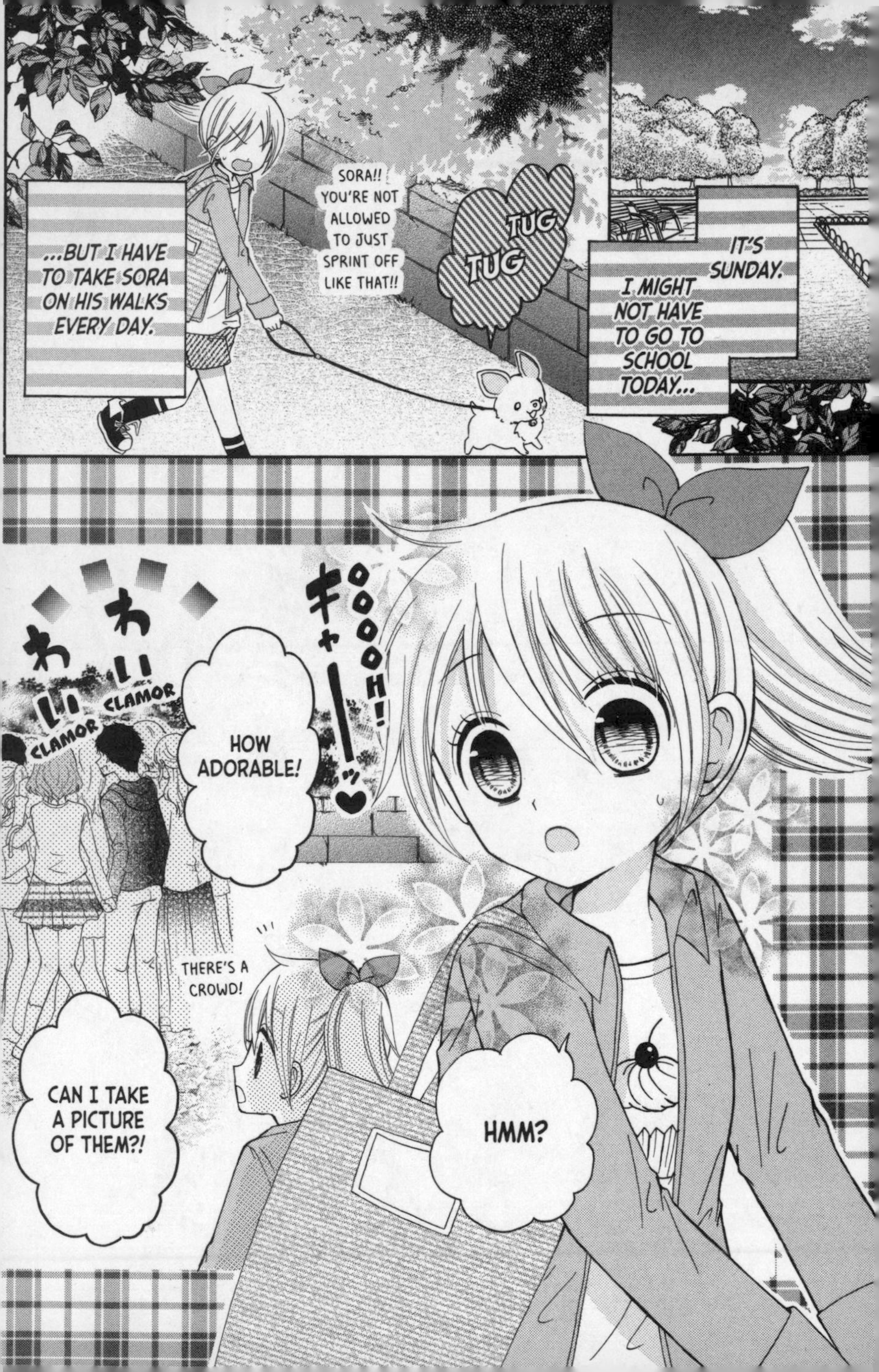
IT'S SUNDAY.
I MIGHT NOT HAVE TO GO TO SCHOOL TODAY...
TUG TUG
SORA!! YOU'RE NOT ALLOWED TO JUST SPRINT OFF LIKE THAT!!
...BUT I HAVE TO TAKE SORA ON HIS WALKS EVERY DAY.
キャー!!
OOOOH!
わいわい
CLAMOR CLAMOR
HOW ADORABLE!
HMM?
THERE'S A CROWD!
CAN I TAKE A PICTURE OF THEM?!

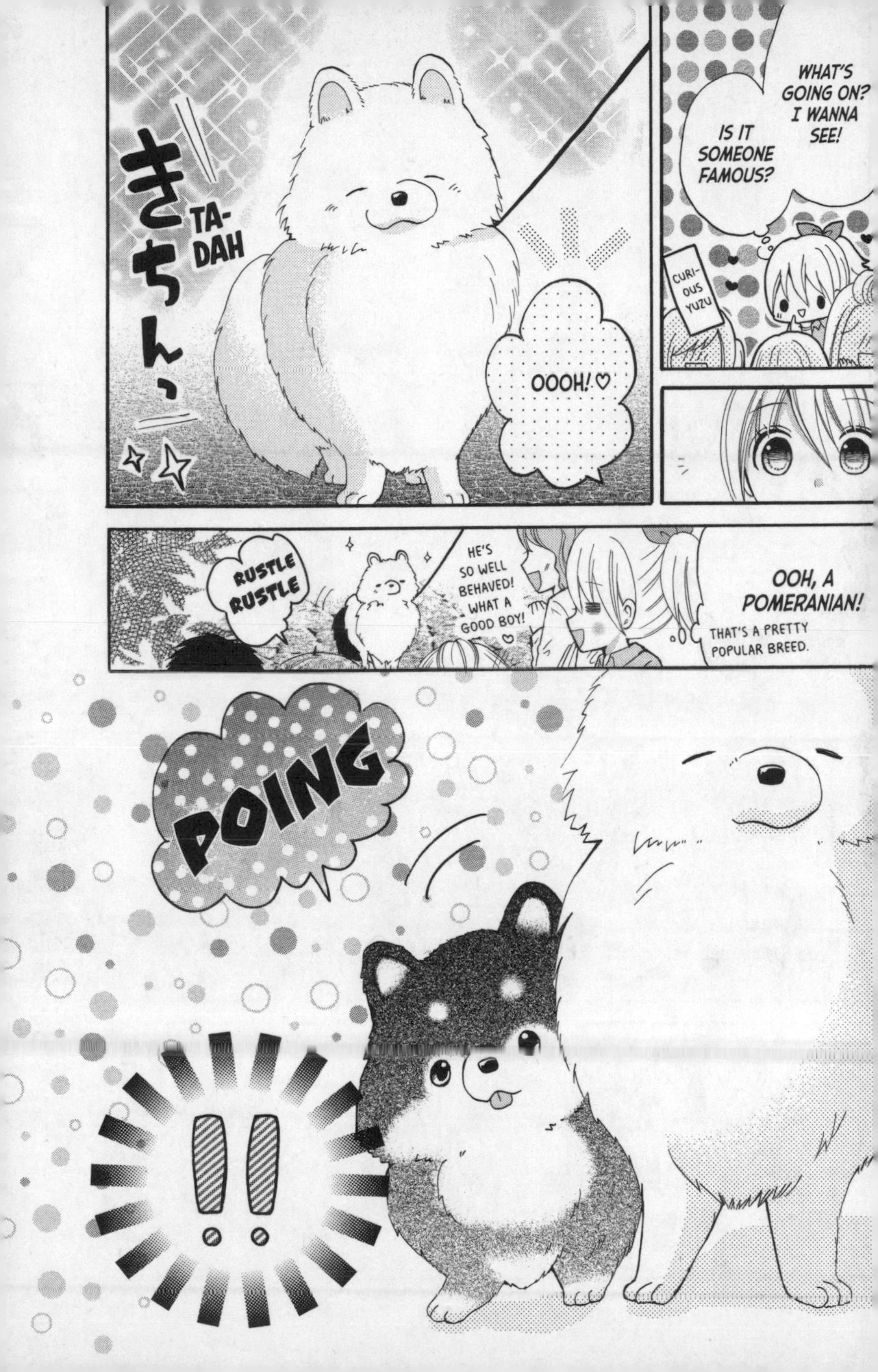
WHAT'S GOING ON? I WANNA SEE!
IS IT SOMEONE FAMOUS?
CURIOUS YUZU
きちんっ
TA-DAH
OOOH! ♡
OOH, A POMERANIAN!
THAT'S A PRETTY POPULAR BREED.
HE'S SO WELL BEHAVED! WHAT A GOOD BOY! ♡
RUSTLE RUSTLE
POING
!!

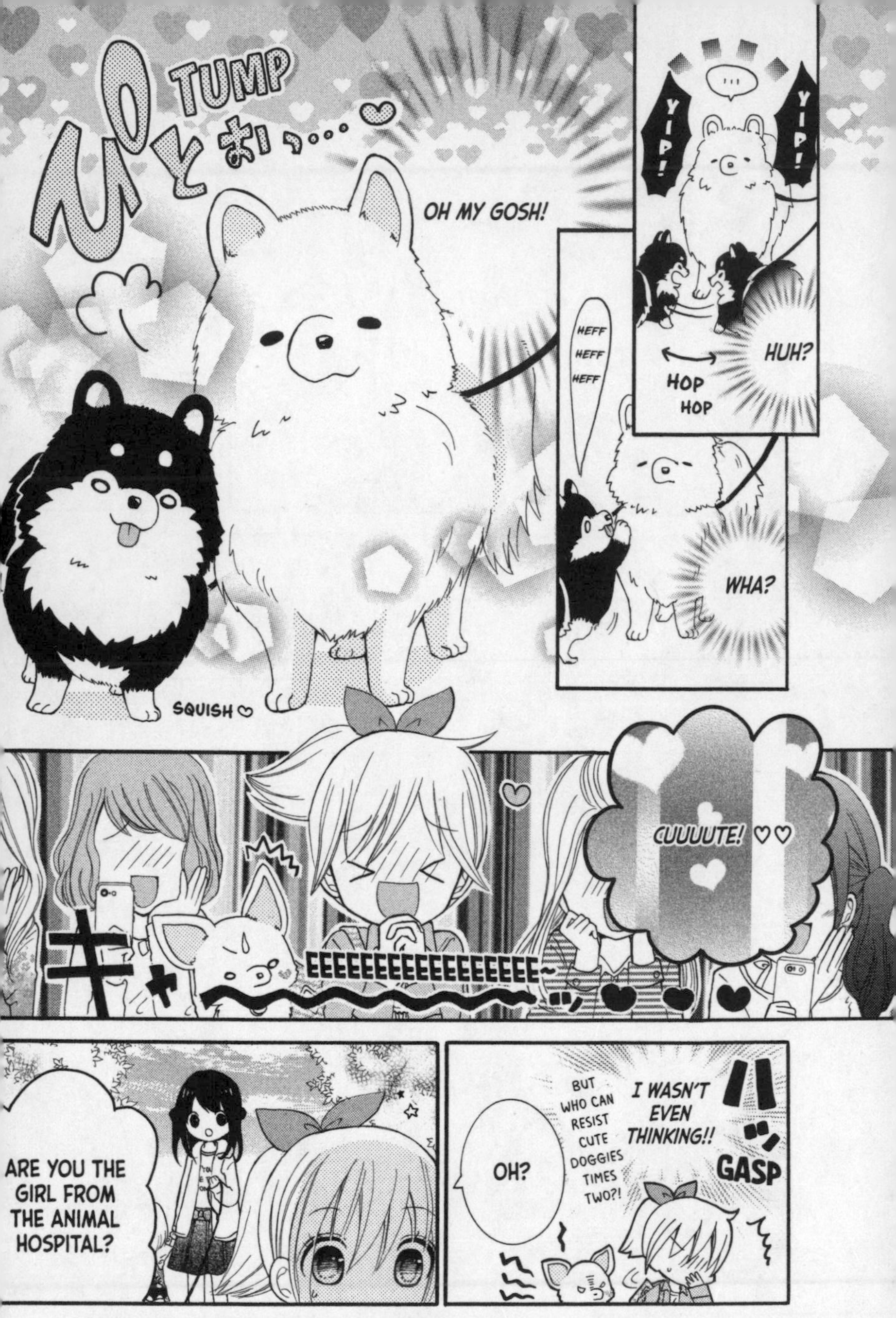
YIP!
YIP!
...
HUH?
HOP HOP
HEFF HEFF HEFF
WHA?
OH MY GOSH!
TUMP
SQUISH ♡
CUUUUTE! ♡♡
EEEEEEEEEEEEEEEEE~
I WASN'T EVEN THINKING!!
GASP
BUT WHO CAN RESIST CUTE DOGGIES TIMES TWO?!
OH?
ARE YOU THE GIRL FROM THE ANIMAL HOSPITAL?

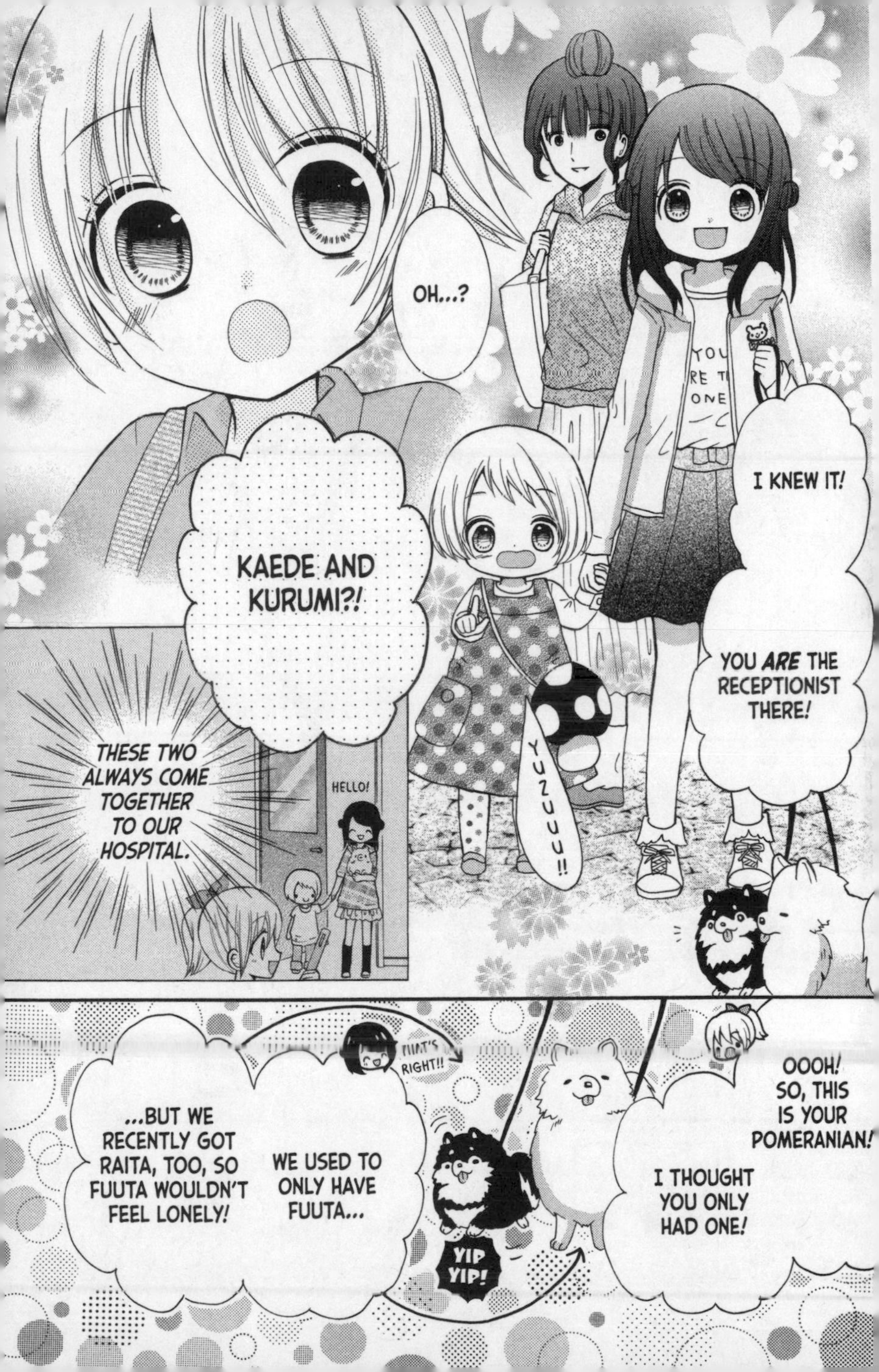
OH...?
KAEDE AND KURUMI?!
I KNEW IT!
YOU *ARE* THE RECEPTIONIST THERE!
YUZUUUU!!
THESE TWO ALWAYS COME TOGETHER TO OUR HOSPITAL.
HELLO!
OOOH! SO, THIS IS YOUR POMERANIAN!
I THOUGHT YOU ONLY HAD ONE!
YIP YIP!
THAT'S RIGHT!!
WE USED TO ONLY HAVE FUUTA...
...BUT WE RECENTLY GOT RAITA, TOO, SO FUUTA WOULDN'T FEEL LONELY!

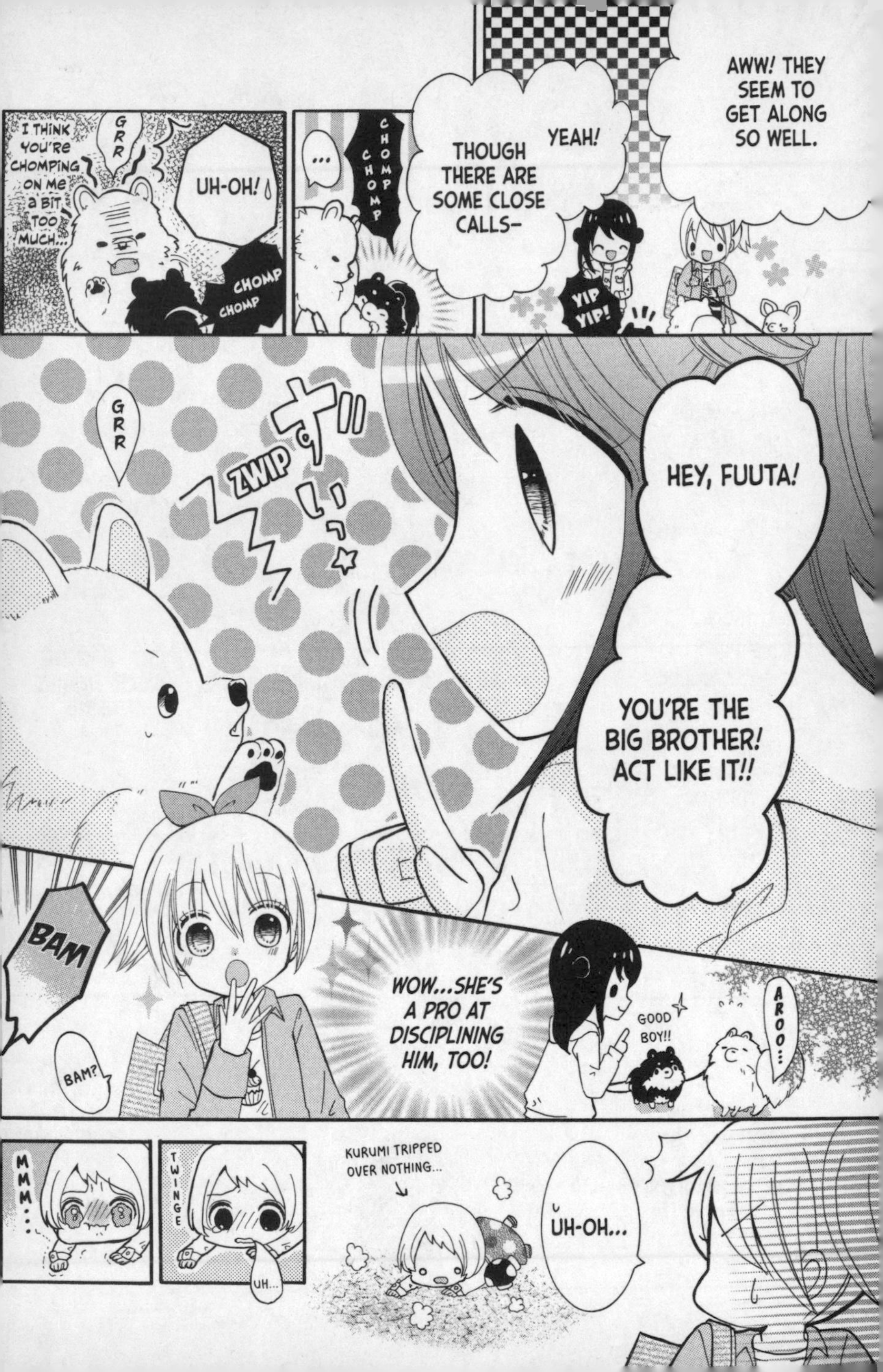
AWW! THEY SEEM TO GET ALONG SO WELL.
YEAH!
THOUGH THERE ARE SOME CLOSE CALLS–
YIP YIP!
CHOMP CHOMP
...
UH-OH!
GRR
I THINK YOU'RE CHOMPING ON ME A BIT TOO MUCH...
CHOMP CHOMP
HEY, FUUTA!
YOU'RE THE BIG BROTHER! ACT LIKE IT!!
ZWIP
GRR
AROO...
GOOD BOY!!
WOW...SHE'S A PRO AT DISCIPLINING HIM, TOO!
BAM
BAM?
UH-OH...
KURUMI TRIPPED OVER NOTHING...
TWINGE
UH...
MMM...

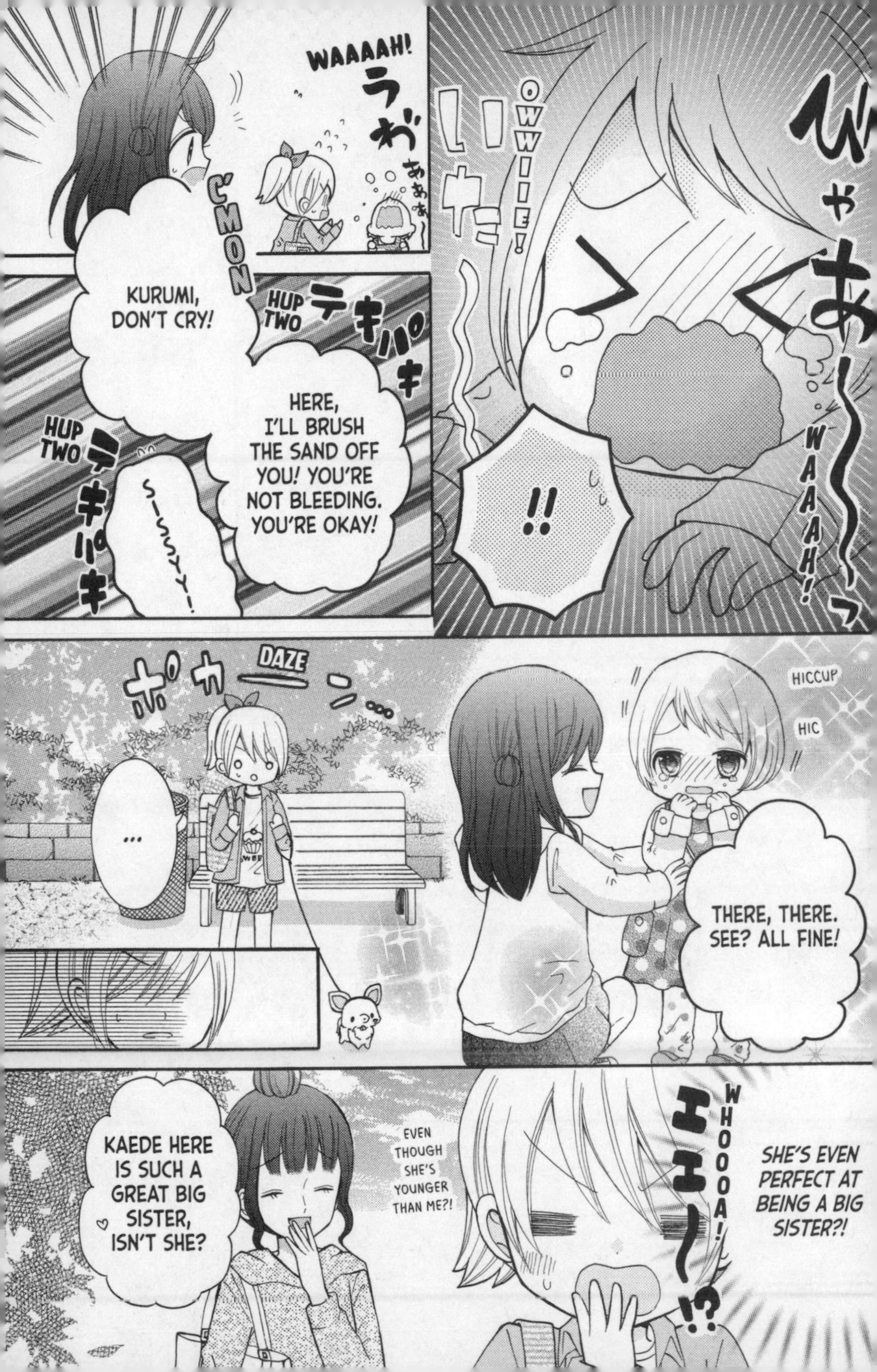

OWWIIE!
WAAAAH!
!!
WAAAAH!
C'MON
KURUMI, DON'T CRY!
HUP TWO
HERE, I'LL BRUSH THE SAND OFF YOU! YOU'RE NOT BLEEDING. YOU'RE OKAY!
HUP TWO
SISSYY~!
HICCUP
HIC
THERE, THERE. SEE? ALL FINE!
DAZE
...
WHOOOA!
SHE'S EVEN PERFECT AT BEING A BIG SISTER?!
EVEN THOUGH SHE'S YOUNGER THAN ME?!
KAEDE HERE IS SUCH A GREAT BIG SISTER, ISN'T SHE?

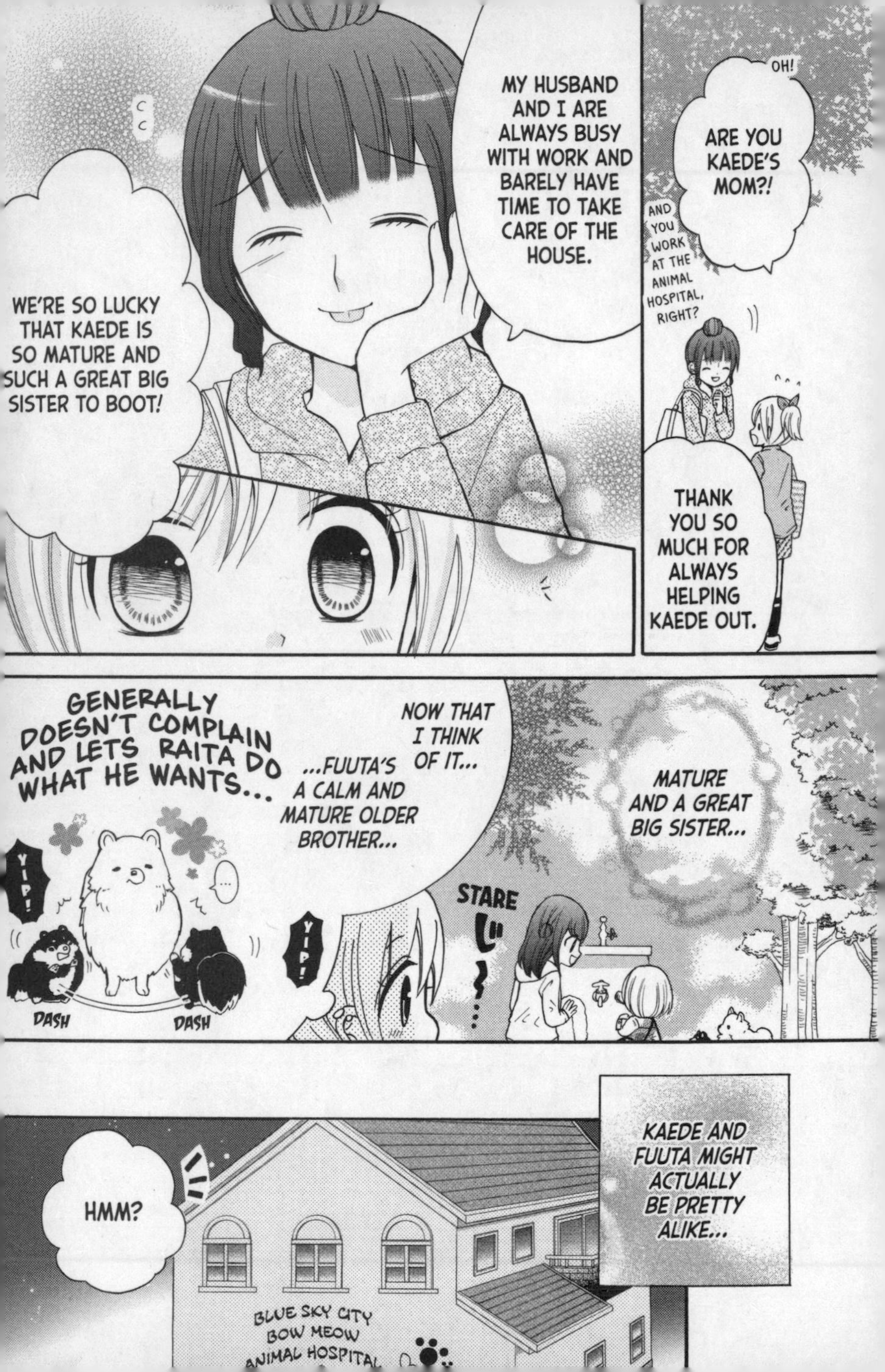
OH!
ARE YOU KAEDE'S MOM?!
AND YOU WORK AT THE ANIMAL HOSPITAL, RIGHT?
THANK YOU SO MUCH FOR ALWAYS HELPING KAEDE OUT.
MY HUSBAND AND I ARE ALWAYS BUSY WITH WORK AND BARELY HAVE TIME TO TAKE CARE OF THE HOUSE.
WE'RE SO LUCKY THAT KAEDE IS SO MATURE AND SUCH A GREAT BIG SISTER TO BOOT!
MATURE AND A GREAT BIG SISTER...
STARE
NOW THAT I THINK OF IT...
...FUUTA'S A CALM AND MATURE OLDER BROTHER...
GENERALLY DOESN'T COMPLAIN AND LETS RAITA DO WHAT HE WANTS...
YIP!
...
YIP!
DASH
DASH
KAEDE AND FUUTA MIGHT ACTUALLY BE PRETTY ALIKE...
HMM?
BLUE SKY CITY BOW MEOW ANIMAL HOSPITAL

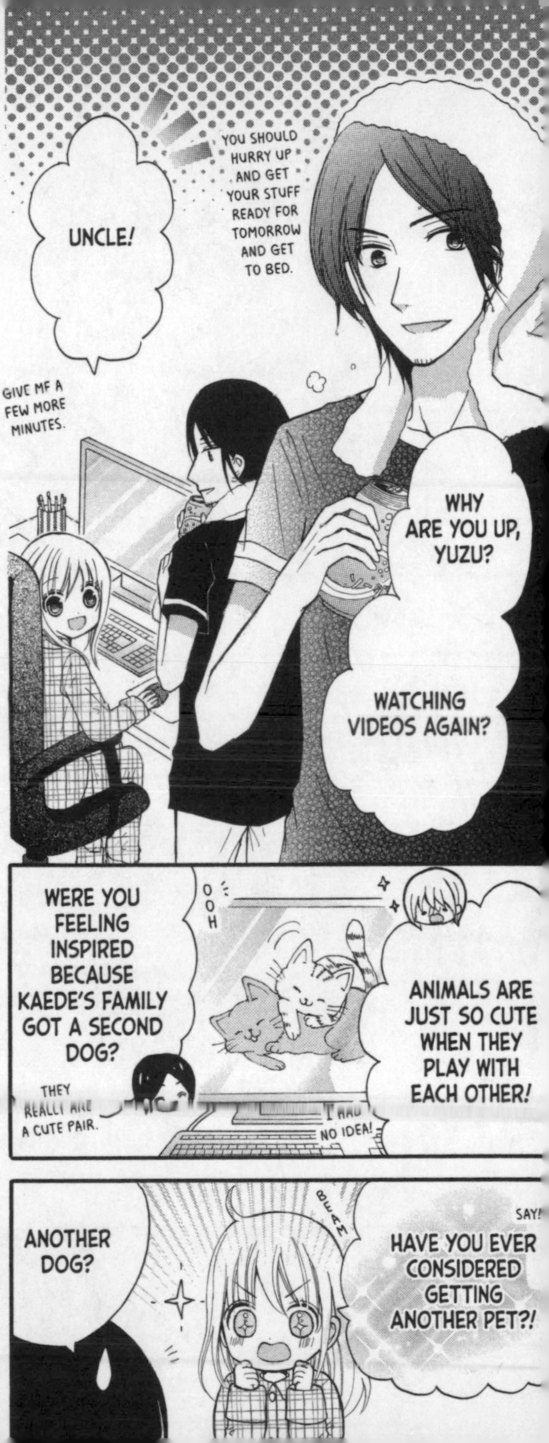
YOU SHOULD HURRY UP AND GET YOUR STUFF READY FOR TOMORROW AND GET TO BED.
UNCLE!
WHY ARE YOU UP, YUZU?
WATCHING VIDEOS AGAIN?
GIVE MF A FEW MORE MINUTES.
ANIMALS ARE JUST SO CUTE WHEN THEY PLAY WITH EACH OTHER!
OOH
I HAD NO IDEA!
WERE YOU FEELING INSPIRED BECAUSE KAEDE'S FAMILY GOT A SECOND DOG?
THEY REALLY ARE A CUTE PAIR.
SAY!
HAVE YOU EVER CONSIDERED GETTING ANOTHER PET?!
BEAM
ANOTHER DOG?

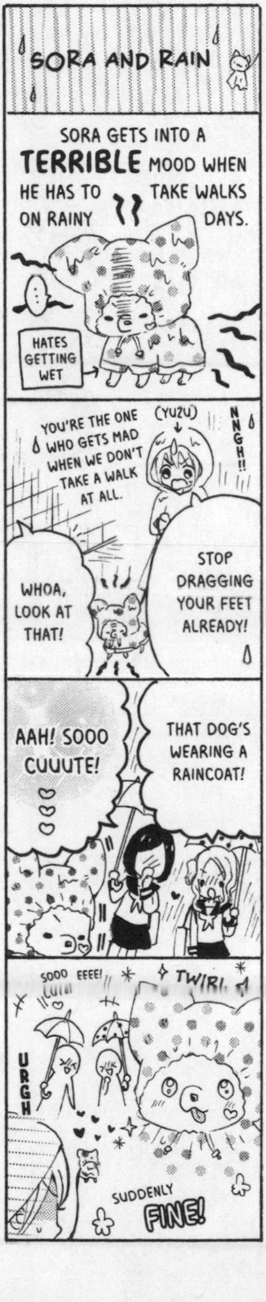
SORA AND RAIN
SORA GETS INTO A TERRIBLE MOOD WHEN HE HAS TO TAKE WALKS ON RAINY DAYS.
...
HATES GETTING WET
(YUZU)
NNGH!!
YOU'RE THE ONE WHO GETS MAD WHEN WE DON'T TAKE A WALK AT ALL.
STOP DRAGGING YOUR FEET ALREADY!
WHOA, LOOK AT THAT!
THAT DOG'S WEARING A RAINCOAT!
AAH! SOOO CUUUTE!
TWIRL
EEEE!
SOOO
URGH
SUDDENLY FINE!

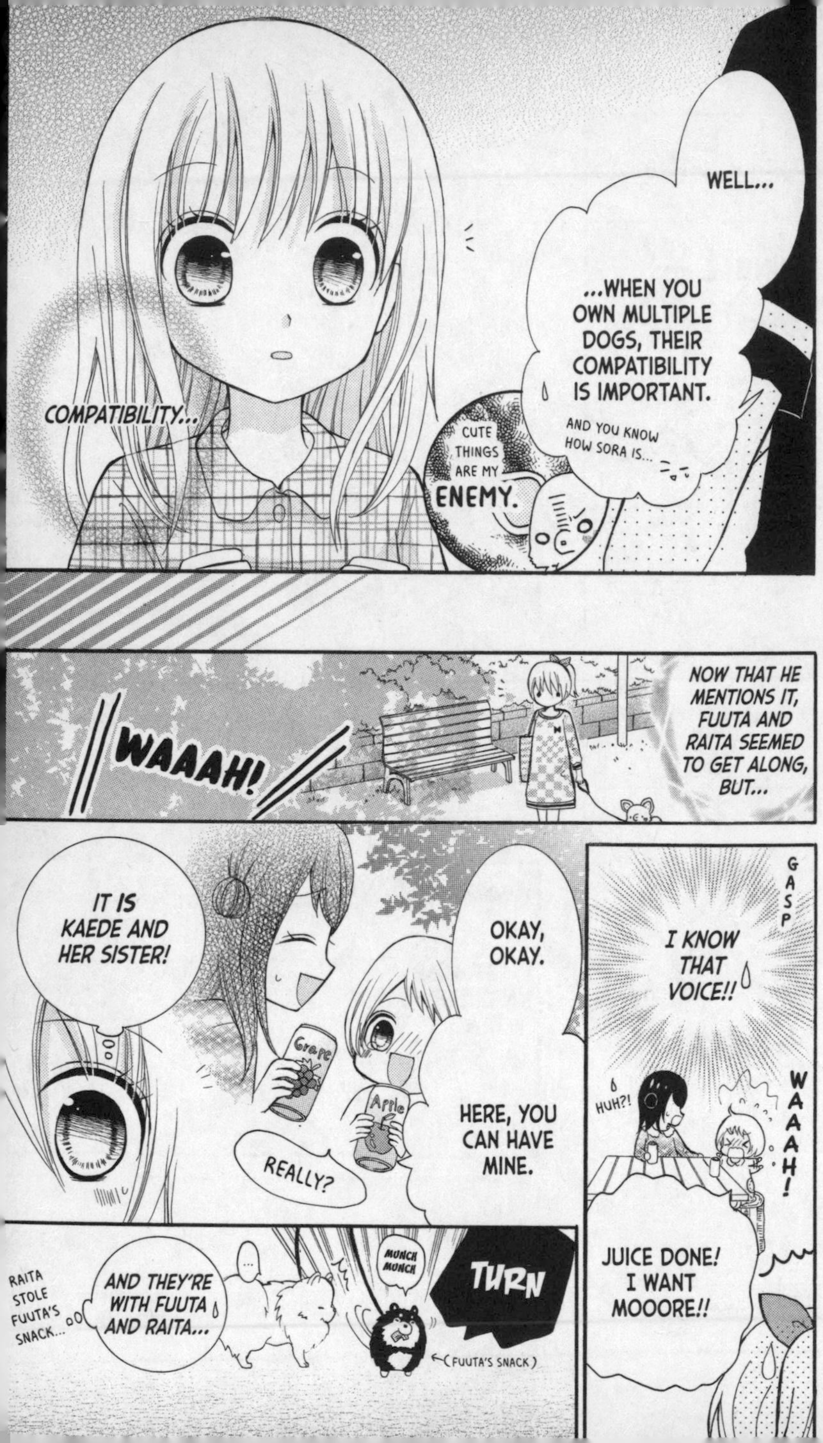
WELL...
...WHEN YOU OWN MULTIPLE DOGS, THEIR COMPATIBILITY IS IMPORTANT.
AND YOU KNOW HOW SORA IS...
CUTE THINGS ARE MY ENEMY.
COMPATIBILITY...
NOW THAT HE MENTIONS IT, FUUTA AND RAITA SEEMED TO GET ALONG, BUT...
WAAAH!
GASP
I KNOW THAT VOICE!!
WAAAH!
HUH?!
JUICE DONE! I WANT MOOORE!!
OKAY, OKAY.
HERE, YOU CAN HAVE MINE.
Grape
Apple
REALLY?
IT IS KAEDE AND HER SISTER!
TURN
MUNCH MUNCH
(FUUTA'S SNACK)
...
AND THEY'RE WITH FUUTA AND RAITA...
RAITA STOLE FUUTA'S SNACK...

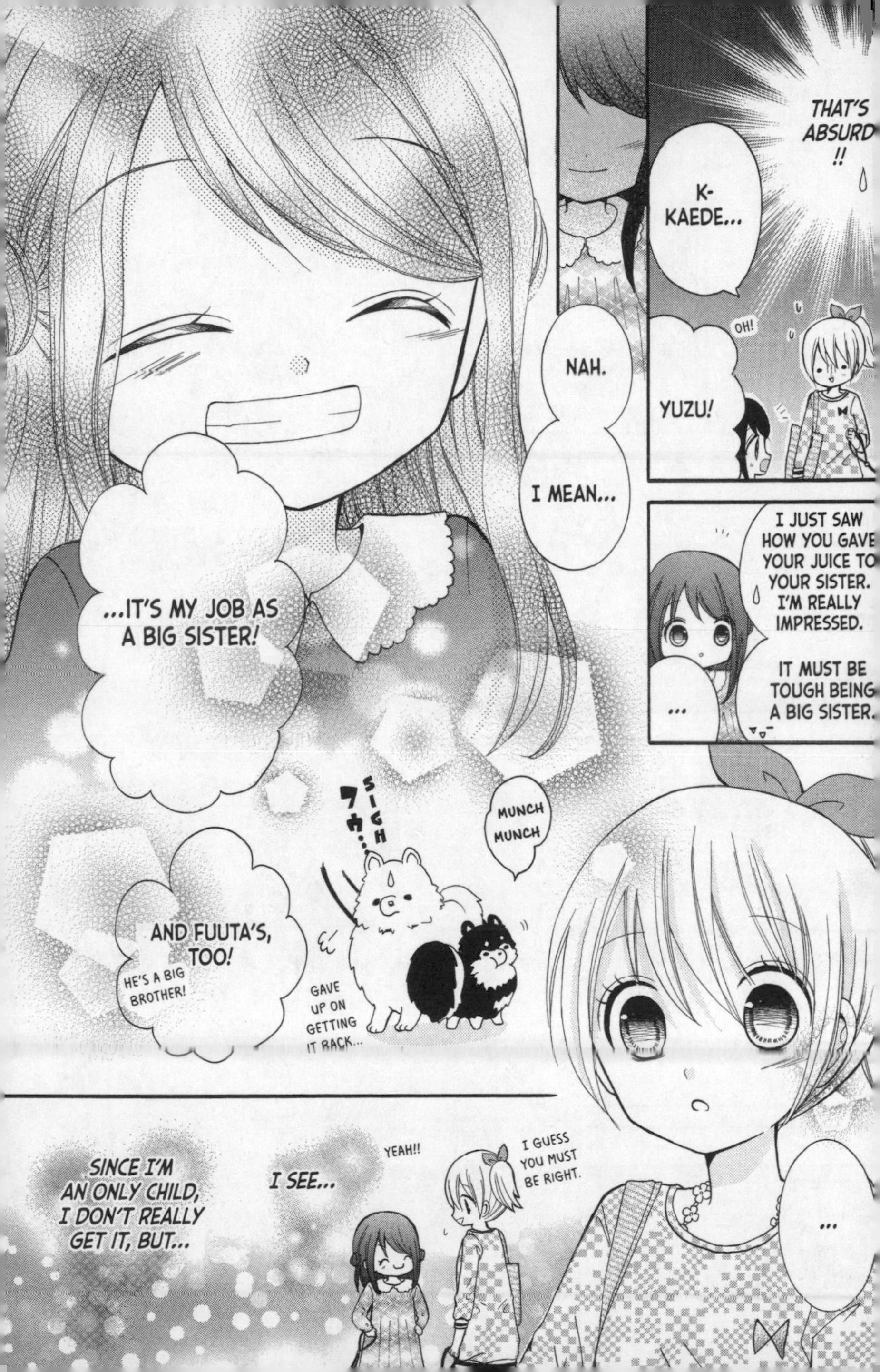
THAT'S ABSURD!!
K-KAEDE...
OH!
YUZU!
I JUST SAW HOW YOU GAVE YOUR JUICE TO YOUR SISTER. I'M REALLY IMPRESSED.
IT MUST BE TOUGH BEING A BIG SISTER.
...
NAH.
I MEAN...
...IT'S MY JOB AS A BIG SISTER!
AND FUUTA'S, TOO!
HE'S A BIG BROTHER!
MUNCH MUNCH
SIGH
GAVE UP ON GETTING IT BACK...
...
I GUESS YOU MUST BE RIGHT.
YEAH!!
I SEE...
SINCE I'M AN ONLY CHILD, I DON'T REALLY GET IT, BUT...

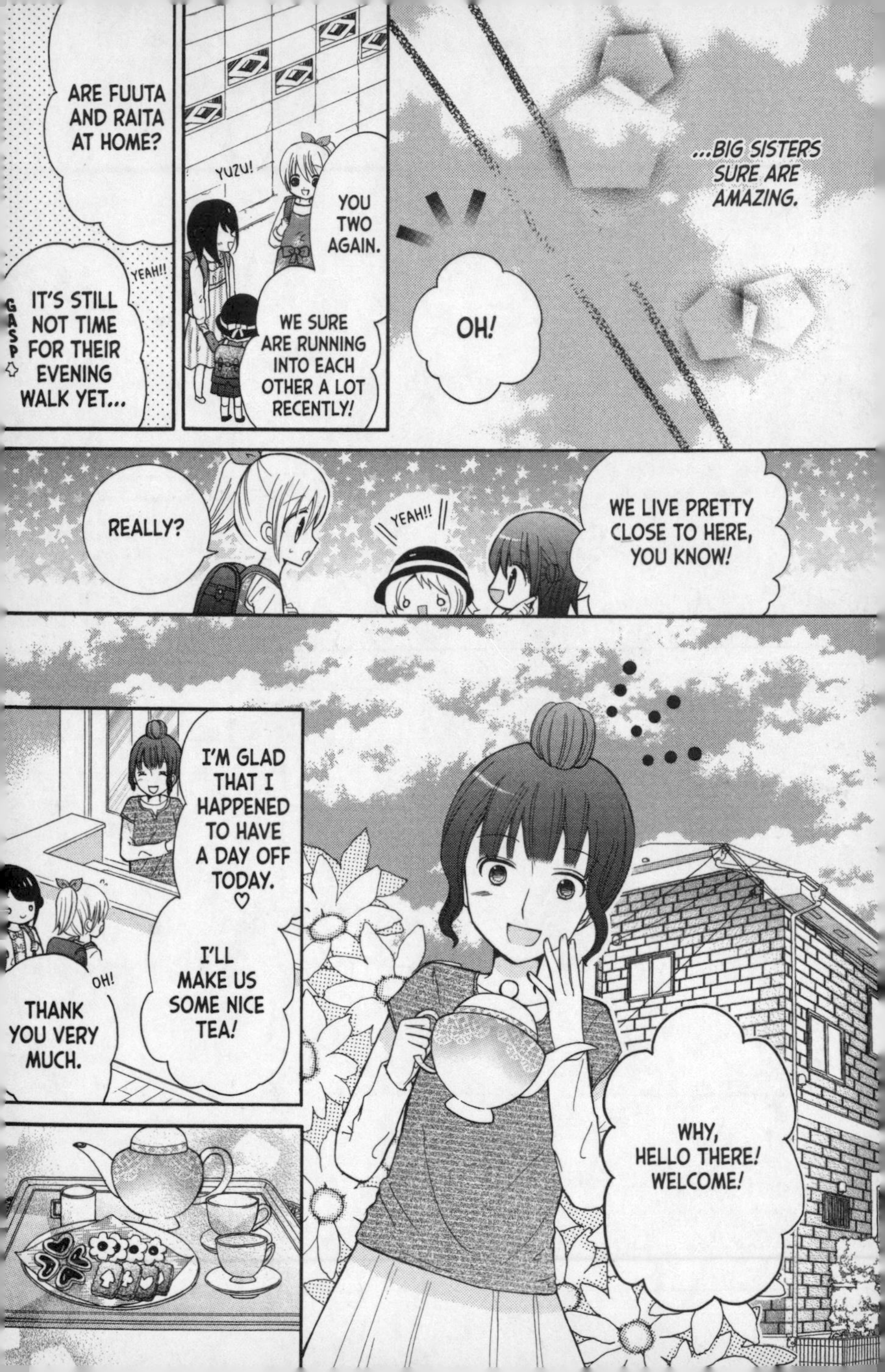
...BIG SISTERS SURE ARE AMAZING.
OH!
YUZU!
YOU TWO AGAIN.
WE SURE ARE RUNNING INTO EACH OTHER A LOT RECENTLY!
ARE FUUTA AND RAITA AT HOME?
YEAH!!
IT'S STILL NOT TIME FOR THEIR EVENING WALK YET...
GASP
WE LIVE PRETTY CLOSE TO HERE, YOU KNOW!
YEAH!!
REALLY?
WHY, HELLO THERE! WELCOME!
I'M GLAD THAT I HAPPENED TO HAVE A DAY OFF TODAY. ♡
I'LL MAKE US SOME NICE TEA!
OH!
THANK YOU VERY MUCH.

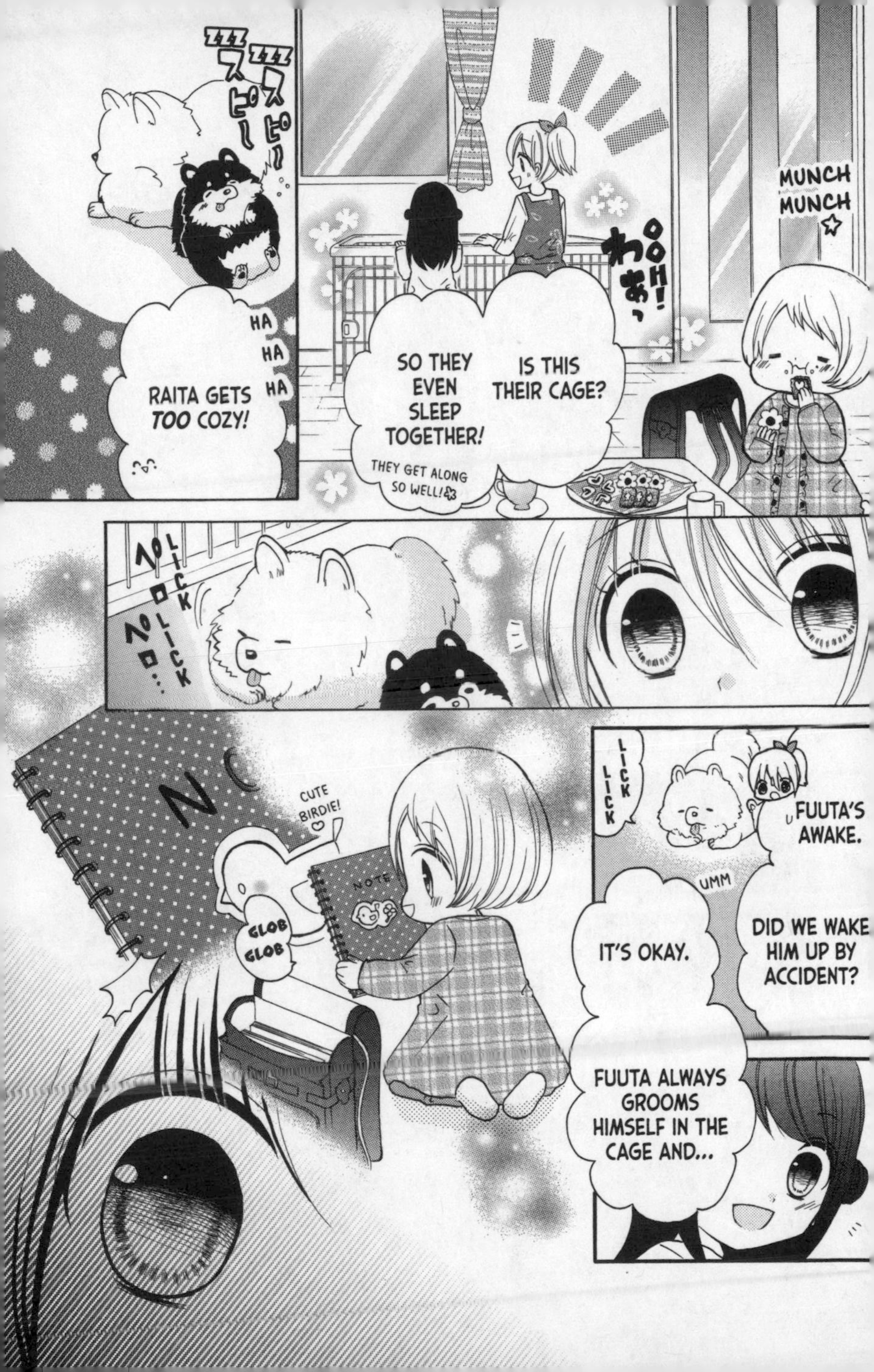
MUNCH MUNCH☆
わぁっ OOH!
IS THIS THEIR CAGE?
SO THEY EVEN SLEEP TOGETHER!
THEY GET ALONG SO WELL!
ZZZ スピー
ZZZ スピー
HA HA HA
RAITA GETS *TOO* COZY!
ペロ LICK
ペロ... LICK
LICK LICK
FUUTA'S AWAKE.
DID WE WAKE HIM UP BY ACCIDENT?
UMM
IT'S OKAY.
FUUTA ALWAYS GROOMS HIMSELF IN THE CAGE AND...
CUTE BIRDIE!
GLOB GLOB
NOTE

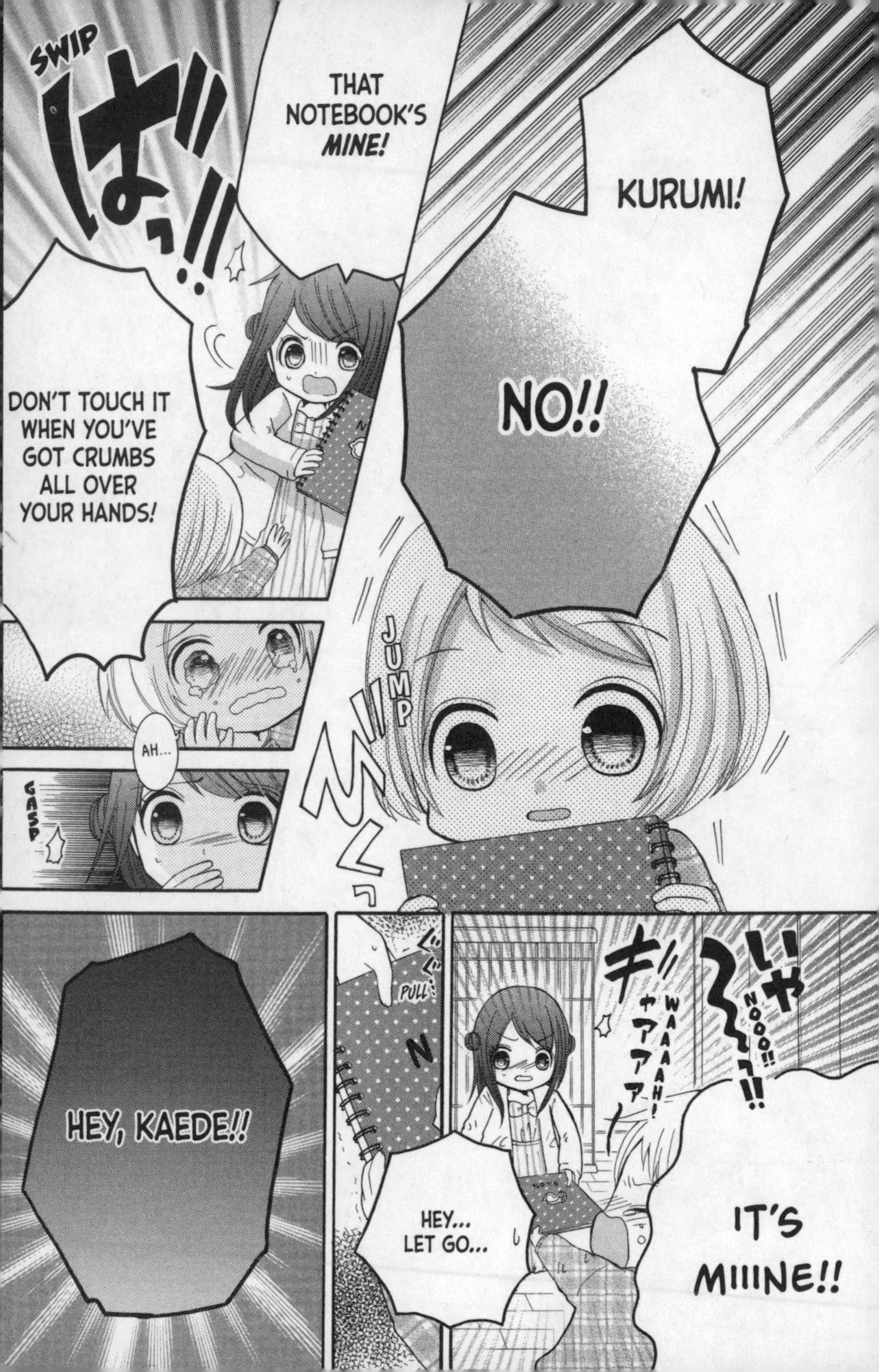
KURUMI!
NO!!
JUMP
SWIP
THAT NOTEBOOK'S MINE!
DON'T TOUCH IT WHEN YOU'VE GOT CRUMBS ALL OVER YOUR HANDS!
AH...
GASP
NOOOO!!
WAAAAH!
IT'S MIIINE!!
PULL
HEY... LET GO...
HEY, KAEDE!!

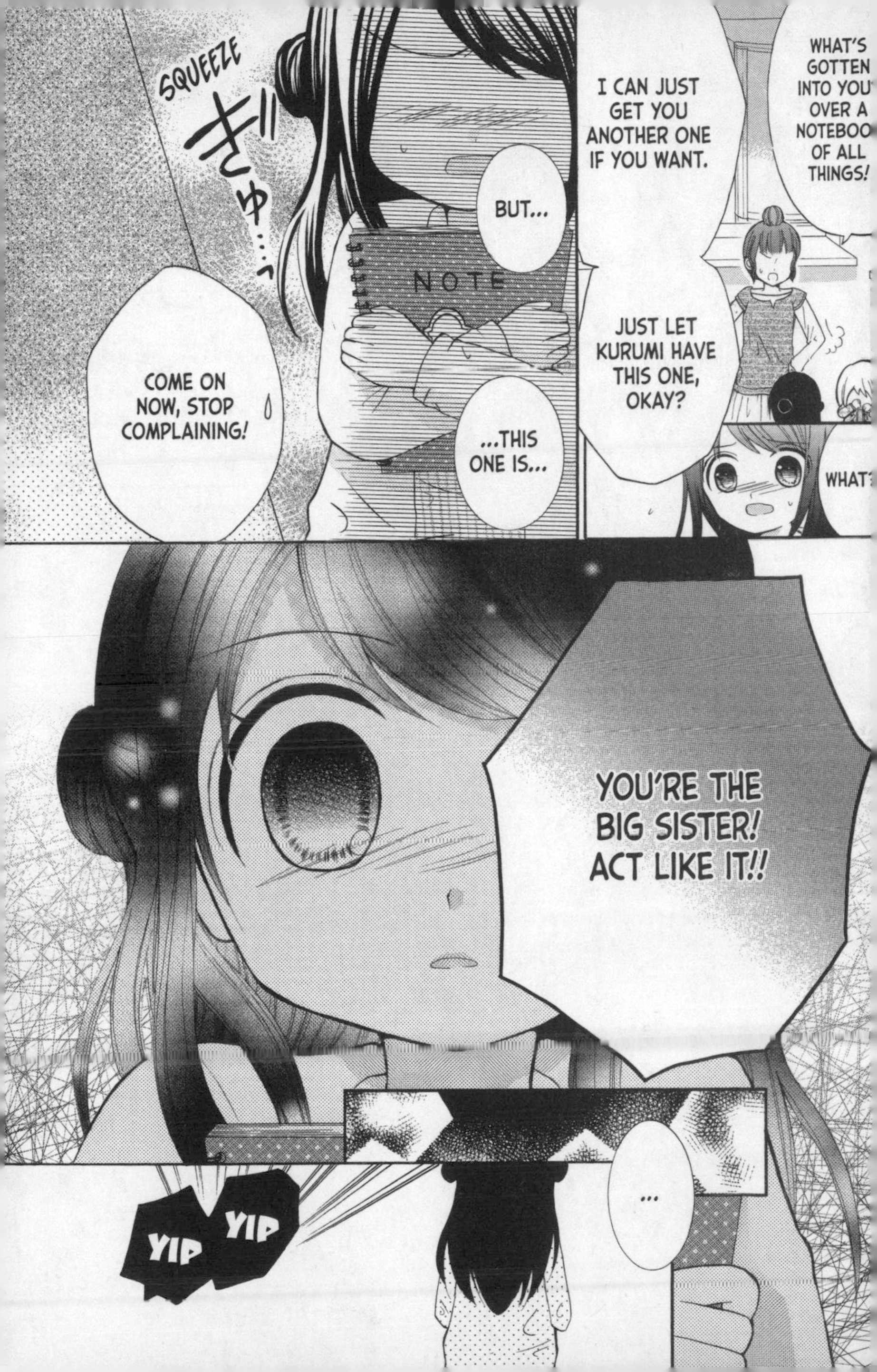
WHAT'S GOTTEN INTO YOU OVER A NOTEBOO OF ALL THINGS!
I CAN JUST GET YOU ANOTHER ONE IF YOU WANT.
JUST LET KURUMI HAVE THIS ONE, OKAY?
WHAT
BUT...
NOTE
...THIS ONE IS...
SQUEEZE
きゅ…
COME ON NOW, STOP COMPLAINING!
YOU'RE THE BIG SISTER! ACT LIKE IT!!
...
YIP
YIP

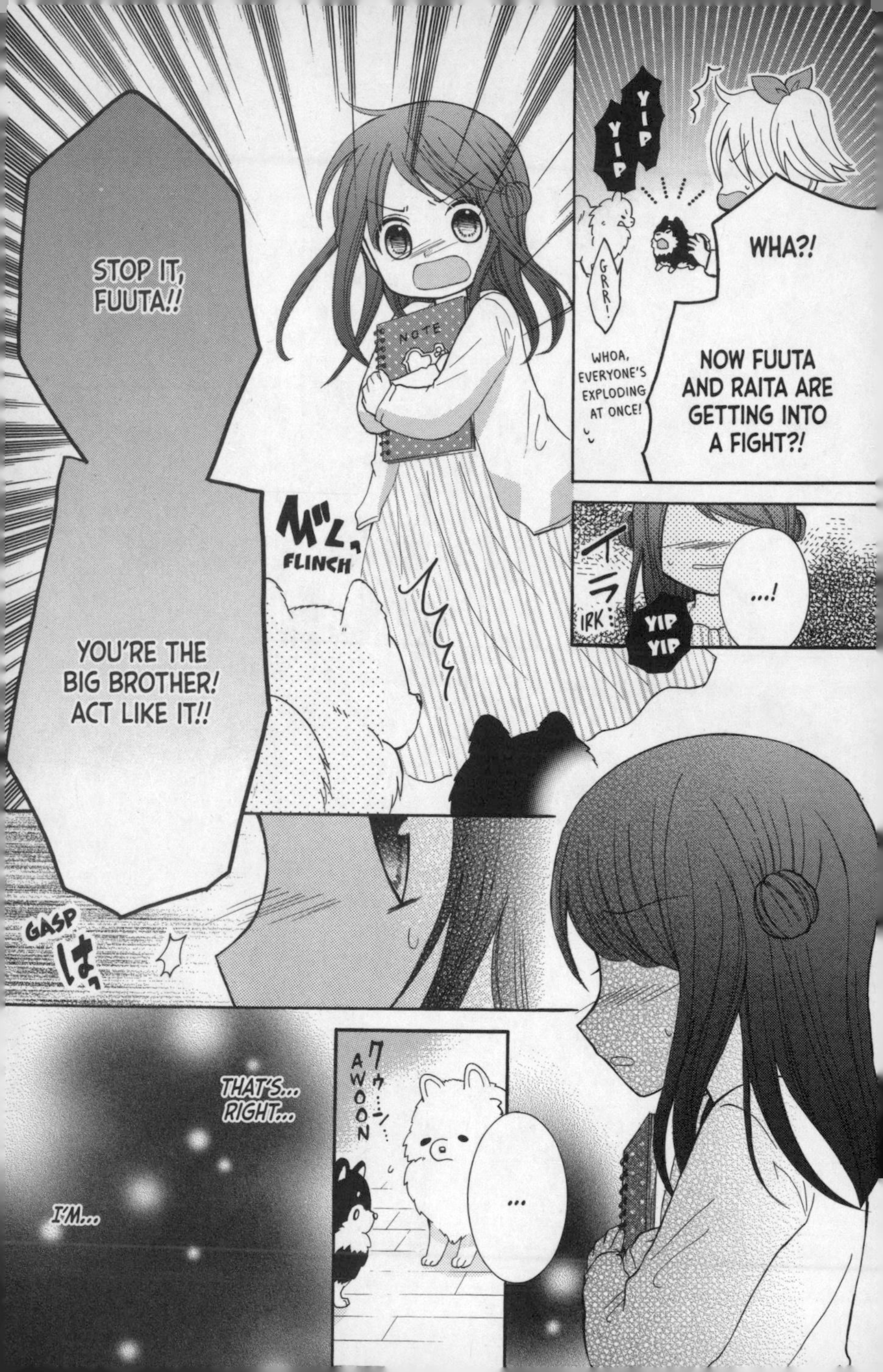
YIP YIP YIP
WHA?!
NOW FUUTA AND RAITA ARE GETTING INTO A FIGHT?!
GRR!
WHOA, EVERYONE'S EXPLODING AT ONCE!
IRK
YIP YIP
...!
STOP IT, FUUTA!!
FLINCH
YOU'RE THE BIG BROTHER! ACT LIKE IT!!
GASP
AWOON
...
THAT'S... RIGHT...
I'M...

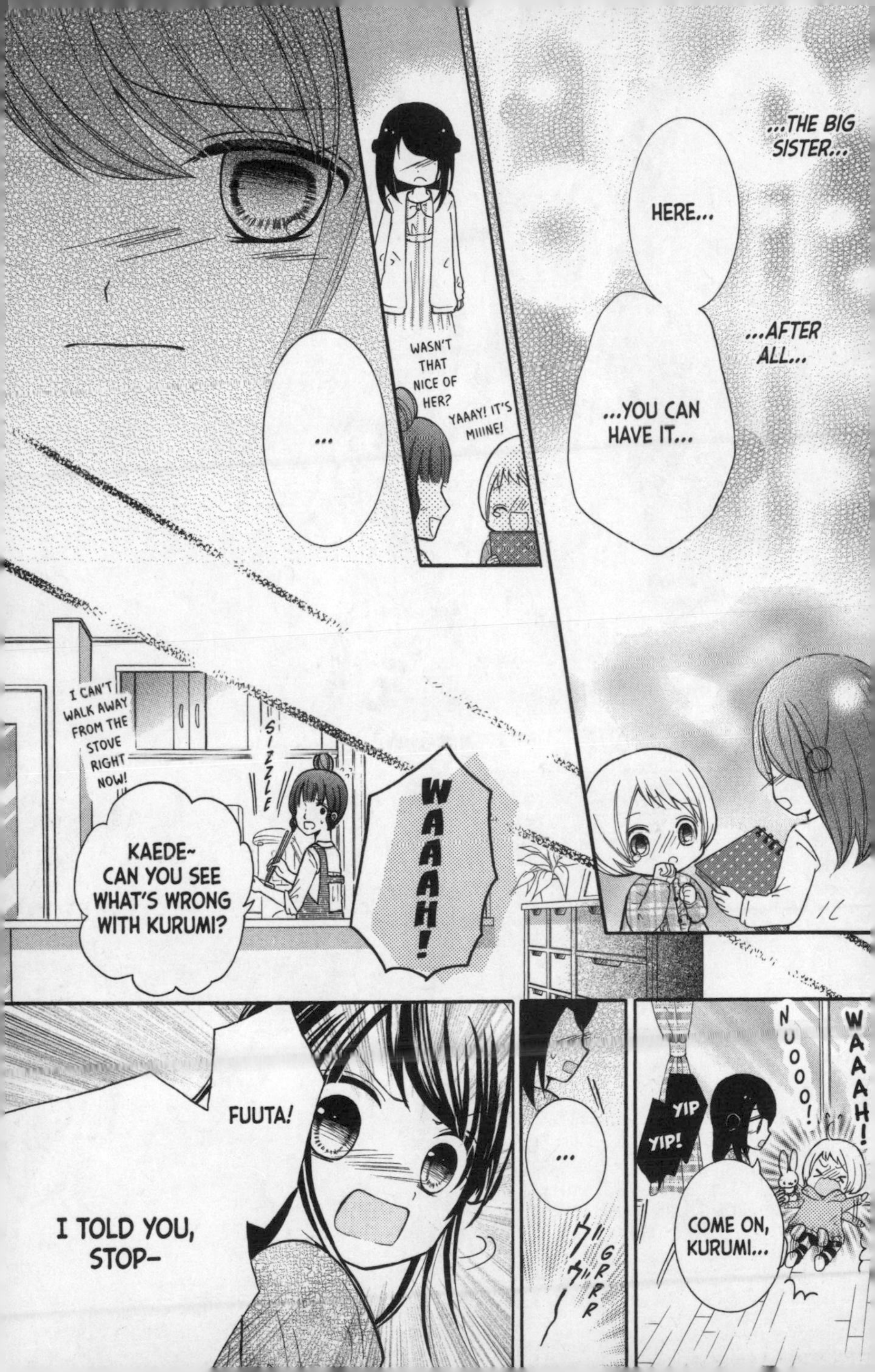
...THE BIG SISTER...
HERE...
...AFTER ALL...
...YOU CAN HAVE IT...
WASN'T THAT NICE OF HER?
YAAAY! IT'S MIIINE!
...
WAAAAH!
I CAN'T WALK AWAY FROM THE STOVE RIGHT NOW!
SIZZLE
KAEDE~ CAN YOU SEE WHAT'S WRONG WITH KURUMI?
WAAAAH!
NUOOOO!
YIP YIP!
COME ON, KURUMI...
...
GRRR
FUUTA!
I TOLD YOU, STOP~

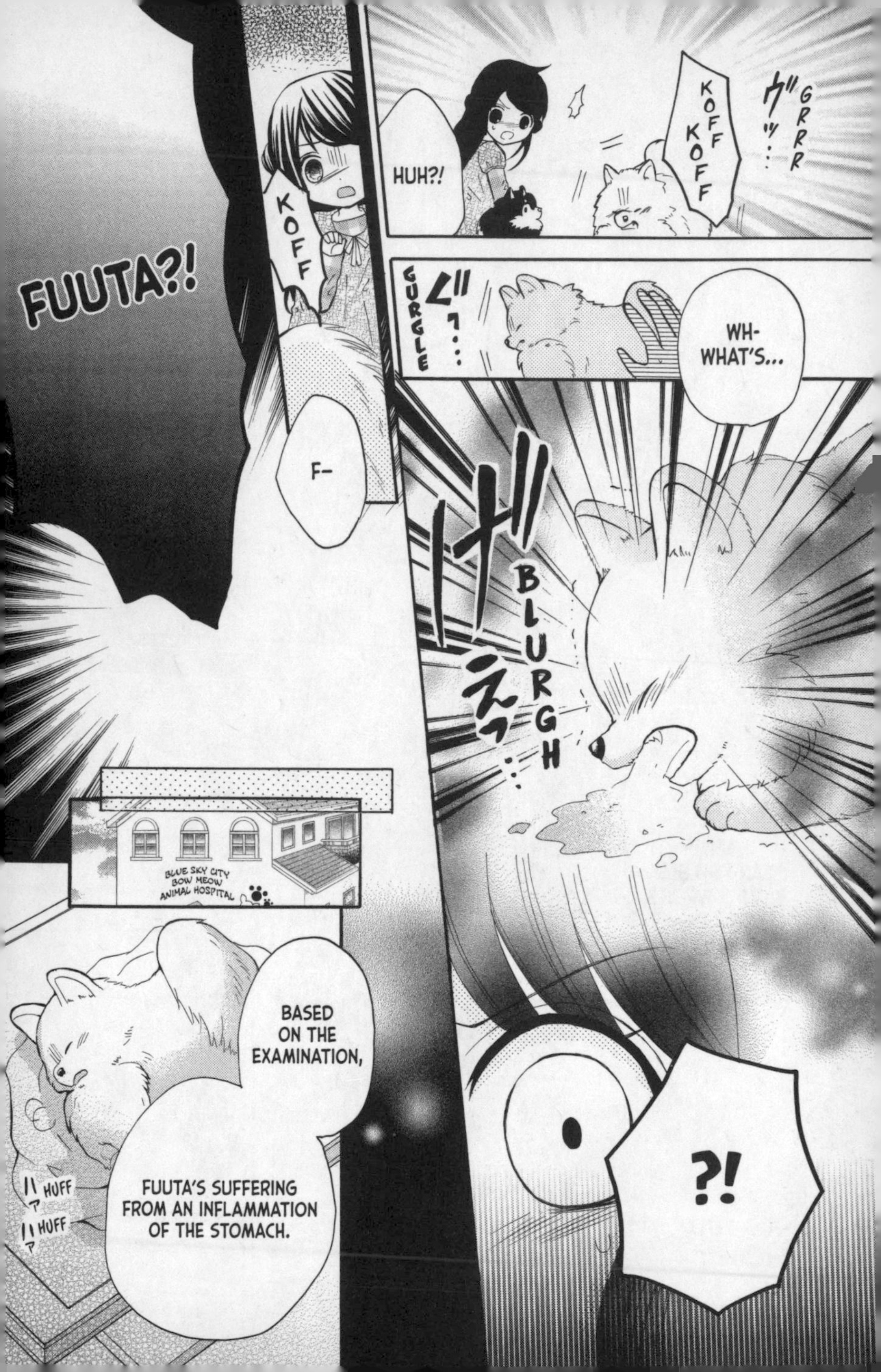
GRRR
KOFF KOFF
HUH?!
GURGLE
WH- WHAT'S...
BLURGH
?!
KOFF
F-
FUUTA?!
BLUE SKY CITY BOW MEOW ANIMAL HOSPITAL
BASED ON THE EXAMINATION,
FUUTA'S SUFFERING FROM AN INFLAMMATION OF THE STOMACH.
HUFF HUFF

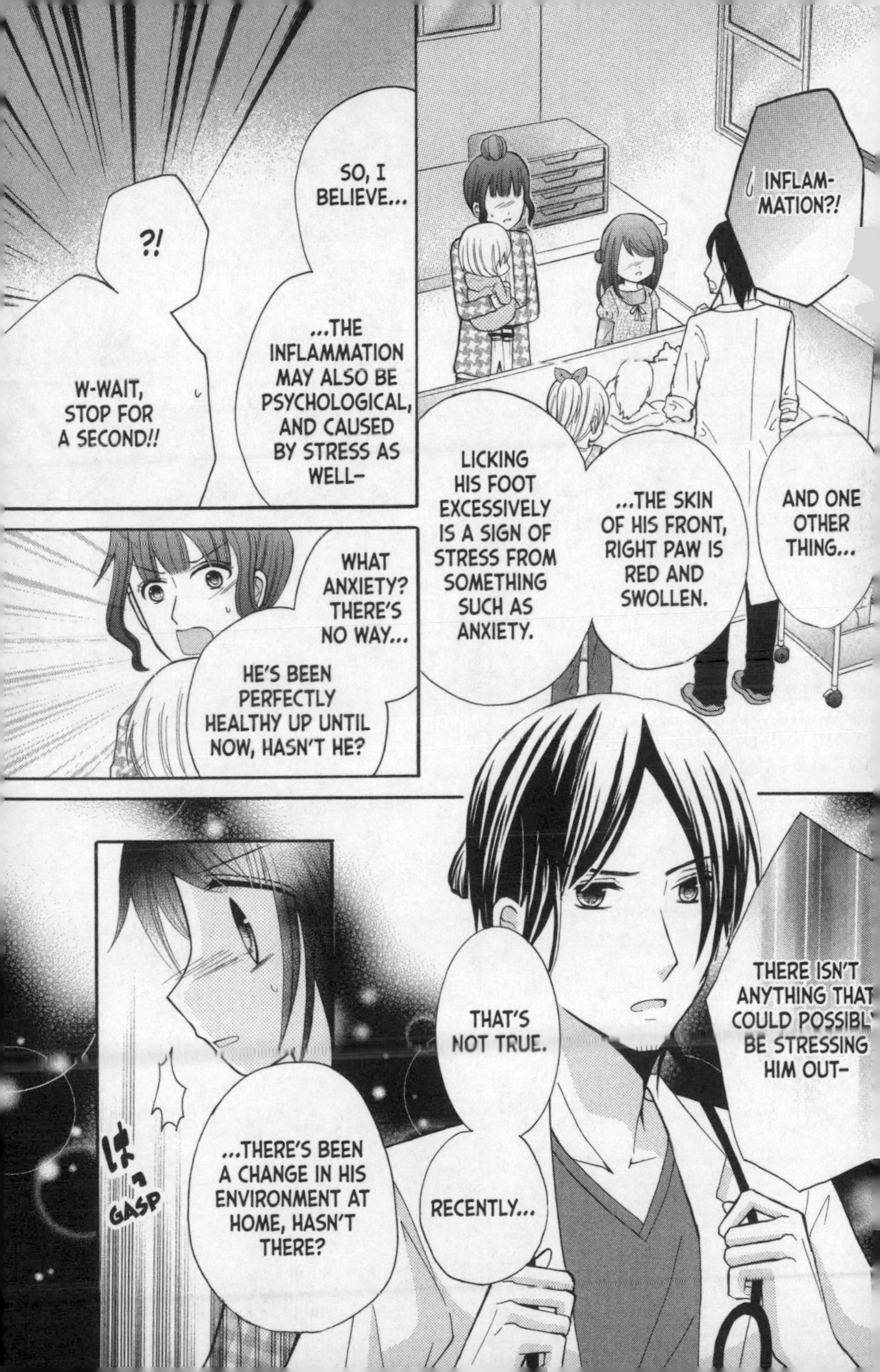
INFLAM-MATION?!
AND ONE OTHER THING...
...THE SKIN OF HIS FRONT, RIGHT PAW IS RED AND SWOLLEN.
LICKING HIS FOOT EXCESSIVELY IS A SIGN OF STRESS FROM SOMETHING SUCH AS ANXIETY.
SO, I BELIEVE...
...THE INFLAMMATION MAY ALSO BE PSYCHOLOGICAL, AND CAUSED BY STRESS AS WELL–
?!
W-WAIT, STOP FOR A SECOND!!
WHAT ANXIETY? THERE'S NO WAY...
HE'S BEEN PERFECTLY HEALTHY UP UNTIL NOW, HASN'T HE?
THERE ISN'T ANYTHING THAT COULD POSSIBL BE STRESSING HIM OUT–
THAT'S NOT TRUE.
RECENTLY...
...THERE'S BEEN A CHANGE IN HIS ENVIRONMENT AT HOME, HASN'T THERE?
はっ
GASP

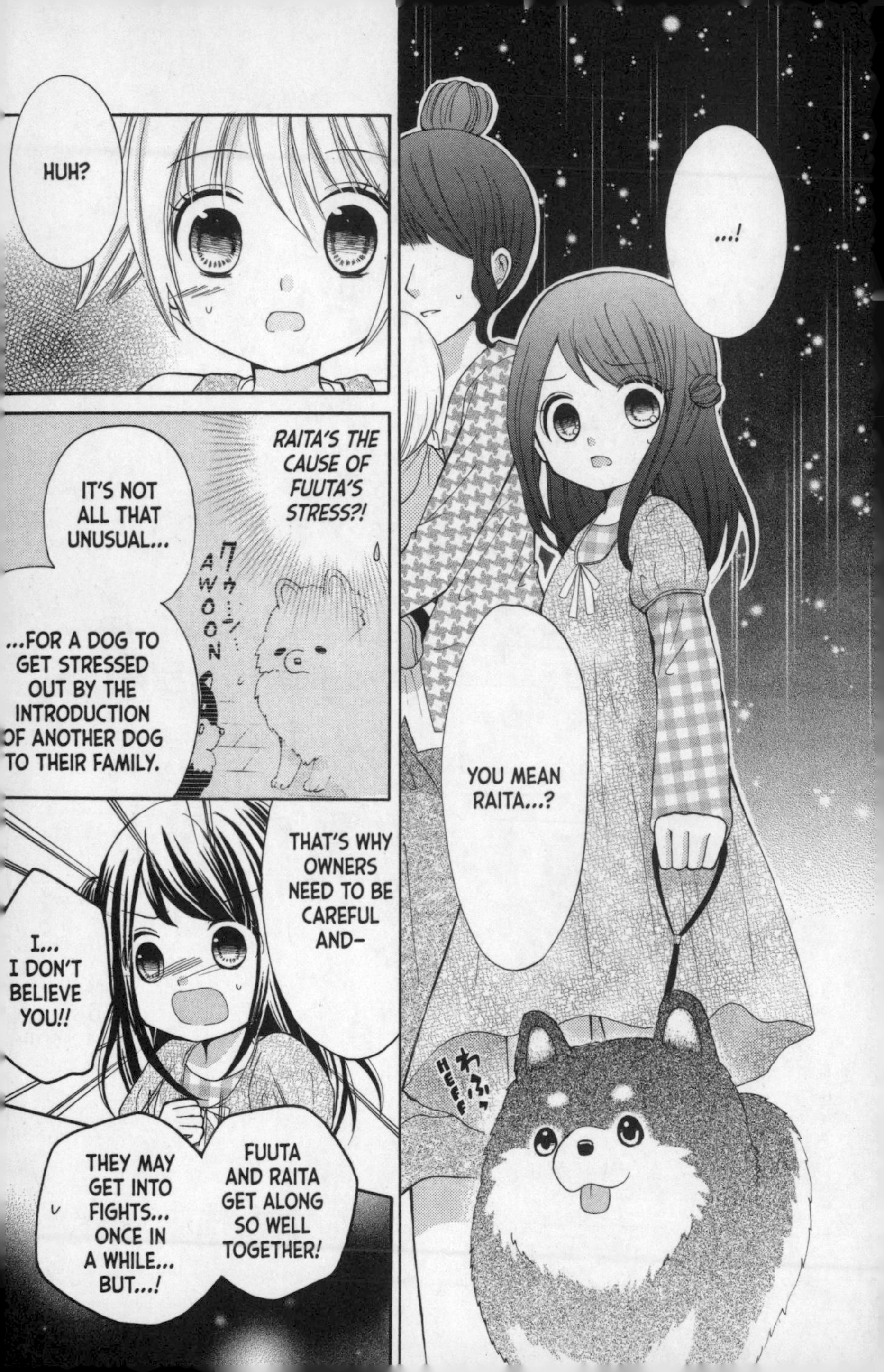
...!
YOU MEAN RAITA...?
HEFF
HUH?
RAITA'S THE CAUSE OF FUUTA'S STRESS?!
IT'S NOT ALL THAT UNUSUAL...
AWOON
...FOR A DOG TO GET STRESSED OUT BY THE INTRODUCTION OF ANOTHER DOG TO THEIR FAMILY.
THAT'S WHY OWNERS NEED TO BE CAREFUL AND-
I... I DON'T BELIEVE YOU!!
FUUTA AND RAITA GET ALONG SO WELL TOGETHER!
THEY MAY GET INTO FIGHTS... ONCE IN A WHILE... BUT...!

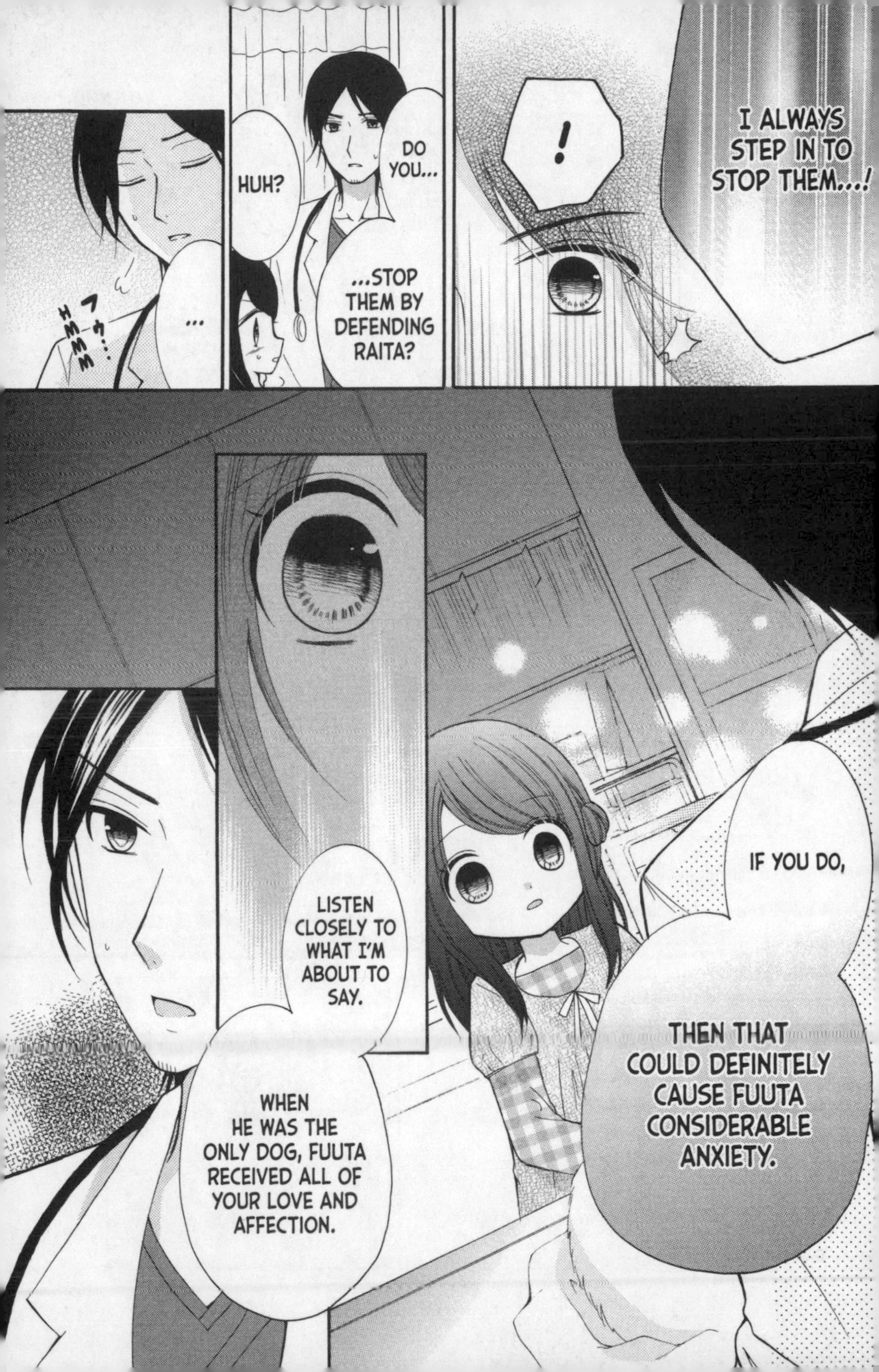
I ALWAYS STEP IN TO STOP THEM...!
!
DO YOU...
HUH?
...STOP THEM BY DEFENDING RAITA?
...
フゥ...
HMMM
IF YOU DO,
THEN THAT COULD DEFINITELY CAUSE FUUTA CONSIDERABLE ANXIETY.
LISTEN CLOSELY TO WHAT I'M ABOUT TO SAY.
WHEN HE WAS THE ONLY DOG, FUUTA RECEIVED ALL OF YOUR LOVE AND AFFECTION.

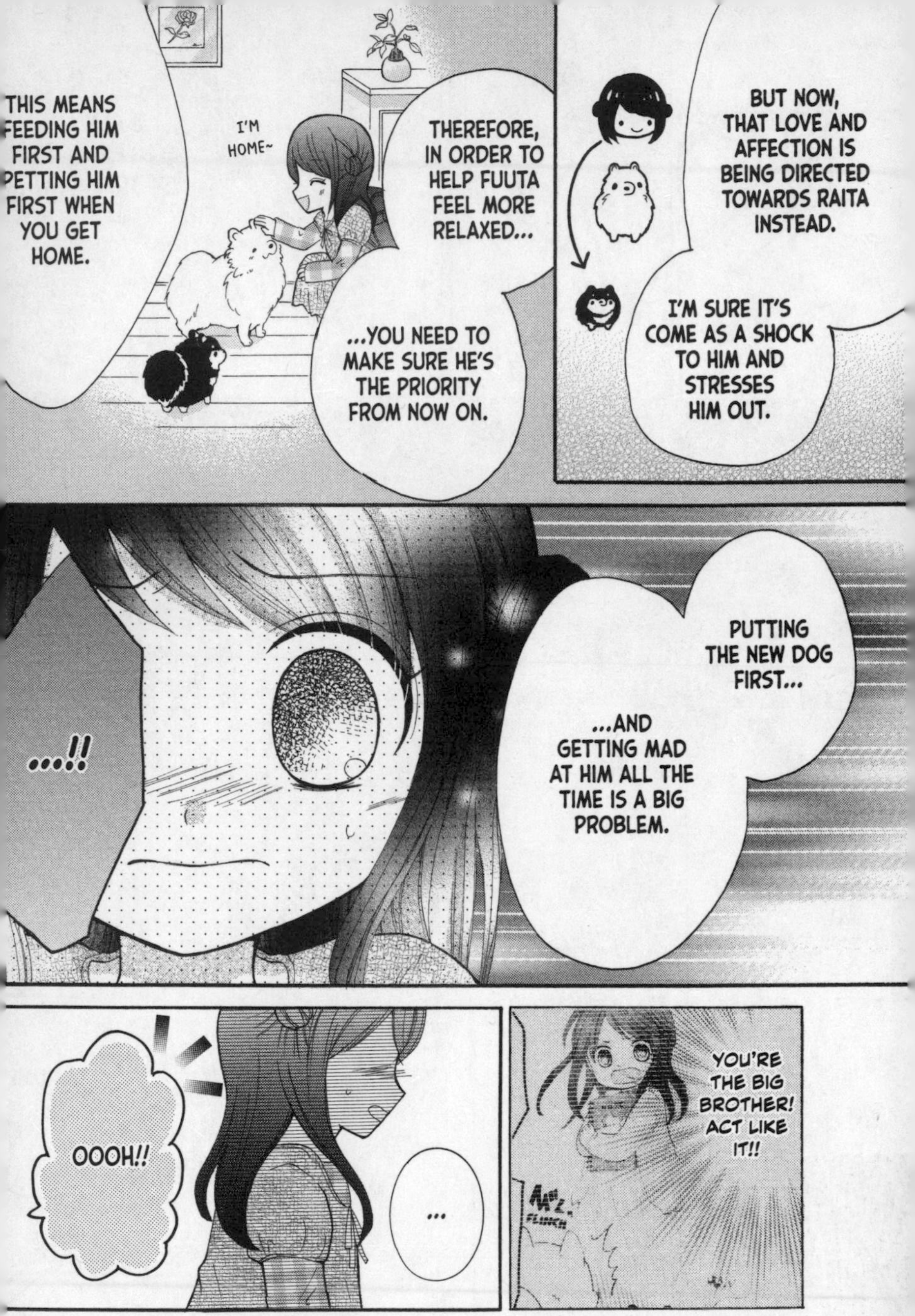
BUT NOW, THAT LOVE AND AFFECTION IS BEING DIRECTED TOWARDS RAITA INSTEAD.
I'M SURE IT'S COME AS A SHOCK TO HIM AND STRESSES HIM OUT.
THEREFORE, IN ORDER TO HELP FUUTA FEEL MORE RELAXED...
...YOU NEED TO MAKE SURE HE'S THE PRIORITY FROM NOW ON.
I'M HOME~
THIS MEANS FEEDING HIM FIRST AND PETTING HIM FIRST WHEN YOU GET HOME.
PUTTING THE NEW DOG FIRST...
...AND GETTING MAD AT HIM ALL THE TIME IS A BIG PROBLEM.
...!!
YOU'RE THE BIG BROTHER! ACT LIKE IT!!
FLINCH
...
OOOH!!

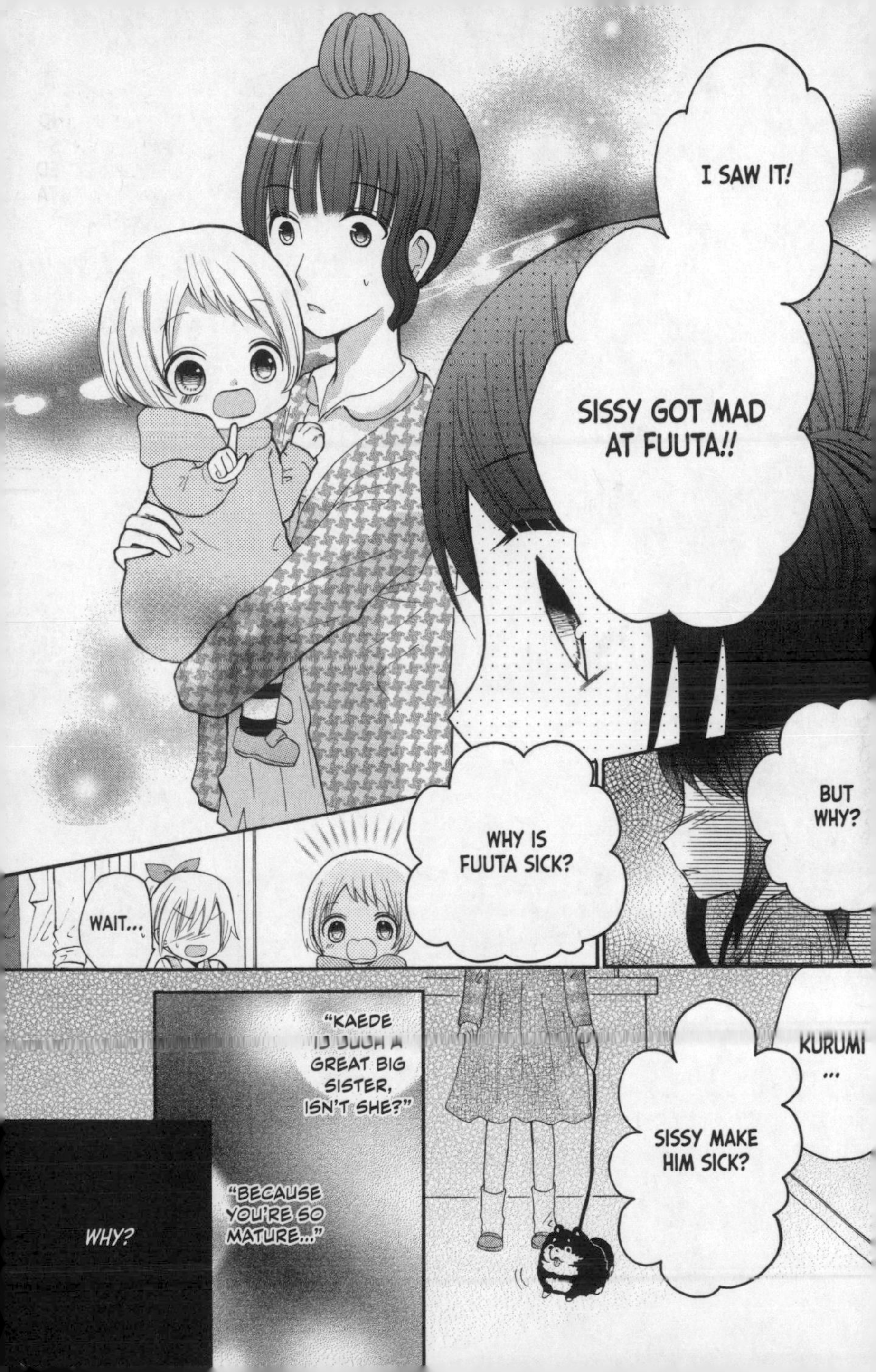
I SAW IT!
SISSY GOT MAD AT FUUTA!!
BUT WHY?
WHY IS FUUTA SICK?
WAIT...
KURUMI ...
SISSY MAKE HIM SICK?
"KAEDE IS SUCH A GREAT BIG SISTER, ISN'T SHE?"
"BECAUSE YOU'RE SO MATURE..."
WHY?

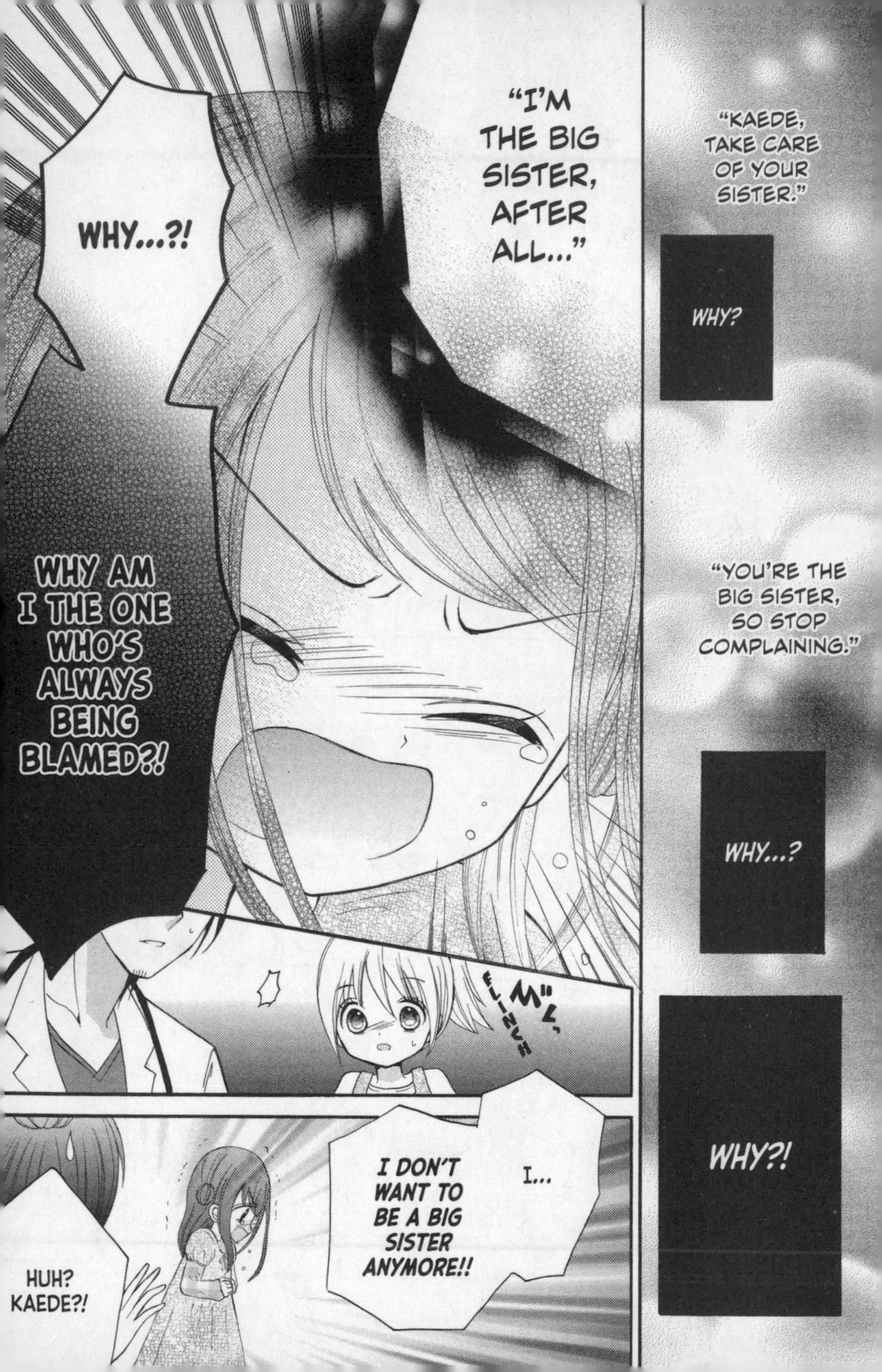
"KAEDE, TAKE CARE OF YOUR SISTER."
WHY?
"YOU'RE THE BIG SISTER, SO STOP COMPLAINING."
WHY...?
WHY?!
"I'M THE BIG SISTER, AFTER ALL..."
WHY...?!
WHY AM I THE ONE WHO'S ALWAYS BEING BLAMED?!
FLINCH
I...
I DON'T WANT TO BE A BIG SISTER ANYMORE!!
HUH? KAEDE?!

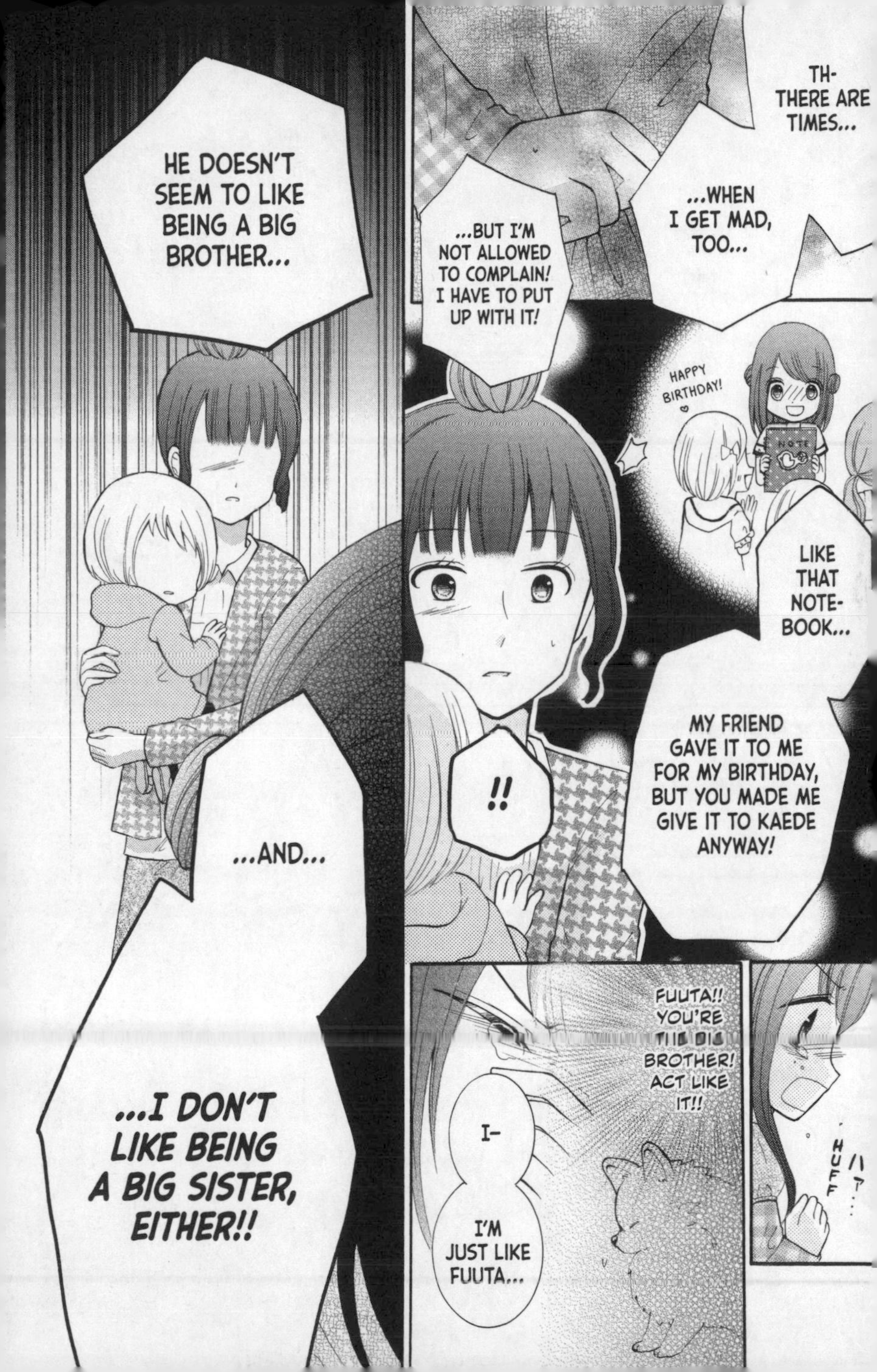
TH- THERE ARE TIMES...
...WHEN I GET MAD, TOO...
...BUT I'M NOT ALLOWED TO COMPLAIN! I HAVE TO PUT UP WITH IT!
HAPPY BIRTHDAY!
NOTE
LIKE THAT NOTEBOOK...
MY FRIEND GAVE IT TO ME FOR MY BIRTHDAY, BUT YOU MADE ME GIVE IT TO KAEDE ANYWAY!
!!
FUUTA!! YOU'RE THE BIG BROTHER! ACT LIKE IT!!
HUFF
ハァ…
I-
I'M JUST LIKE FUUTA...
HE DOESN'T SEEM TO LIKE BEING A BIG BROTHER...
...AND...
...I DON'T LIKE BEING A BIG SISTER, EITHER!!

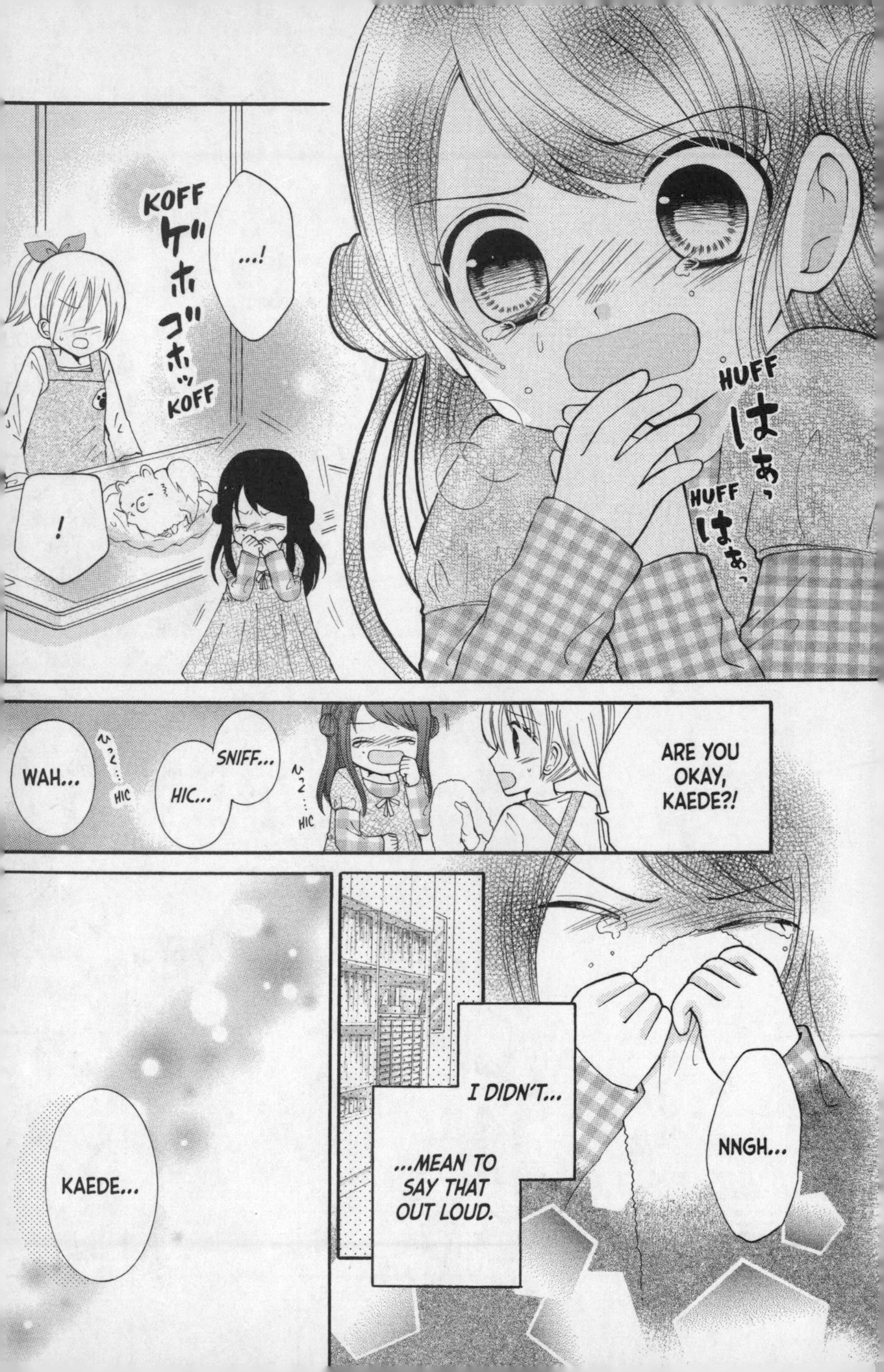

HUFF
はぁ
HUFF
はぁ
...!
KOFF
ゲホゴホッ
KOFF
!
ARE YOU OKAY, KAEDE?!
ひっく...
HIC
SNIFF...
HIC...
ひっく...
HIC
WAH...
NNGH...
I DIDN'T...
...MEAN TO SAY THAT OUT LOUD.
KAEDE...

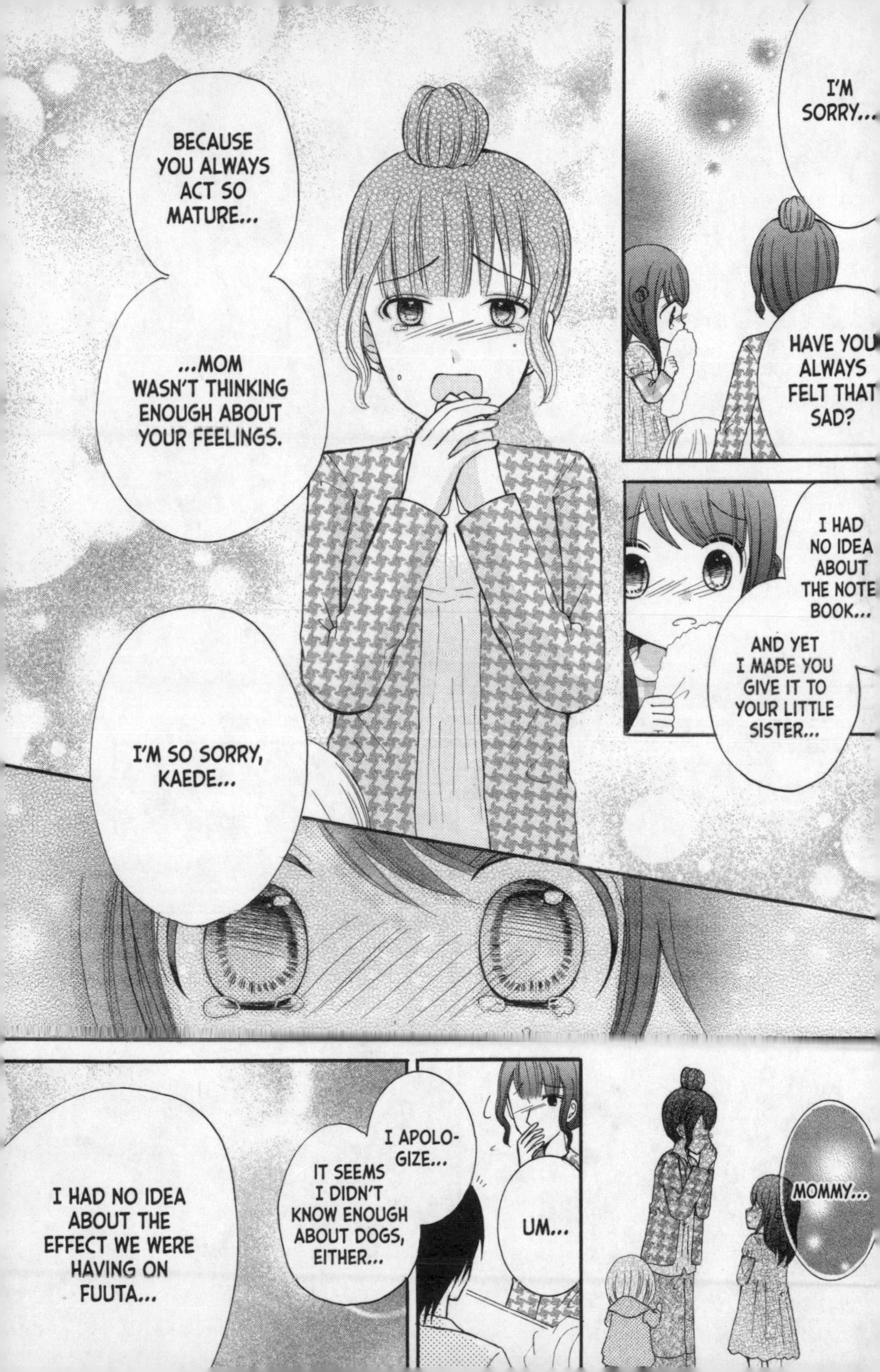
I'M SORRY...
HAVE YOU ALWAYS FELT THAT SAD?
I HAD NO IDEA ABOUT THE NOTE BOOK...
AND YET I MADE YOU GIVE IT TO YOUR LITTLE SISTER...
BECAUSE YOU ALWAYS ACT SO MATURE...
...MOM WASN'T THINKING ENOUGH ABOUT YOUR FEELINGS.
I'M SO SORRY, KAEDE...
MOMMY...
UM...
I APOLOGIZE...
IT SEEMS I DIDN'T KNOW ENOUGH ABOUT DOGS, EITHER...
I HAD NO IDEA ABOUT THE EFFECT WE WERE HAVING ON FUUTA...

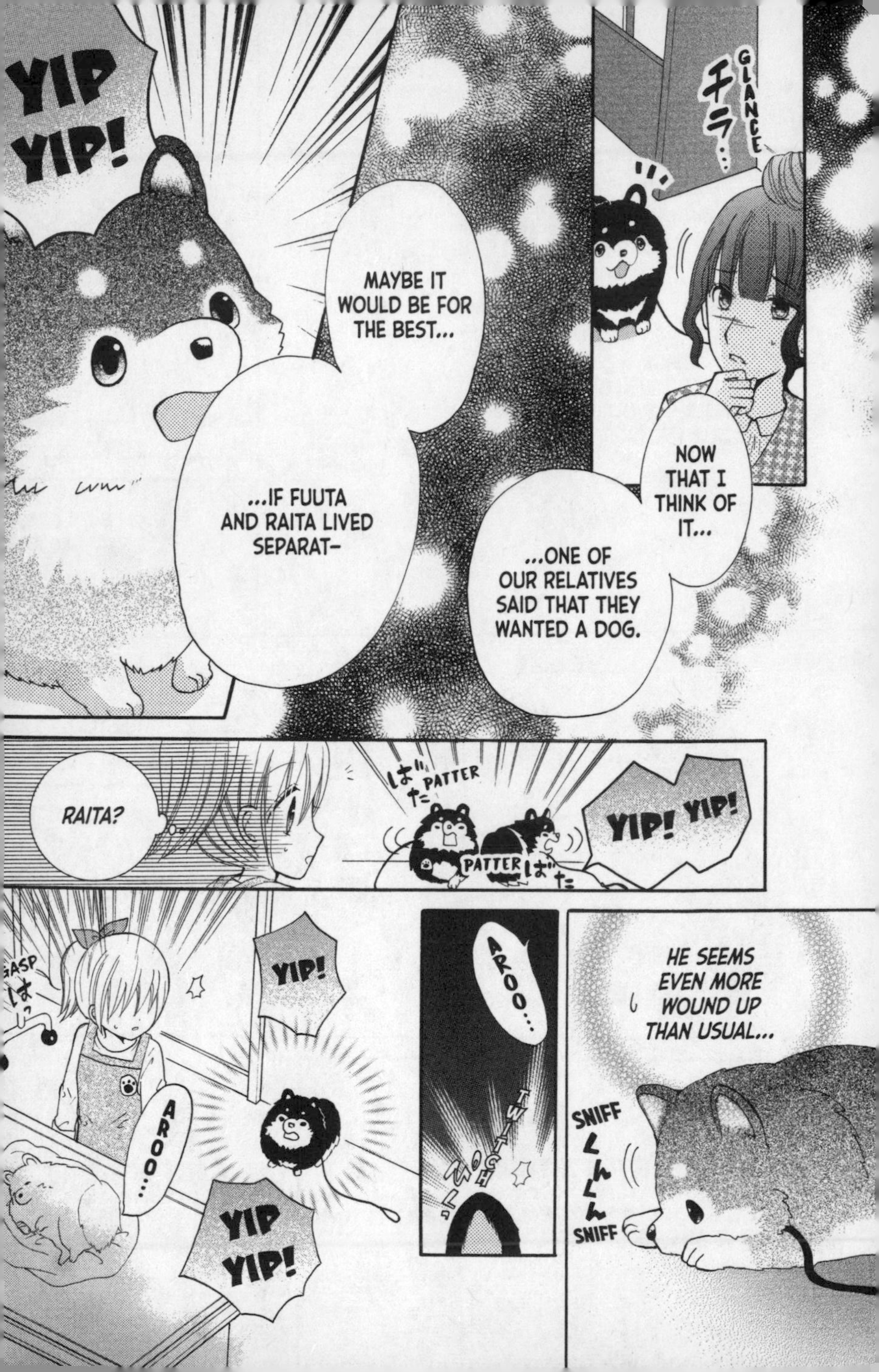
GLANCE
チラ…
NOW THAT I THINK OF IT...
...ONE OF OUR RELATIVES SAID THAT THEY WANTED A DOG.
MAYBE IT WOULD BE FOR THE BEST...
...IF FUUTA AND RAITA LIVED SEPARAT-
YIP YIP!
YIP! YIP!
ぱた PATTER
PATTER ぱた
RAITA?
HE SEEMS EVEN MORE WOUND UP THAN USUAL...
SNIFF くんくん SNIFF
AROO...
TWITCH
GASP はっ
YIP!
AROO...
YIP YIP!

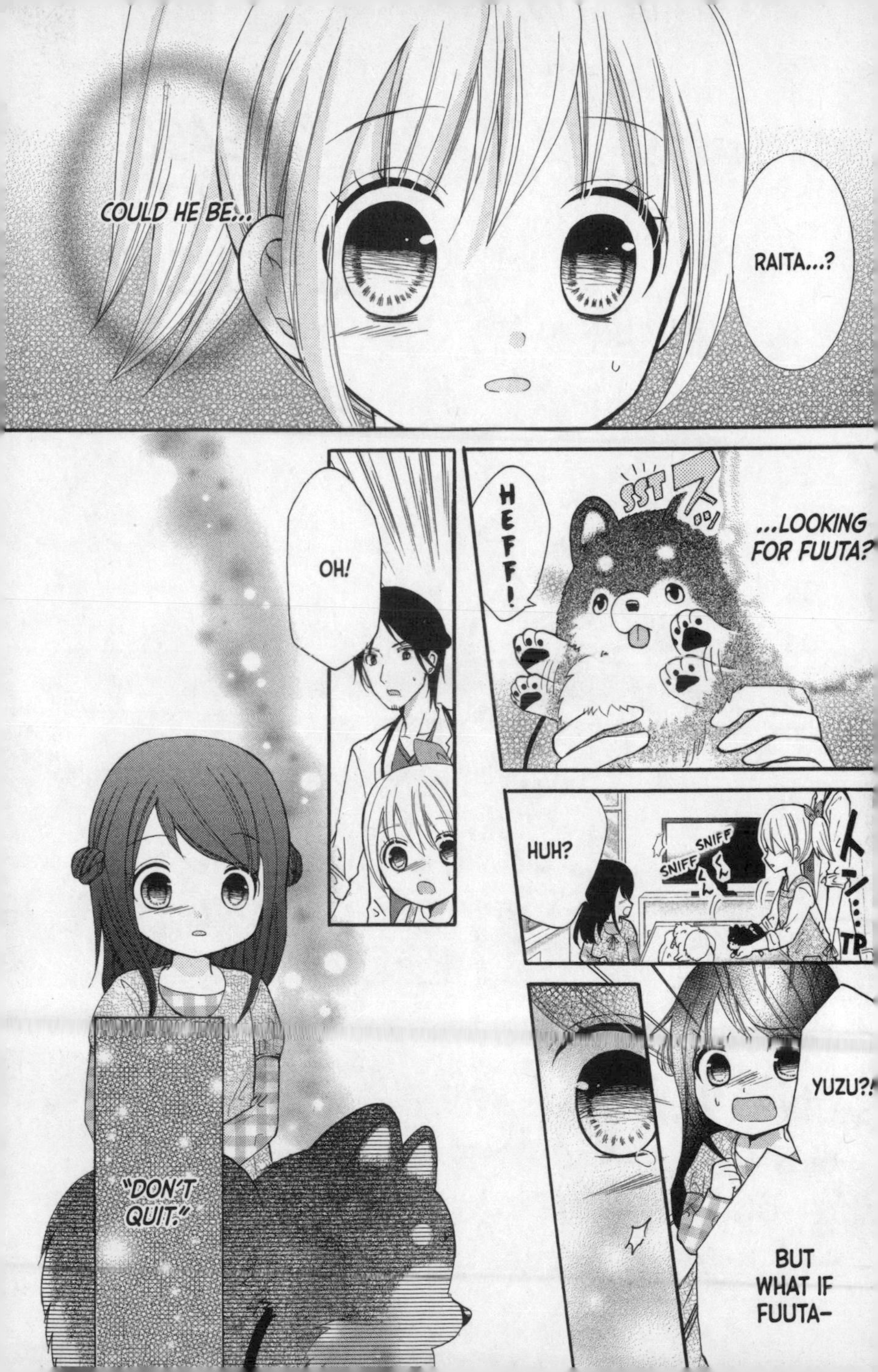
RAITA...?
COULD HE BE...
...LOOKING FOR FUUTA?
SST
HEFF!
OH!
HUH?
SNIFF SNIFF
TP
YUZU?!
BUT WHAT IF FUUTA-
"DON'T QUIT."

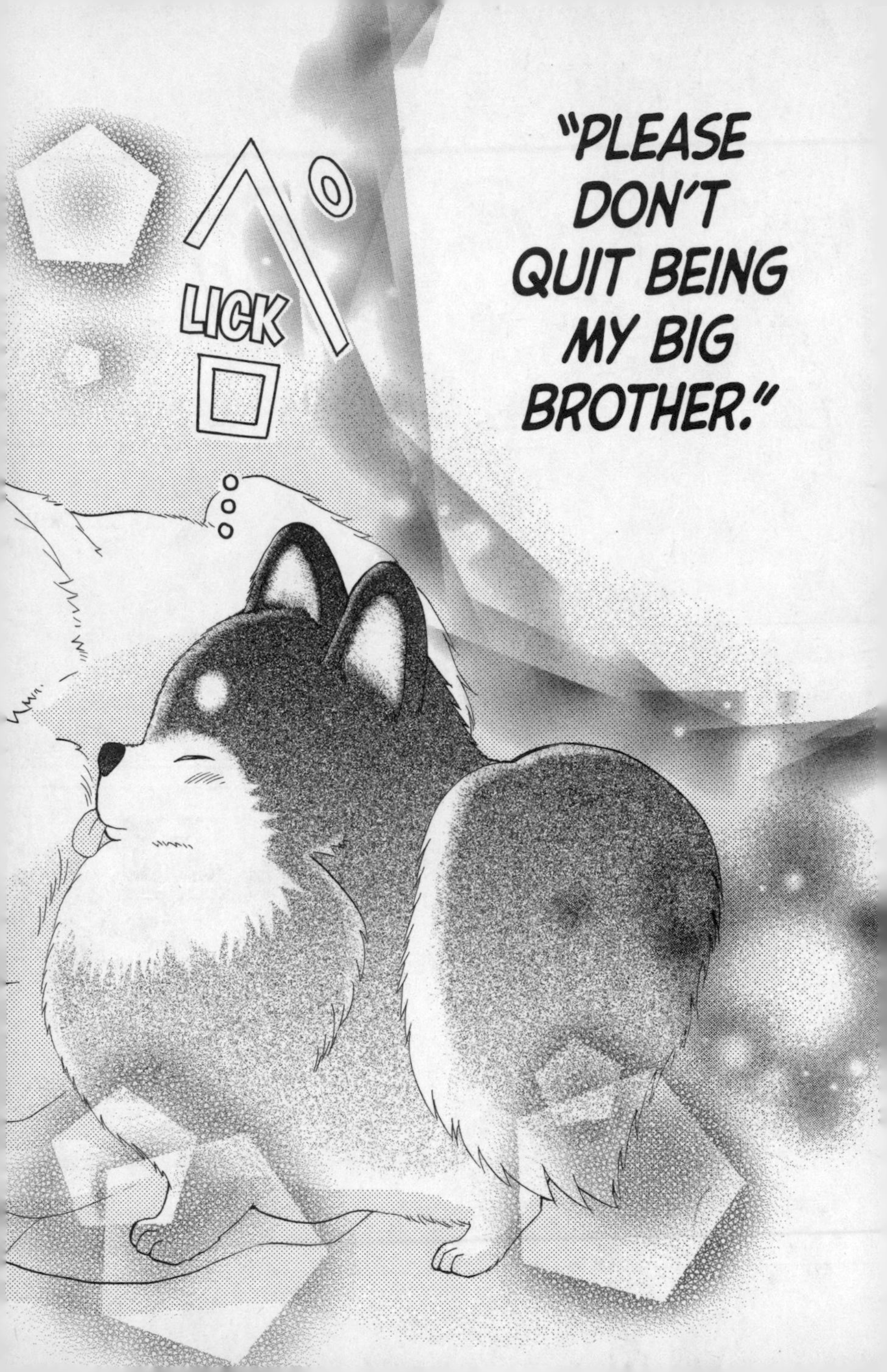
"PLEASE DON'T QUIT BEING MY BIG BROTHER."
LICK

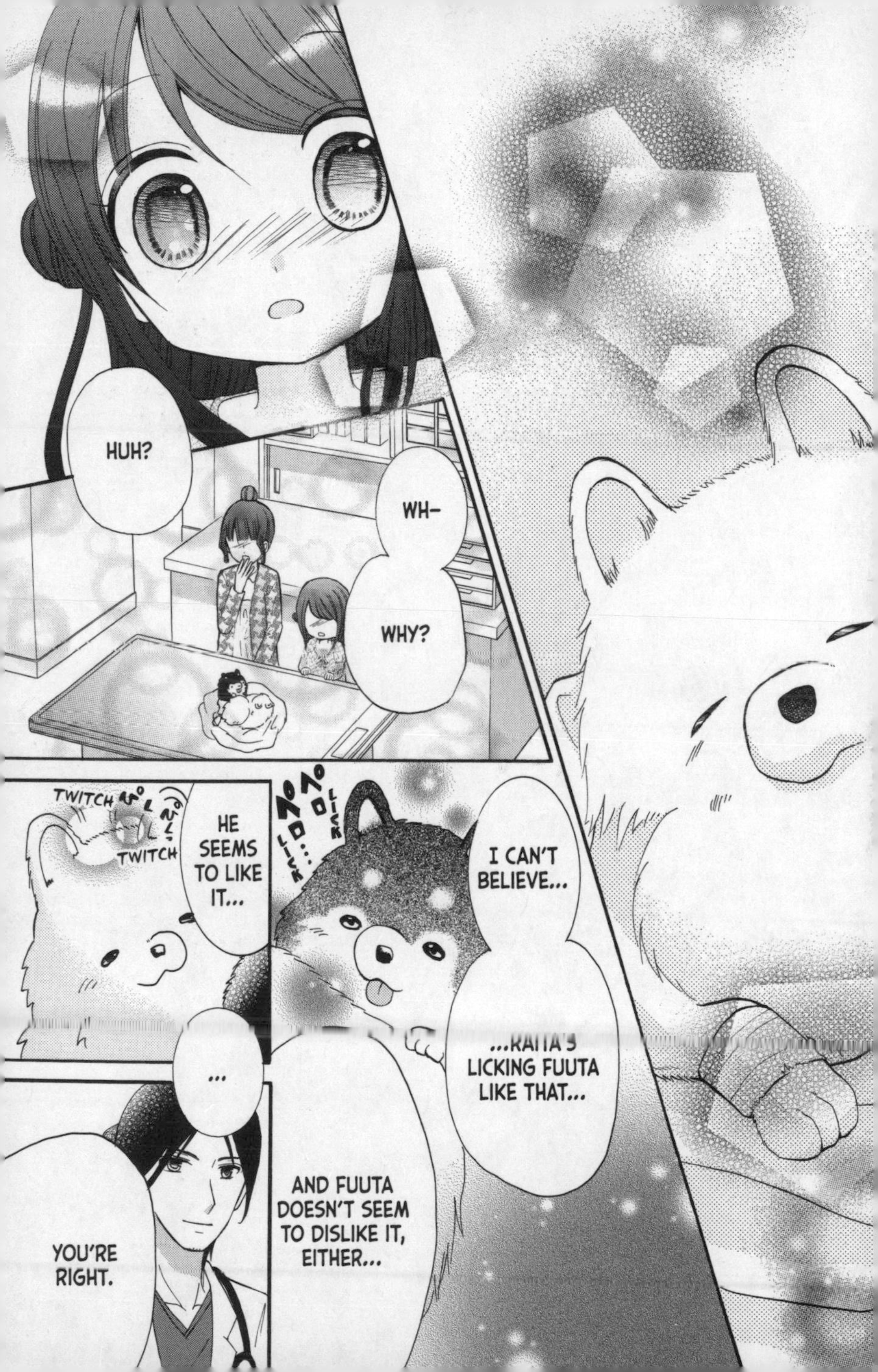
HUH?
WH-
WHY?
LICK
LICK
I CAN'T BELIEVE...
...RAITA'S LICKING FUUTA LIKE THAT...
HE SEEMS TO LIKE IT...
TWITCH
TWITCH
AND FUUTA DOESN'T SEEM TO DISLIKE IT, EITHER...
...
YOU'RE RIGHT.

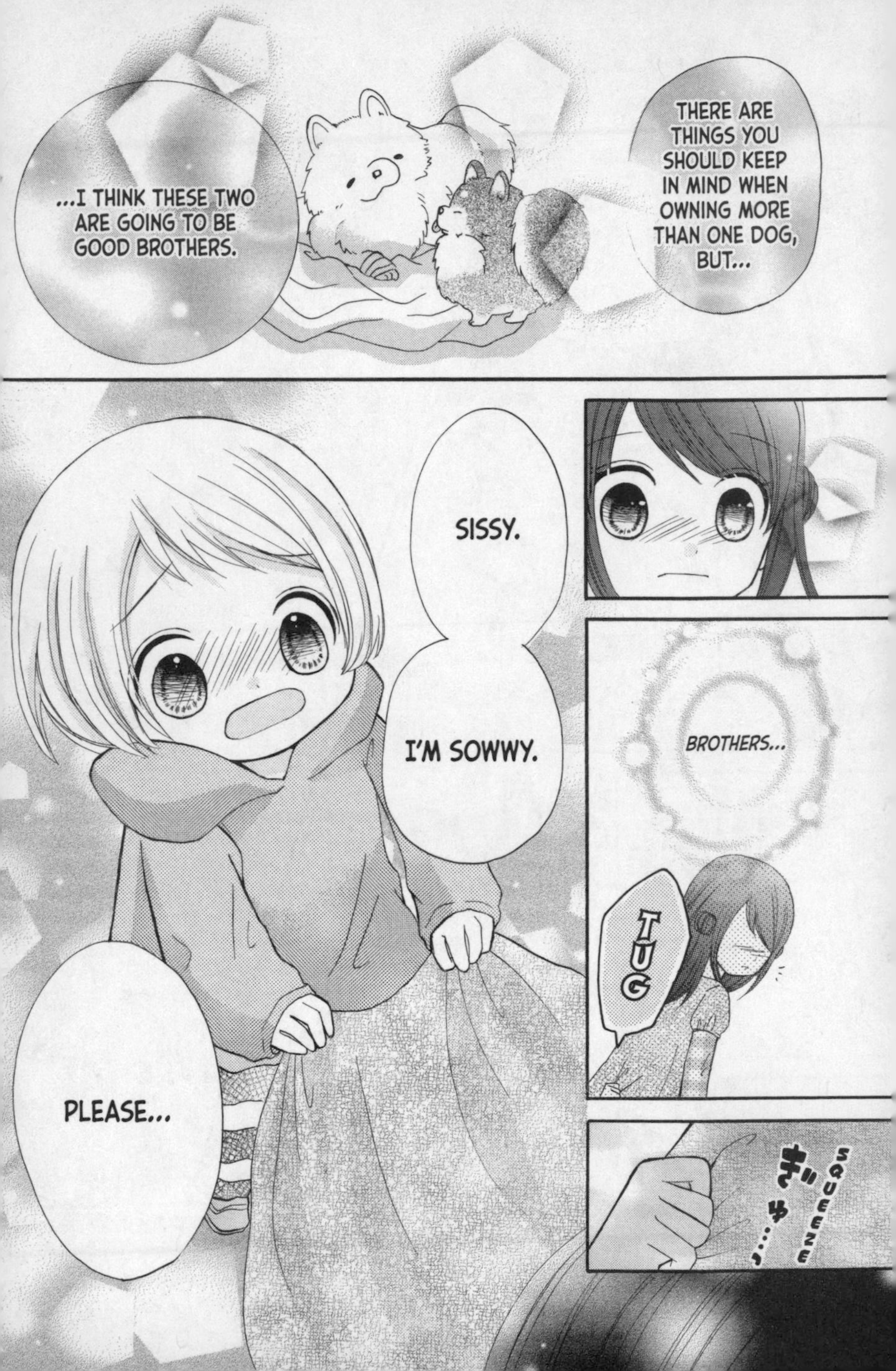
THERE ARE THINGS YOU SHOULD KEEP IN MIND WHEN OWNING MORE THAN ONE DOG, BUT...
...I THINK THESE TWO ARE GOING TO BE GOOD BROTHERS.
BROTHERS...
TUG
SQUEEZE
SISSY.
I'M SOWWY.
PLEASE...

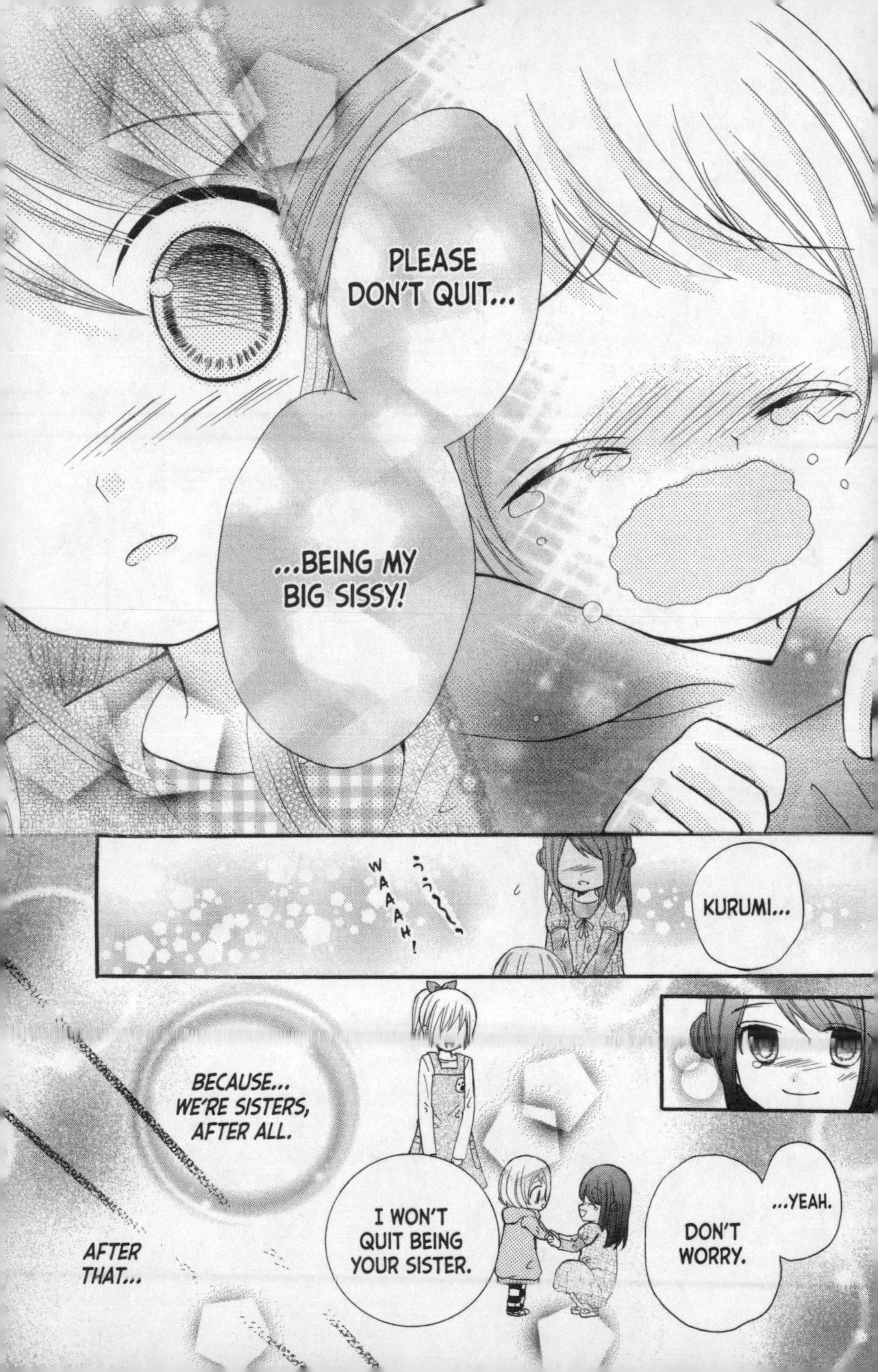
PLEASE DON'T QUIT...
...BEING MY BIG SISSY!
KURUMI...
WAAAAH!
...YEAH.
DON'T WORRY.
I WON'T QUIT BEING YOUR SISTER.
BECAUSE... WE'RE SISTERS, AFTER ALL.
AFTER THAT...

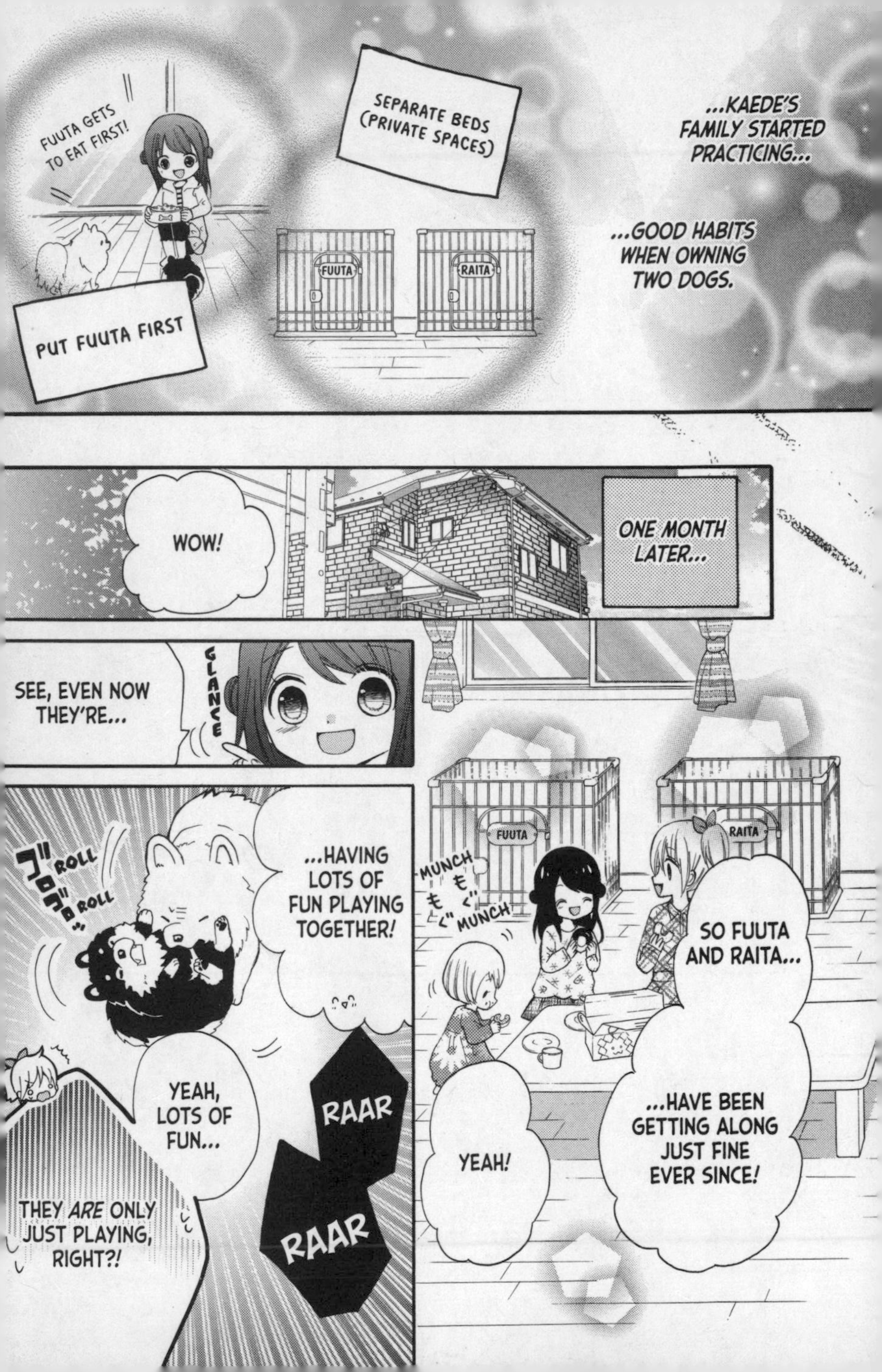
...KAEDE'S FAMILY STARTED PRACTICING...
...GOOD HABITS WHEN OWNING TWO DOGS.
SEPARATE BEDS (PRIVATE SPACES)
RAITA
FUUTA
FUUTA GETS TO EAT FIRST!
PUT FUUTA FIRST
ONE MONTH LATER...
WOW!
SO FUUTA AND RAITA...
...HAVE BEEN GETTING ALONG JUST FINE EVER SINCE!
RAITA
FUUTA
MUNCH MUNCH
YEAH!
SEE, EVEN NOW THEY'RE...
GLANCE
...HAVING LOTS OF FUN PLAYING TOGETHER!
ROLL ROLL
RAAR
RAAR
YEAH, LOTS OF FUN...
THEY *ARE* ONLY JUST PLAYING, RIGHT?!

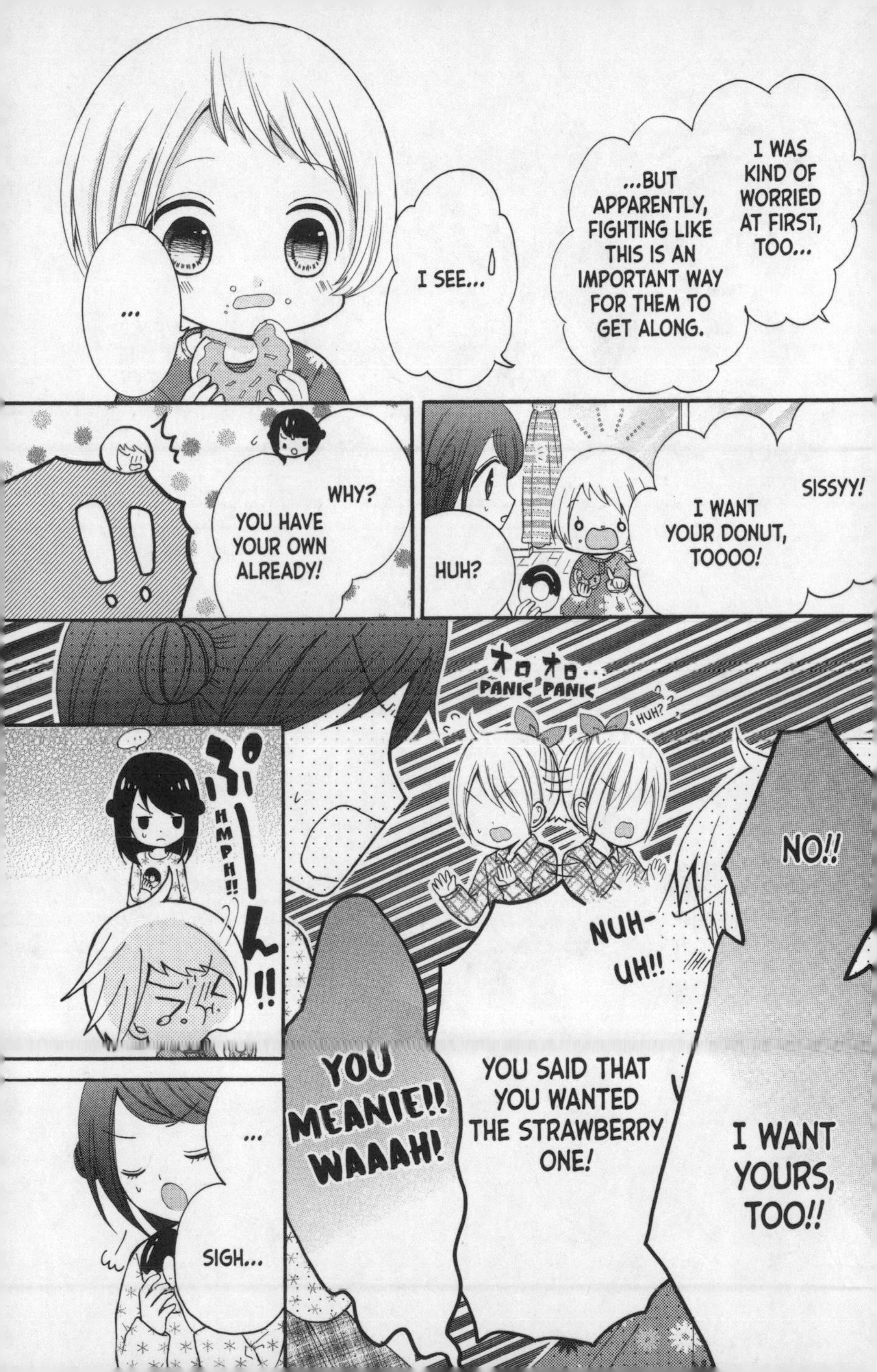
I WAS KIND OF WORRIED AT FIRST, TOO...
...BUT APPARENTLY, FIGHTING LIKE THIS IS AN IMPORTANT WAY FOR THEM TO GET ALONG.
I SEE...
...
SISSYY!
I WANT YOUR DONUT, TOOOO!
HUH?
WHY?
YOU HAVE YOUR OWN ALREADY!
!!
オロオロ...
PANIC PANIC
HUH?
NO!!
NUH-UH!!
I WANT YOURS, TOO!!
YOU SAID THAT YOU WANTED THE STRAWBERRY ONE!
YOU MEANIE!! WAAAH!
ぷーん!!
HMPH!!
...
SIGH...

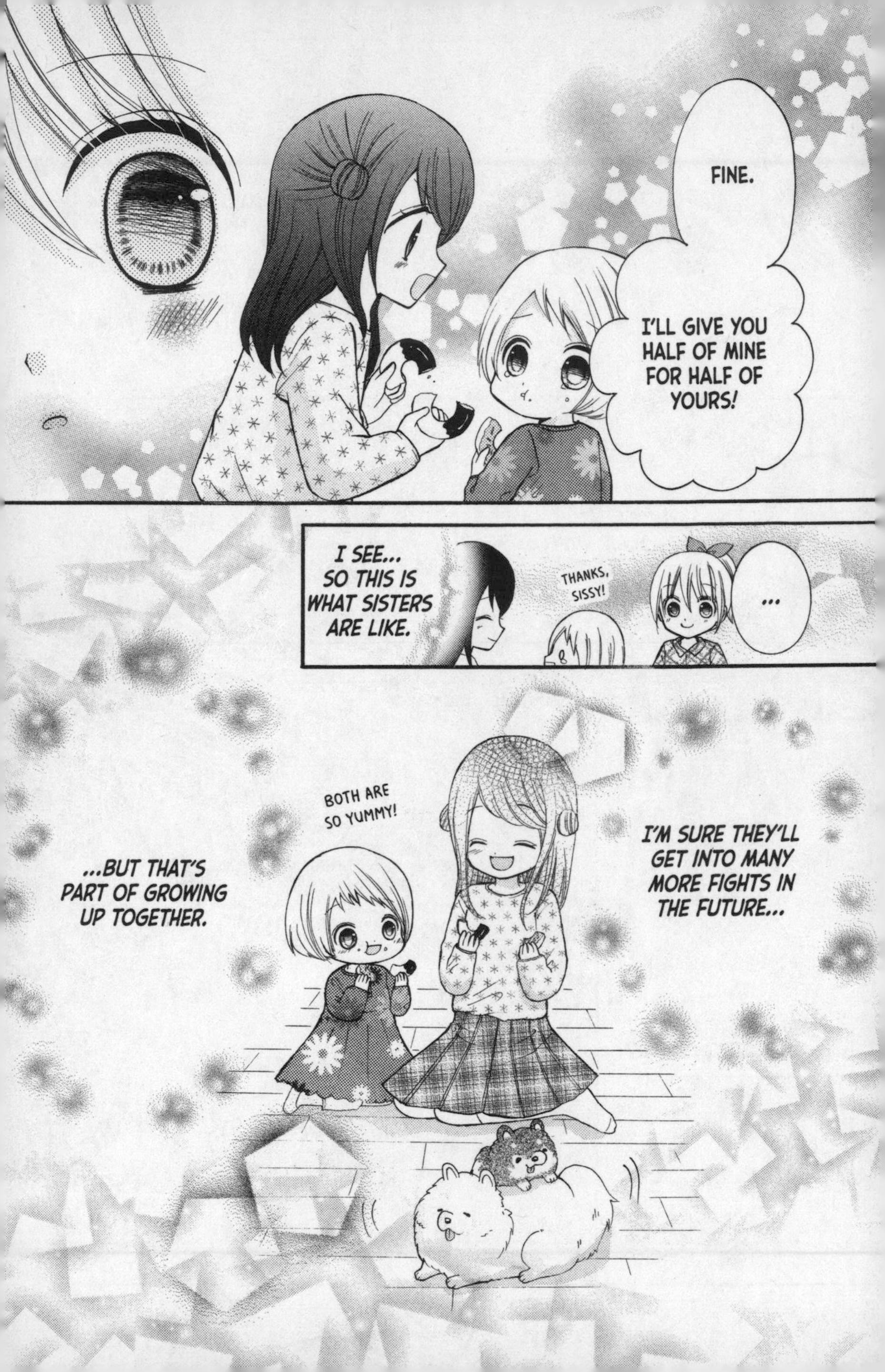
FINE.
I'LL GIVE YOU HALF OF MINE FOR HALF OF YOURS!
...
THANKS, SISSY!
I SEE... SO THIS IS WHAT SISTERS ARE LIKE.
I'M SURE THEY'LL GET INTO MANY MORE FIGHTS IN THE FUTURE...
BOTH ARE SO YUMMY!
...BUT THAT'S PART OF GROWING UP TOGETHER.

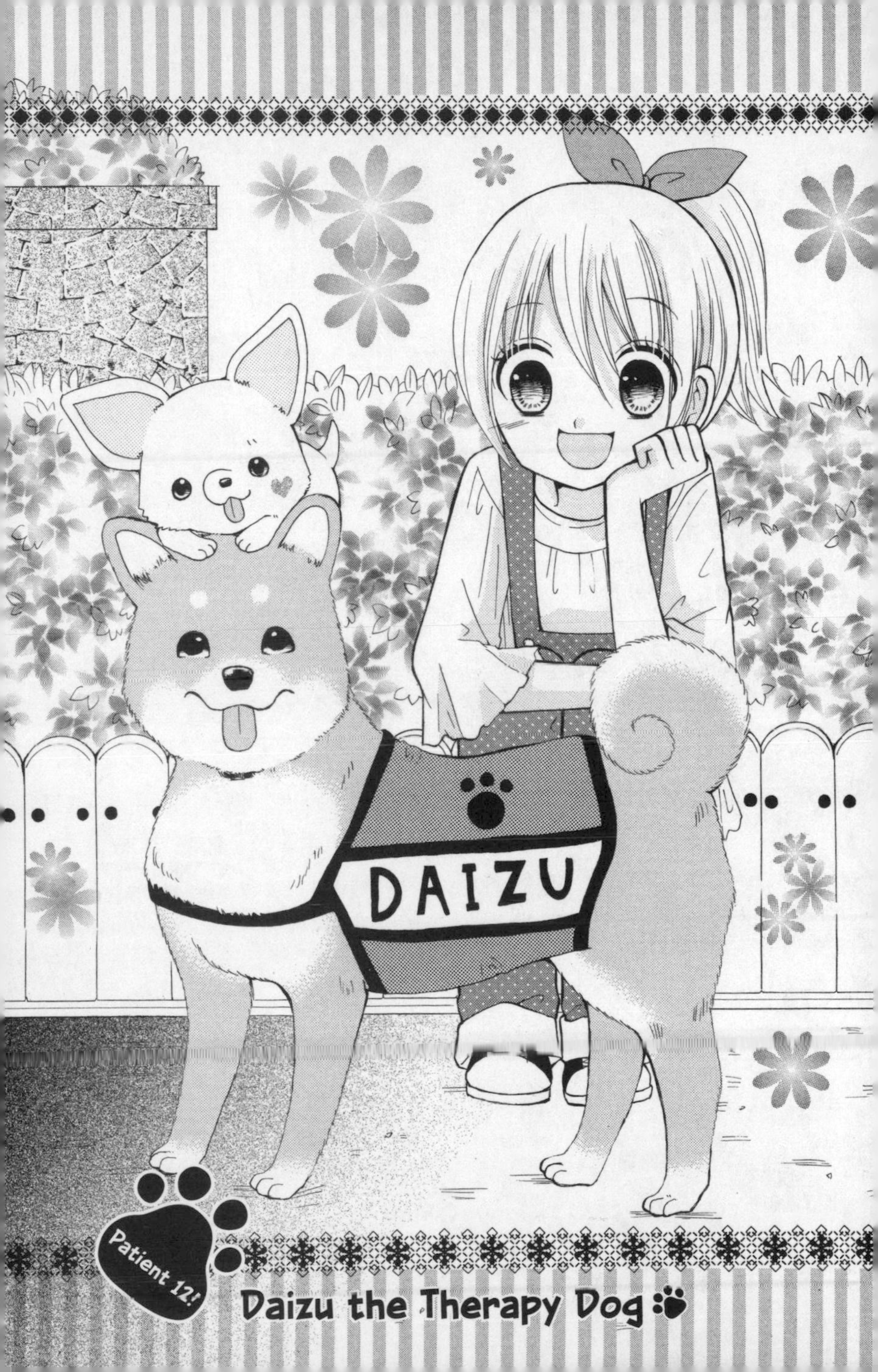
DAIZU
Patient 17!
Daizu the Therapy Dog

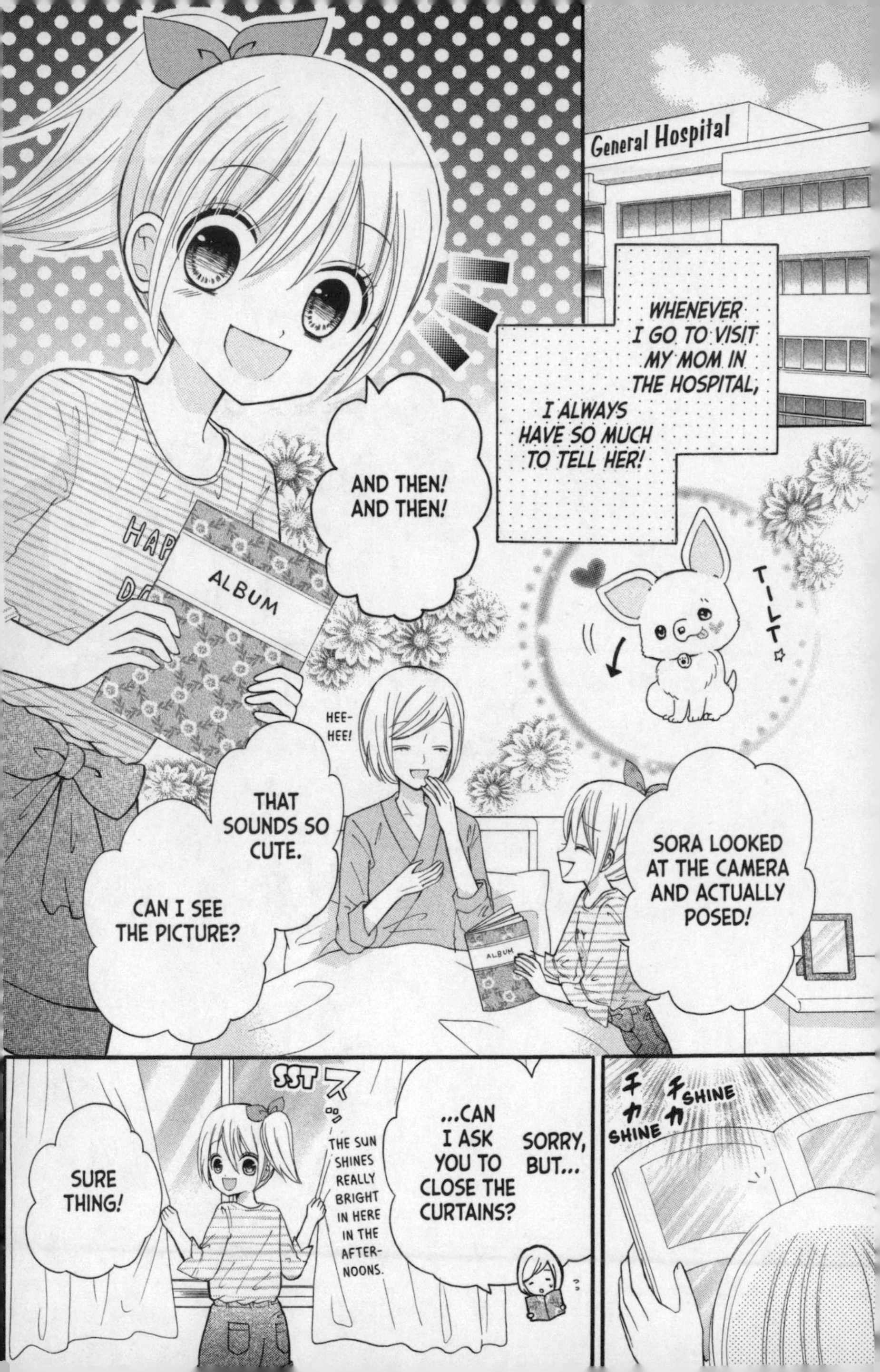
General Hospital
WHENEVER I GO TO VISIT MY MOM IN THE HOSPITAL, I ALWAYS HAVE SO MUCH TO TELL HER!
AND THEN! AND THEN!
ALBUM
TILT☆
SORA LOOKED AT THE CAMERA AND ACTUALLY POSED!
HEE-HEE!
THAT SOUNDS SO CUTE.
CAN I SEE THE PICTURE?
ALBUM
チカ SHINE
チカ SHINE
SORRY, BUT...
...CAN I ASK YOU TO CLOSE THE CURTAINS?
ス SST
THE SUN SHINES REALLY BRIGHT IN HERE IN THE AFTERNOONS.
SURE THING!

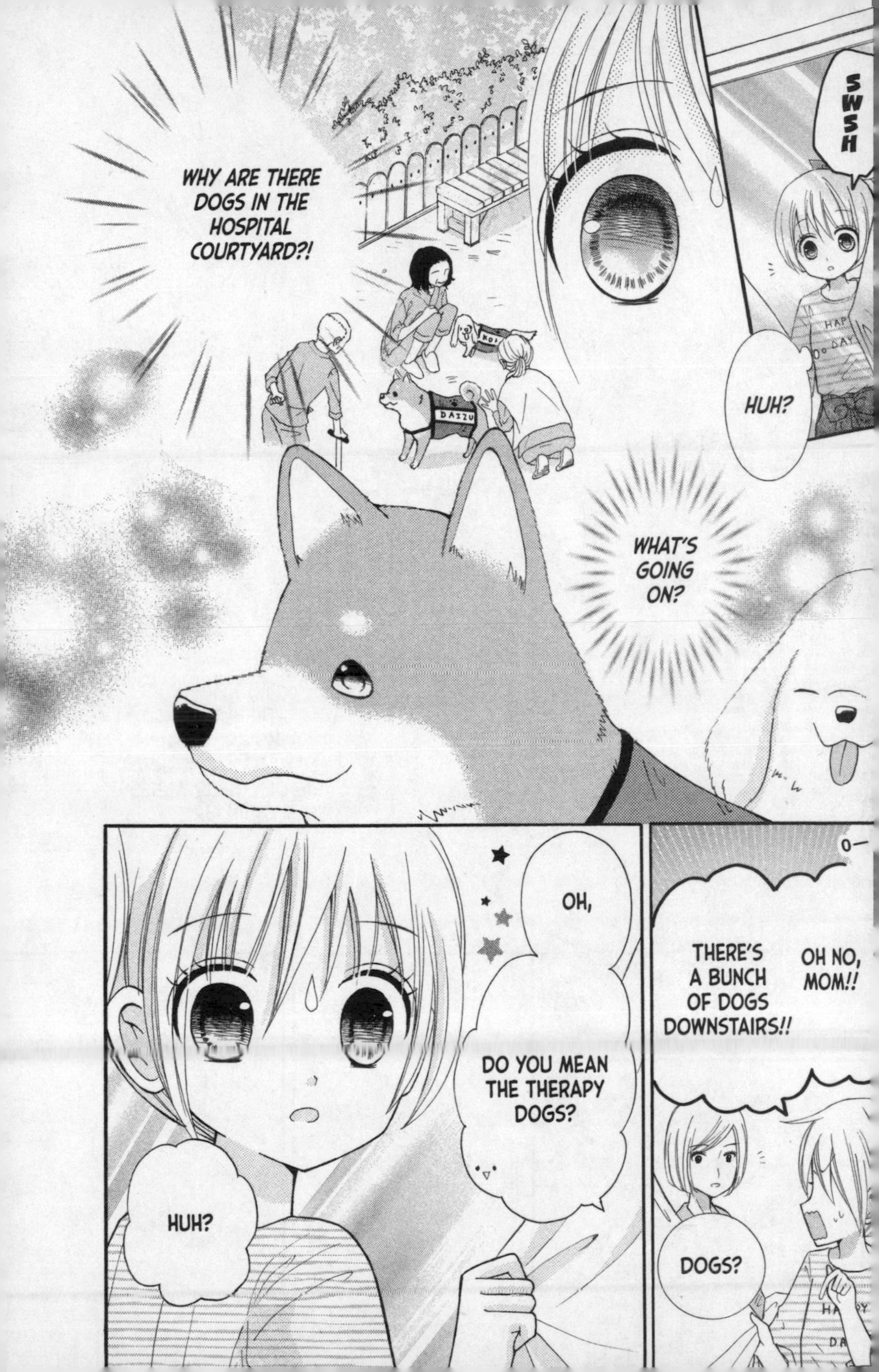
SWSH
HUH?
WHY ARE THERE DOGS IN THE HOSPITAL COURTYARD?!
WHAT'S GOING ON?
O—
OH NO, MOM!!
THERE'S A BUNCH OF DOGS DOWNSTAIRS!!
DOGS?
OH,
DO YOU MEAN THE THERAPY DOGS?
HUH?

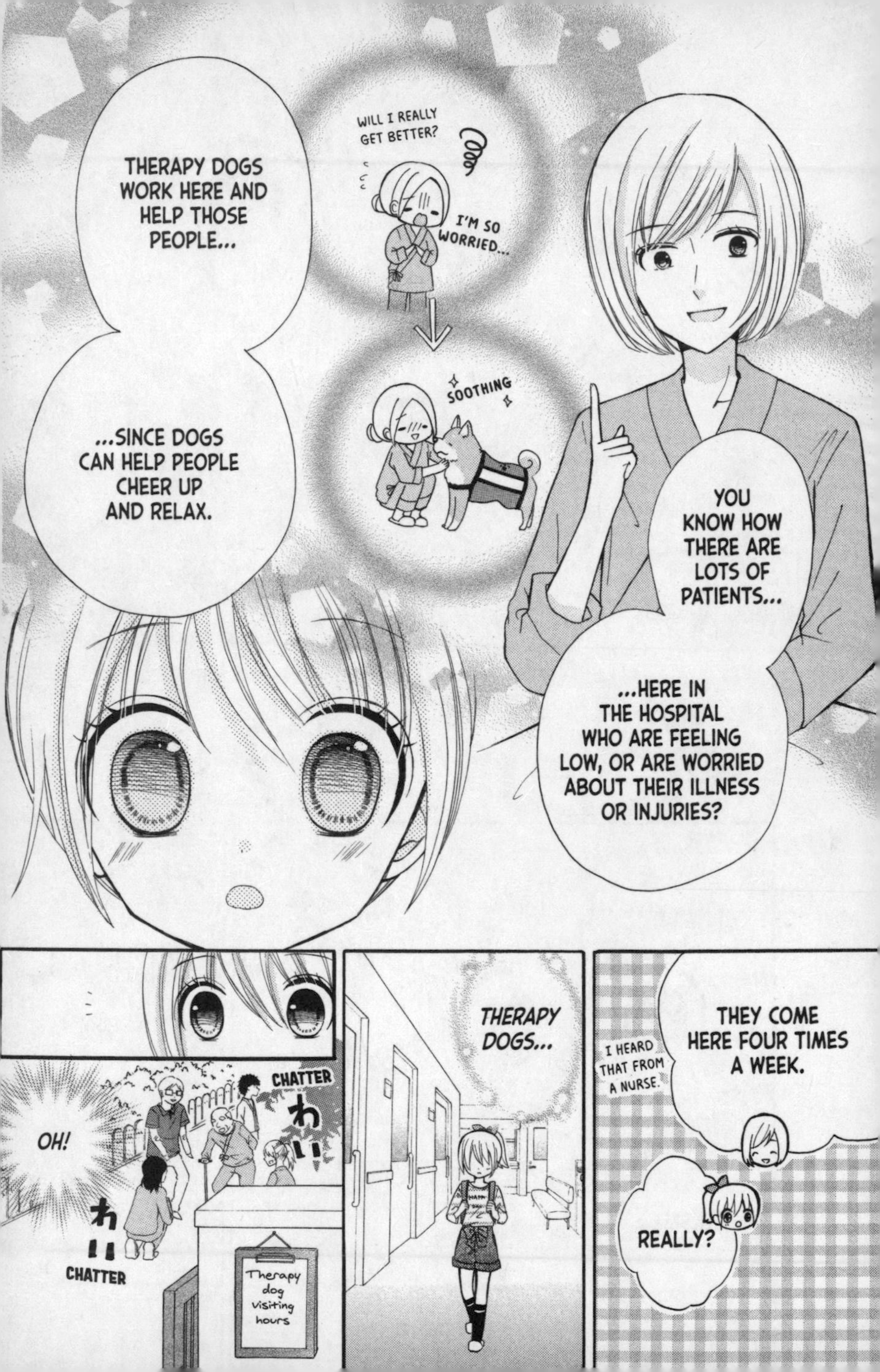
YOU KNOW HOW THERE ARE LOTS OF PATIENTS...
...HERE IN THE HOSPITAL WHO ARE FEELING LOW, OR ARE WORRIED ABOUT THEIR ILLNESS OR INJURIES?
WILL I REALLY GET BETTER?
I'M SO WORRIED...
SOOTHING
THERAPY DOGS WORK HERE AND HELP THOSE PEOPLE...
...SINCE DOGS CAN HELP PEOPLE CHEER UP AND RELAX.
THEY COME HERE FOUR TIMES A WEEK.
I HEARD THAT FROM A NURSE.
REALLY?
THERAPY DOGS...
CHATTER
わい
OH!
CHATTER
Therapy dog visiting hours

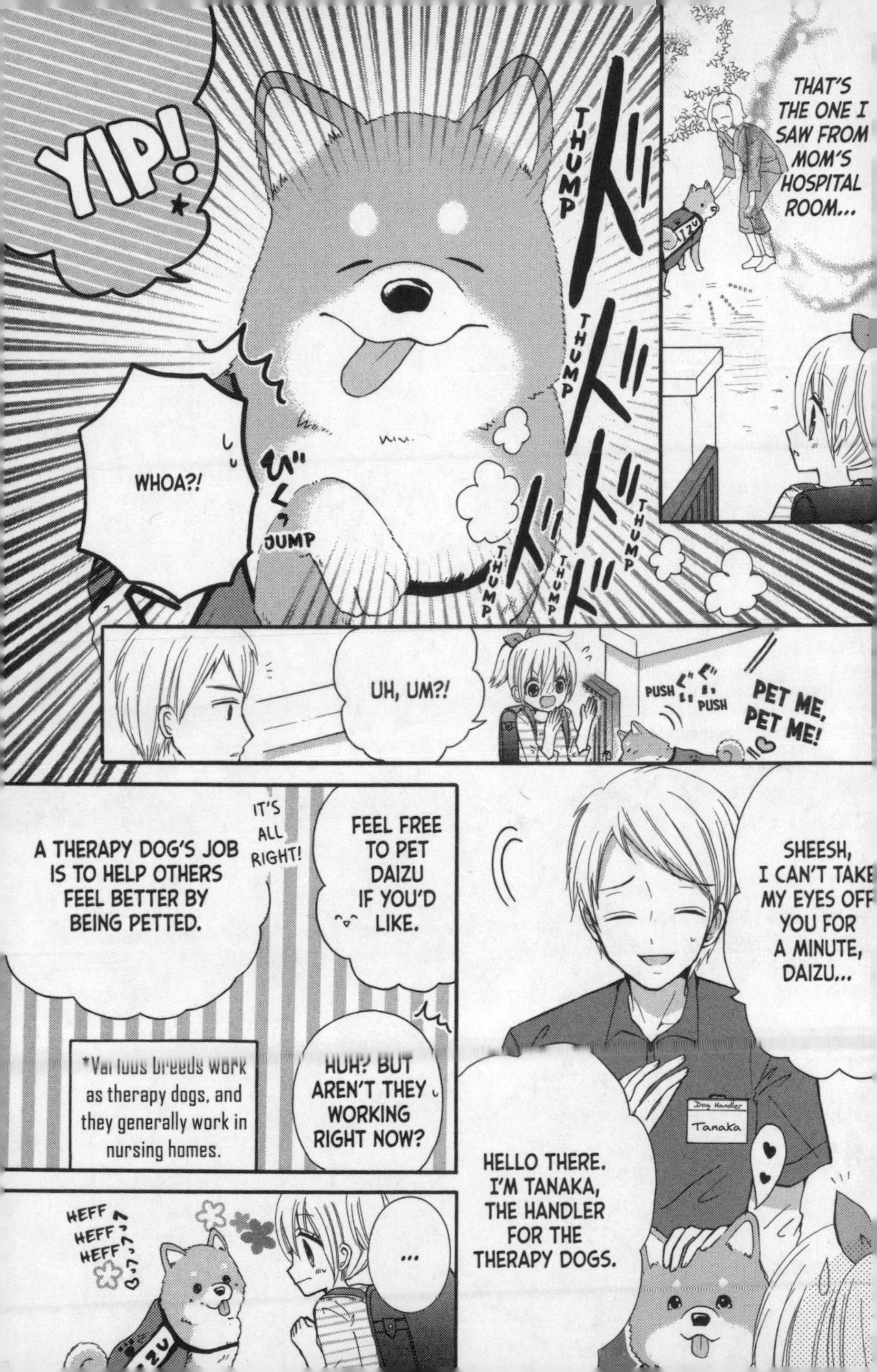
THAT'S THE ONE I SAW FROM MOM'S HOSPITAL ROOM...
THUMP THUMP THUMP THUMP THUMP
YIP!★
WHOA?!
JUMP
PET ME, PET ME!
PUSH PUSH
UH, UM?!
SHEESH, I CAN'T TAKE MY EYES OFF YOU FOR A MINUTE, DAIZU...
HELLO THERE. I'M TANAKA, THE HANDLER FOR THE THERAPY DOGS.
Dog Handler
Tanaka
IT'S ALL RIGHT!
FEEL FREE TO PET DAIZU IF YOU'D LIKE.
A THERAPY DOG'S JOB IS TO HELP OTHERS FEEL BETTER BY BEING PETTED.
HUH? BUT AREN'T THEY WORKING RIGHT NOW?
*Various breeds work as therapy dogs, and they generally work in nursing homes.
...
HEFF HEFF HEFF

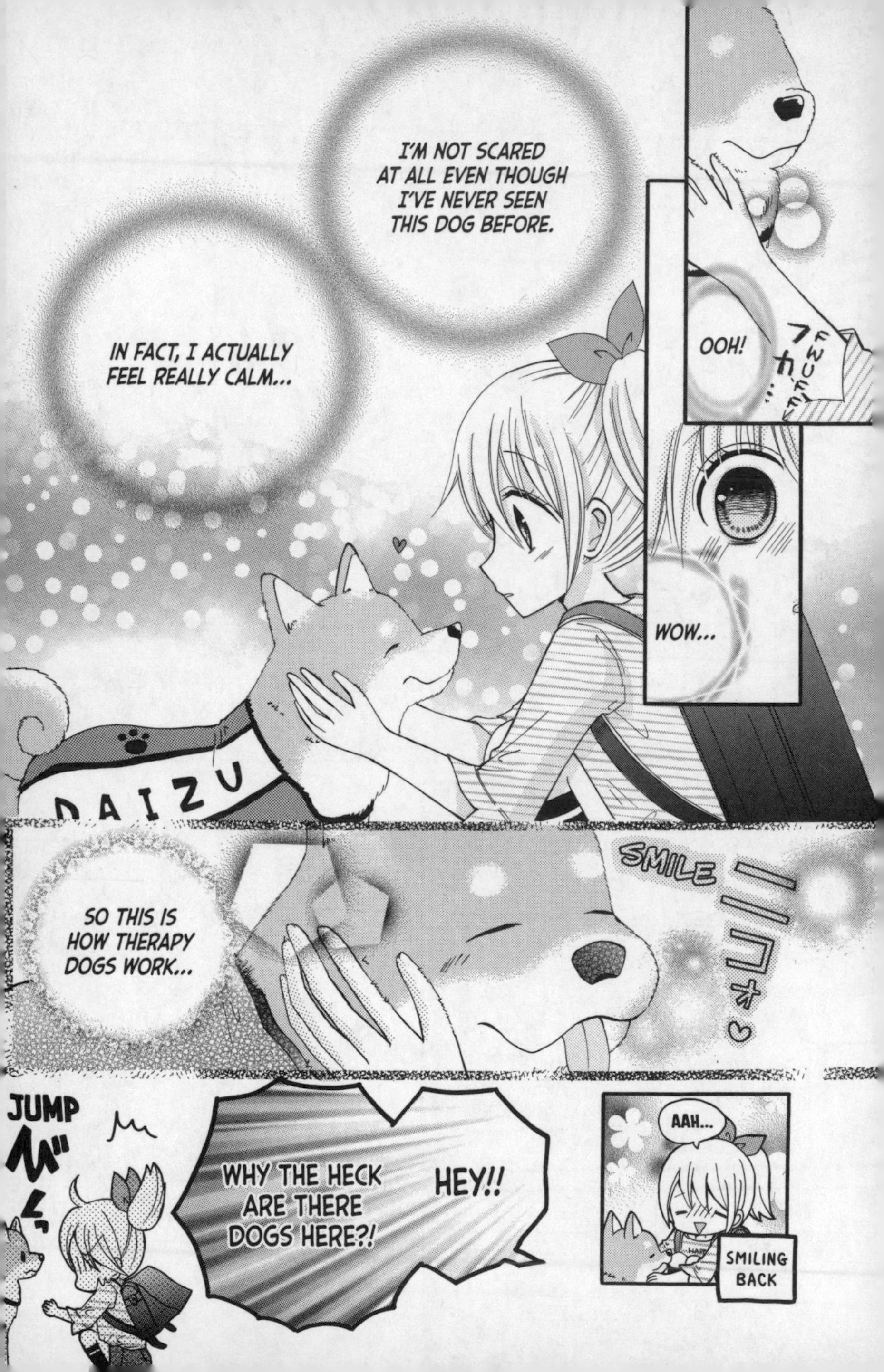
OOH!
FWUFF
WOW...
I'M NOT SCARED AT ALL EVEN THOUGH I'VE NEVER SEEN THIS DOG BEFORE.
IN FACT, I ACTUALLY FEEL REALLY CALM...
DAIZU
SMILE
SO THIS IS HOW THERAPY DOGS WORK...
AAH...
SMILING BACK
HEY!!
WHY THE HECK ARE THERE DOGS HERE?!
JUMP

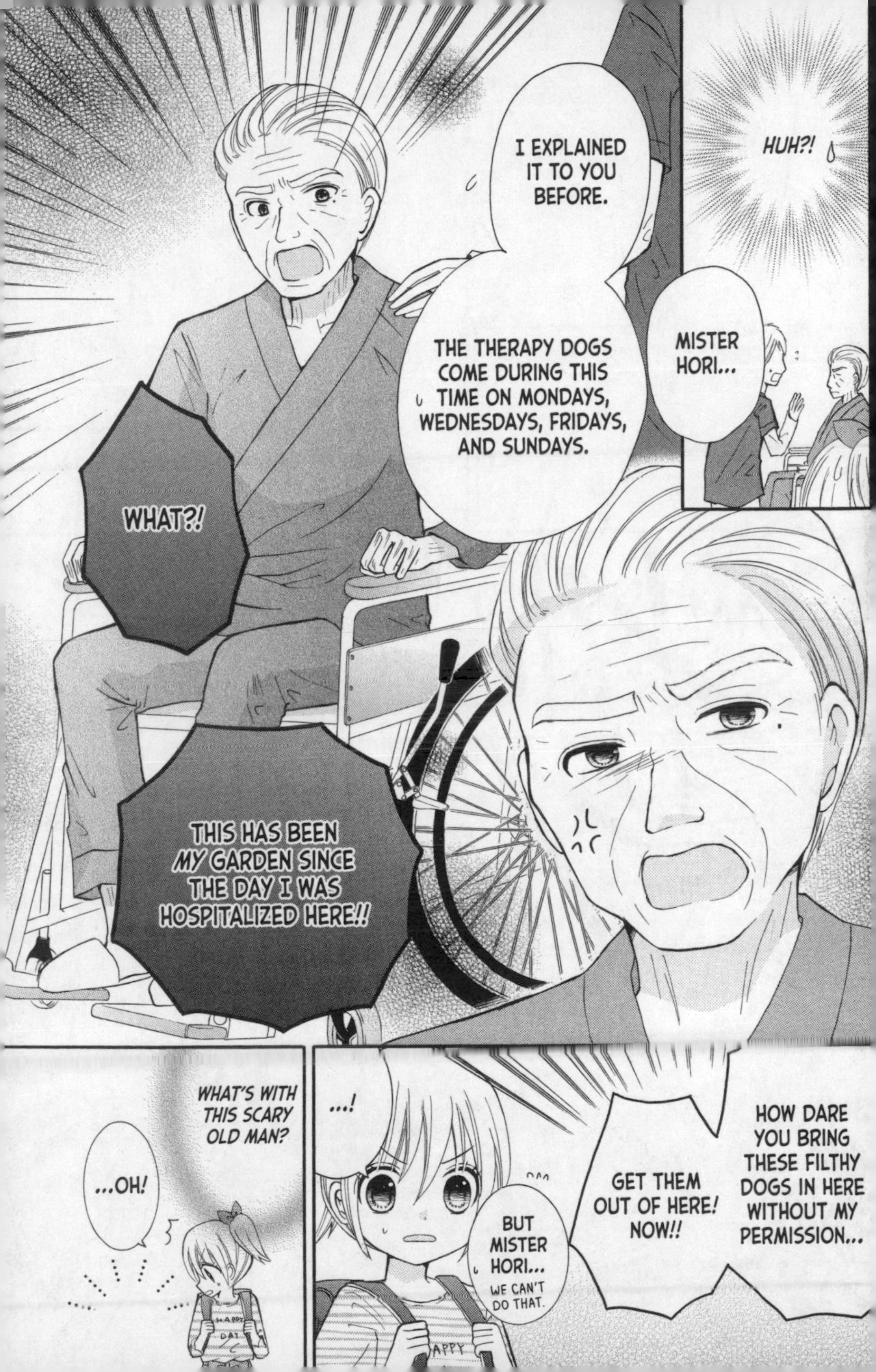
HUH?!
MISTER HORI...
I EXPLAINED IT TO YOU BEFORE.
THE THERAPY DOGS COME DURING THIS TIME ON MONDAYS, WEDNESDAYS, FRIDAYS, AND SUNDAYS.
WHAT?!
THIS HAS BEEN *MY* GARDEN SINCE THE DAY I WAS HOSPITALIZED HERE!!
HOW DARE YOU BRING THESE FILTHY DOGS IN HERE WITHOUT MY PERMISSION...
GET THEM OUT OF HERE! NOW!!
...!
BUT MISTER HORI... WE CAN'T DO THAT.
WHAT'S WITH THIS SCARY OLD MAN?
...OH!

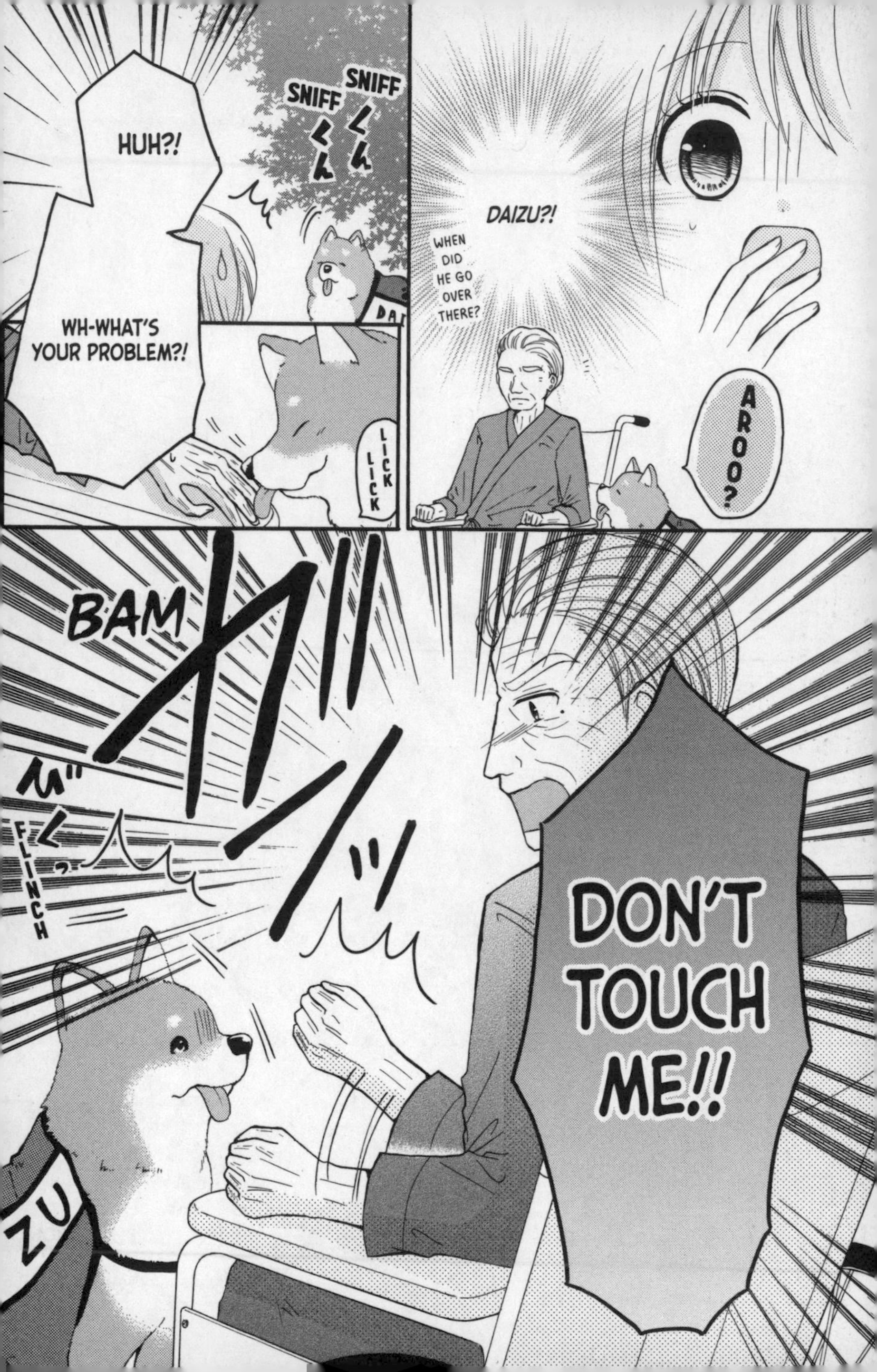
DAIZU?!
WHEN DID HE GO OVER THERE?
AROO?
SNIFF
SNIFF
HUH?!
WH-WHAT'S YOUR PROBLEM?!
LICK LICK
DON'T TOUCH ME!!
BAM
FLINCH

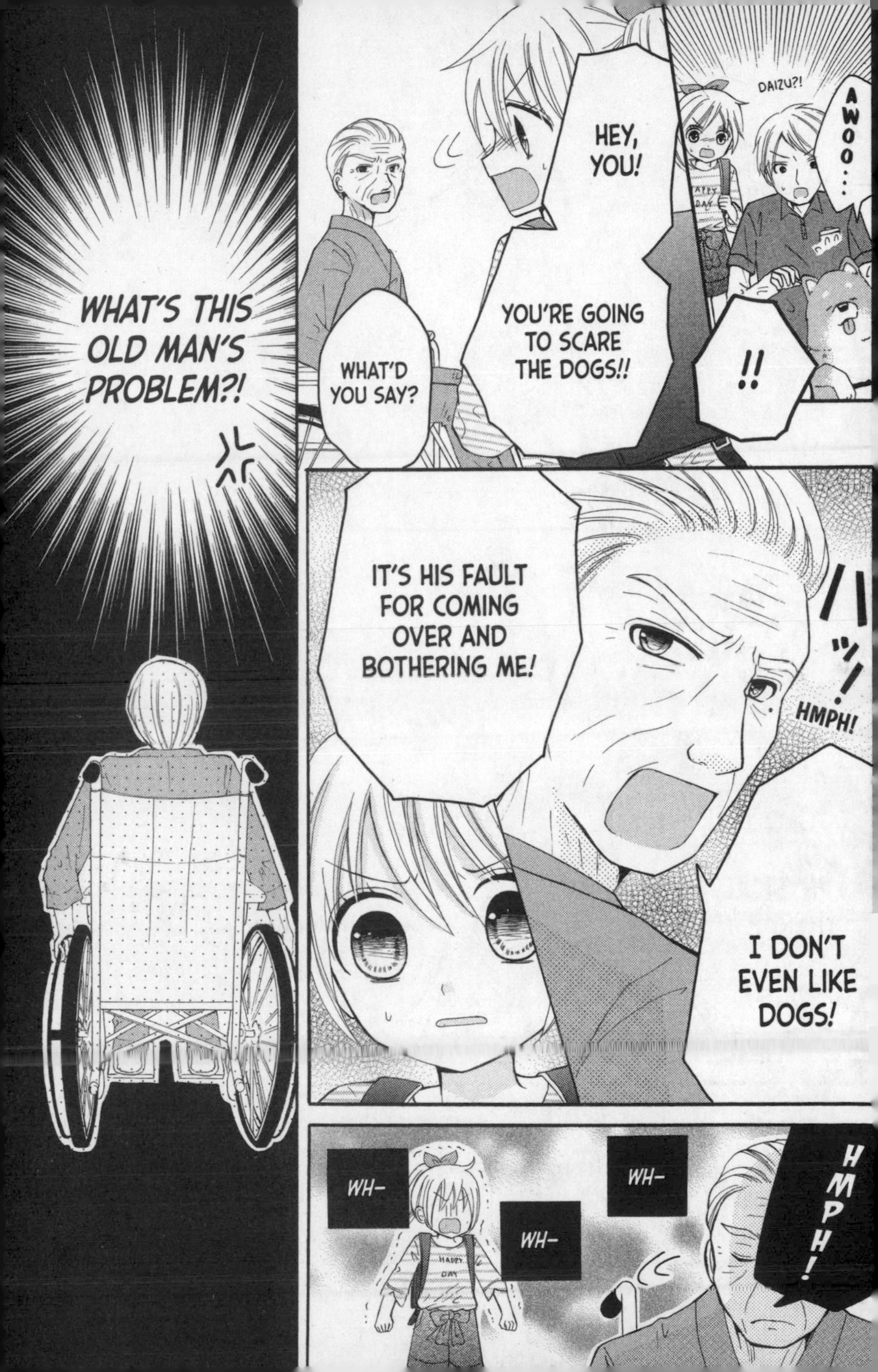
DAIZU?!
AWOO...
!!
HEY, YOU!
YOU'RE GOING TO SCARE THE DOGS!!
WHAT'D YOU SAY?
IT'S HIS FAULT FOR COMING OVER AND BOTHERING ME!
HMPH!
I DON'T EVEN LIKE DOGS!
HMPH!
WH-
WH-
WH-
WHAT'S THIS OLD MAN'S PROBLEM?!

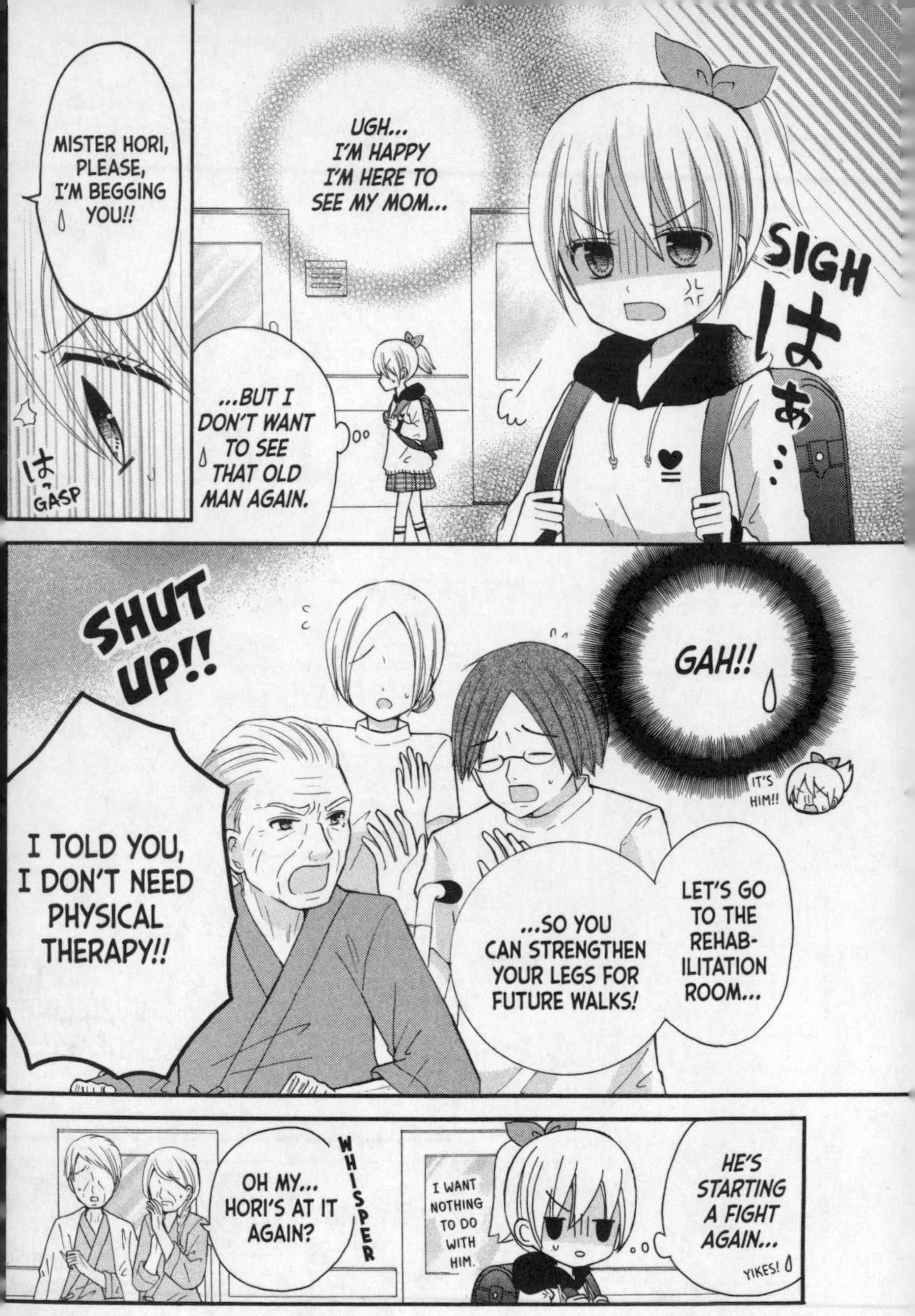
UGH... I'M HAPPY I'M HERE TO SEE MY MOM...
SIGH はぁ…
...BUT I DON'T WANT TO SEE THAT OLD MAN AGAIN.
MISTER HORI, PLEASE, I'M BEGGING YOU!!
はっ GASP
GAH!!
IT'S HIM!!
LET'S GO TO THE REHAB-ILITATION ROOM...
...SO YOU CAN STRENGTHEN YOUR LEGS FOR FUTURE WALKS!
SHUT UP!!
I TOLD YOU, I DON'T NEED PHYSICAL THERAPY!!
HE'S STARTING A FIGHT AGAIN...
YIKES!
I WANT NOTHING TO DO WITH HIM.
WHISPER
OH MY... HORI'S AT IT AGAIN?

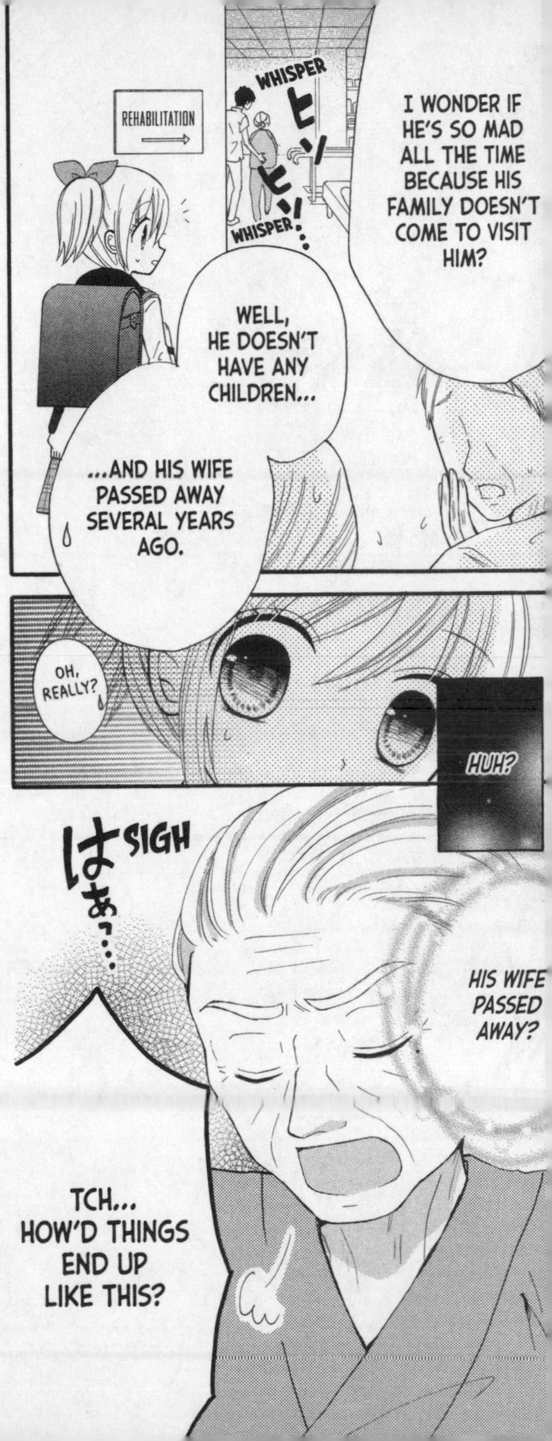
REHABILITATION
I WONDER IF HE'S SO MAD ALL THE TIME BECAUSE HIS FAMILY DOESN'T COME TO VISIT HIM?
WHISPER
WHISPER...
WELL, HE DOESN'T HAVE ANY CHILDREN...
...AND HIS WIFE PASSED AWAY SEVERAL YEARS AGO.
OH, REALLY?
HUH?
HIS WIFE PASSED AWAY?
SIGH
TCH... HOW'D THINGS END UP LIKE THIS?

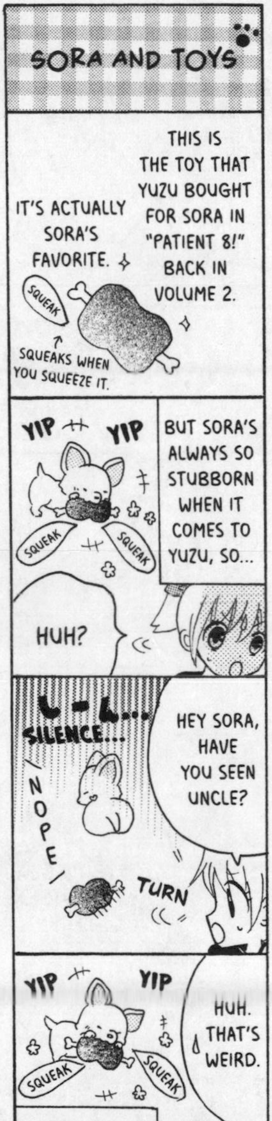
SORA AND TOYS
THIS IS THE TOY THAT YUZU BOUGHT FOR SORA IN "PATIENT 8!" BACK IN VOLUME 2.
IT'S ACTUALLY SORA'S FAVORITE.
SQUEAK
SQUEAKS WHEN YOU SQUEEZE IT.
BUT SORA'S ALWAYS SO STUBBORN WHEN IT COMES TO YUZU, SO...
YIP YIP
SQUEAK
SQUEAK
HUH?
HEY SORA, HAVE YOU SEEN UNCLE?
SILENCE...
NOPE
TURN
HUH. THAT'S WEIRD.
YIP YIP
SQUEAK
SQUEAK
I WONDER WHERE HE WENT.
SORA'S ALWAYS PRETENDING TO ACT INDIFFERENT AROUND YUZU.

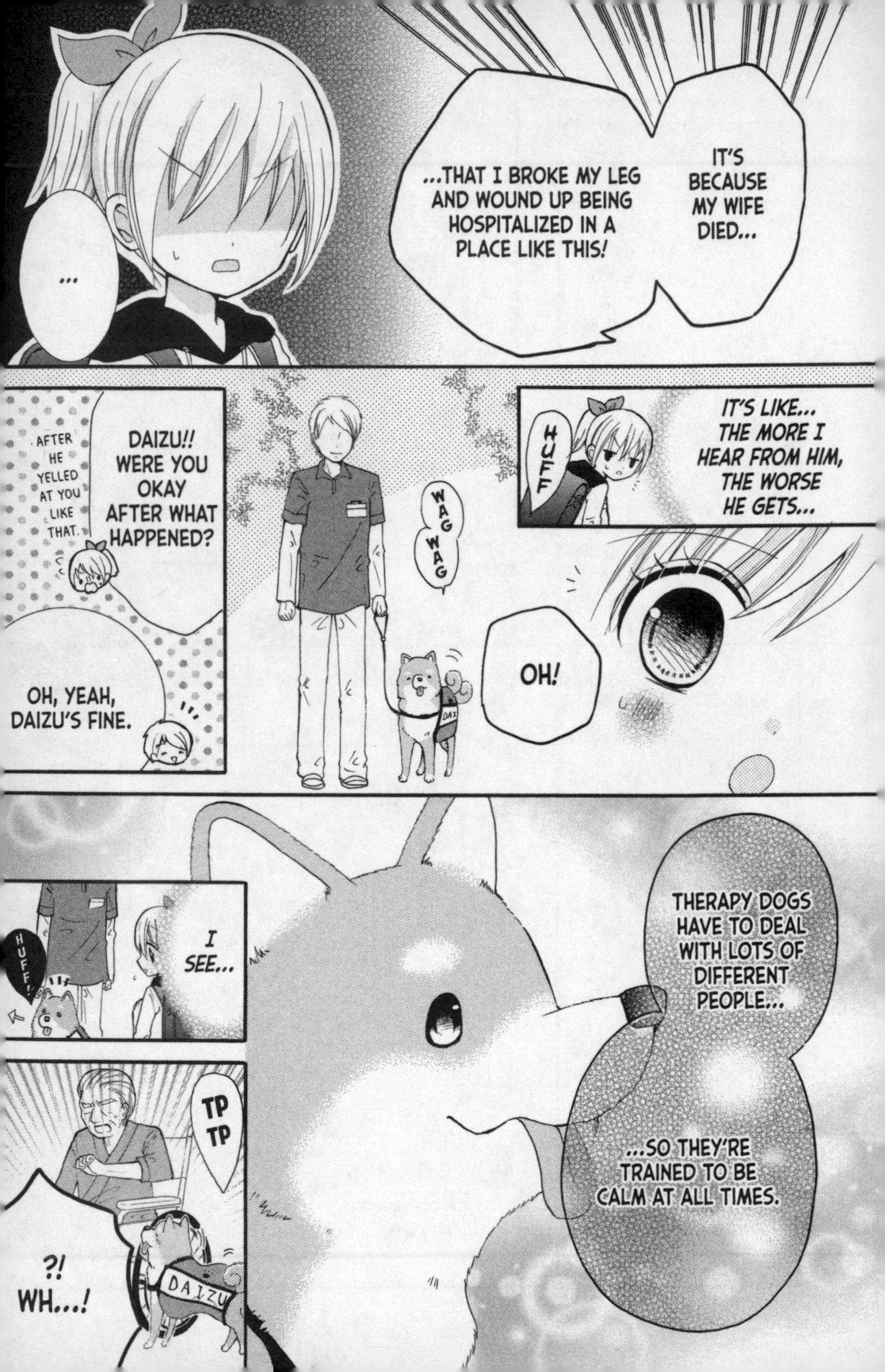
IT'S BECAUSE MY WIFE DIED...
...THAT I BROKE MY LEG AND WOUND UP BEING HOSPITALIZED IN A PLACE LIKE THIS!
...
HUFF
IT'S LIKE... THE MORE I HEAR FROM HIM, THE WORSE HE GETS...
OH!
WAG WAG
DAIZU!! WERE YOU OKAY AFTER WHAT HAPPENED?
AFTER HE YELLED AT YOU LIKE THAT.
OH, YEAH, DAIZU'S FINE.
THERAPY DOGS HAVE TO DEAL WITH LOTS OF DIFFERENT PEOPLE...
...SO THEY'RE TRAINED TO BE CALM AT ALL TIMES.
I SEE...
HUFF!
TP TP
?! WH...!
DAIZU

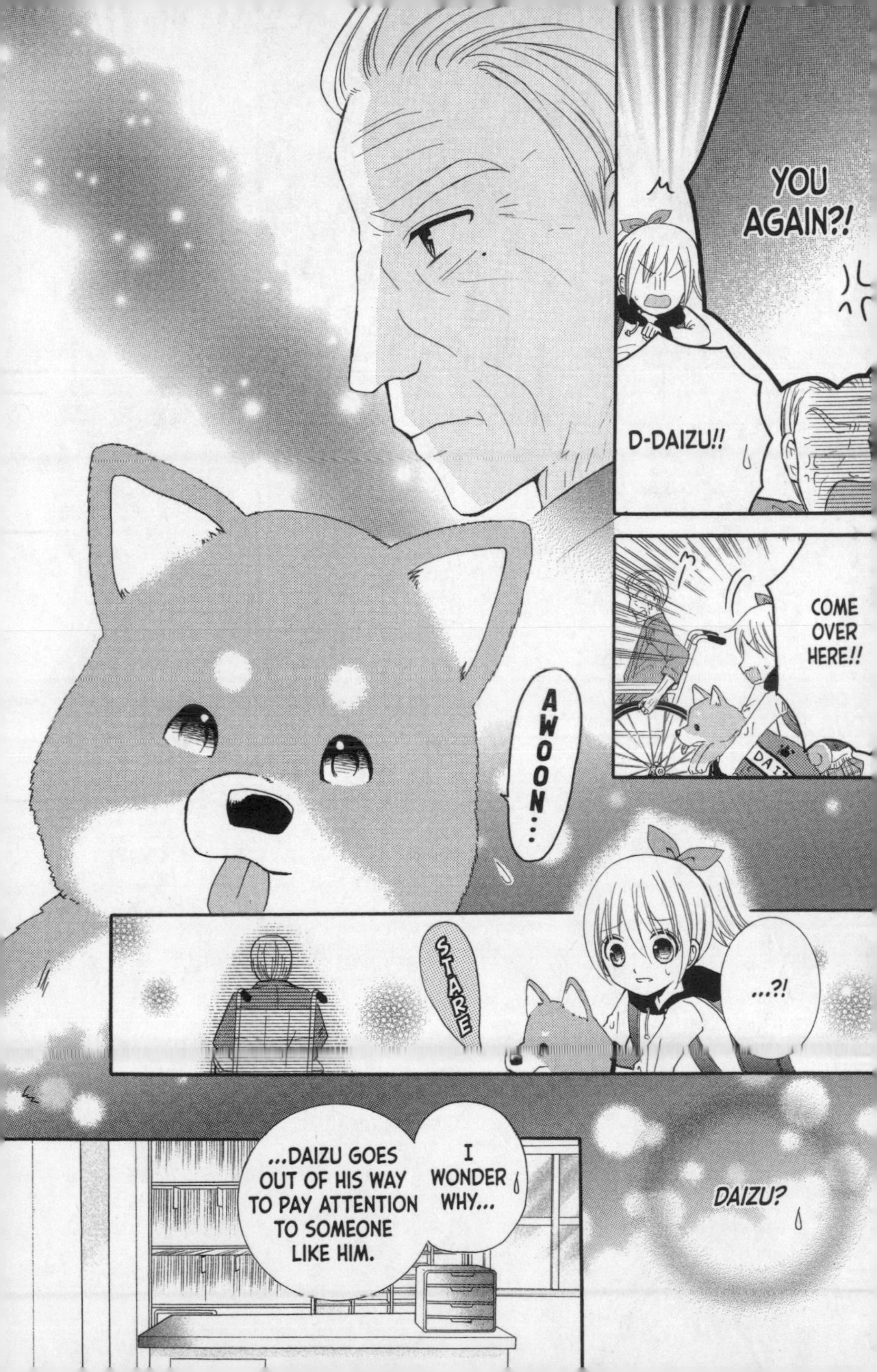
YOU AGAIN?!
D-DAIZU!!
COME OVER HERE!!
AWOON...
...?!
STARE
DAIZU?
I WONDER WHY...
...DAIZU GOES OUT OF HIS WAY TO PAY ATTENTION TO SOMEONE LIKE HIM.

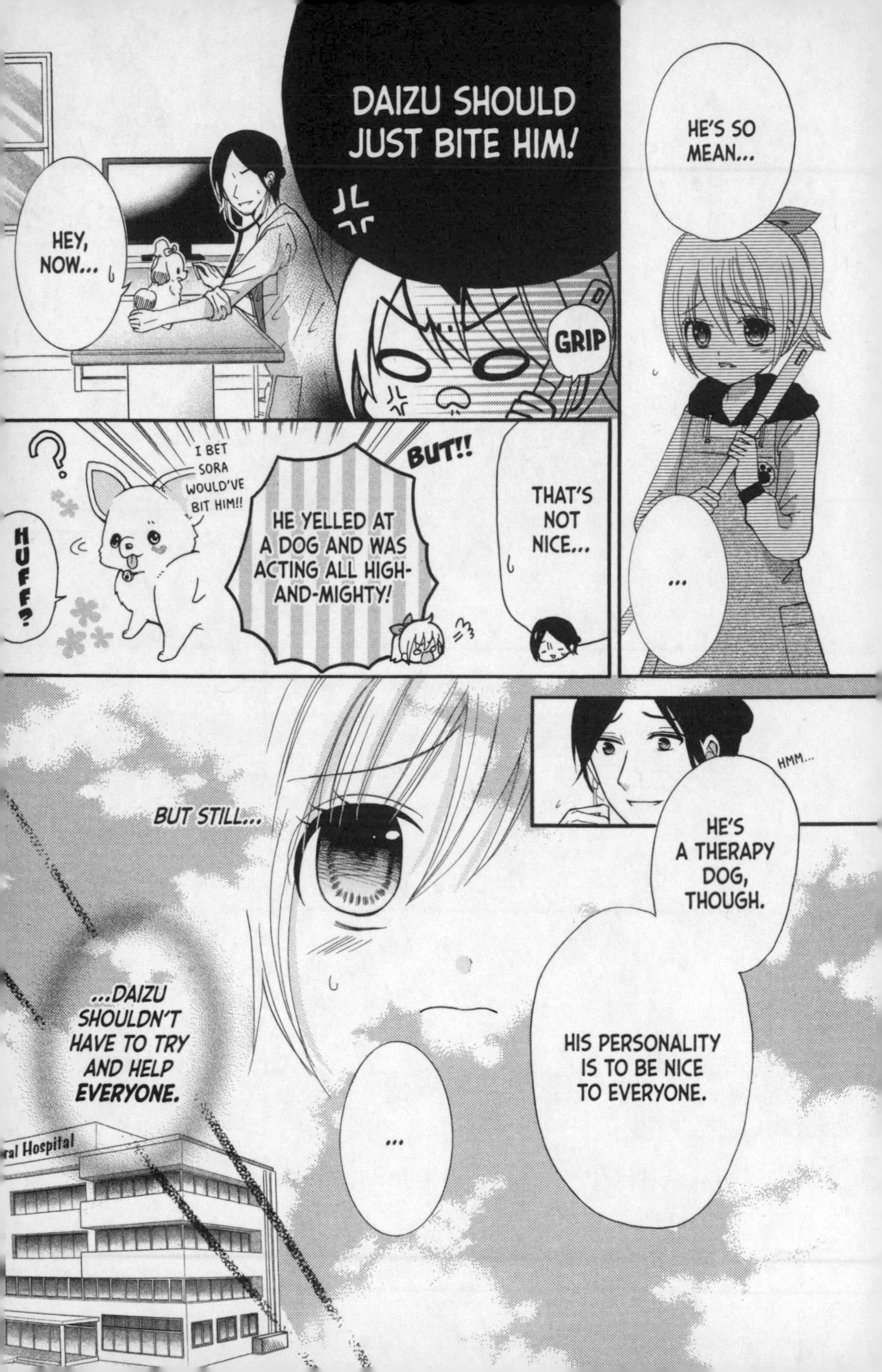
HE'S SO MEAN...
...
DAIZU SHOULD JUST BITE HIM!
GRIP
HEY, NOW...
THAT'S NOT NICE...
BUT!!
HE YELLED AT A DOG AND WAS ACTING ALL HIGH-AND-MIGHTY!
I BET SORA WOULD'VE BIT HIM!!
HUFF?
HMM...
HE'S A THERAPY DOG, THOUGH.
HIS PERSONALITY IS TO BE NICE TO EVERYONE.
...
BUT STILL...
...DAIZU SHOULDN'T HAVE TO TRY AND HELP EVERYONE.
ral Hospital

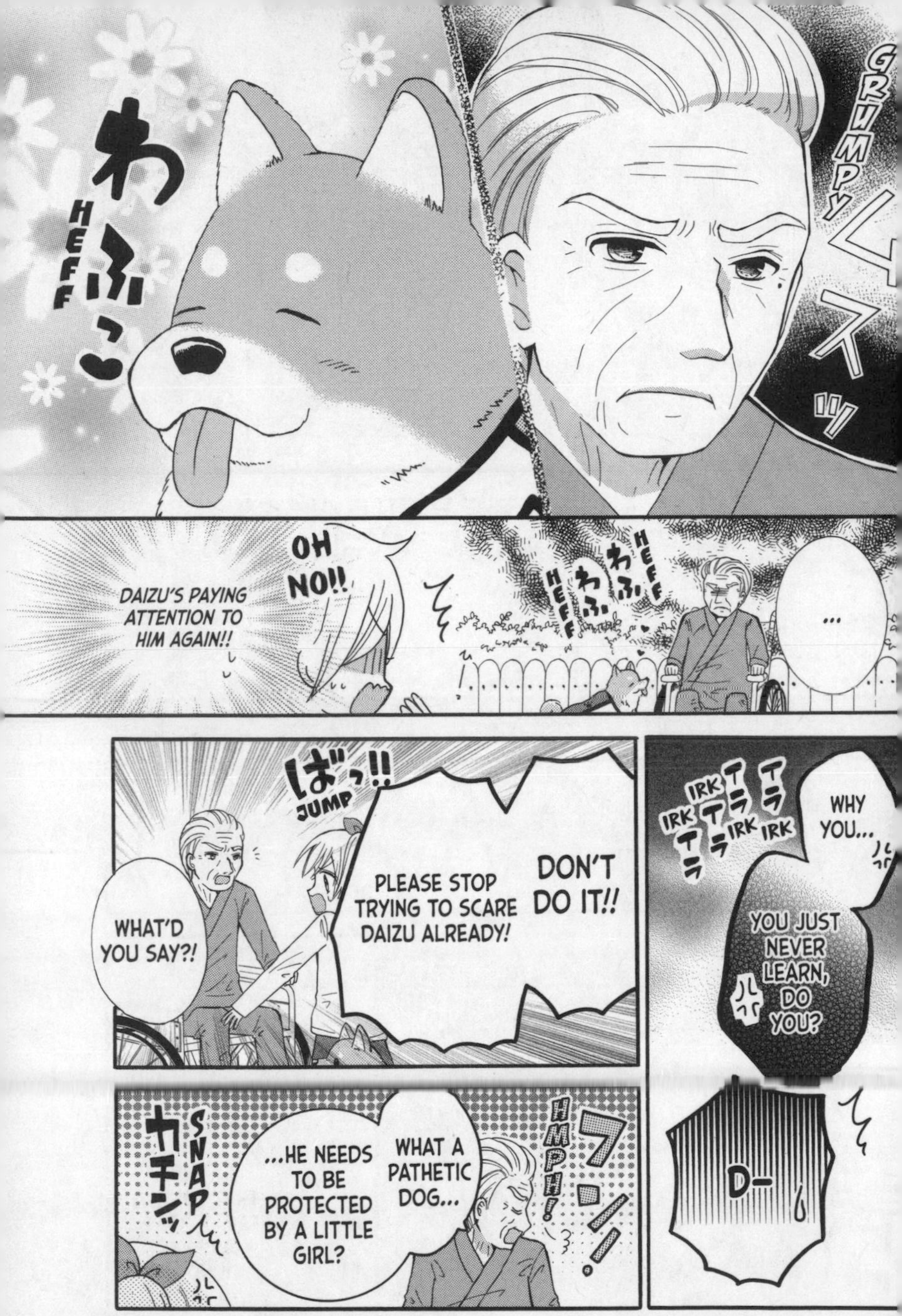
ムスッ
GRUMPY
わふっ
HEFF
...
わふ わふ
HEFF HEFF
OH NO!!
DAIZU'S PAYING ATTENTION TO HIM AGAIN!!
イラ イラ イラ イラ
IRK IRK IRK IRK
WHY YOU...
YOU JUST NEVER LEARN, DO YOU?
D-
ばっ!!
JUMP
DON'T DO IT!!
PLEASE STOP TRYING TO SCARE DAIZU ALREADY!
WHAT'D YOU SAY?!
フンッ
HMPH!
WHAT A PATHETIC DOG...
...HE NEEDS TO BE PROTECTED BY A LITTLE GIRL?
カチンッ
SNAP

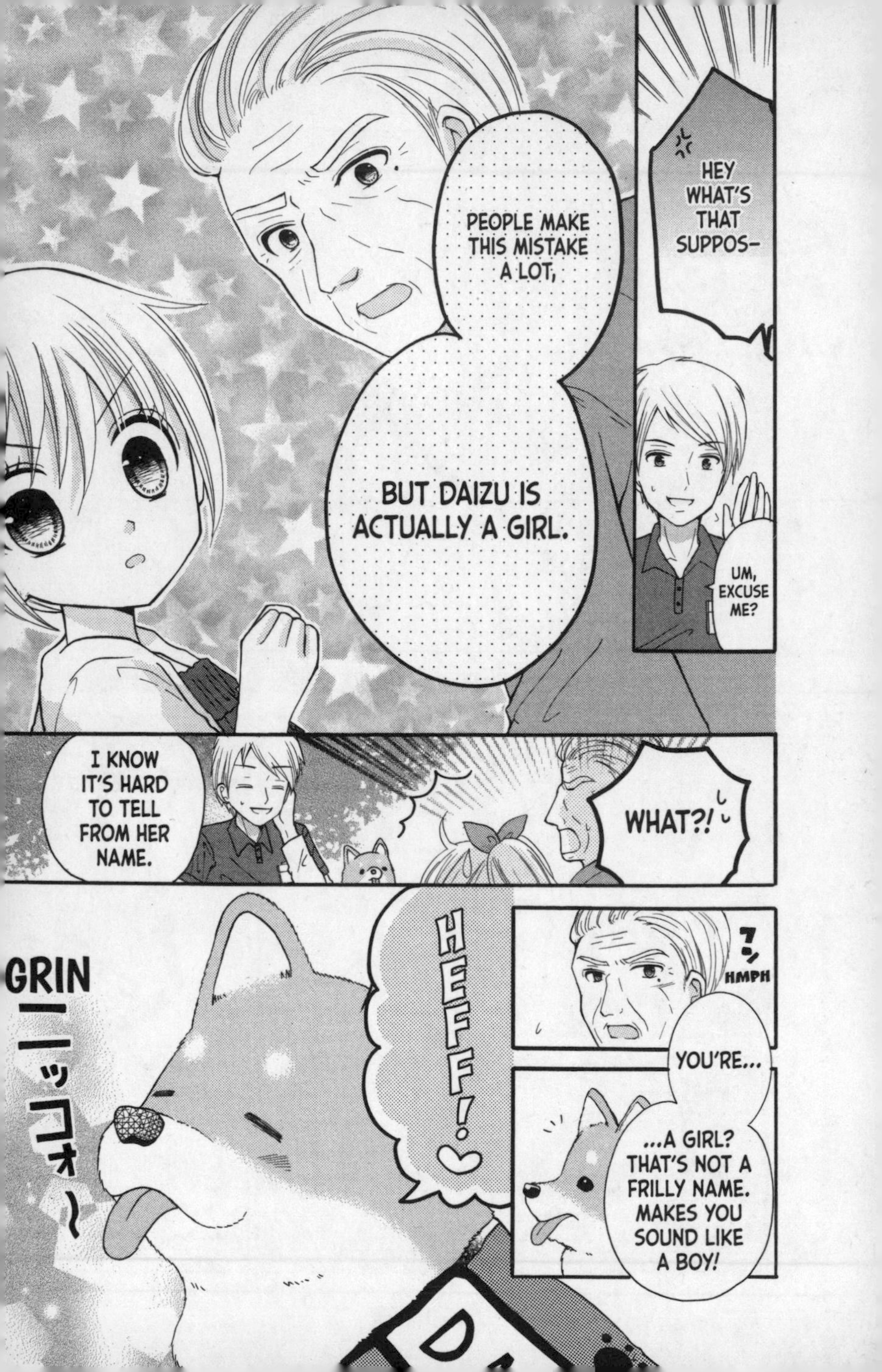
HEY WHAT'S THAT SUPPOS-
UM, EXCUSE ME?
PEOPLE MAKE THIS MISTAKE A LOT,
BUT DAIZU IS ACTUALLY A GIRL.
WHAT?!
I KNOW IT'S HARD TO TELL FROM HER NAME.
HMPH
YOU'RE...
...A GIRL? THAT'S NOT A FRILLY NAME. MAKES YOU SOUND LIKE A BOY!
HEFF!
GRIN
ニッコォ～

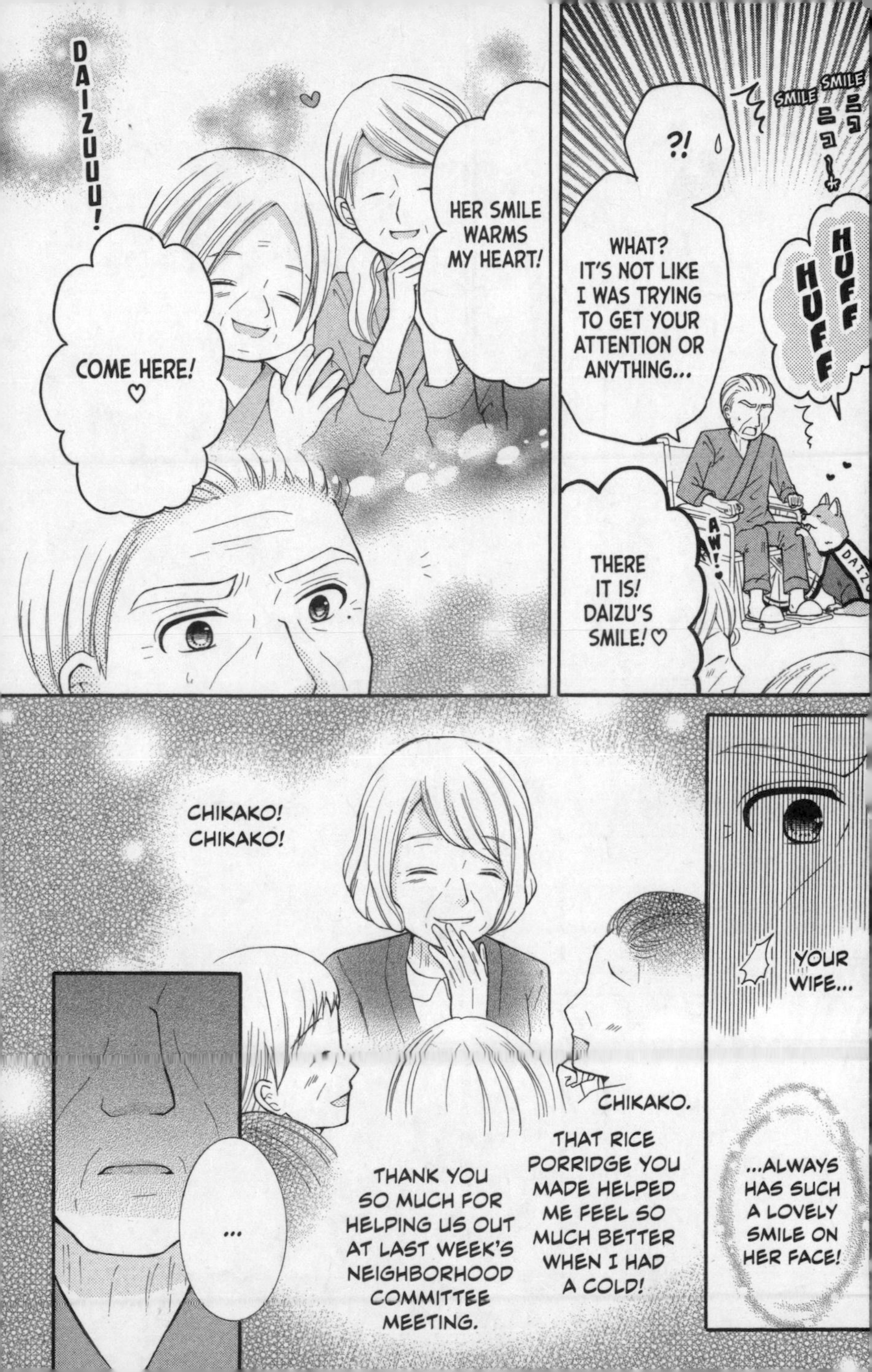
SMILE SMILE
?!
HUFF HUFF HUFF
WHAT? IT'S NOT LIKE I WAS TRYING TO GET YOUR ATTENTION OR ANYTHING...
AW! ♥
DAIZU
THERE IT IS! DAIZU'S SMILE! ♡
DAIZUUUU!
HER SMILE WARMS MY HEART!
COME HERE! ♡
YOUR WIFE...
...ALWAYS HAS SUCH A LOVELY SMILE ON HER FACE!
CHIKAKO! CHIKAKO!
CHIKAKO.
THAT RICE PORRIDGE YOU MADE HELPED ME FEEL SO MUCH BETTER WHEN I HAD A COLD!
THANK YOU SO MUCH FOR HELPING US OUT AT LAST WEEK'S NEIGHBORHOOD COMMITTEE MEETING.
...

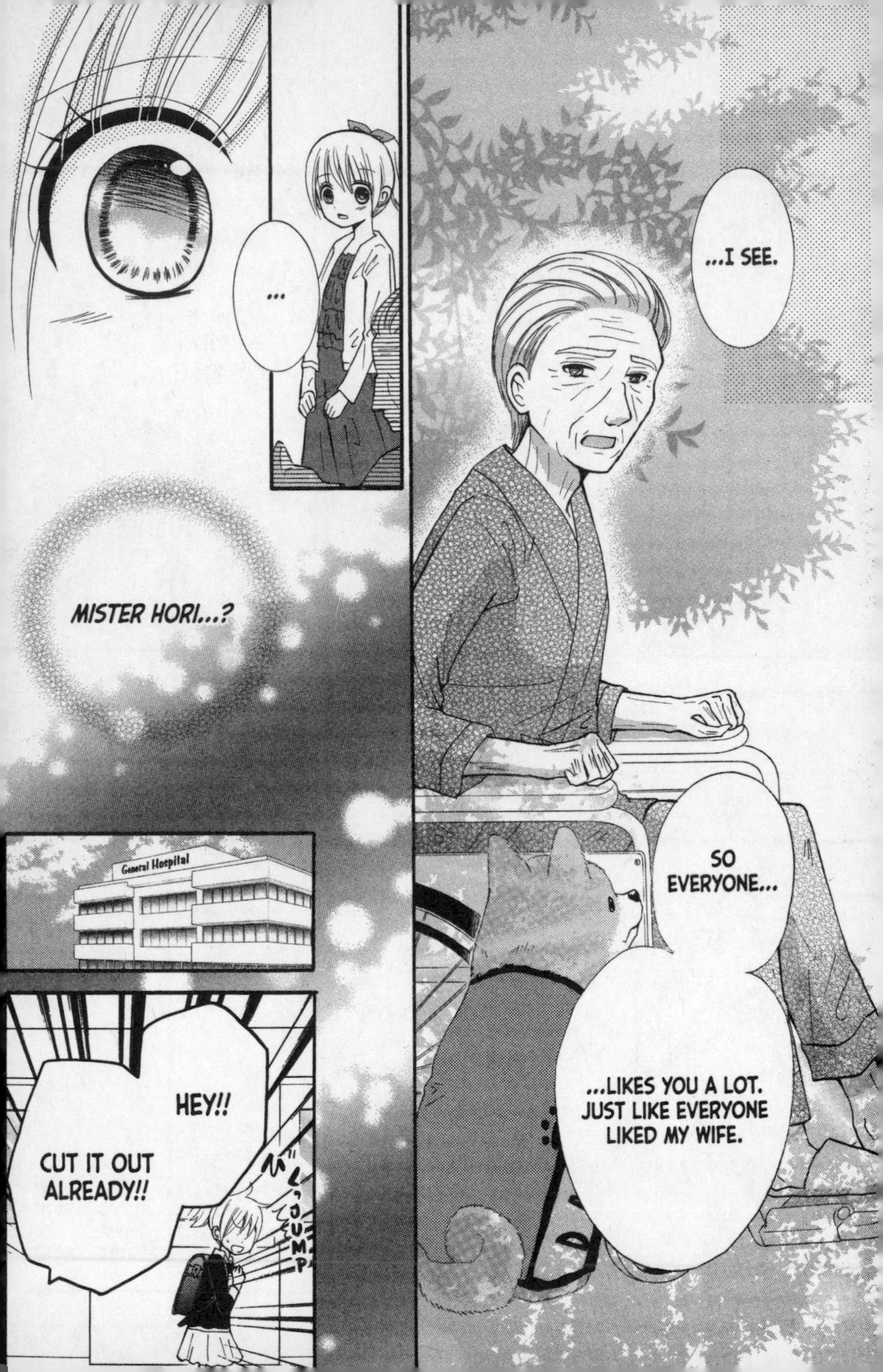
...I SEE.
SO EVERYONE...
...LIKES YOU A LOT. JUST LIKE EVERYONE LIKED MY WIFE.
...
MISTER HORI...?
General Hospital
HEY!!
CUT IT OUT ALREADY!!
JUMP

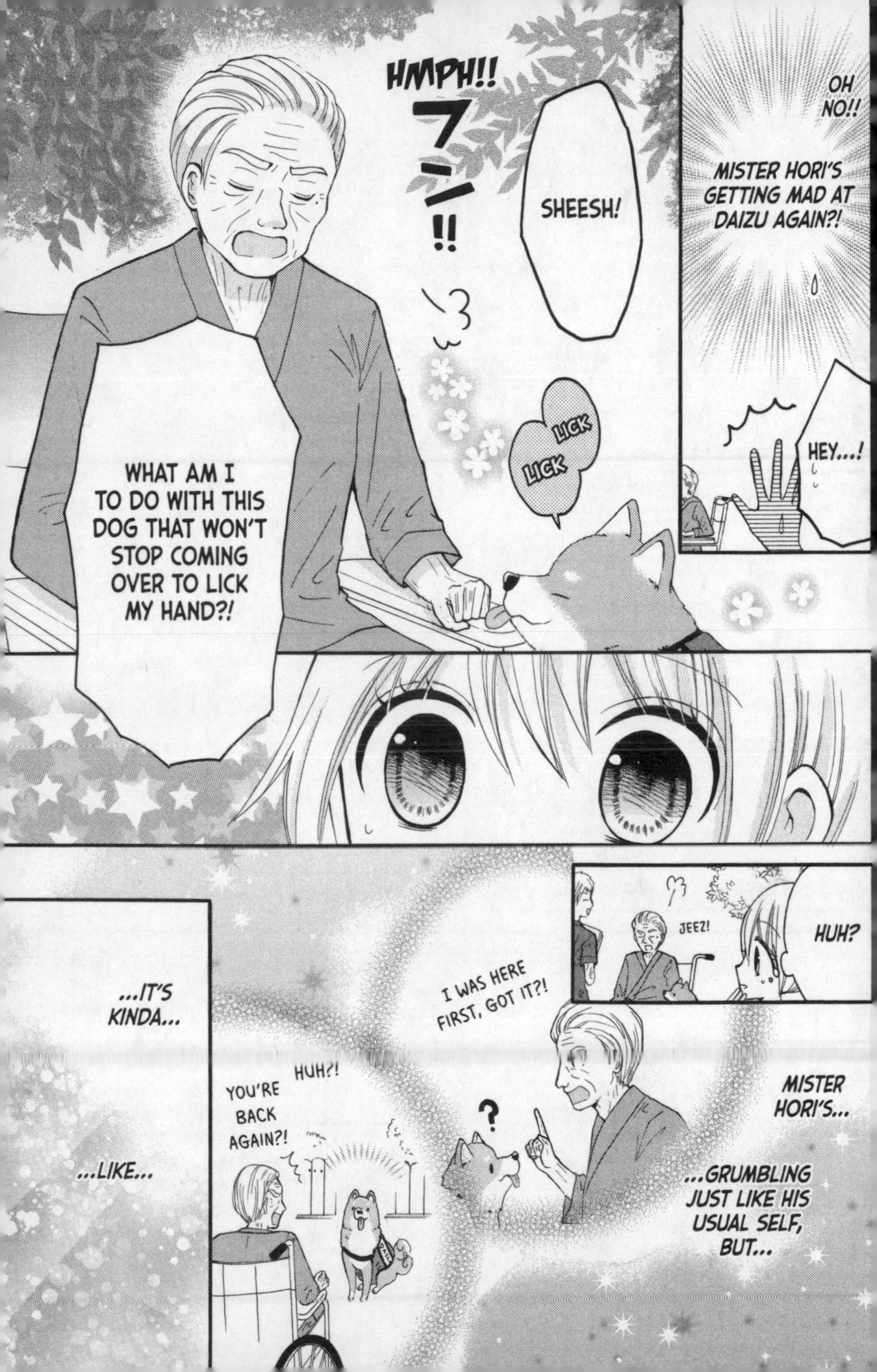
OH NO!!
MISTER HORI'S GETTING MAD AT DAIZU AGAIN?!
HEY...!
HMPH!!
SHEESH!
LICK LICK
WHAT AM I TO DO WITH THIS DOG THAT WON'T STOP COMING OVER TO LICK MY HAND?!
HUH?
JEEZ!
MISTER HORI'S...
...GRUMBLING JUST LIKE HIS USUAL SELF, BUT...
I WAS HERE FIRST, GOT IT?!
HUH?!
YOU'RE BACK AGAIN?!
...IT'S KINDA...
...LIKE...

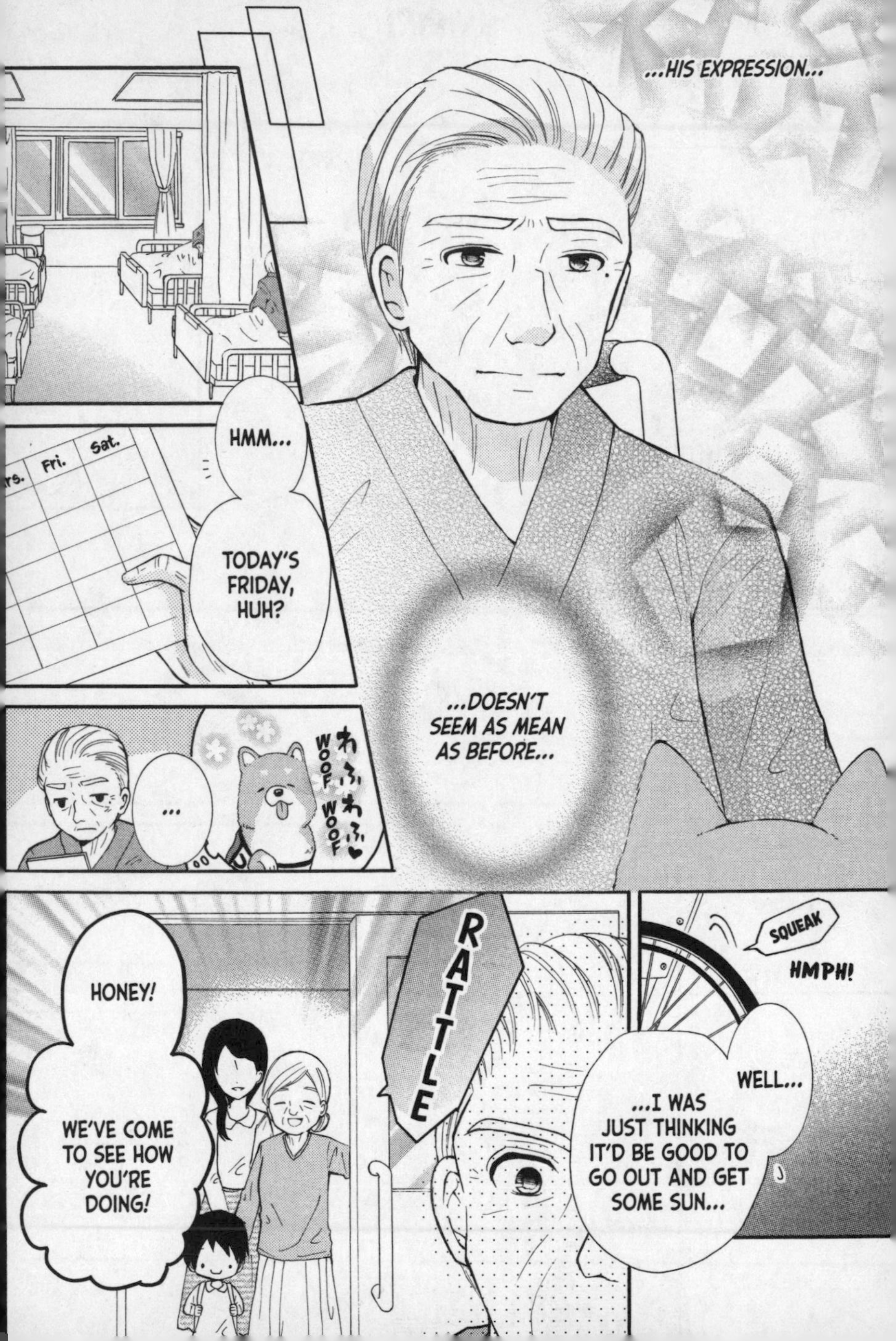
...HIS EXPRESSION...
...DOESN'T SEEM AS MEAN AS BEFORE...
Fri.
Sat.
HMM...
TODAY'S FRIDAY, HUH?
わふわふ
WOOF WOOF
...
SQUEAK
HMPH!
WELL...
...I WAS JUST THINKING IT'D BE GOOD TO GO OUT AND GET SOME SUN...
RATTLE
HONEY!
WE'VE COME TO SEE HOW YOU'RE DOING!

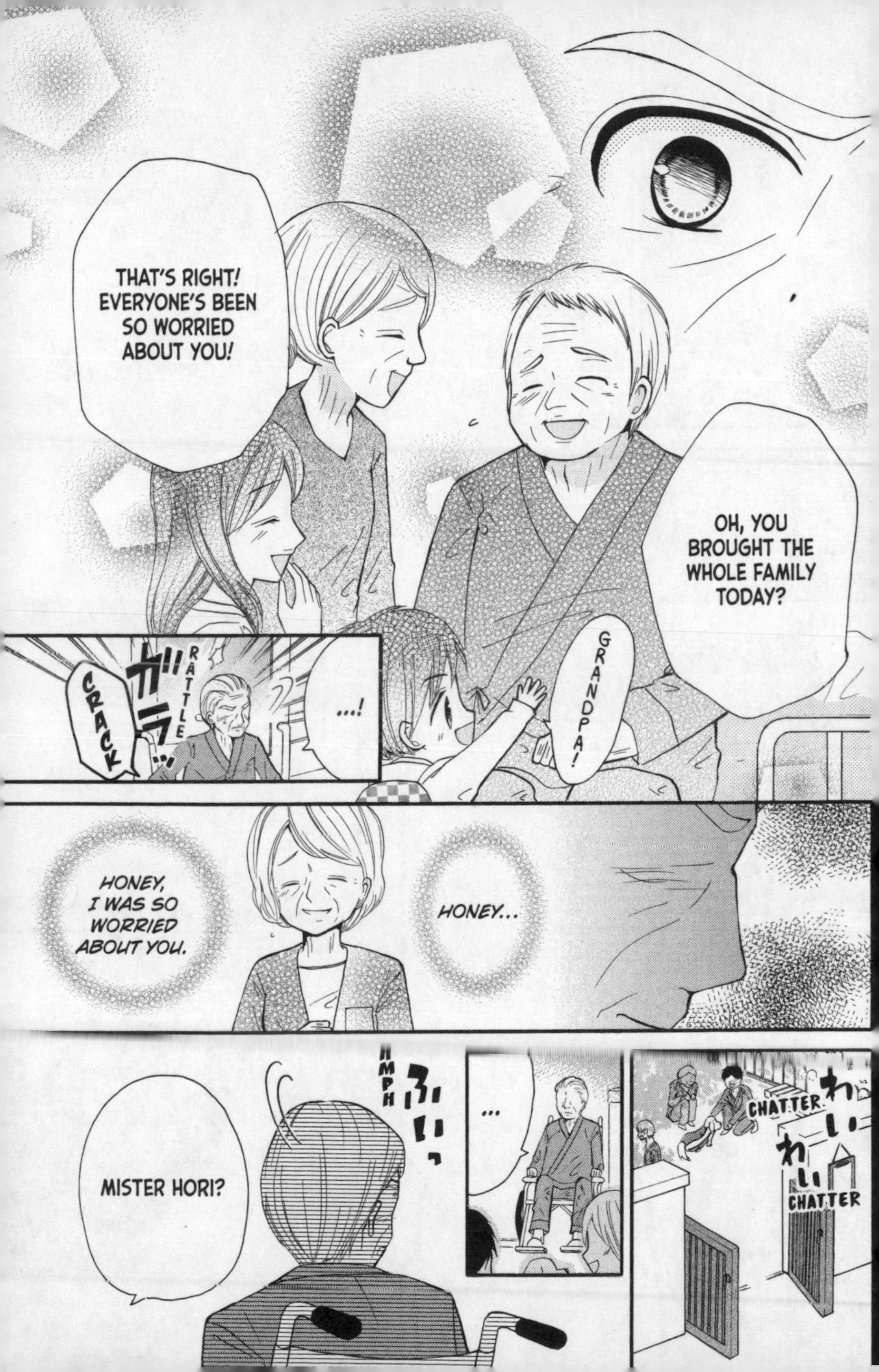
OH, YOU BROUGHT THE WHOLE FAMILY TODAY?
THAT'S RIGHT! EVERYONE'S BEEN SO WORRIED ABOUT YOU!
GRANDPA!
ガラッ
RATTLE
CRACK
...!
HONEY...
HONEY, I WAS SO WORRIED ABOUT YOU.
わいわい
CHATTER
わい
CHATTER
...
ふいっ
HMPH
MISTER HORI?

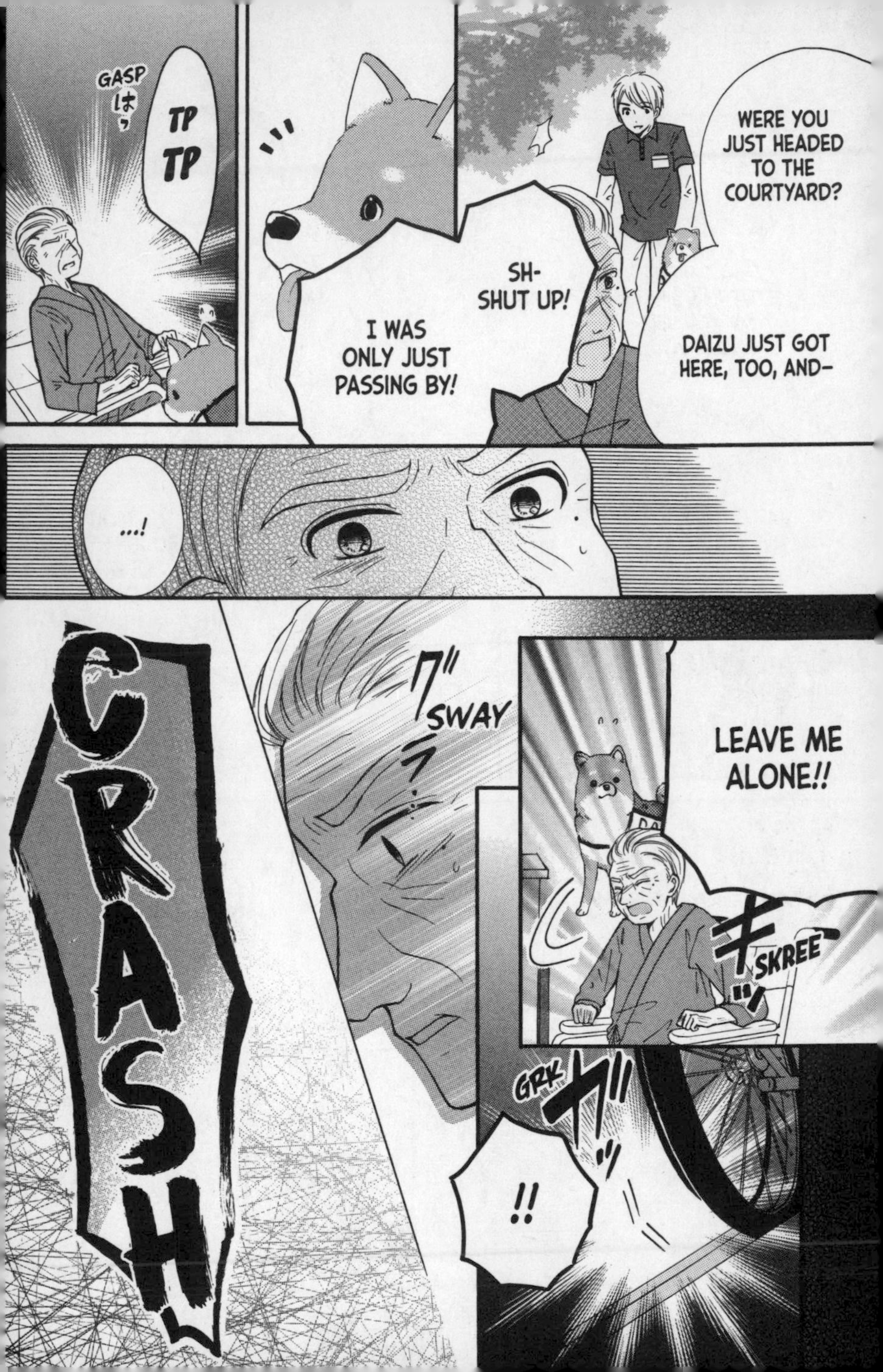
WERE YOU JUST HEADED TO THE COURTYARD?
DAIZU JUST GOT HERE, TOO, AND—
SH- SHUT UP!
I WAS ONLY JUST PASSING BY!
GASP はっ
TP TP
...!
LEAVE ME ALONE!!
キー SKREE
ガッ GRK
!!
グラ SWAY
CRASH

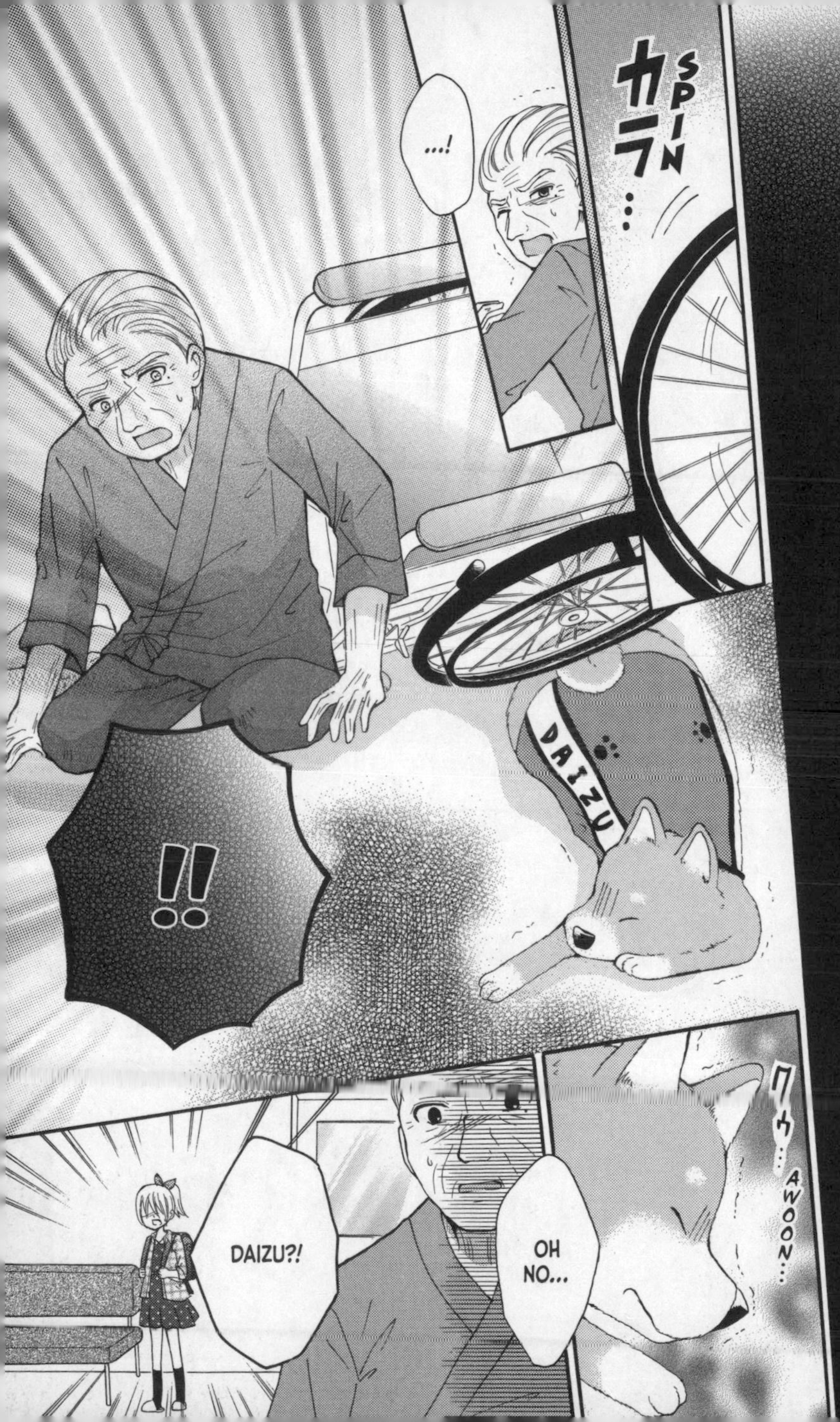
カラ… SPIN
...!
!!
DAIZU
ワゥ… AWOOON...
OH NO...
DAIZU?!

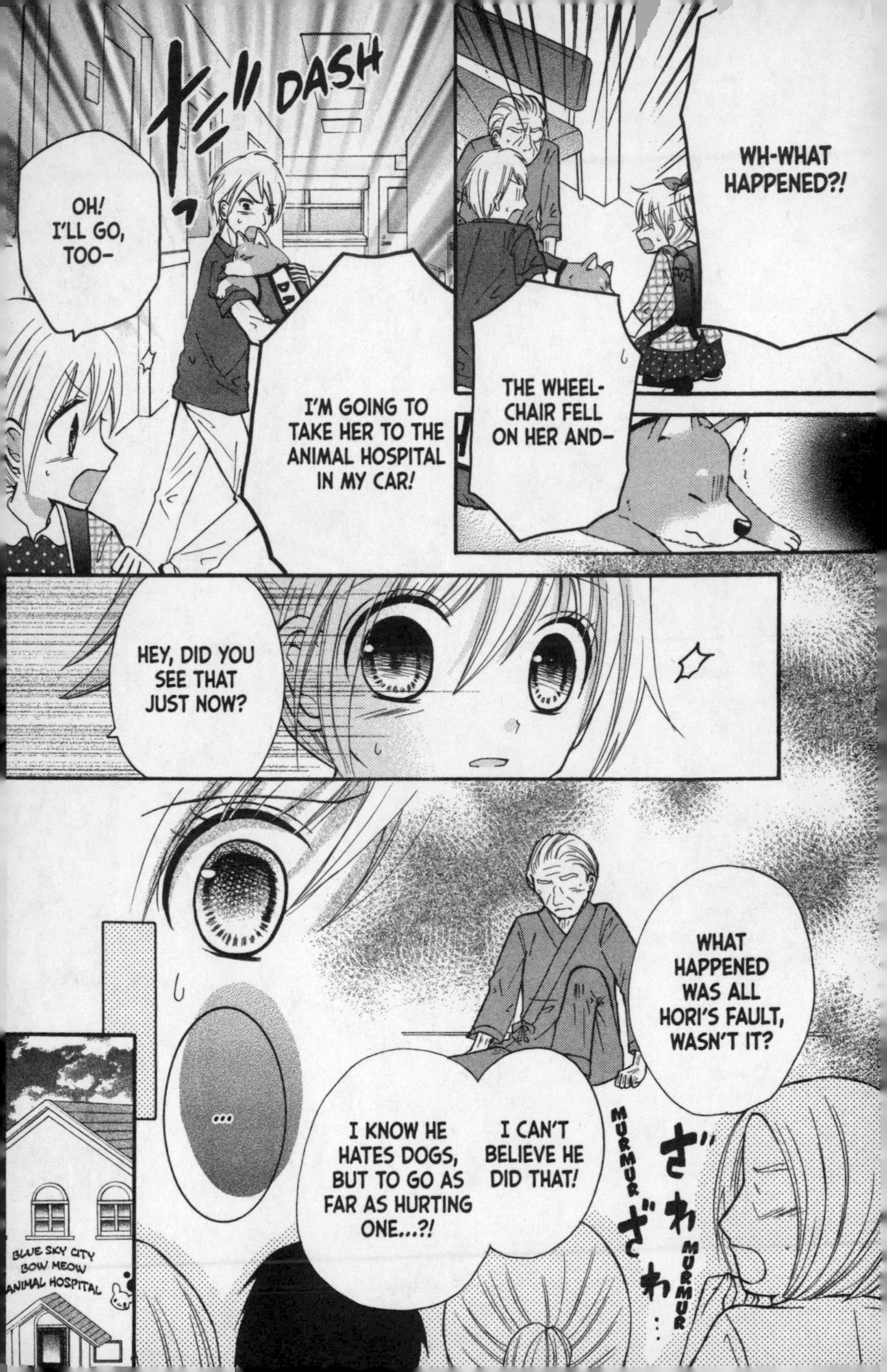
WH-WHAT HAPPENED?!
THE WHEEL-CHAIR FELL ON HER AND-
DASH
I'M GOING TO TAKE HER TO THE ANIMAL HOSPITAL IN MY CAR!
OH! I'LL GO, TOO-
HEY, DID YOU SEE THAT JUST NOW?
WHAT HAPPENED WAS ALL HORI'S FAULT, WASN'T IT?
MURMUR MURMUR
ざわ ざわ…
I CAN'T BELIEVE HE DID THAT!
I KNOW HE HATES DOGS, BUT TO GO AS FAR AS HURTING ONE...?!
...
BLUE SKY CITY BOW MEOW ANIMAL HOSPITAL

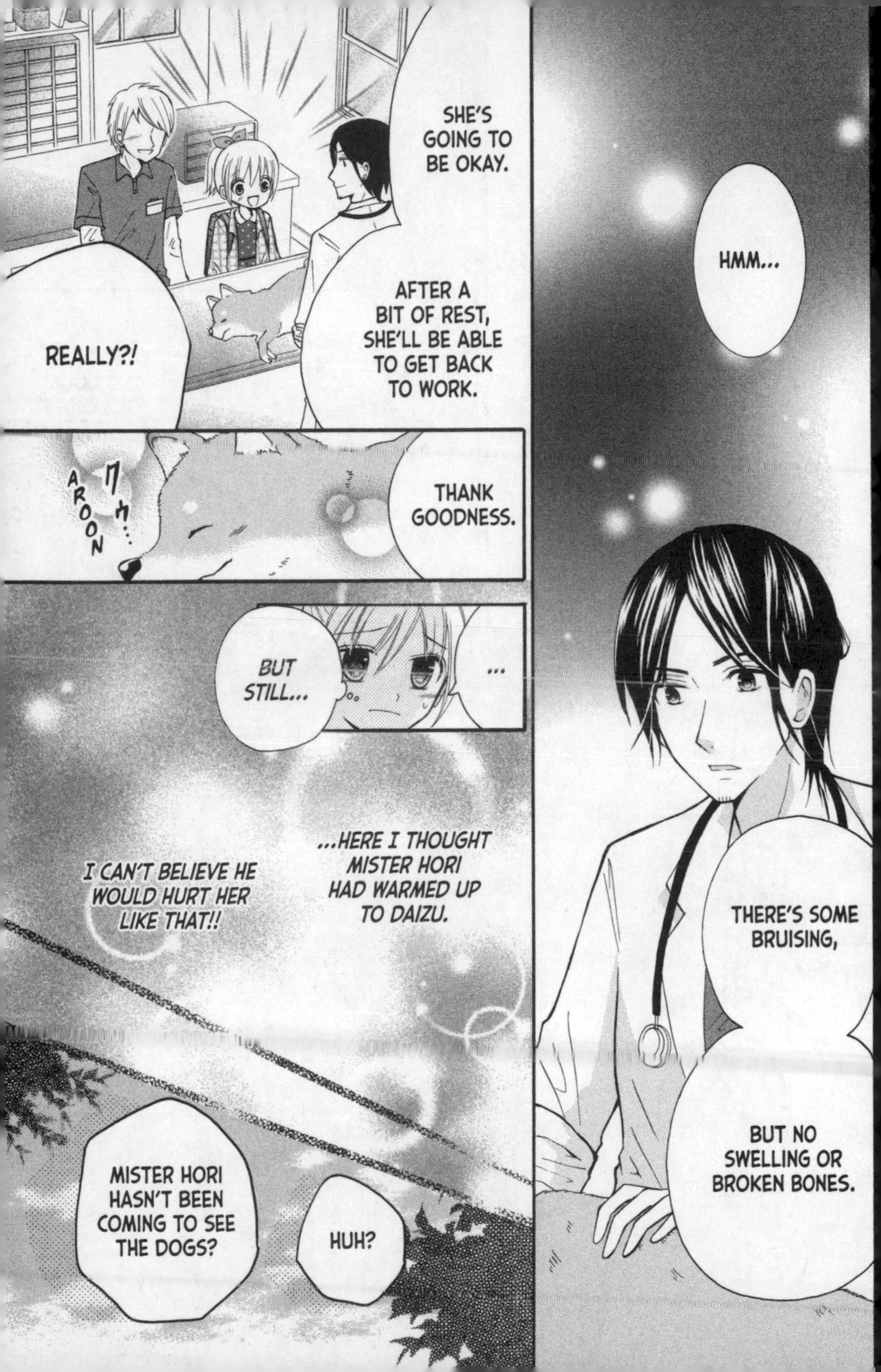
HMM...
THERE'S SOME BRUISING,
BUT NO SWELLING OR BROKEN BONES.
SHE'S GOING TO BE OKAY.
AFTER A BIT OF REST, SHE'LL BE ABLE TO GET BACK TO WORK.
REALLY?!
THANK GOODNESS.
AROON
...
BUT STILL...
...HERE I THOUGHT MISTER HORI HAD WARMED UP TO DAIZU.
I CAN'T BELIEVE HE WOULD HURT HER LIKE THAT!!
MISTER HORI HASN'T BEEN COMING TO SEE THE DOGS?
HUH?

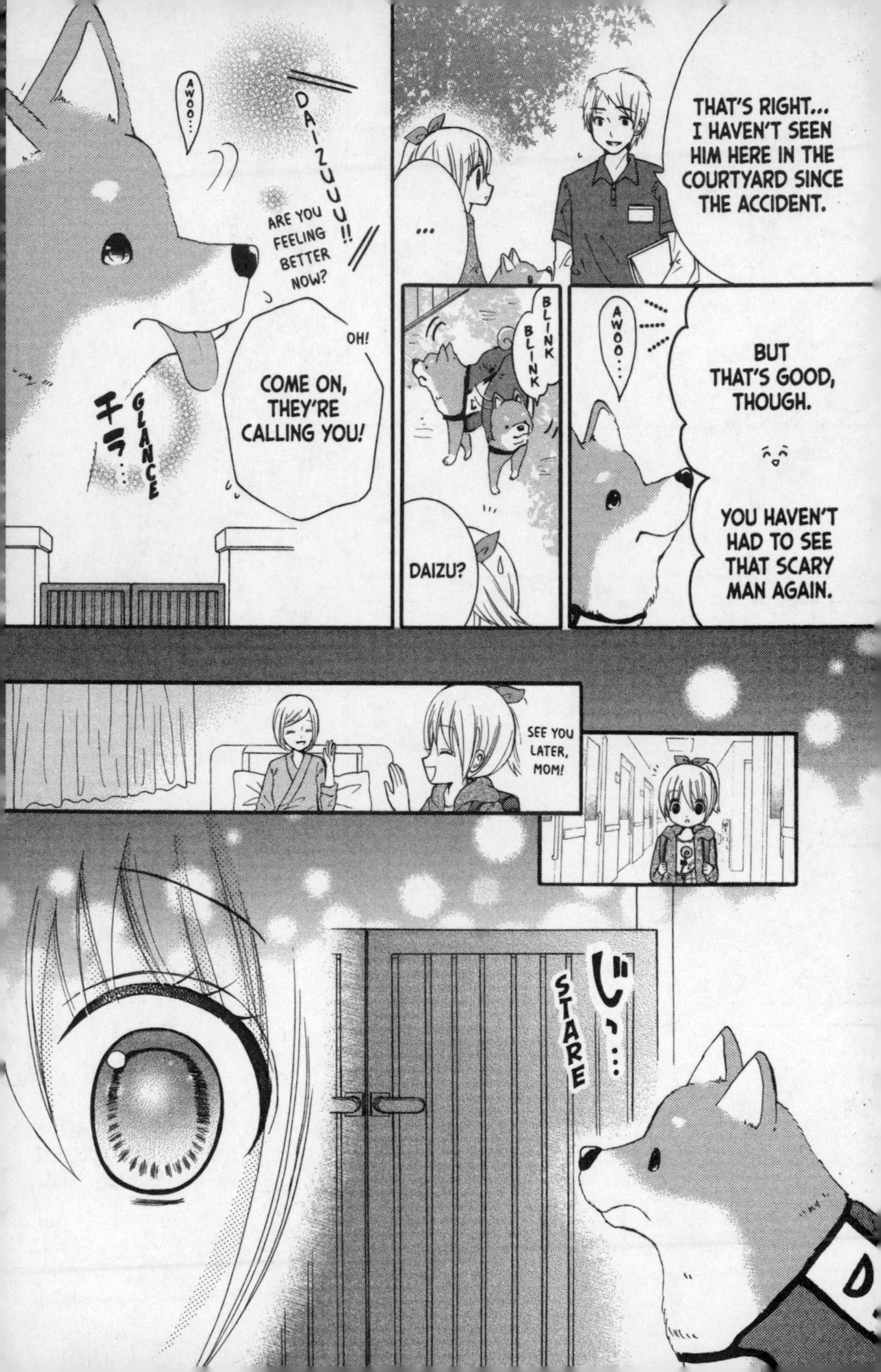
THAT'S RIGHT... I HAVEN'T SEEN HIM HERE IN THE COURTYARD SINCE THE ACCIDENT.
...
AWOO...
BUT THAT'S GOOD, THOUGH.
YOU HAVEN'T HAD TO SEE THAT SCARY MAN AGAIN.
BLINK BLINK
DAIZU?
AWOO...
DAIZUUUU!!
ARE YOU FEELING BETTER NOW?
OH!
COME ON, THEY'RE CALLING YOU!
チラ... GLANCE
SEE YOU LATER, MOM!
じっ... STARE

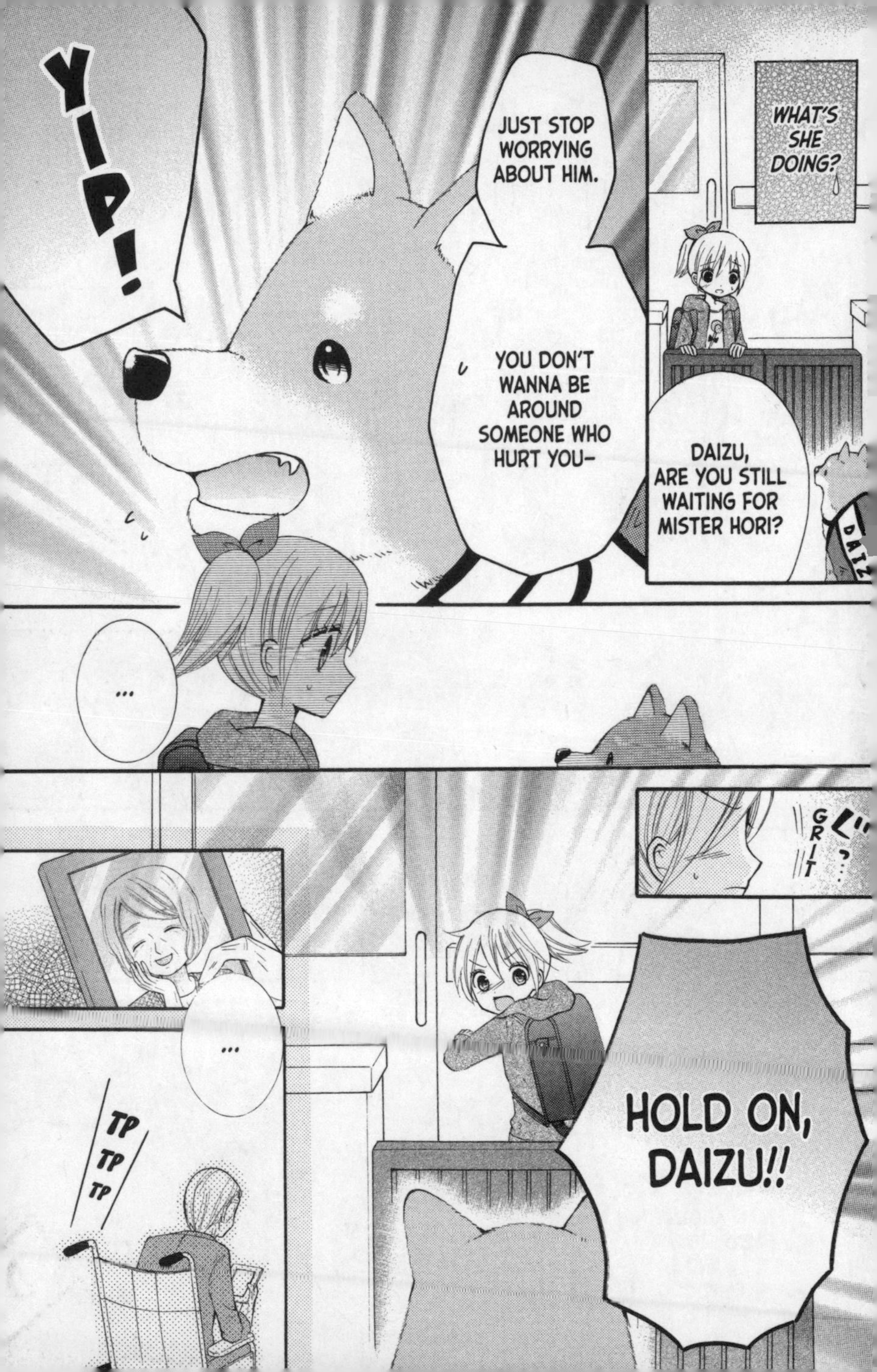
WHAT'S SHE DOING?
DAIZU, ARE YOU STILL WAITING FOR MISTER HORI?
JUST STOP WORRYING ABOUT HIM.
YOU DON'T WANNA BE AROUND SOMEONE WHO HURT YOU–
YIP!
...
GRIT
HOLD ON, DAIZU!!
...
TP TP TP

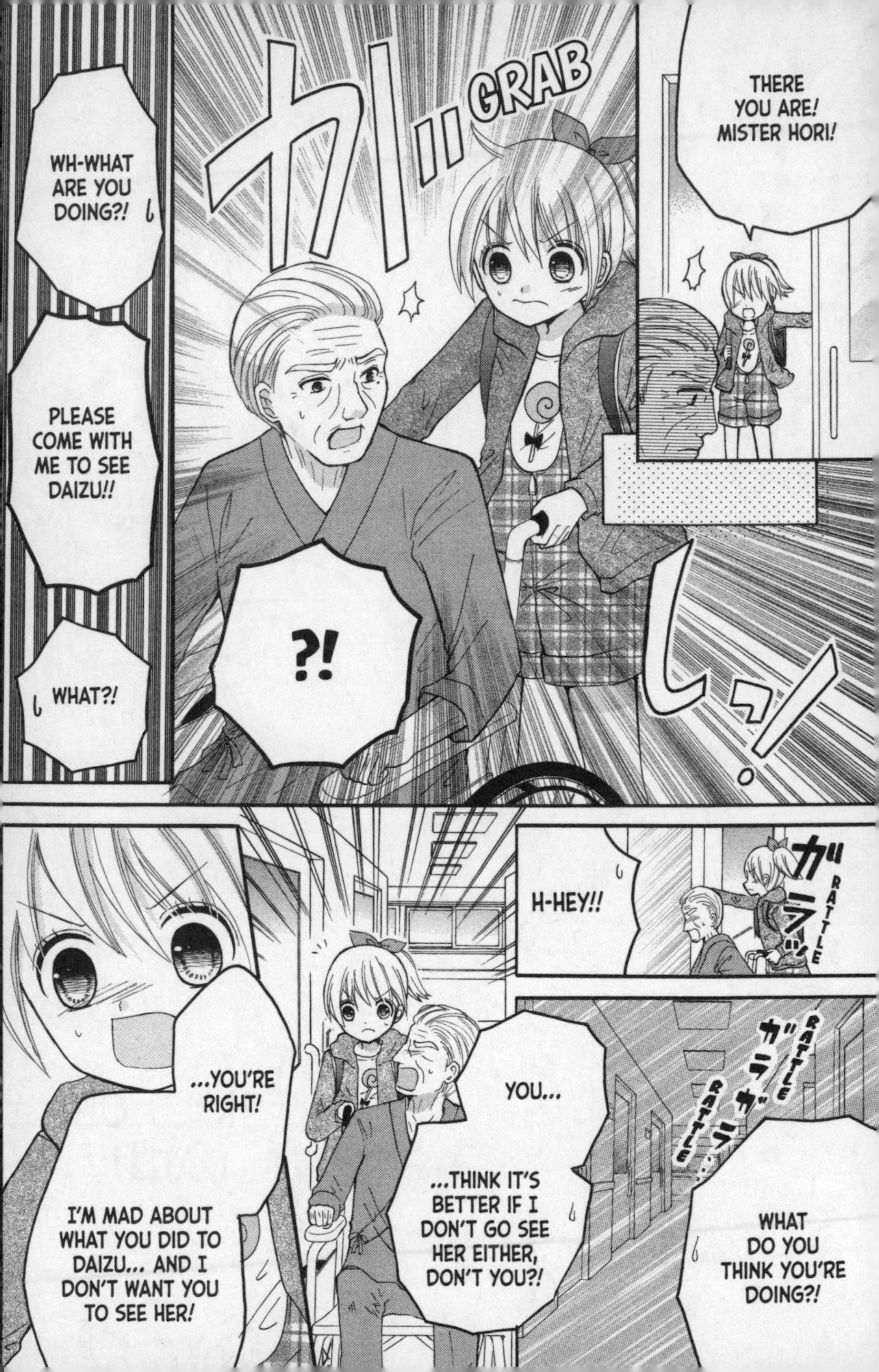
THERE YOU ARE! MISTER HORI!
GRAB
?!
WH-WHAT ARE YOU DOING?!
PLEASE COME WITH ME TO SEE DAIZU!!
WHAT?!
H-HEY!!
RATTLE
WHAT DO YOU THINK YOU'RE DOING?!
RATTLE
RATTLE
YOU...
...THINK IT'S BETTER IF I DON'T GO SEE HER EITHER, DON'T YOU?!
...YOU'RE RIGHT!
I'M MAD ABOUT WHAT YOU DID TO DAIZU... AND I DON'T WANT YOU TO SEE HER!

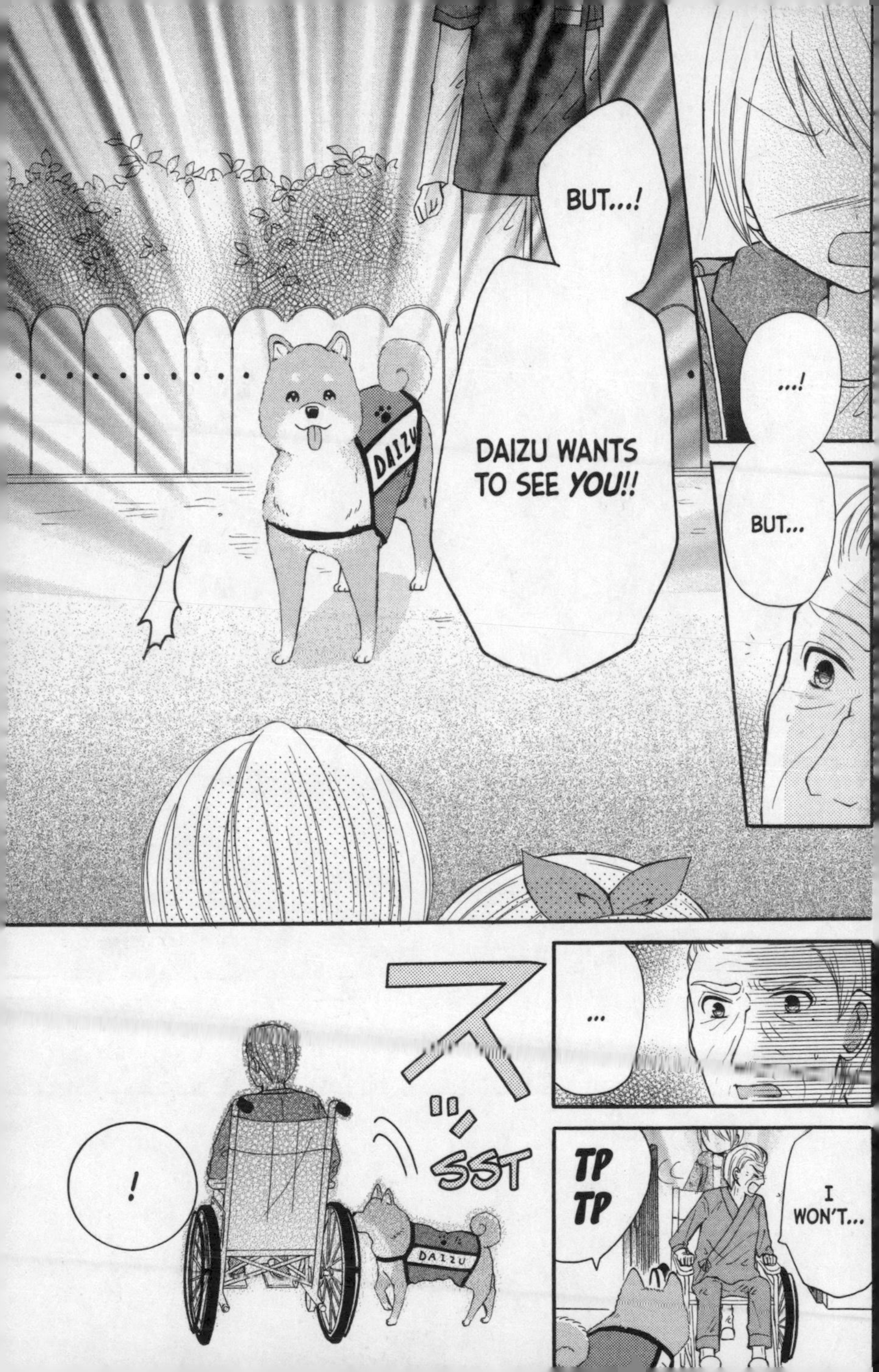
...!
BUT...
BUT...!
DAIZU WANTS TO SEE YOU!!
...
I WON'T...
TP TP
ス
SST
!

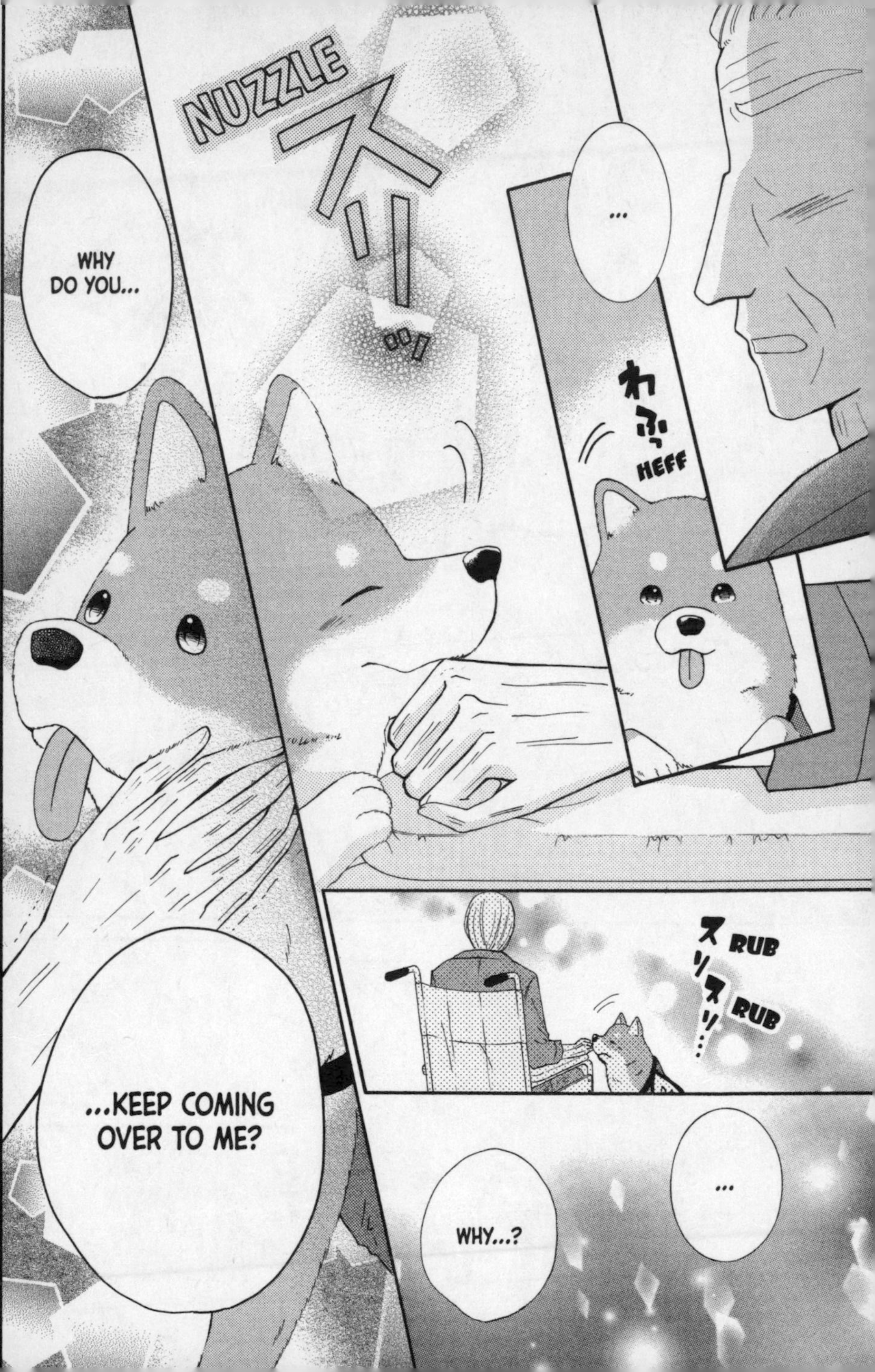
...
わふっ
HEFF
NUZZLE
スーッ
WHY DO YOU...
...KEEP COMING OVER TO ME?
スリスリッ
RUB
RUB
...
WHY...?

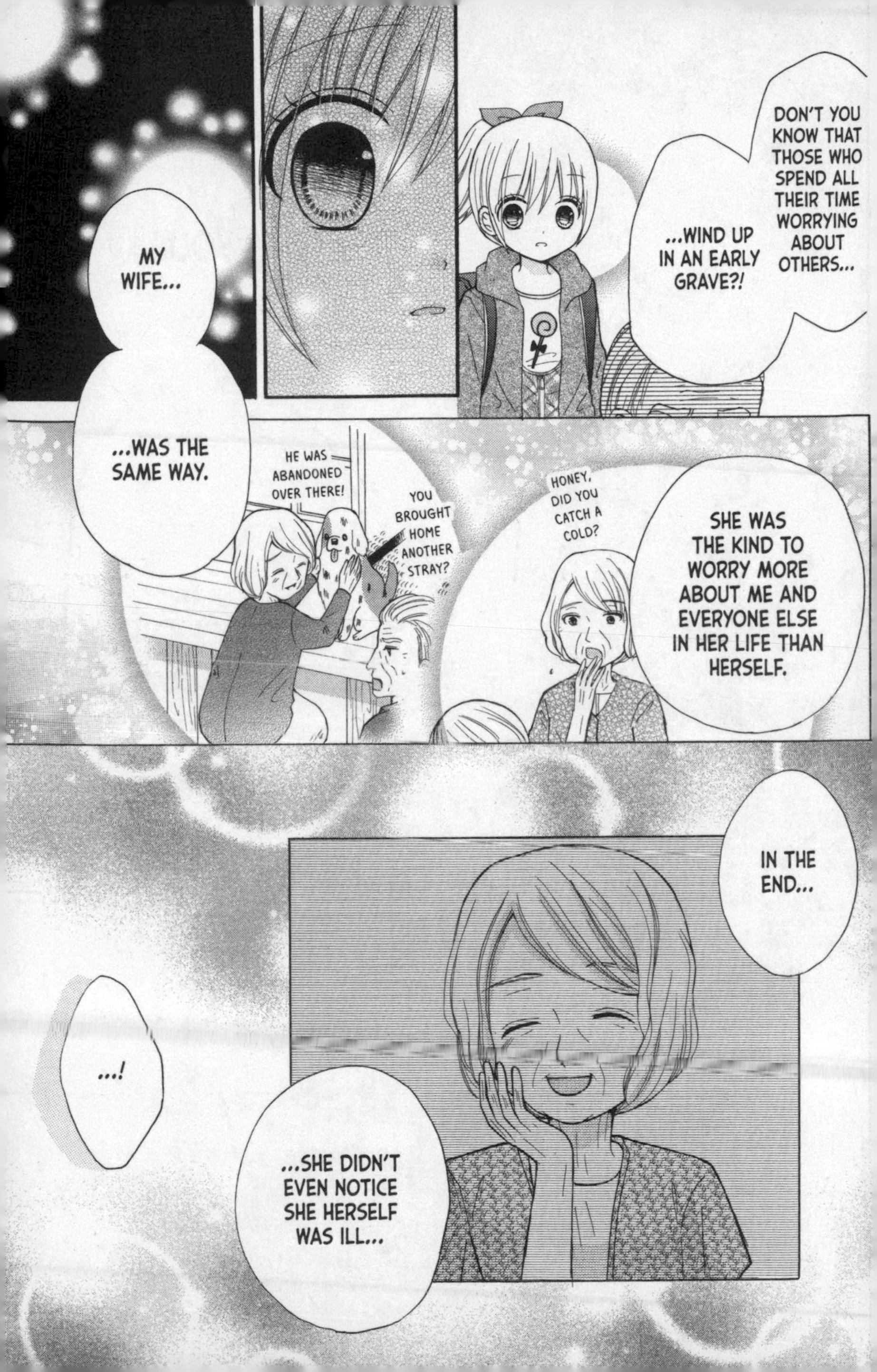
DON'T YOU KNOW THAT THOSE WHO SPEND ALL THEIR TIME WORRYING ABOUT OTHERS...
...WIND UP IN AN EARLY GRAVE?!
MY WIFE...
...WAS THE SAME WAY.
SHE WAS THE KIND TO WORRY MORE ABOUT ME AND EVERYONE ELSE IN HER LIFE THAN HERSELF.
HONEY, DID YOU CATCH A COLD?
YOU BROUGHT HOME ANOTHER STRAY?
HE WAS ABANDONED OVER THERE!
IN THE END...
...SHE DIDN'T EVEN NOTICE SHE HERSELF WAS ILL...
...!

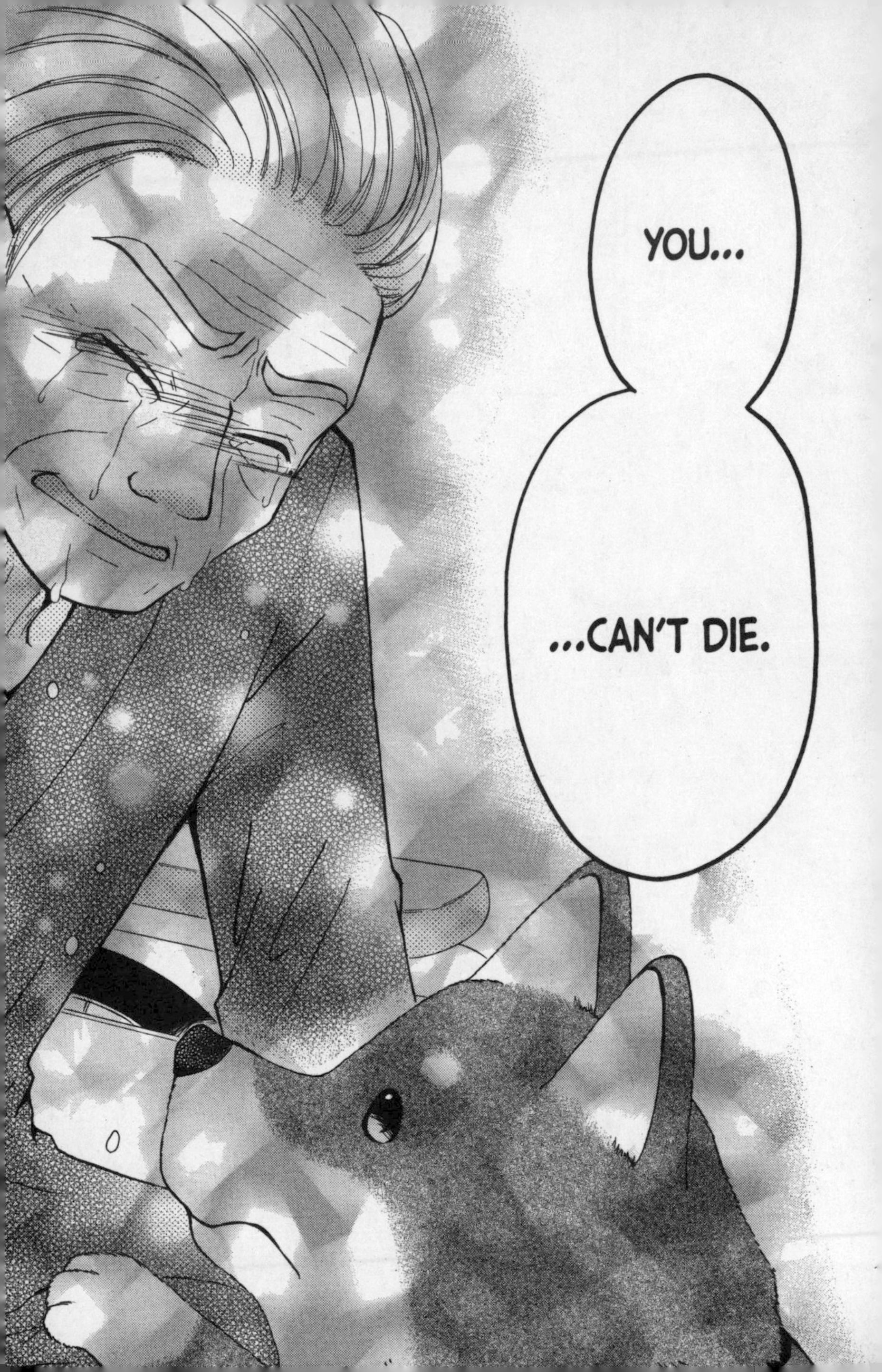
YOU...
...CAN'T DIE.

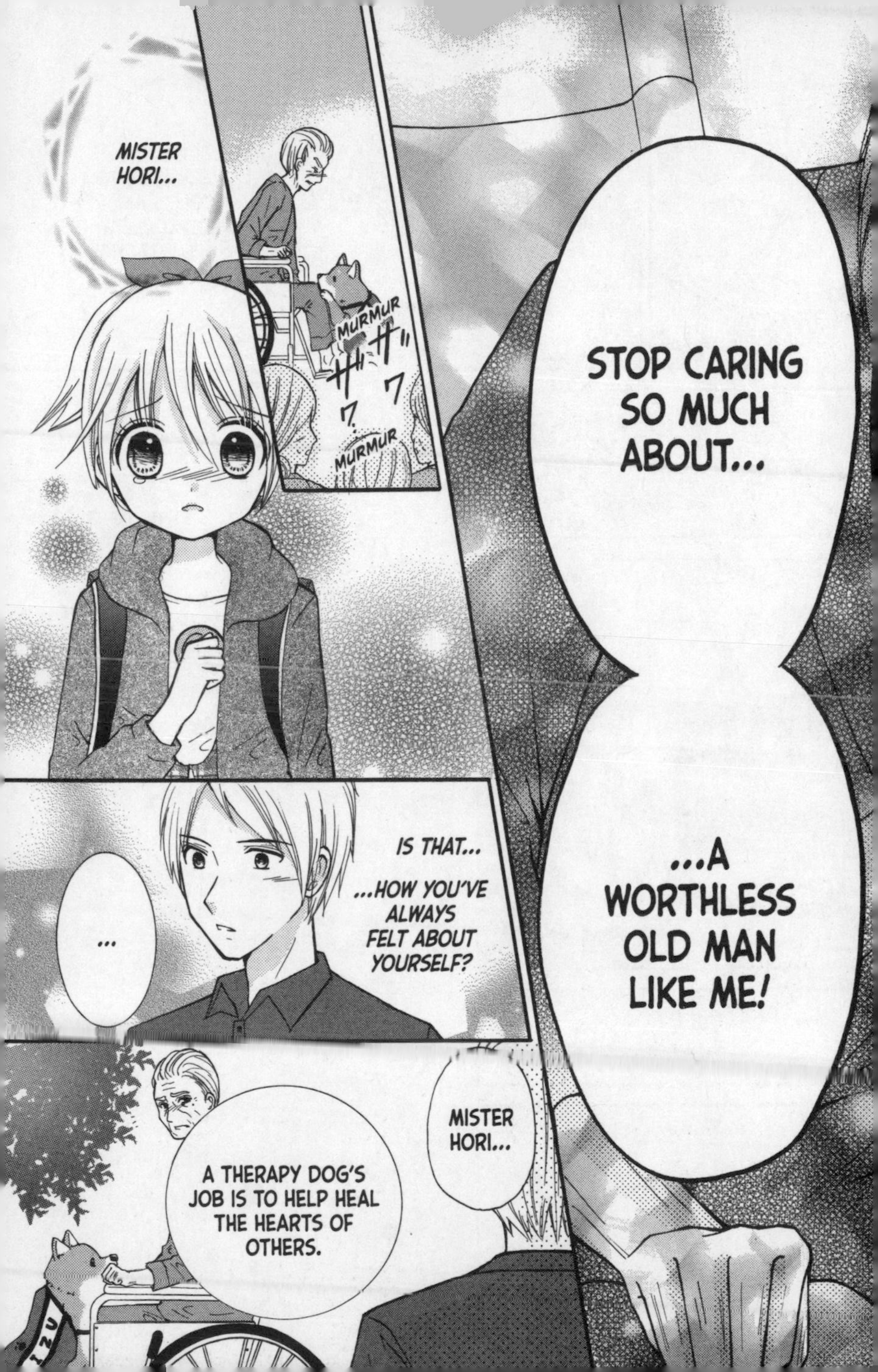
STOP CARING SO MUCH ABOUT...
...A WORTHLESS OLD MAN LIKE ME!
MURMUR
MURMUR
MISTER HORI...
IS THAT...
...HOW YOU'VE ALWAYS FELT ABOUT YOURSELF?
...
MISTER HORI...
A THERAPY DOG'S JOB IS TO HELP HEAL THE HEARTS OF OTHERS.
IZU

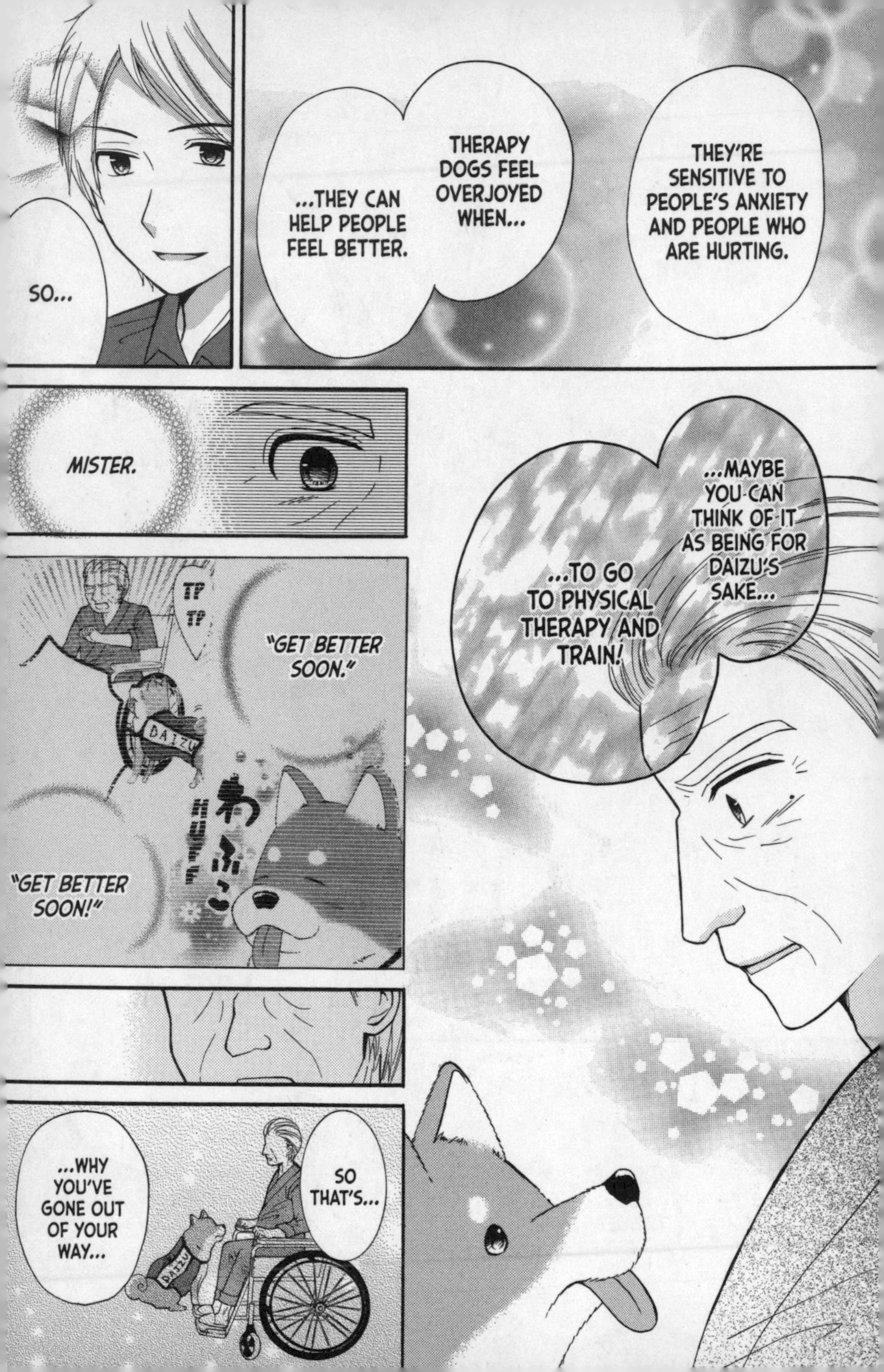
THEY'RE SENSITIVE TO PEOPLE'S ANXIETY AND PEOPLE WHO ARE HURTING.
THERAPY DOGS FEEL OVERJOYED WHEN...
...THEY CAN HELP PEOPLE FEEL BETTER.
SO...
...MAYBE YOU CAN THINK OF IT AS BEING FOR DAIZU'S SAKE...
...TO GO TO PHYSICAL THERAPY AND TRAIN!
MISTER.
TP TP
"GET BETTER SOON."
DAIZU
わふっ
HUFF
"GET BETTER SOON!"
SO THAT'S...
...WHY YOU'VE GONE OUT OF YOUR WAY...
DAIZU

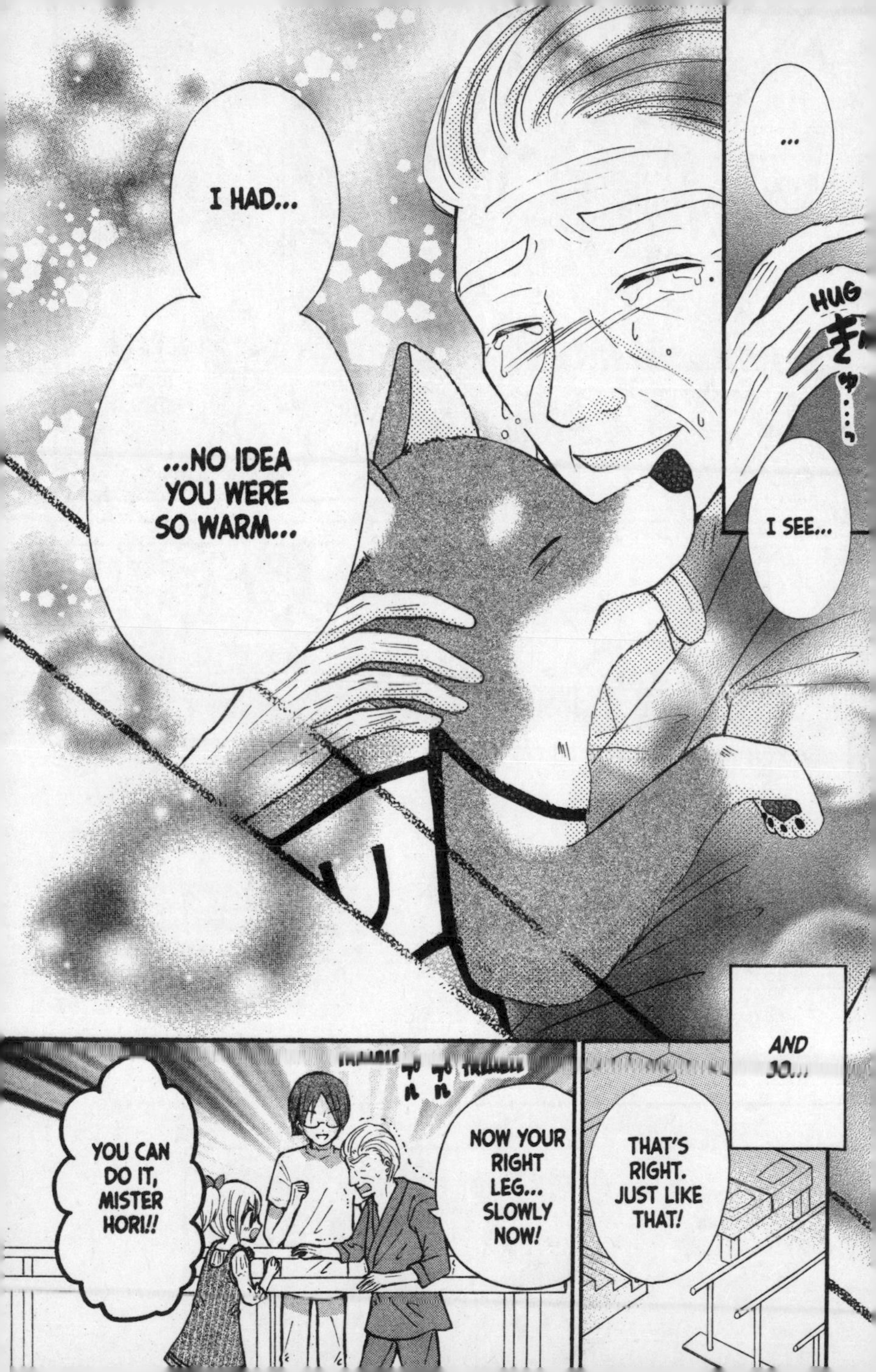
...
HUG
I SEE...
I HAD...
...NO IDEA YOU WERE SO WARM...
AND SO...
THAT'S RIGHT. JUST LIKE THAT!
NOW YOUR RIGHT LEG... SLOWLY NOW!
YOU CAN DO IT, MISTER HORI!!

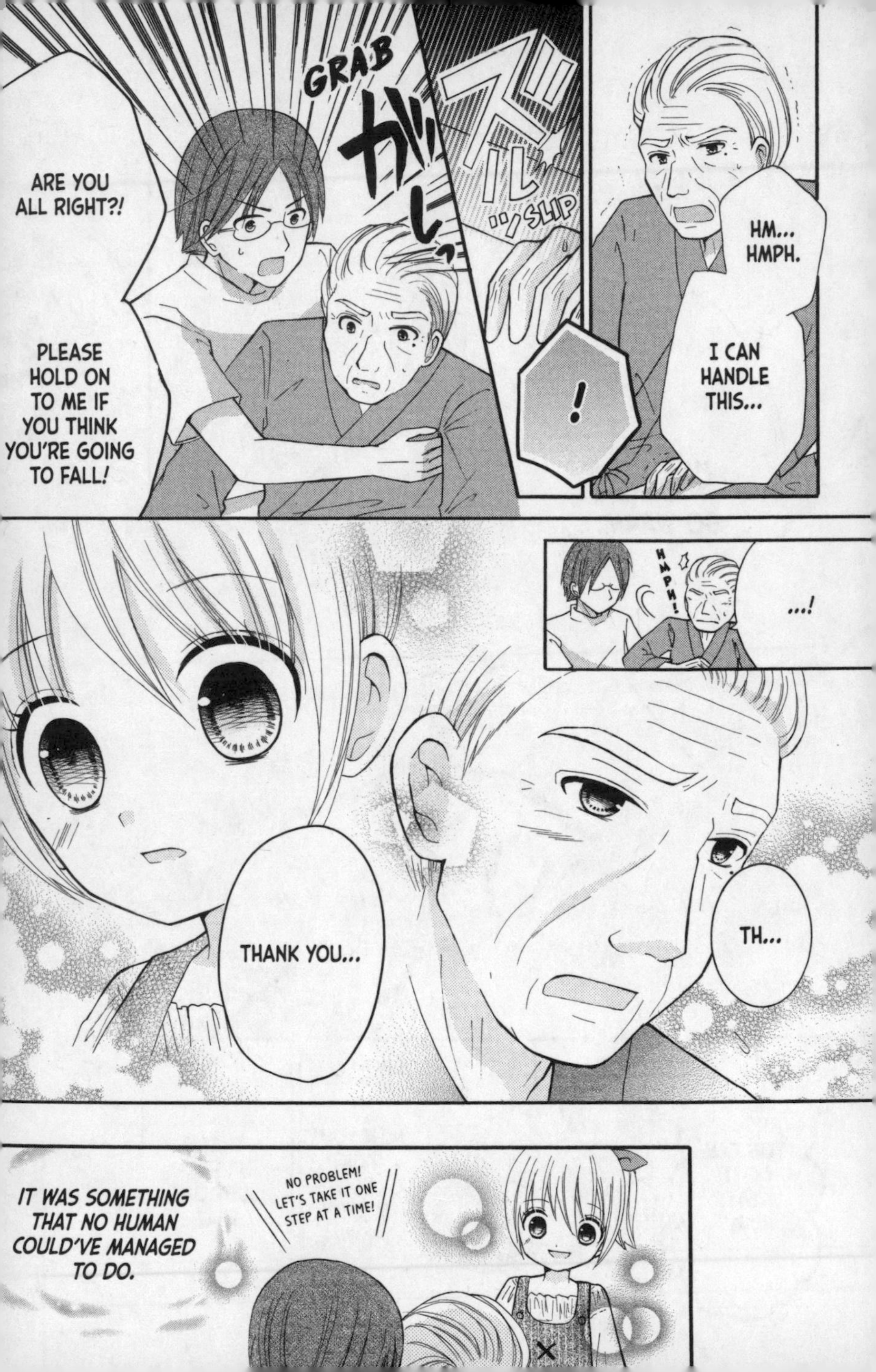
HM... HMPH.
I CAN HANDLE THIS...
SLIP
!
GRAB
ARE YOU ALL RIGHT?!
PLEASE HOLD ON TO ME IF YOU THINK YOU'RE GOING TO FALL!
HMPH!
...!
TH...
THANK YOU...
NO PROBLEM! LET'S TAKE IT ONE STEP AT A TIME!
IT WAS SOMETHING THAT NO HUMAN COULD'VE MANAGED TO DO.

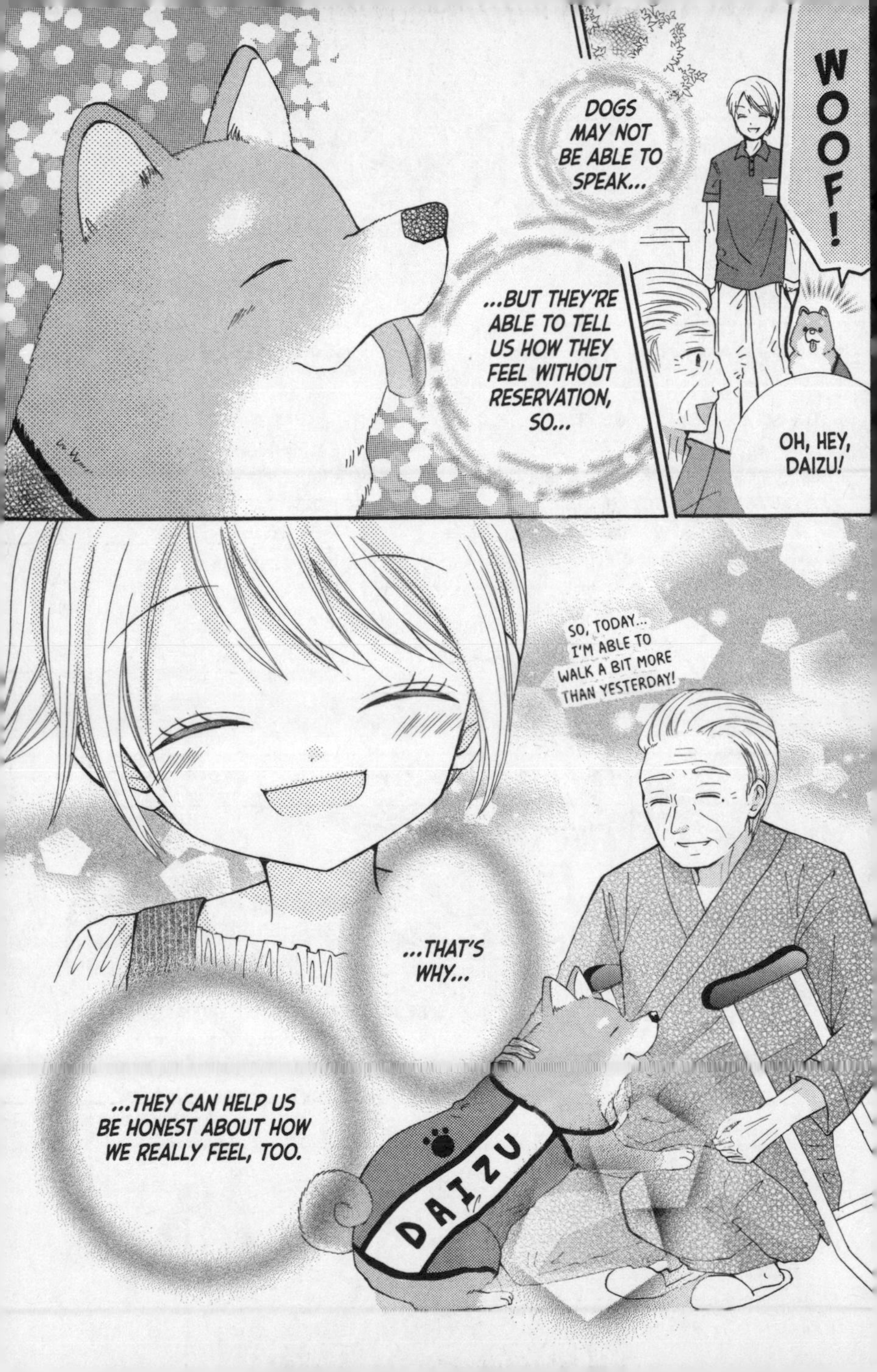
WOOF!
OH, HEY, DAIZU!
DOGS MAY NOT BE ABLE TO SPEAK...
...BUT THEY'RE ABLE TO TELL US HOW THEY FEEL WITHOUT RESERVATION, SO...
SO, TODAY... I'M ABLE TO WALK A BIT MORE THAN YESTERDAY!
...THAT'S WHY...
...THEY CAN HELP US BE HONEST ABOUT HOW WE REALLY FEEL, TOO.
DAIZU

BEHIND THE SCENES

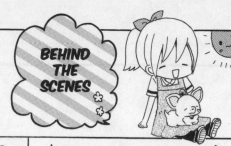

THERE ARE SOME SPOILERS WRITTEN HERE, SO PLEASE READ THIS SECTION AFTER YOU READ THE REST OF THE BOOK!

CHAPTER 9

<PUDDING THE PAMPERED POOCH>

THERE'S ACTUALLY A REAL DOG THAT I BASED PUDDING ON—AN AMERICAN COCKER SPANIEL OWNED BY ONE OF MY FAVORITE CELEBRITIES.

THEIR DOG WAS JUST TOO CUTE NOT TO! ALTHOUGH THEIR DOG ISN'T AS PLUMP AS PUDDING IS (HEHE).

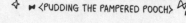

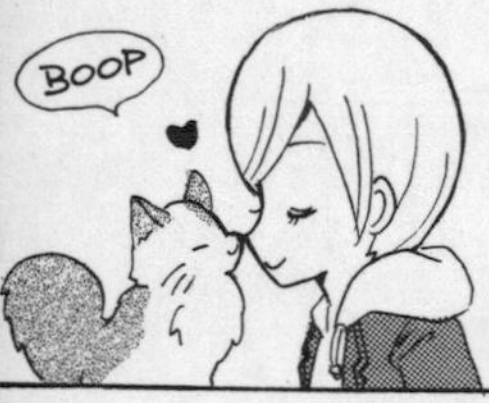

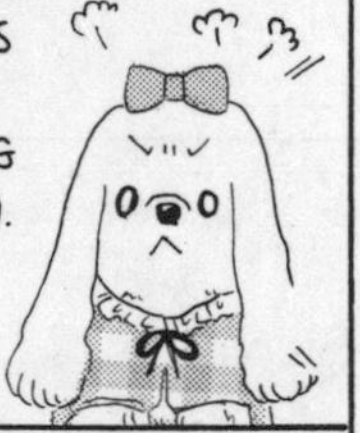

CHAPTER 10

<MUGI THE HIDE-AND-SEEK-LOVING CAT>

IT'S SO HARD TO SAY GOODBYE TO A BELOVED PET, ISN'T IT? IT WAS ESPECIALLY HARD FOR ME TO DRAW THE ENDING TO THIS CHAPTER. I PRAY THAT ASUKA AND MUGI WILL SOMEDAY BE REUNITED AT THE RAINBOW BRIDGE BEFORE HEAVEN.

BOOP

CHAPTER 11

<FUUTA AND RAITA, BROTHER DOGS>

I'M ACTUALLY A BIG SISTER AS WELL, SO I COULD REALLY RELATE TO HOW KAEDE AND FUUTA FELT WHILE I WAS WORKING ON THIS CHAPTER! OLDER SIBLINGS OFTEN END UP HAVING TO GRIN AND BEAR IT, DON'T THEY?! I LOVE THE LAST PAGE WHERE FUUTA AND RAITA REALLY GET ALONG.

CHAPTER 12

<DAIZU THE THERAPY DOG>

I'VE BEEN WANTING TO DRAW A SHIBA DOG FOR A WHILE! THE WAY THEY CURL UP THEIR TAILS IS JUST SO CUTE, DON'T YOU THINK? ♡ I THINK THE HEALING POWER OF PETTING A FLUFFY ANIMAL IS TREMENDOUS!

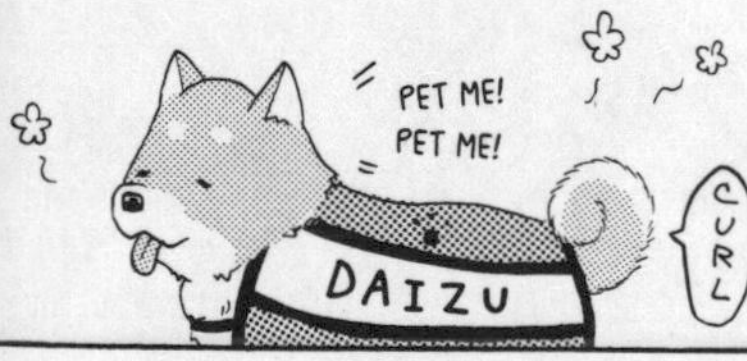

PET ME!
PET ME!
DAIZU
CURL

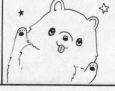

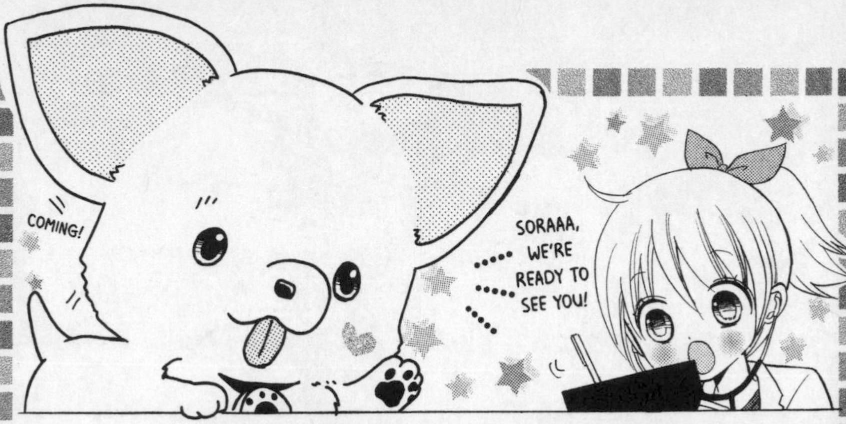
SORAAA, WE'RE READY TO SEE YOU!
COMING!

SPECIAL THANKS

- IN COLLABORATION WITH NIPPON COLUMBIA CO., LTD.
- SUPERVISOR: TAISEI HOSOIDO

- EDITORS: NAKAZATO
  NAGANO
- DESIGNER: KOBAYASHI
- EVERYONE FROM NAKAYOSHI MAGAZINE'S EDITORIAL DEPARTMENT

- MANUSCRIPT ASSISTANTS: ANCHAN
  NAOCHAN
  MEIRA ISHIZAKA
  KOUTEI PENGUIN DX
  BONCHI

PLEASE SEND YOUR LETTERS TO THE FOLLOWING ADDRESS!!

PLEASE SEND ME LETTERS WITH YOUR THOUGHTS ABOUT THE MANGA, OR IF YOU JUST WANT TO BRAG ABOUT YOUR PETS! ☆

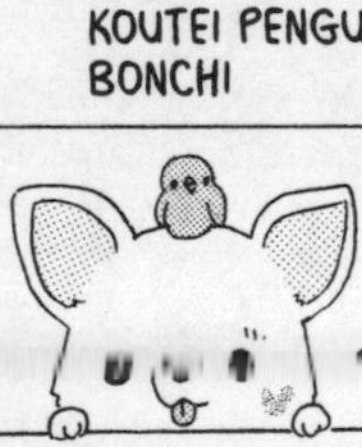

MINGO ITO
KODANSHA COMICS
451 PARK AVE. SOUTH,
7TH FLOOR
NEW YORK, NY 10016

BLOG
MINGOROKU
http://ameblo.jp/itoumingo/

twitter
@itoumingo

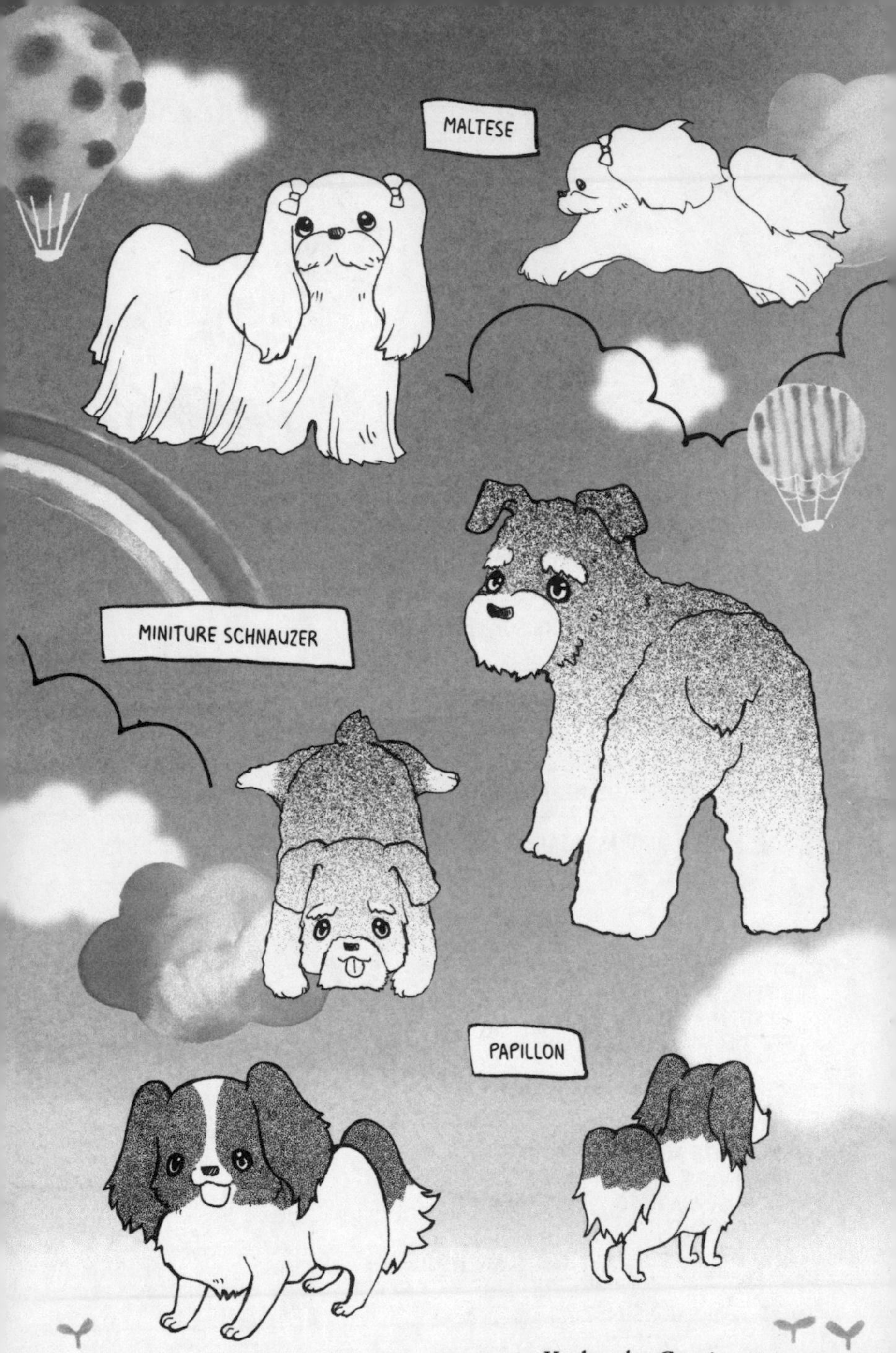
MALTESE
MINITURE SCHNAUZER
PAPILLON

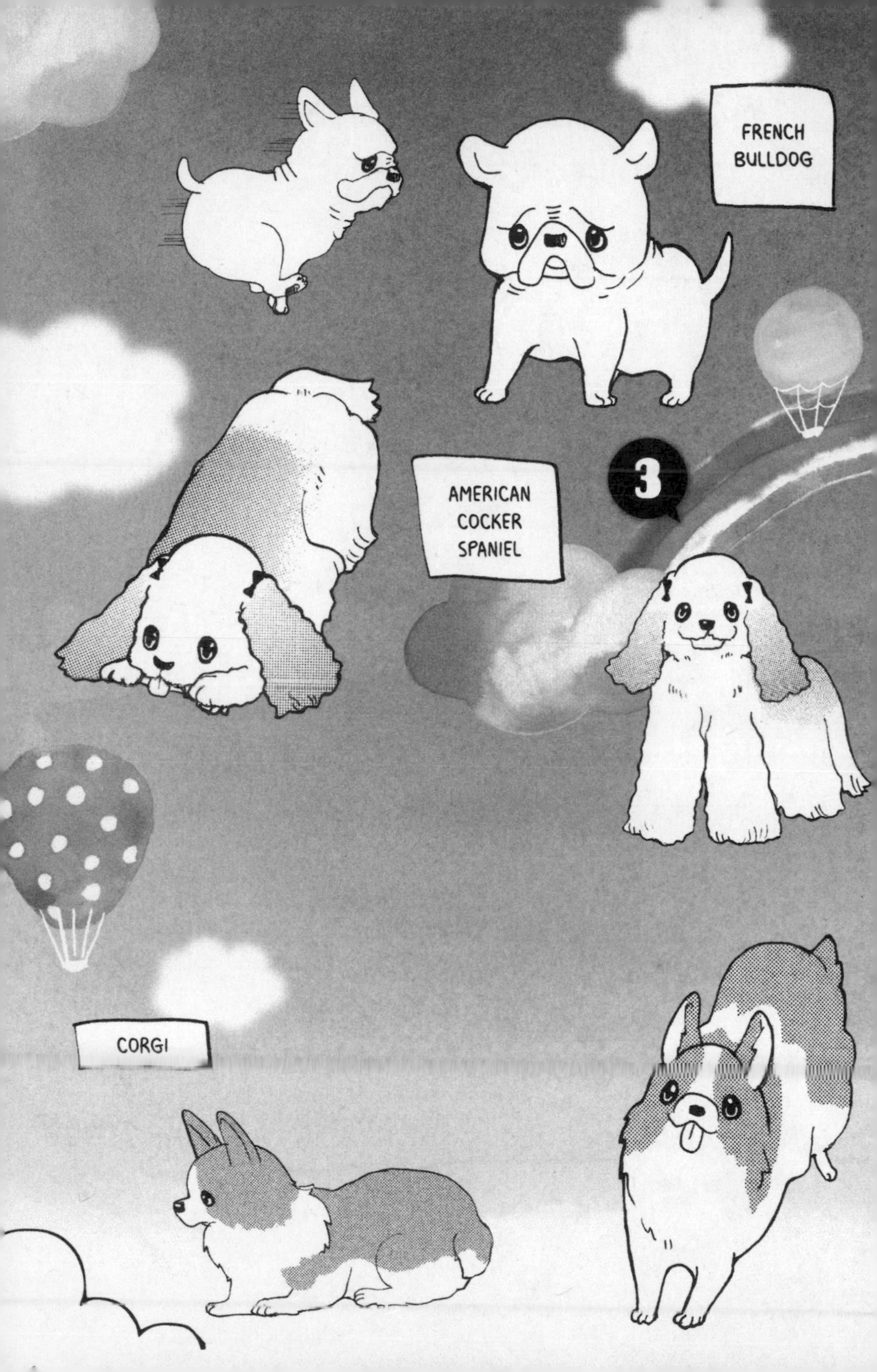
FRENCH BULLDOG
3
AMERICAN COCKER SPANIEL
CORGI

Translation Notes

Mugi, page 41
Mugi means "wheat" in Japanese.

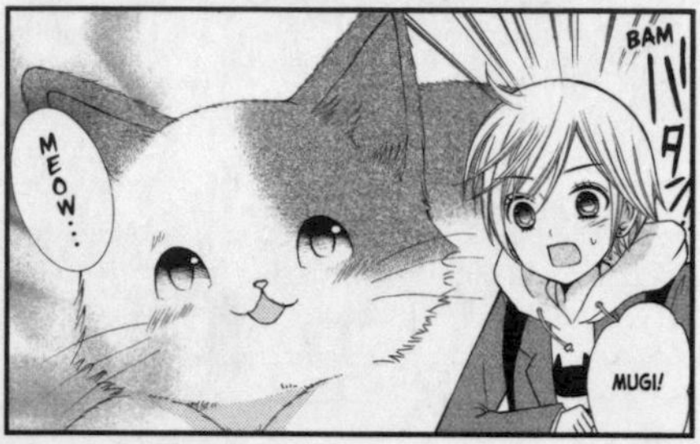
BAM
MUGI!
MEOW...

Daizu, page 115
Daizu means "soybean" in Japanese.

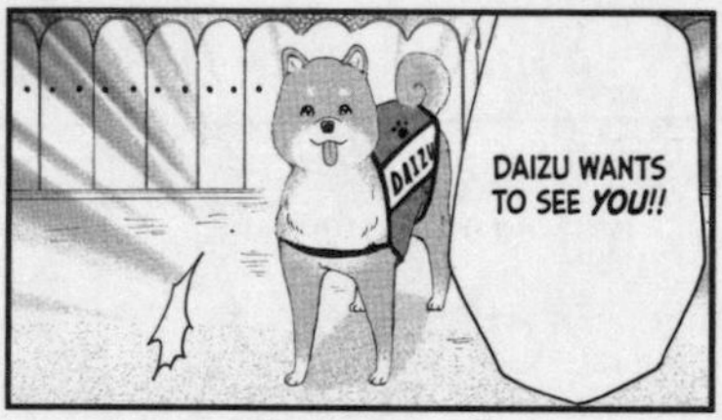
DAIZU WANTS TO SEE *YOU!!*
DAIZU

Rice porridge, page 115
Rice porridge (called *okayu* in Japanese) is what people in Japan typically eat when they're sick, like how people in the US often eat chicken noodle soup.

A Kodansha Comics Trade Paperback Original
Yuzu the Pet Vet 3 copyright © 2017 Mingo Ito © 2017 NIPPON COLUMBIA CO., LTD.
English translation copyright © 2020 Mingo Ito © NIPPON COLUMBIA CO., LTD.

Published in the United States by Kodansha Comics, an imprint of Kodansha USA Publishing, LLC, New York.

Publication rights for this English edition arranged through Kodansha Ltd., Tokyo.

First published in Japan in 2017 by Kodansha Ltd., Tokyo
as *Yuzu no Doubutsu Karute ~Kochira Wan Nyan Doubutsu Byouin~*, volume 3.

ISBN 978-1-64651-012-2

Original cover design by Tomoko Kobayashi

Printed in the United States of America.

www.kodanshacomics.com

9 8 7 6 5 4 3 2 1
Translation: Julie Goniwich
Lettering: David Yoo
Editing: Haruko Hashimoto
Kodansha Comics edition cover design by Matthew Akuginow

Publisher: Kiichiro Sugawara

Director of publishing services: Ben Applegate
Associate director of operations: Stephen Pakula
Publishing services managing editor: Noelle Webster
Assistant production manager: Emi Lotto, Angela Zurlo
Logo and character art ©Kodansha USA Publishing, LLC

The adorable new odd-couple cat comedy manga from the creator of the beloved *Chi's Sweet Home*, in full color!

Sue & Tai-chan

Konami Kanata

Sue is an aging housecat who's looking forward to living out her life in peace... but her plans change when the mischievous black tomcat Tai-chan enters the picture! Hey! Sue never signed up to be a catsitter! *Sue & Tai-chan* is the latest from the reigning meow-narch of cute kitty comics, Konami Kanata.

HOW TO READ MANGA

Japanese is written right to left and top to bottom. This means that for a reader accustomed to Western languages, Japanese books read "backwards." Since most manga published in English now keep the Japanese page order, it can take a little getting used to—but once you learn how, it's a snap!

Here you can see pages 24-25 from *Yuzu the Pet Vet* volume 1. The speech balloons have been numbered in the order you should read them in.

Page 24—read this page first!

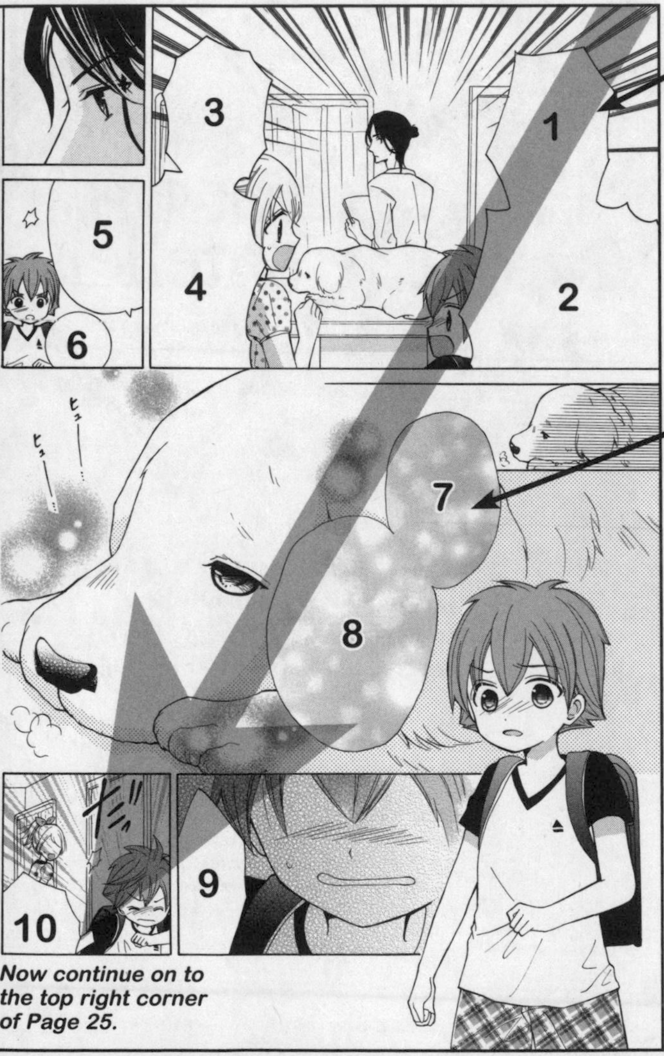

1
2
3
4
5
6
7
8
9
10

Start here, at the top right corner of the right-hand page.

Read right to left, then top to bottom.

Now continue on to the top right corner of Page 25.

After a few pages, you'll be reading manga like a pro!

Page 25—read the page on the **right-hand side** first!

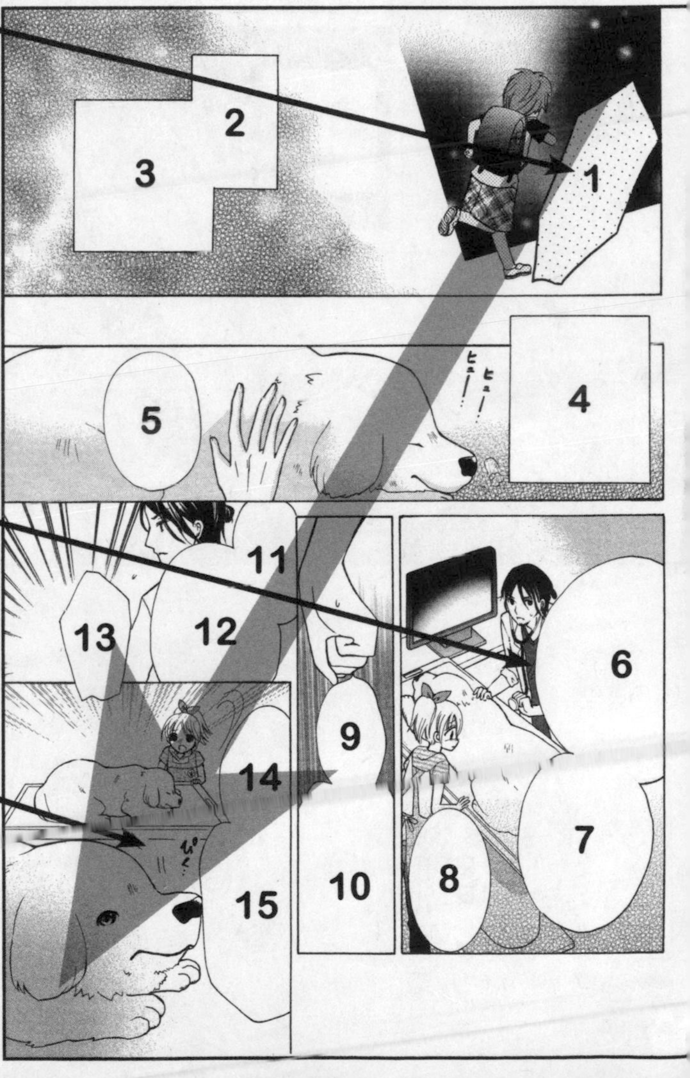
1
2
3
4
5
6
7
8
9
10
11
12
13
14
15

Start at the top right corner for this page, too!

Don't forget to move back to the right side.

This is the bottom left-most panel, so it's **read last.**

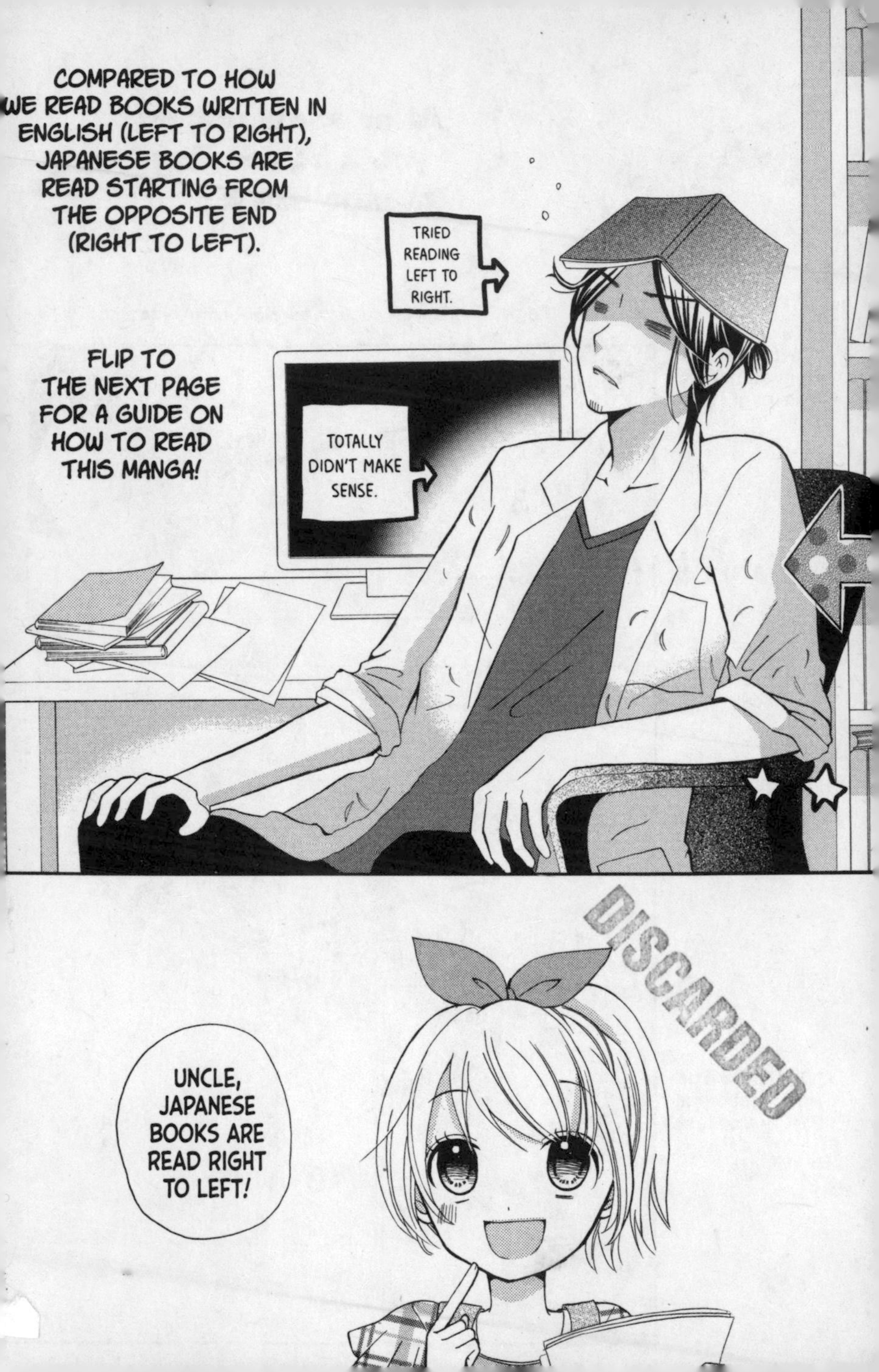
COMPARED TO HOW WE READ BOOKS WRITTEN IN ENGLISH (LEFT TO RIGHT), JAPANESE BOOKS ARE READ STARTING FROM THE OPPOSITE END (RIGHT TO LEFT).
TRIED READING LEFT TO RIGHT.
TOTALLY DIDN'T MAKE SENSE.
FLIP TO THE NEXT PAGE FOR A GUIDE ON HOW TO READ THIS MANGA!
UNCLE, JAPANESE BOOKS ARE READ RIGHT TO LEFT!